Setting a Course
American Women in the 1920s

American Women in the Twentieth Century

Series Editor: Barbara Haber, The Schlesinger Library on the History of Women in America, Radcliffe College

Pulling together a wealth of widely scattered primary and secondary sources on women's history, *American Women in the Twentieth Century* is the first series to provide a chronological history of the changing status of women in America. Each volume presents the experiences and contributions of American women during one decade of this century. Written by leading scholars in American history and women's studies, *American Women in the Twentieth Century* meets the need for an encyclopedic overview of the roles women have played in shaping modern America.

Also Available:

Holding Their Own: American Women in the 1930s
Susan Ware
The Home Front and Beyond: American Women in the 1940s
Susan M. Hartman
Mothers and More: American Women in the 1950s
Eugenia Kaledin

Forthcoming Titles:

American Women in the 1960s
Carol Hurd Green
American Women in the 1970s
Winifred Wandersee
American Women 1900–1920
Barbara Miller Solomon

"The New Woman"
Drawing by Van Werveke
Copyright © 1927, Current History, Inc.

Setting a Course
American Women in the 1920s

Dorothy M. Brown

Twayne Publishers • Boston
A Division of G.K. Hall & Co.

Setting a Course
American Women in the 1920s

Copyright © 1987 by G.K. Hall & Co.
All Rights Reserved
Published by Twayne Publishers
A Division of G.K. Hall & Co.
70 Lincoln Street, Boston, Massachusetts 02111

Copyediting supervised by Lewis DeSimone
Produced by Janet Zietowski
Designed by Marne B. Sultz
Typeset in Janson by Compset, Inc., Beverly, Massachusetts

First Paperback Edition

Printed on permanent/durable acid-free paper
and bound in the United States of America

Library of Congress Cataloging in Publication Data

Brown, Dorothy M. (Dorothy Marie), 1932–
Setting a course.

(American women in the twentieth century)
Includes index.
1. Women—United States—History—20th century.
I. Title. II. Series.
HQ1420.B75 1987   305.4′0973   86-22898
ISBN 0-8057-9906-0
ISBN 0-8057-9908-7 (pbk.)

To friends and teachers,
who in my life have been synonymous

Contents

About the Author

Dorothy M. Brown is professor of history and coordinator of academic planning at Georgetown University in Washington, D.C. Her other work on an aspect of women in the 1920s is *Mabel Walker Willebrandt: A Study in Power, Loyalty, and Law.*

Preface

In 1977, Paul A. Carter, in his trenchant introduction to *Another Part of the Twenties*, observed that when he talked with his father or mother or others who had lived through the decade, their memories or perceptions did not square with historians' accounts. Carter concluded: "If it is ever proper to generalize from few examples, somewhere between the period's various polar opposites—bond salesman and Bohemian, prude and rebel, snob and sweated worker, all the liberated women and all the sad young men—there seems to have stretched a broad continuum of Americans whose stories have never been read into the record."[1]

Carter merely swelled a growing chorus on the need to reexamine this extraordinary period, to study the "other parts" and to find the missing. Certainly the largest number of stories that remained to be read into the record were those of American women. In 1974, Estelle B. Freedman surveyed the historiography in her masterful article, "The New Woman: Changing Views of Women in the 1920s," and found that the "failure to consider the women's movement in the 1920s is not an uncommon oversight among historians."[2] Historians of the women's movement carried the story through the Progressive Era and the suffrage victory and stopped. "Beyond suffrage" virtually remained terra incognita. Paradoxically, Freedman found that women, in the existing studies of the decade, were either ignored or stereotyped. The assessments of the first historians of the 1920s, Frederick Lewis Allen, in his jaunty and influential *Only Yesterday*, and Preston W. Slosson, in his study of social trends in *The Great Crusade and After*, were accepted and reiterated. Women were depicted as flappers, partners in the alleged "revolution in manners and morals," and as ineffectual voters and political organizers. They were also credited with finally achieving full social and economic equality. Into the 1960s, Freedman observed, historians claimed either everything or nothing for women of the 1920s.

Even worse, they tended to generalize about American *women*, as if they were not divided by class, race, region, and ethnicity.[3]

In the 1960s historians, against the background of President Kennedy's conference on the status of women and the emergence of the New Left, questioned why feminism failed to consolidate and achieve further reforms in the 1920s. By 1986, the burgeoning interest of the 1960s, spurred on by the women's movement of the 1970s, had produced an outpouring of studies on the social feminist reformers, the radical feminists of the National Woman's party, the continuing gender separation on the job, the birth control movement, and trends in the higher education of women.

This volume, like its predecessors in this series, is an attempt to bring together the various parts of the whole. It is a task reminiscent of a story related by an advertising executive of the 1920s. As a man walked down a muddy street, he spied a straw hat in a puddle, poked at it with a stick, and discovered that the hat was on a head. "Is it as deep as that?" he asked. "It's deeper than you think," was the reply. "I'm standing on a bus."[4] There is a daunting depth to the history of the 1920s and the history of the generations of women who peopled it. This study is only part of an ongoing effort to get to the bottom of it.

Twelve years ago when I was ending a lecture on the novelists of the lost generation in my course on the United States in the twentieth century at Georgetown University, a young woman asked, "Weren't there any women in the lost generation?" I was appalled at my omission and immediately reeled off the usual names—Edna St. Vincent Millay, Zelda Fitzgerald, and Dorothy Parker. During the course of researching for this volume, I have encountered hundreds of other women who demand further consideration. I have also concluded that I would be slower in responding, because what has emerged is that women were never quite as lost as their brothers in the 1920s. In the courage and the staunchness of their self-discovery, they had much to contribute to a nation in search of itself.

This book would not have been completed without the assistance, advice, and encouragement of many friends. Georgetown colleagues Susan Vroman and Elizabeth McKeown were helpful in their suggestions for the chapters on work and religion. Margaret Steinhagen and Mary McBride gave a valuable critique to the chapter on education. Mary McHenry and Josephine Trueschler suggested sources and read the sections on literature and the arts. Nancy Malan of the staff of the

National Archives lent her valuable time and expertise to tracking down the pictures and suggesting a format. Georgette Dorn of the Library of Congress continued her indefatigable support of researchers. David Hagan contributed his photographer's skills. Archivists Sister Bridget Marie Engelmeyer of the College of Notre Dame of Maryland and Elaine D. Trehub of Mount Holyoke College were generous in researching their picture files. Kathleen Colquohon, Mark Sherry, Donna Riley, and Linda Turbyville helped in the research. Student research has always extended my knowledge and teaching; three essays by Frances Magovern, Tracy Primrose, and Deborah Daw were helpful in this study. Maura E. Fay and Janet Doehlert shared their precise talents in proofing. Bertrand deCoquereaument intervened at a crucial moment to make my IBM user-friendly and offered suggestions on the text. Throughout, Carol Hurd Green, who has already contributed so much to women's history through *Notable American Women: The Modern Period*, shared her knowledge of sources and trends. Finally, no one could have had more encouragement or patience from her editors, Barbara Haber, who conceived this series, and Anne M. Jones of G. K. Hall. All omissions or errors are, of course, my own.

Dorothy M. Brown

Georgetown University

Clockwise from top left: 1928 drawing of Amelia Earhart. Ford advertisement. Ku Klux Klan women parade down Pennsylvania Ave., 1928.

CHAPTER ONE

The Twenties: At the Crossroads

Prosperity is more than an economic condition; it is a state of mind.

For better or worse, American culture was remade in the 1920s. Robust with business styles, technologies, educational policies, manners, and leisure habits which are identifiably our own, the decade sits solidly at the base of our culture.

This was the first serious attempt of Americans to make their peace with the twentieth century.[1]

Few decades have been so labeled, stereotyped, celebrated, or derided as the 1920s in America. Beginning with Frederick Lewis Allen's record in *Only Yesterday* of the "charming, crazy days" of the Ballyhoo Years, historians have piled alliterative titles onto the Roaring Twenties: Fords, Flappers, and Fanatics, the Decade of the Dollar, the Period of the Psyche, the Time of Tremendous Trifles, Alcohol and Al Capone, and the Dry Decade. They have stretched this alliteration to describe the tensions—Babbitts and Bohemians, City and Countryside—and exclamation points litter the historical landscape. Revolutions were announced; a renaissance proclaimed. Liberal historians wrote off the politics of the Republican ascendancy as an "unfortunate interregnum" or "the shame of the Babbitts." In analyses of the crash of 1929, the historical rhetoric escalated. Morison and Commager in their much used textbook harshly asserted: "Seldom has a generation bequeathed so little that was of permanent value and so much that was troublesome." In the 1960s, Paul Carter summed up the conventional view of the 1920s as "Babylon on wheels with nobody in the driver's seat, even though there were signs that the road ahead might be rough." But he added presciently, "The superficial froth of the period may have been sprayed forth from some deep and terrifying ocean currents indeed." Most encompassing, and the departure point for this volume, is the assessment of the twenties as "really the formative years of modern American history."[2]

Tantalizingly benchmarked by the devastation and brutality of World War I and the cataclysm of the crash and the Great Depression, the twenties has always seemed a distinct period with a style, content, and mood of its own. To contemporaries it marked a deep divide, a changing of the guard from the nineteenth to the twentieth century. The world, wrote journalist Mark Sullivan, was out of balance, its equilibrium gone. More succinctly, Willa Cather observed: "The world broke in two in 1922 or thereabouts." The signs of change and the evidence of struggle between the old and the new were everywhere. The economy of abundance challenged the old Horatio Alger formula of thrift, hard work, and sobriety as the American way to success; advances in technology and science transformed the workplace and the home and triggered new tensions in the churches between the fundamentalists and the modernists. The "new woman" edged in front of the genteel "true woman"; newer Americans crowding the cities threatened the mores of the countryside and of old stock "100 percent Americans." A new generation, teethed on Freud and Jung, called for new freedoms. There was, observed Allen in *Only Yesterday*, a revolution in manners and morals. He added, "If the decade was ill-mannered, it was also unhappy. With the old order of things had gone a set of values which had given richness and meaning to life, and substitute values were not easily found."[3]

The velocity of change was unnerving. In mid-decade, sociologists Robert and Helen Lynd took a team of researchers to Muncie, Indiana, to analyze a representative community. Tracking changes from the 1890s to the mid-1920s, they concluded in their massive study, *Middletown*, that this was "one of the eras of greatest rapidity of change in the history of human institutions." In Muncie, disguised as Magic Middletown, they found, "A citizen has one foot on the relatively solid ground of established habits and the other fast to an escalator careening madly in several directions at a bewildering variety of speeds. . . . Living under such circumstances consists first of all in maintaining some sort of equilibrium." Meanwhile a citizen had to hold on for dear life. Small wonder that the Lynds believed "these people are afraid of something." Their anxiety was described by European visitor Andre Siegfried as "a vague uneasy fear of being overwhelmed from within, and of suddenly finding one day that they are no longer themselves."[4]

The prelude year, 1919, was a harbinger of things to come—a dizzying mix of endings and beginnings. The world, observed a Harvard historian, was one "in which two and two make three or five . . . but never four. . . . It is easy to see that the United States is a new country." The euphoria of the Armistice quickly gave way to grim reality and the political infighting over the Versailles Treaty. While Congress, with the aid of the illness and intransigence of Wilson, spiked the plans for peace, there were no such careful designs for domestic reconversion. Wilson's crusade was "over there." Americans, he stated, did not want to be coached and led. Demobilization began without a clear plan for mustering out 4.5 million troops; it began so quickly that some trains en route to boot camp were reversed in transit. In spite of shouts of "Lafayette, we are still here," by the end of August only forty thousand men remained in Europe. Veterans returned home with sixty dollars in their pockets and bronze or silver buttons in their lapels as a mark of their service. They entered the job market in competition with their younger brothers, the 9 million who had worked in war industries, and the blacks and women who had won new opportunities during the war. Industrial reconversion was also abrupt. Government contracts were rapidly terminated; more than three thousand boards involved in the war effort disbanded. Plants geared up to fill consumer orders; realtors and construction companies planned new housing units and office buildings. In the ensuing boom, there was dislocation but unemployment totaled only 950,000. More troublesome was the high cost of living. Food prices soared 84 percent, clothing 114.5 percent, and furniture, 125 percent. By December 1919, the $5 weekly wage instituted by Henry Ford in 1914 was worth only $2.40.[5]

The economic tension engendered by inflation was exacerbated by more than three thousand strikes. Four million workers walked off their jobs to hold onto wartime gains in working conditions and to increase salaries. In an international environment of Bolshevik success in Russia, uprisings in Hungary, unrest in Germany, and on the homefront, the formation of the Communist and Communist Labor parties, strikes over bread-and-butter issues were quickly translated into a full-blown Red Scare. The American Defense Society, the National Security League, and the 250,000-member American Protective League, formed to guard against the enemy within during the war, girded to thwart the radical. The new American Legion pledged its 650,000 members to 100 percent Americanism.

The carryover of wartime patriotism and the fear of Bolshevism led to bizarre and violent incidents. In Hammond, Indiana, a naturalized citizen killed an alien who said, "To hell with the United States," and was acquitted by a jury in two minutes. In Washington, an enraged sailor fired three shots to the cheers of the crowd into the back of a man who refused to stand for "The Star-Spangled Banner." Ironically, the Left was riven with divisions. The socialist leader, Eugene Debs, was in prison for his stand against the war. The Industrial Workers of the World (IWW) was decimated by federal raids and indictments. Even though the *Atlantic Monthly* carried a sober assessment of Socialist party membership at thirty-nine thousand, the Communist party totals at thirty thousand to sixty thousand, and the Communist Labor party at ten thousand to thirty thousand members, or an estimated one-tenth of 1 percent of the adult population, the fear did not subside.[6]

The labor-related Red Scare began in February 1919. In Seattle, the American Protective League rounded up twenty-eight IWW aliens and sent them on a "Red Express" to Ellis Island for deportation. Shipyard workers, on strike to maintain their high wartime wages, were backed by the Central Labor Council, which was dominated by the American Federation of Labor (AFL). Union walkouts brought the first major general strike in American history. Mayor Ole Hanson, citing an IWW statement that "every strike is a small revolution and a dress rehearsal for the big one," refused to treat with the "revolutionists." The *Chicago Tribune* thundered a warning that "it is only a middling step from Petrograd to Seattle." Though the strikers kept open vital services and avoided violence, troops were brought in. The strike ended in failure, and Hanson went on a triumphal tour speaking on "Americanism versus Bolshevism."[7] Seven months later Boston was rocked by a strike by policemen who wanted the right to join the AFL. Again troops were brought into a city, this time to prevent looting. Again the crisis provided a political hero, Governor Calvin Coolidge, who said in his rebuke: "There is no right to strike against the public safety by anybody anywhere, anytime."

Broader in its impact and implications was the steel strike in September. Through the intervention of the National War Labor Board, the steelworkers had won the eight-hour day and seven wage increases during the war months. In 1919, management determined on an open-shop policy; the AFL massed a major organizational drive led by former socialist and IWW member, Big Bill Foster. By April, the steelworkers were pouring into the AFL ranks. Ninety-eight percent agreed to strike if management refused to negotiate on wages, hours, and conditions. On 22 September, after six months of frustration, 356,000 launched the strike. The New York Socialist paper, the *Call*, hailed what might be "the last battle with the entrenched overlords of America." The Communist party urged support for the workers in their battle to crush the capitalists. The National Association of Manufacturers, dredging up Foster's past, excoriated the leadership of "Red Foster" and warned, "Beware the Agitator who Makes Labor a Catspaw for Bolshevism." In Gary, Indiana, where radicals did have a dominant role, violence resulted in martial law. By January, with twenty dead and $112 million lost in wages, the strike ended. Six weeks after the steelworkers walked out, 394,000 United Mine Workers began a strike that proved equally unsuccessful. In each of the strikes from Seattle to West Virginia, the issues were traditional bread-and-butter ones, the workers were cheered by the Socialists and Communists, and management used Red Scare tactics.[8]

The scare was fueled by bomb blasts and bomb scares. In April, Mayor Ole Hanson received a crude and leaking bomb in the mail. Though this was discovered and defused, a bomb mailed to a conservative Alabama jurist exploded. A New York postal clerk, hearing the description of the packages, remembered sixteen other boxes wrapped in Gimbels paper and labeled "novelty" ready for delivery on May Day. Two months later bombs exploded in eight cities, one in the backyard of Attorney General A. Mitchell Palmer. Though uninjured, the shaken Palmer, now convinced that a revolution was in the offing, marshaled the resources of the Justice Department and launched a series of raids that were decried by one civil libertarian as "the greatest executive restriction of personal liberty in the history of this country." In December 1919, as part of his "Ship or Shoot" policy, Palmer had 249 aliens, including Emma Goldman, rounded up to sail on the "Soviet Ark" the *Buford*. In January 1920, federal agents raided the headquarters of the Communist and Communist Labor parties and arrested six thousand. Meanwhile, thirty-two state legislatures passed restrictive laws and instituted teacher loyalty oaths. The most destructive bomb explosion occurred September 1920 outside of J.P. Morgan's Wall Street offices. Twenty-nine were instantly killed, two hundred hospitalized; damages were more than $2 million. Yet the worst of the hysteria seemed over. The Red tide was not sweeping over Europe; there seemed little evidence of actual fire behind the smoke. Jack Dempsey and Babe Ruth were providing more beguiling pyrotechnics and hysteria yielded to circuses.[9]

Yet the fear and intolerance that launched the decade remained. In

1922, writer Katherine Fullerton Gerould noted in *Harper's*: "America is no longer a free country in the old sense, and liberty is increasingly a mere rhetorical figure. . . . No thinking citizen can express in freedom more than a part of his honest convictions . . . everywhere, on every hand, free speech is choked off in one direction or another. The only way an American citizen who is really interested in all the social problems of his country can preserve any freedom of expression is to choose the mob that is most sympathetic to him, and abide under the shadow of that mob." The most graphic example of the legacy of the Red Scare and the fear and intolerance that haunted the decade was the Sacco-Vanzetti case. Sacco and Vanzetti were Italian anarchists arrested and indicted on flimsy evidence during the Red Scare; their dignified demeanor and their cause won an increasing outpouring of support by the Left in America, Europe, and Latin America. Their execution on 22 August 1927 was hailed as martyrdom and given as proof of both the fear and the vulnerability of Coolidge prosperity.[10]

Yet it was Coolidge prosperity, or the "Golden Glow," that was the central reality of the decade. After a postwar boom and a severe recession in 1921 that drove the GNP down 10 percent, toppled 30,000 businesses, brought 500,000 mortgage foreclosures, and left 5 million jobless, America had seven biblical fat years. From 1922 to 1929, "the prosperity bandwagon rolled down Main Street." In those seven years, America amassed two-fifths of the world's wealth. Economist T. N. Carver, observing the outpouring of goods, concluded: "The economic changes now occurring in the United States are significant in their relation to the whole history of Western Civilization—as significant perhaps as the Industrial Revolution in England at the close of the eighteenth century."[11] The basic problems of production seemed solved. America had the technology, resources, and organization to produce as much as it needed; the challenge shifted to distribution and consumption.

The Golden Glow was fueled from a variety of sources. With new discoveries of oil fields in Texas, Oklahoma, and California, America controlled nearly half of the world's total power resources. American industry was 70 percent electrified by the end of the decade, a 40 percent jump from 1913. Henry Ford led in the application of technology to production problems. The continuous flow of his mechanized production line produced, as a demonstration of its efficiency in October 1925, a complete Model T every ten seconds. Scientific management, the time-and-motion studies introduced by Frederick W. Taylor, was not only increasingly utilized by management but accepted by Samuel Gompers and the AFL. Mechanization brought an estimated 50 percent increase in horsepower per worker and a 65 percent rise in manufacturing output.[12]

While increased power and technology stimulated production, the expansion of the housing boom and the emergence of new industries and products provided a more dramatic push to Coolidge prosperity. The spurt in the housing industry continued through mid-decade. Single-family dwellings remained the standard. By 1926, 16 million homes were wired for electricity, providing a vast market for new electric appliances. Thirty-seven percent of those households had a vacuum cleaner, 25 percent a clothes washer, 80 percent an electric iron. Refrigerators replaced the ice box and made the "cool cellar" obsolete. By the end of the decade when housing starts declined, builders had produced apartment units and continued breaking urban skylines with skyscrapers. In 1929, New York architects and builders vied for the "tallest" title with the elegant seventy-seven-story Chrysler Building winning a temporary victory before its eclipse by the eighty-six-story Empire State Building. While the construction industry was a major catalyst, the automobile provided the crucial fuel for the Golden Glow. Historian William Leuchtenburg asserted, "The development of the industry in a single generation was the greatest achievement of modern technology."[13]

The roar of the twenties was partially the roar of new urban traffic. In 1919, there were 6.7 million passenger cars in the United States; ten years later there were 23.1 million, a total that surpassed the number of telephones in use. In Middletown, the Lynds reported two cars for every three families. Automobiles consumed 80 percent of the rubber, 50 percent of the plate glass, 11 percent of the steel, 65 percent of the leather upholstery, and 8 percent of the copper produced, as well as 7 billion gallons of gasoline. The Federal Highways Act of 1916 was producing a network of roads, providing construction jobs and stimulating new businesses along the highways from restaurants to garages. Florida, California, and Arizona became tourist meccas. National parks were developed and expanded. City councils pondered new traffic laws and voted appropriations to purchase new red and green traffic signals. Buses replaced the interurban trolley lines and trucks dried up the traffic of many railroad branch lines.

Henry Ford was the early leader in the production miracles. At once practical and visionary, Ford boasted that, through centralized management, control of raw materials, precision tools, and a high-speed mechanized production line, iron ore arriving at the docks at his new River Rouge plant at eight o'clock on a Monday would form a completed Ford car by Wednesday noon. Ford envisioned the production of a people's car. He paid his workers five dollars a day, determined that every Ford worker would be able to buy a Ford automobile. His dynamic logic of mass production was to lower unit costs until the price matched buying power. The Model T became the Volkswagen of the 1920s; the Tin Lizzie, the "family pet of the nation." It did not lack for competition; Chrysler and Dodge, Studebaker and Packard, produced elegant rivals. General Motors, under the leadership of Alfred Sloan, utilized Du Pont organization and management expertise to sharply challenge Ford with the low-cost Chevrolet. Ford's response in 1927 was to shut down and retool to produce the Model A. Five hundred thousand customers made down payments sight unseen. They bought mobility and freedom with their purchase. The automobile created a nation of nomads, and it changed every aspect of American life.[14]

Other new or expanding industries contributed to the boom. The chemical industry, freed from German competition during the war, developed new synthetics, rayon and celluloid, Pyrex glass, and antifreeze. The tobacco, safety razor, and watch industries spurted as veterans returned from their European experience smoking cigarettes rather than cigars and ready to abandon straight razors and watch fobs. War stimulated interest in and spurred development of a fledgling aviation industry. *Time, Reader's Digest, Vanity Fair, American Mercury*, and the *New Yorker* were launched, providing wider outlets for a burgeoning advertising industry.

In communications, three industries linked Americans more closely: the telephone, the radio, and the movies. Radio had the most meteoric rise. In 1922, radio sales totaled $60 million; by 1929 sales had increased 1400 percent to $852 million. The airways were so cluttered by mid-decade that the federal government, through the leadership of Secretary of Commerce Herbert Hoover, created the Federal Radio Commission; AT&T and the National Broadcasting Company combined to form the first national network system. While radio provided ears, the movies provided eyes. Louis B. Mayer began the organization of his successful star-studded studio. Mary Pickford, Charlie Chaplin, Barbara Swanson, Rudolph Valentino, and Greta Garbo were directed in a galaxy of money-making films by Cecil B. deMille, Eric von Stroheim, and Clarence Brown. Each week 100 million went to the movies in the more than 20,500 new theaters.[15]

Industrial expansion was matched by corporate consolidation. The 1920s brought the second age of the "big merge." Unlike the trustification of the United States that had marked the turn of the century, the holding company was the structure most utilized in the twenties, with the Insull utility combine as the classic example. By 1920, ten companies controlled 72 percent of the nation's electric power. In banking, 1 percent of the banks controlled 46 percent of the banking resources. Four meat packers controlled 70 percent of the production; four tobacco companies controlled 94 percent of the cigarette market. Goodyear, Firestone, U.S. Rubber, and Goodrich dominated rubber, and General Electric and Westinghouse were the major brands for refrigerators. In retailing the A&P was the chain-store leader; by 1928 it had 17,500 branch stores doing an annual business of $750 million.[16]

The proliferation of holding companies and industrial consolidation was paralleled by the emergence of new trade associations. The war had demonstrated the benefits of working together. Secretary of Commerce Herbert Hoover, believing the business of the government was to help to "rationalize" business, was an eager midwife in the development of associations. Each shared information on prices, production methods, credit rating, and cost accounting and served as a watchdog on federal regulation. Each developed a code of ethics stressing the commitment to service. A vice president of the Chemical National Bank of New York summed up business idealism: "We know that real success in business is not attained at the expense of others. Business can succeed only in the long run by acquiring and holding the goodwill of people."[17]

If this was not enough to allay the antitrust anxieties of prewar reformers, business was armed with new public relations experts to help inform the public that what was good for General Motors was good for the United States. More important were the new professional managers who were setting policies for the giant combines. Gerald Swope of General Electric and Walter Gifford at AT&T had worked with Jane Addams at Hull House. Significant numbers of new executives were beginning to emerge from Harvard's new Graduate School of Business Administration, the Wharton School and others. With increased mergers and new managers, there was increased separation of ownership and management. By 1929, AT&T boasted of $5 billion in assets, 454,000 employees, and 567,694 stockholders. The president of Illinois Central declared, "It is Main Street and not Wall Street that runs the railroads today."[18]

Government was a solid partner in the Golden Glow. President Harding's pledge of "less government in business and more business in government" was affirmed by his successors. By 1925, Harding and Coolidge appointments had transformed the Federal Trade Commission. The commission announced its policy in 1927 as "helping business to help itself whenever and wherever it can be done." The chairman believed that "the legitimate interests of business are in perfect harmony with the true interests of the public." The Antitrust Division of the Justice Department was similarly well disposed; it managed to settle almost 50 percent of its cases between 1925 and 1929 by consent decrees. The Tariff Commission was headed by the former editor of the *Protectionist* magazine. Congress supported business growth through passage of the Fordney-McCumber tariff in 1921, the highest protective tariff in American history. By 1926, the trickle-down tax proposals of Secretary of Treasury Andrew Mellon were in place. A taxpayer with $1 million annual income now paid an income tax of $200,000 rather than $600,000. Mellon himself received a larger tax reduction than all the citizens of the state of Nebraska. Still, government receipts totaled $4 billion, while expenditures averaged $3 billion. The national debt was trimmed down from $24 billion to $16 billion. Though the number of millionaires escalated, there was also an increase in real wages on an average of 8 percent. The nation's total realized income also increased during Coolidge prosperity from $74.3 billion to $89 billion.[19]

The Golden Glow was boosted not only by statistics but by rhetoric and idealism. Business was regarded with reverence. Coolidge intoned, "The man who builds a factory builds a temple; the man who works there worships there." Advertising pioneer Bruce Barton forged the business-religion linkage more surely in his 1925–26 best-seller *The Man Nobody Knows*, marveling at the business expertise of Jesus who "picked up twelve men from the bottom ranks of business and forged them into an organization that conquered the world." A Metropolitan Casualty Insurance Company pamphlet hailed Moses as one of the greatest salesmen and real estate promoters. Democratic national chairman and General Motors executive John J. Raskob, agreeing with Coolidge that the era of people's capitalism had arrived, wrote an article for *Ladies Home Journal* in 1929 entitled "You Ought to Be Rich." He detailed how an investment of $15 a month wisely invested with dividends plowed back could bring a 400 percent return, or $80,000, in twenty years. His positive thinking was reflected in America's infatuation with Frenchman Emile Coué's formula for success through repetition of the simple refrain "Every day, and in every way, I am becoming better and better."

The *Chicago Tribune* presented a "Portrait of a Businessman" in September 1927, asserting, "He is too busy to defend himself. He has to be busy. He has the whole country resting on his shoulders and if he weakens everybody is miserable. He keeps the country going. He provides work which buys the shoes, the steaks, the house furniture and the automobile. Yes, he commercializes everything and makes it possible to exist." *Nation's Business*, the organ of the Chamber of Commerce, editorially exhorted, "Dare to be a Babbitt." Most sweeping was a litany by Edward Purinton in the *Independent*: "What is the finest game? Business. The soundest science? Business. The truest art? Business. The fullest education? Business. The fairest opportunity? Business. The cleanest philanthropy? Business. The sanest religion? Business." Historian James Truslow Adams in *Our Business Civilization* saw that America was "resting her civilization on the ideas of businessmen," and questioned, "Can a great civilization be built up or maintained upon the philosophy of the counting-house and the sole basic idea of a profit?"[20]

More challenging to the concept of business beneficence was the presence of those who, as Frederick Lewis Allen put it, were unable or did not choose to climb aboard Uncle Sam's prosperity wagon: organized labor, the embattled farmers, and the intellectuals and artists of the lost generation.

Organized labor, reeling from the Red Scare and in the wake of a series of disastrous strikes, entered the twenties on the defensive. In thirty-four years the AFL had organized just over 4 million members; one in five working Americans belonged to a union, the lowest percentage of any major industrial nation. Even this total declined as labor faced a series of daunting challenges throughout the decade. Though European immigration was restricted by new quota legislation, the workplace was crowded with refugees from the countryside. More than 19 million emigrated to the cities during the decade. They were joined in a continuing migration of hope by black Americans from the South and by women wage earners, up 27 percent by 1929. None had union experience; and blacks and women had traditionally not been welcomed by the AFL. Increased mechanization with the concomitant emphasis on speed eroded the bargaining power of skilled workers. The

Lynds found the working class in Middletown anxious about frequent layoffs. Throughout the nation seasonal and technological unemployment averaged more than 200,000 each year. Coal miners faced 30 percent unemployment; workers in other sick industries—textiles, shoes and leather, and shipbuilding—experienced shutdowns and relocation. Workers on the production line complained of feeling like part of the machine and Ford's River Rouge plant was described as "not a happy place."[21]

Labor's defensive stance was aggravated by management's offensive. Committed to the open shop, the National Association of Manufacturers (NAM) and other business groups stressed the "American plan," which translated into a "kill them with kindness policy." President John Edgerton of the NAM explained: "The responsibilities of industrial managers imposed on them a vast duty. It required them to give workers a square deal in industry." Industries developed or expanded stock-sharing programs, group life insurance opportunities, and old-age pensions. Through picnics and dances and baseball teams companies sought worker identity. Ford's Sociological Department was only the most ambitious and most paternalistic of these efforts. In 1927, Elton Mayo and a Harvard Business School team began a project with a group of Western Electric Company workers at Hawthorne, Illinois, experimenting with a shortened workday, regular breaks, and refreshments to try to expand productivity. Output increased appreciably, they discovered, primarily because the workers felt part of the project, felt that someone cared about how they worked. Western Electric, which paid good wages, provided paid vacations, pension plans, and a company hospital, confirmed the truism that happy workers are better workers.[22]

The AFL was particularly ill equipped to meet this broad management offensive. Samuel Gompers, who had led the organization for all but one year of its existence, died in 1924. He was succeeded by United Mine Workers (UMW) executive William Green. Described by columnist Westbrook Pegler as an "All-American mushmouth," Green lacked the charisma and leadership of Gompers. The only major industrial union within the AFL was the UMW. Steel, rubber, automobiles remained unorganized as the AFL continued its emphasis on craft unions.[23]

Debacles in three major strikes graphically demonstrated the problems facing organized labor. In 1922, railroad shopmen struck for better wages and conditions. When management proved intransigent, the railroad brotherhoods supported the shopmen by suddenly and dramatically stopping twelve transcontinental trains and stranding twenty-five hundred passengers. Four hundred thousand workers joined in the first nationwide railroad strike since 1894. Harding's attorney general, Harry Daugherty, sought and won an injunction so sweeping that the AFL and the brotherhoods began an unsuccessful impeachment movement. Workers were forbidden to picket. They could not speak or act to dissuade workers from returning to the job. In June of the same year, sixty thousand bituminous miners struck in the Midwest for a $7.50 a day wage. Management argued they could not meet the competition of nonunionized West Virginia companies. In Herrin, Illinois, a UMW town, violence broke out when strikebreakers were brought in. Strikers blew up the pumping station, cut off the food supply, and stood ready with a thousand rifles trained on the shaft. A hastily arranged truce and safe conduct broke down, and seventeen corpses were left in the streets. The union's leader John L. Lewis blamed communist agitators. The miners won their wage increase but lost the war. More than 3,300 bituminous mines closed by 1929, and 250,000 of the 400,000 United Mine Workers lost their jobs. Finally, in the textile industry, the AFL affiliate United Textile Workers union faced the relocation of plants from New England to the nonunion South. By 1929, they represented only 3 percent of the textile workers. In 1929, the Communist National Textile Workers tried to organize workers in Gastonia, North Carolina. In the ensuing violence and trial of the union leaders for murder, one of them fled to the Soviet Union, ending the decade for organized labor as it had begun with charges of Reds in the unions.[24]

By 1929, union membership declined to 4,330,000, a drop of 20 percent over the decade. One in eight American adult workers was organized. A *Liberty* magazine editorial observed, "American conditions have just about wiped out the proletariat." To workers in the twenties the promise of steady employment and higher earnings seemed more important than industrial freedom. In Middletown, the Lynds found class was a reality, but class consciousness was not a winning weapon for organized labor in the Coolidge years. The AFL was ill prepared in organization and ideas to meet the onslaught of the depression years.

While organized labor faced lean years, the farmers were on "perhaps the most terrible toboggan slide in all-American agricultural history." Accepting the slogan, "Food will Win the War," farmers had plowed 45 million new acres from 1914 to 1919. The Lever, or Food Control Act of 1917 had encouraged expanded production with guaranteed prices. When the war closed, the government price for wheat stood at $2.20 a bushel. Peace brought the end of price supports and the collapse of the export market to Europe. Responding to the inflation in the boom months at the end of the war, the Federal Reserve Board tightened credit. Faced with overproduction and lowered demand, farmers grappled with high costs and tight credit. Transportation costs had risen in some areas in the Midwest over 50 percent. Iowa farmers who had paid $199 an acre during the war were left with high mortgages. Farm laborers were leaving for the higher wages of the city; new mechanized plows and equipment raised costs. Property taxes were raised to finance road costs and other state expansion; in some counties in Ohio, Indiana, and Wisconsin, one-third of farmers' income was devoted to taxes. Finally, changes in American diet and dress had an impact. Fresh vegetables and dairy products profited, while beef, wheat, and cotton all faced a decline in demand. By November 1920 farm prices were down 33 percent; by the summer of 1921, they had dropped 85 percent. The price for a bushel of wheat had fallen to 67 cents.[25]

As in the severe agricultural depression of the 1890s, the farmers of the 1920s looked for villains. Again, the middleman was a prime candidate. Secretary of Agriculture Henry C. Wallace estimated that the farmers received at most only 50 percent of the consumer's dollar. One Texas farmer testified that he had sold his cabbage for six dollars a ton and it had brought the middleman two hundred dollars a ton. Another farmer reportedly paid more for a pair of calfskin shoes than he received for the calf. Armed with the knowledge of their distress, the farmers did not lack for organization or muscle to seek some redress. Although the Grange was the most venerable of the farmers' organizations, the American Farm Bureau Federation and the Farmers' Union were the most effective lobbyists in the 1920s. In the Senate, they built a farm bloc of twenty-six supporters, and in the House they could count on the backing of ninety-five or ninety-six representatives. From 1921 through 1923, they were able to achieve some gains: inclusion of commodities in the Fordney-McCumber tariff, broad exemption of cooperatives from antitrust action, and better regulation of the stockyards. Tariff protection remained a major objective with the overall goal of the farmers to achieve parity, a fair exchange level for what they bought with what they sold.[26]

A measure of the farmers' economic desperation and the intransigence of the two major parties in responding to their pleas for parity was the decision of some to join forces with leaders in organized labor and the Socialists in forming the Progressive party in 1924. Presidential standard-bearer "Fighting Bob" La Follette and vice-presidential candidate Burton K. Wheeler fought for a cluster of issues from the Populist-Progressive years, arguing again for trust-busting and federal regulation of the railroads. Handicapped by a late start, technical difficulties in getting on state ballots, a lack of organization, and a weak campaign chest, La Follette could expend only four cents for every Coolidge dollar. Still the seriousness of the Progressive ticket could be measured by the sharpness of the attack mounted by Coolidge and the Republicans. La Follette and his backers were painted as radicals; sloganeering stressed "Coolidge or Chaos." In spite of a rise in wheat prices, which hurt the La Follette candidacy in some midwestern states, the Progressive ticket, beyond an expected victory in La Follette's home state of Wisconsin, garnered second place in Idaho, California, Minnesota, Iowa, North and South Dakota, Washington, Montana, Wyoming, Nevada, and Oregon. The Progressives gained 4.8 million votes, 17 percent of the vote, and, combined with the Democratic tally in major northeastern cities, edged out the Republicans in urban America. La Follette's death in 1925 and labor's differences with the Socialists effectively buried the Progressive party.[27]

The farm organizations, aided by the strong support of Secretary Wallace, did achieve an important gain in 1924 with the introduction of the first of the McNary-Haugen bills which accepted the right of farmers to a fair purchasing power. American Farm Bureau head Gray Silver testified, "We are sick nigh unto death." Others, pointedly arguing that "you can't sell a plow to a busted customer," tried to convince the business community and politicians that Coolidge prosperity could not survive a continuing agricultural depression. Finally passed in 1927 and 1928, the McNary-Haugen bills were twice vetoed by Calvin Coolidge, who denounced the measures as preferential class legislation. By the end of his administration farm income had dropped to 9 percent of the national total. Herbert Hoover called a special session of Congress in March 1929 to deal with the continuing emergency. The congressional response was to establish a Federal Farm Board. Armed with a $500 million appropriation, it was given the mandate to work with cooperatives to try to "rationalize" agriculture. In years of surpluses, the Farm Board would buy and store nonperishable commodities to try to achieve parity. By 1931, the Farm Board had 257 million bushels of wheat stored and had failed to sustain the price. The exodus from the farms continued, but the farmers, unlike organized labor, had an agenda and a program at the onset of the depression and New Deal.[28]

While farmers and labor struggled to share in the Golden Glow, the artists and intellectuals of the lost generation excoriated the values and materialism of Coolidge prosperity. The decade, wrote poet Hart Crane, was "appalling and dull at the same time." America's business civilization was hostile territory. Middle-class society, explained Malcolm Cowley, was "something alien . . . it was a sort of parlor car in which we rode, over smooth tracks, toward a destination we should never have chosen for ourselves." The vehemence of their rejection of the dominant values was matched by the poignancy of their search for new values, for a way to live with dignity in a world "loose at all ends."[29]

The sources of their discontent were many. Their experience in the war and disillusion with the peace left them disgusted with systems and sham. The closeness and randomness of death bred an irony articulated in Randall Jarrell's poem "Losses": "When we died they said / Our casualties were low." They determined, as John Dos Passos observed, "not to die for God, country, and for Yale." On their return, they joined an ongoing critique of America voiced by an earlier generation. Van Wyck Brooks described the thinness of the culture and asserted that "old American things are old as nothing else anywhere in the world is old, old without majesty, old without mellowness, old without pathos, just shabby and bloodless and worn out." Sinclair Lewis was scalding in his depiction of Gopher Prairie values: "It is contentment . . . the contentment of the quiet dead, who are scornful of the living for their restless waking. It is negation canonized as the one positive virtue. It is the prohibition of happiness. . . . It is dullness made God." The village virus of Gopher Prairie was part of a nationwide pressure for conformity that left the artist, according to Ezra Pound, "thwarted with systems / Helpless against control." The sage of Baltimore Henry L. Mencken, the "chief tomtom beater," summed up the trouble as "Puritanism compounded by evangelicalism and political moralism soured and coarsened by money grubbing."[30]

Mencken, through his magazine articles and as editor of *American Mercury*, and Lewis, in *Main Street* and *Babbitt*, combined to lash American customs and values. America, asserted Mencken, was a paradise of the third-rate; Americans were the "booboisie"; the citizen was a "lumpish, peasant oaf" or worse, "a gaping primate." Of *Babbitt*,

Mencken declared: "I know of no American novel that more accurately presents the real America." Daniel Boone and Horatio Alger were only distant cousins of this new American character. Lewis had created, according to one critic, "almost a perfectly conceived poetic vision of a perfectly standardized money society; it is our native Inferno of the mechanized heartland." Political philosopher Walter Lippmann, not always an enchanted commentator on American life, examined the furor created by the barbs of Mencken and Lewis and quipped, "Who knows having read Mencken and Lewis . . . what kind of world will be left when all the boobs and yokels have crawled back in their holes and have died in shame?"[31]

Mencken was included among the pundits and observers approached by young Harold Stearns to contribute to his compendium, *Civilization in the United States.* Stearns gave a press conference summarizing the criticisms and asserting that the younger generation was in "revolt". It disliked, "almost to the point of hatred and certainly to the point of contempt, the type of people who actually run things." He made his statements on the dock when he was about to leave for Europe.[32]

He joined a stream of artists following the lead of Ezra Pound, seeking a culture that could nurture art and seeking in Paris a laboratory of how to live. Malcolm Cowley has movingly detailed the search in his *Exile's Return.* Hemingway's Jake Barnes spoke for a wounded generation in exile in *The Sun Also Rises,* stating: "I did not care what it was all about. All I wanted to know was how to live in it. Maybe if you found out how to live in it, you learned what it was all about."[33] Hemingway's code, a stoic grace under pressure, was one of the few answers advanced on how to live. The exiles tried to escape to art, to the primitive, to nature, to Mexico, to the country of their youth. France had brought perspective to America, if not acceptance. One of Dos Passos's characters in *Manhattan Transfer* announced as he prepared to return home: "It's all the same in France. You are paid badly and live well; here you are paid well and live badly."[34]

The writing of the young artists who remained at home was portrayed by disapproving critic Henry S. Canby. "Taught by the social philosophers and war's disillusions that Denmark is decaying," he wrote, "they do not escape to Cathay or Bohemia, but stay at home and pessimistically narrate what Denmark has done to them." Their novels were diaries. The plot was drearily the same. The hero encountered disillusion after disillusion. "At the age of seven or thereabout he sees through his parents and characterizes them in a phrase. At fourteen he sees through his education and begins to dodge it. At eighteen he sees through morality and steps over it. At twenty he loses respect for his home town, and at twenty-one discovers that our social and economic system is ridiculous. At twenty-three his story ends because the author has run through society to date and does not know what to do next. Life is ahead of the hero, and presumably a new society of his own making." F. Scott Fitzgerald's *This Side of Paradise* in 1920 was the perfect exemplar. His hero, Amory Blaine, having grown up "to find all Gods dead, all wars fought, all faiths in man shaken," leaves Princeton with the pronouncement "I know myself and that is all." *This Side of Paradise* "haunted the decade like a song." In capturing the desperate rhythm of the fast life, Fitzgerald shocked and alarmed his older readers. The young generation claimed him for its own. Fitzgerald became the voice of all the sad young men, yearning for a lost world of virtue and values. In 1929 in *The Modern Temper*, a sweeping reflection on the peril of the individual in a world in the process of radical transformation, Joseph Wood Krutch described the "expectant hopelessness" of his generation. "The certainty had departed from life," Frederick Lewis Allen summarized, "the purpose of life was undiscoverable, the ends of life were less discoverable still; in all this fog there was no solid thing on which a man could lay hold and say, This is real; this will abide."[35]

The whirl of change creating a crisis of culture in the 1920s was stirred by the rapid advance of science and technology. Science promised a new authority, a possible way to control a changing external world and to order the inner life. In their visits to America in 1921, Albert Einstein and Madame Curie were lionized. AT&T invested $15 million annually to support two thousand scientists in research in the Bell Labs. Life expectancy lengthened to 57.1 years during the decade; new vitamins were discovered and became part of the American diet. Popularizers of biology and anthropology gave the general impression that humans "were merely animals of a rather intricate variety," a conclusion that was challenged in the widely publicized Scopes "monkey trial."

But psychology was the science that dominated the decade. Freud had lectured in America in 1909, and two hundred books had been published on his theories before 1920. Popularizers and interpreters found a ready market for his ideas on individual freedom and development. Allen humorously summarized the impact. Sex, he explained, made the world go around. "Almost every human motive was attributable to it; if you were patriotic or liked the violin, you were in the grip of sex—in a sublimated form. The first requirement of mental health was to have an uninhibited sex life. If you would be well and happy you must obey your libido." Researchers and reporters began to tabulate Americans' changing sexual practices. One account in *Harper's* in 1928 traced the 1,358 love affairs of 200 married couples, an average of 7 each. Less scientifically, journalist Elmer Davis counted 259 affairs of one benighted heroine in a postwar novel and observed that she did not get "an emotional wallop out of any of them." With sex so available, social workers reported that the number of brothels had declined. Prostitutes were being replaced by call girls and nightclub hostesses. New sex magazines and movies depicted the sexual revolution, one movie ad promising "Neckers, petters, white kisses, red kisses, pleasure-mad daughters, sensation-craving mothers, the truth—bold, naked, sensational." The speakeasy gave men and women a place to drink together; the automobile provided the privacy to be together. Jazz, the wailing saxophone, the new dances of the decade, and the craze of dance marathons were part of the revolution. The new sexual freedom rolled forward, concluded one historian, "as implacably as a tank division advancing across an agricultural plain, its weight and speed flattening everything in its path."[36]

Coolidge prosperity brought the leisure to make whoopee in a variety of ways. Money spent on amusement and recreation rose by 300 percent. Movies, dances, and sports absorbed most of the dollars. Americans took up golf and tennis, but increasingly, in an age of Babe Ruth, Red Grange, Jack Dempsey, and Man o' War, they became spectators. Boxing's million-dollar gates and the heavy gambling at bouts and the racetracks was another challenge to the morality of an older America. Heywood Broun depicted the obsession with sports and the collision of values in an imaginative account of the arrival of conservative preacher John Roach Straton into heaven. Straton urged God to rain fire down on Yankee Stadium where forty thousand had gathered for Sunday baseball. God was willing, but as he watched Babe Ruth come to the plate, he suggested, "Let's at least wait until the inning's over."[37]

Cultural issues roused political passions and set the political agenda. The dividing lines were sharp: rural / urban, dry / wet, 100 percent old-stock America / ethnic America. Culturally, old America faced the challenge of new America. The census report of 1920 for the first time recorded that more Americans lived in cities than in the countryside. It was a bare 51 percent and twenty-five hundred citizens made a city, but the trend to a metropolitan America seemed clear. Rural and old-stock America moved to the defensive. Blue laws, insistence on clean movies, the Scopes trial, the flow of nostalgic writing celebrating village life, the success of fundamentalist preachers like Aimee Semple McPherson—all marked the effort to retain familiar American values.

The central test was the noble experiment, Prohibition. The Eighteenth Amendment became law in January 1920. The campaigns of the Anti-Saloon League and the Women's Christian Temperance Union had won ratification of the amendment in forty-six states. The battle to dry up America seemed won. Yet in 1919, the "applejack" gubernatorial campaign in New Jersey was a harbinger of wet America's intransigence. Before Wilson's veto of the Volstead Act, enforcing Prohibition, was overridden in October, Democratic candidate Edward I. Edwards campaigned on a pledge to make New Jersey as wet as the Atlantic Ocean. His Republican opponent thundered it was a contest of the Constitution and law and order versus sedition, of patriotic Americans versus aliens. Edwards won the vote of New Jersey's newer urban Americans; some loyalists even walked to their old bars after Edwards's inauguration, hoping to find them open again. The Democrats maintained their loyalty in each off-year election in the twenties. Although enforcement was initially successful and 1920 was probably the driest year in American history, the cities became increasingly damp. Enforcement was estimated as 95 percent in Kansas, but only 5 percent in New York City.[38]

In their frustration, rural old-stock America found scapegoats: it must be the Reds; it must be the Catholics; it must be the Jews; it must be the immigrants. In April 1921 emergency legislation to restrict the flow of immigrants passed the House of Representatives in eight hours. The *Congressional Record* included State Department assessments of those who crowded American shores in 1920: the Poles were "beaten folk"; those from the Russian Caucasus were "not only illiterate" but years of unsettled conditions had caused them "to lose the habit of work." More disturbing, they might be impregnated with Bolshevism. The 1921 legislation was followed by the Johnson Quota Act of 1924, setting a quota based on national origin. In 1927, the total allowed to enter was set at 150,000 annually. Americans still welcomed the tired and the poor, but they preferred them to come from northern or western Europe and from sturdy Protestant stock. Under the quota, 65,700 Irish were allowed in; Italians were limited to 5,000.

While legislators barred the golden door to keep undesirables out, the Ku Klux Klan reemerged to preserve America within. By 1921 it boasted an estimated 100,000 members; by 1924 it had grown to be the most powerful nativist organization in American history. Its membership spread from Atlanta to Los Angeles. The organization controlled Indiana politics, and its largest membership was in Chicago. The targets of its vigilance were blacks, ethnics, and WASPs who did not live what the Klan construed as a morally upright life. Facing the Klan challenge to their Americanism, blacks and newer Americans responded in a variety of ways. Some returned to their homelands. Most of them were determined to prove how American they were. They identified with the success of their countrymen: Poles cheered the prowess of Al Simmons (Syzmanski) of the Chicago White Sox; Irish and other ethnics hailed the rise of Al Smith. A third group emphasized their heritage. The Fascist League of North America formed; the Zionist movement expanded. Most dramatic was the rise of Marcus Garvey's United Negro Improvement Association. Headquartered in New York City, Garvey's movement claimed a membership of more than ten thousand in Detroit, Philadelphia, Pittsburgh, Cleveland, and Cincinnati. His rallying cry was "Up, up, you mighty race." He gloried in the rich heritage of Africa and the courage of Nat Turner; he insisted that black was beautiful. His announcement of the creation of the Black Star shipping line with black management and black capital immediately attracted $100,000 from black shareholders. Though the company foundered and Garvey was indicted for mail fraud, he was a powerful spokesman for the urban black. He was known, declared Langston Hughes, the length and breadth of the west coast of Africa.[39]

Whereas cultural and ethnic tensions hardly ruffled the Republican party, they almost destroyed the Democratic coalition resting on the "boss wing" of urban, ethnic, wet America and the rural, dry, 100 percent American South. In 1924, the divisions were dramatic. Reporter Arthur Krock described the "snarling, cursing, tedious, tenuous, suicidal, homicidal roughhouse" of the Democratic convention. Hoping to capitalize on the Harding scandals, the Democrats had no shortage of presidential candidates. One leading contender was Californian William Gibbs McAdoo. Woodrow Wilson's son-in-law and former secretary of the treasury, McAdoo brought progressive credentials to the convention; he also brought the uninvited endorsement of the Ku Klux Klan. Although he did not seek it, he did not reject it either. At his nomination, the opposition raucously shouted "Ku, Ku McAdoo." The other major contender was New York's progressive governor Alfred E.

Smith. A Catholic, Smith had risen through the ranks of Tammany Hall, and his accent was a constant reminder of his origins in the wettest city in America. The opposition shouted from the galleries, "Booze, booze, booze!" A third candidate, Oscar Underwood of Alabama, architect of the Underwood tariff and foe of the Klan, urged with the Smith forces that the convention adopt a plank denouncing the Klan. In the ensuing passionate debate, highlighted by the exhortations for compromise of William Jennings Bryan, the delegates voted 542 3/20th to 541 3/20th not to condemn the Klan. With a two-thirds vote needed for the nomination, it was obvious that neither the McAdoo forces nor the Smith forces would be victorious. But it had to be proven ballot after ballot. Will Rogers finally quipped, "This thing has got to come to an end. New York invited you as guests, not to live." On the 103d ballot, the Democrats finally chose a compromise candidate, John W. Davis of West Virginia, and balanced the ticket with William Jennings Bryan's brother, Charles. With a third-party ticket headed by La Follette and Wheeler, a normal Republican majority, the masterful defusing of the scandal issue by incumbent Coolidge, and the country enjoying Coolidge prosperity, the Democrats had no chance.[40]

Four years later the cultural conflicts still centered within the Democratic party. McAdoo was no longer a contender. Al Smith had been resoundingly reelected governor in 1926. He had a solid record of accomplishment in a powerful state. To reject his candidacy in 1928 would be to threaten the support of the boss wing of the urban Northeast. Seeking to hold the party together, the delegates nominated Smith for president and gave him as vice-presidential running mate Joseph Robinson of Arkansas. Smith, the first Catholic candidate, had signed the law repealing New York State's Prohibition revision. He was the quintessential representative of urban, wet, ethnic America. Walter Lippmann summed it up: "Quite apart even from the severe opposition of the prohibitionists, the objection to Tammany, the sectional objection to New York, there is an opposition to Smith which is as authentic, and it seems to me, as poignant as his support. It is inspired by the feeling that the clamorous life of the city should not be acknowledged as the American ideal."[41]

The Republicans gathered in Kansas City. Although they were divided on solutions for the farmer, there were no major cultural divides. Their presidential nominee Herbert Hoover was the mirror image of Al Smith, the ideal of 100 percent America. Born in rural Iowa, the son of a blacksmith and a teacher, Hoover had been orphaned at an early age. He worked his way through Stanford University and became an internationally respected engineer and a millionaire before he was forty. During World War I, he began his career of public service. Winning wide acclaim for his relief work in Belgium, he served as food czar under Wilson, and then as secretary of commerce under Harding and Coolidge. Author of *American Individualism*, he was a perfect reflection of his own philosophy of success: "The winner is he who shows the most conscientious training, the greatest ability, the greatest character."[42]

The intensity of the issues in the election of 1928 brought a 70 percent voter turnout. Hoover carried forty states and amassed 21 million votes. The solid South was broken. Smith, though he lost his home state, garnered 15 million votes, more than any other previous losing candidate. More important was his strength in the cities. The Democrats carried Boston (66.8 percent), Milwaukee (53.7 percent), New Orleans, with its heavy Catholic population (79.5 percent). The party increased its percentage of the vote in every city outside the South. The cultural issues, "rum and Romanism," had dominated the debate and a nasty whispering campaign. In their assessments of the outcome, contemporaries, while noting voter loyalties and shifts, acknowledged the drawing power of prosperity. Hoover could stand on the Republican record of seven good years. Coolidge had proudly addressed Congress in December 1928: "No Congress of the United States ever assembled on serving the state of the union has met with a more pleasing prospect than that which appears at the present time."[43]

Yet in 1928, the failure of the American economy to solve the problems of distribution and consumption was becoming obvious. Coal, textiles, and railroads were "sick," and agriculture was still depressed. Construction was in a slump; inventories were building up in automobiles and durable goods. When the state governors met in 1928, they discussed setting up reserve funds for public works should the private sector falter. Most businesses tried to continue Coolidge prosperity by advertising and offered the installment plan as an incentive to the consumer. The slogan was "Enjoy while you pay." By 1929, consumers had $6 billion tied up in installment payments. A study that year by the Brookings Institution revealed more alarming statistics; 60 percent of Americans had an annual income of less than two thousand dollars, the estimated income needed to maintain a family at a minimum level of decency. Seventy-eight percent had incomes of less than three thousand dollars. One chart showed that thirty-six thousand at the top had the same income as 12 million at the bottom. While wages had increased during the Coolidge years, corporate profits soared to 63 percent. Profits of financial institutions stood at 150 percent.[44]

This mounting evidence of an economy out of balance was partially obscured by the continuing boom of the Coolidge bull market. In 1928, the stock market was carrying the economy. Between 1925 and 1929 the value of stocks rose from $27 billion to $87 billion, a 300 percent increase. Mergers and the creation of investment trusts swelled the market with new stocks. Goldman Sachs Trading Corporation spawned subsidiary investment trust companies that issued $250 million in securities in less than a month. The major banks had investment subsidiaries. National City Bank in New York had National City Company aggressively marketing stock. Hoover complained, "Some of the so-called bankers in New York were not bankers at all. They were stock promoters. . . . Their social instinct belonged to an early Egyptian period." Bankers extended loans to brokers for call money; brokers allowed clients to buy on margin. By 1929, $8 billion in brokers' loans were extended, a total that was one-half the national debt. Nick Carraway observed in *The Great Gatsby*, "Everybody I knew was in the bond business."

It was an exaggeration. Only about a million and a half Americans were investing, but the excitement was pervasive. Cabdrivers stopped at lunch to read ticker tape. Many had stories of Uncle Fred and his killing on the market. In mid-decade the Federal Reserve Board, acting to help shore up Britain's economy as it restored the pound to its prewar level, lowered the rediscount rate to 3.5 percent and bought government bonds. Expanding credit and the money supply stimulated the market boom. Insiders, sometimes working with financial columnists, pushed up prices and then pulled the plug, skimming off a handsome profit. Radio (RCA) was promoted to a high of 109 a share in 1928 only to plummet to 87 when the insiders pulled out. Economist William Z. Ripley described the machinations pumping up the market as "prestidigitation, double-shuffling, honey-fugling, hornswoggling and skulduggery." As early as 1927, he had advised Coolidge, "The first duty is to face the fact that there is something the matter. The house is not falling down—no fear of that! But there are queer little noises about as of rats in the wall or of borers in the timbers." Sinclair Lewis, without benefit of economic analysis, stood looking at Wall Street a year later and said, "Within a year this country will have a terrible financial panic. I don't think, I know. Can't you see it, smell it? I can see people jumping out of the windows."

There were warnings by economists in 1929 of an overheated market in the *New York Times* and the *Commercial and Financial Chronicle*. The Federal Reserve Board acted to try to curb bank loans for call money to brokers. In August it raised the rediscount rate. Yet the market rolled on. In the spring and summer of 1929, the average of the *New York Times* industrials rose 110 points. Bernard Baruch asserted that "the economic condition of the world seems on the verge of a great forward movement."[45]

In a Labor Day column, economist Roger Babson had a different assessment, warning that sooner or later a crash was coming, adding, "it may be terrific." Within three weeks the market was jarred as the Bank of England raised its interest rates and nervous foreign investors sold off some of their American holdings. On 15 October analysts noted some of the big investors were selling large blocks of stock. The market shuddered and then stabilized. But 24 October became Black Thursday. Thirteen million shares were traded. In the midst of the slide representatives of the major banks gathered in the Morgan offices. They dispatched Morgan representative Richard Whitney to bid for ten thousand shares of U.S. Steel as a signal that the bankers would stem the flow. Newspaper pictures the next day depicted crowds standing on the street staring blankly. When the market opened on Monday, General Electric fell 48 points, and Westinghouse and AT&T dropped 34. On 29 October the bottom fell out. Sixteen and a half million shares were traded. There was an average decline of 40 points. The *New York Times* reported the next day that efforts to estimate the losses in dollars were futile. "Everyone wanted to tell his neighbor how much he had lost. Nobody wanted to listen. It was too repetitious a tale." On 2 November the *Commercial and Financial Chronicle* stated, "The present week has witnessed the greatest stock market catastrophe of all the ages." In the next four months $40 billion in stock values vanished. An editor at *American* magazine, which specialized in success stories, posted a sign: "Horatio Alger Doesn't Work Here Any More."[46]

The crash and the depression delivered only the final challenge of the 1920s to the old ways and values. Horatio Alger like Casey at the bat had been swinging and missing through much of the decade. In a brilliant essay, historian Warren Susman used three culture heroes, Bruce Barton, Henry Ford, and Babe Ruth to fashion a three-strikes-

and-out analogy showing the erosion of the thrift, hard work, and sobriety roads to American success. Barton, the founder of the advertising agency Batten, Barton, Durstine and Osborn took aim at thrift in
his "Creed of an Advertising Man." "Advertising," he asserted, "sustains
a new system . . . the American Way of Life." The salesman was the
new hero, the consumer more valuable to the new society than the
saver. Henry Ford's assembly line struck at the old concept of work;
Ford's world was the "world of the hired hand." Babe Ruth, the Sultan
of Swat, was a rags-to-riches American hero whose prodigious records
at the bat were matched by his lusty living off the field. Ruth also
exemplified the new American hero, a combination of talent, organization, and promotion. Great in his own right, he was celebrated by
talented sportswriters like Grantland Rice and Heywood Broun, and
promoted by one of the best organizations in baseball.[47]

Yet the greatest hero of the 1920s was Charles Lindbergh, the Lone
Eagle. He was, asserted John William Ward, the symbol of the age,
perfectly capturing the tension between the individual and the organization. He was "Horatio Alger, Tom Swift, and Frank Merriwell rolled
into one," a young Lochinvar out of the West. The *New York Evening
World* wrote of his solo Atlantic flight in 1927 as "the greatest feat of a
solitary man in the records of the human race." Lindbergh entitled his
own story of the flight, *We.* It was a partnership of man and machine
and corporations. The flight of the *Spirit of St. Louis* involved the effort
of one hundred companies. Lindbergh's feat reminded Americans of old
frontiers and gave them hope for new ones. It made graphic the odds
against conquering those frontiers alone.[48]

Tellingly, no woman was advanced as a candidate for symbol of the
age. Yet the 1920s began with high hope that the new woman would
conquer some frontiers of her own.

Four generations of the Wendall family of Washington, D.C., ca. 1920.

CHAPTER TWO

The New Woman: Across the Generations

My feminism tells me that woman can bear children, charm her
lovers, boss a business, swim the channel, stand at Armageddon
and battle for the Lord—all in a day's work.

Cornelia Bryce Pinchot, "In Search of Adventure"

If you set a course and bend your sails to every wind to further
the journey always trusting that the course is right, it will, in
fact, be right even though the ship itself may go down at any
time during the voyage.

Margaret Mead, Blackberry Winter: My Earlier Years[1]

The "new woman" entered the 1920s in many guises. Her coming had
been announced, heralded, and denounced since 1900. By 1920 her
numbers included veteran reformers, victorious suffragists, powerful
athletes, pioneering scientists, Marxists, bohemians, and aviators. With
victory in the suffrage campaign, the new woman seemed to face a new
day—equal, at least at the polling place, and free to turn to new issues.
The magazines of the decade were filled with attempts to cut through
the variety, to predict her course and the implications for American
society, and to sort out just *who* this new woman was.

Although all Americans carried the cultural baggage of Horatio Alger into the 1920s (though it was usually translated that any American
boy, through thrift, hard work, and sobriety, could succeed), women
carried the additional formula for achieving true womanhood. Well described by historian Barbara Welter, the cult of true womanhood was
the defense of nineteenth-century Americans against the incursions of

industrialism. Woman was the anchor in a world of change. Though a "hostage in the home," her virtues of piety, purity, submissiveness, and domesticity provided a comforting surety to anxious husbands and children. It could not last. The continuing onslaught of industrialism and urbanization and the rigorous challenge by suffragists and reformers blurred the public and private spheres that defined the true woman's place at hearth and home.[2]

By the turn of the century, the magazines, which had affirmed the cult of the true woman, began to be filled with laments at her demise. Caroline Ticknor, in the July 1901 issue of the staid *Atlantic Monthly*, graphically portrayed the changing world in "The Steel-Engraving Lady and the Gibson Girl." The steel-engraving lady, who had so elegantly graced magazine illustrations, sat peacefully looking out from the casement window of her apartment. "Her eyes were dreamy, and her embroidery frame lay idly upon the little stand beside her." Her sleeve "fell back, revealing the alabaster whiteness of her hand and wrist. Her glossy abundant hair was smoothly drawn over her ears, and one rose nestled in the curl of her dark locks." Her repose was interrupted by the abrupt arrival of the Gibson Girl to carry out her assignment of writing a paper on "extinct types." Sunburned and fit, the Gibson Girl wore a "short skirt and heavy square-toed shoes, a mannish collar, cravat and vest, and a broad-brimmed felt hat tipped jauntily upon one side." When the steel-engraving lady expressed concern at her dress and her assertiveness, the Gibson Girl proclaimed the new dispensation: "When a man approaches, we do not tremble and droop our eyelids or gaze adoringly while he lays down the law. We meet him on a ground of perfect fellowship and converse freely on any topic." But "does he like it?" persisted the steel-engraving lady. "Whether he *likes* it or not makes little difference," was the response. "*He* is no longer the one whose pleasure is to be consulted. The question now is, not 'What does man like?' but 'What does woman prefer?' " The Gibson Girl, as she explained, had "a liberal education," adding, "I can do everything my brothers do, and do it rather better. . . . My point of view is free from narrow influences and quite outside of the home boundaries." At the continued remonstrances of the steel-engraving lady, the Gibson Girl exclaimed, "We're not a shy, retiring, uncomplaining generation. We're up to date and up to snuff, and every one of us is self-supporting."

When the Gibson Girl finally ended the interview, the steel-engraving lady began to strum her guitar, only to be interrupted by the arrival of Reginald, who crossed the room, dropped to one knee, raised her white hand to his lips, and whispered, "My queen, my lady love." The Gibson Girl left her golfing partner by the side of the road. He planned to meet her for a round the next day, but said, "If I don't show up, you'll know I've had a chance to join that hunting trip. Ta-ta!" Ticknor drove home the moral: "Hail the new woman—behold she comes apace! Woman, once man's superior now his equal."[3]

Articles in the quality magazines after 1910 continued to sigh for "The Return of the Gentlewoman" and "The Vanishing Lady." The new woman, sunburned and with hair flying in the wind, moved across the pages "with such a stride." One alarmed author, condemning the "swiftness and dash," described the scene of an eighty-year-old woman tottering into the gutter to avoid being trampled by an oncoming trio of new women, arms locked, oblivious to any obstacles. Another worried that the example of the new young woman was infecting her mother's generation. The lady of leisure now raced from one thing to another like "a hunted hare." When she "rides for pleasure, her joy consists in going so fast that it is impossible to see anything but the speedometer. . . . She has no time to read or converse, or think, or grow."[4]

The new woman, summarized Margaret Deland in "The Change in the Feminine Ideal," was "almost ceasing to be entirely a joke; for there is something more than a joke in all this curious turning upside-down of traditions and theories in regard to women." Deland's new woman was "a wholesome loveable creature with surprisingly bad manners. [She] has gone to college, and when she graduates she is going to earn her own living. She declines to be dependent upon a father and mother amply able to support her. She will do settlement work; she won't go to church; she has views upon marriage and the birth-rate, and she utters them calmly, while her mother blushes with embarrassment; she occupies herself, passionately, with everything, except the things that used to occupy the minds of girls." She knew how to say I want and I will and I must, but she had not learned how to say I ought.[5]

This new woman, already well defined by alarmed elders, was joined by an even more troubling version in the 1920s—the flapper. "Mr. Grundy," writing in the *Atlantic Monthly* in May 1920, described the coming of this new generation. Restless, excited, noisy, "they trot like foxes, limp like lame ducks, one-step like cripples, and all to the barbaric yawp of strange instruments which transform the whole scene into a moving-picture of a fancy ball in bedlam." Manners were worsening. No longer did a blushing old-fashioned girl drop a rose in the

path of her ardent pursuer; her granddaughter now seized a roll at a
dinner party and, dexterously slinging it across the table at her young
man, shouted, "Hi there! Catch it, you boob."[6]

Contemporary historian Preston W. Slosson drew a slightly more
restrained picture:

Thus the flapper of the 1920s stepped onto the stage of history, breezy, slangy
and informal in manner; slim and boyish in form; covered with silk and fur
that clung to her as close as onion skin; with carmined lips, plucked eyebrows
and close-fitting helmet of hair; gay, plucky and confident. . . . She cared little
for approval or disapproval and went about her "act," whether it were a Mara-
thon dancing contest, driving an automobile at seventy miles an hour, a Channel swim, a political campaign or a social-service settlement. Eventually she
married her dancing partner, that absurdly serious young man with plastered
hair, baby-smooth chin and enormous Oxford bags, and then they settled down
in a four-room kitchenette apartment to raise two children, another "younger
generation" to thrust them back stage among the "old fogies."[7]

Psychologist Beatrice Hinkle produced another reading of the flapper phenomenon and the restlessness of the young. Women, she asserted, were in a "mighty struggle towards differentiation and an individual direction." They were "demanding recognition as individuals
first, and as wives and mothers second." They were "claiming the right
to dispose of themselves according to their own needs and capacities."[8]
The famous expert on the psychology of adolescence, G. Stanley Hall,
agreed that woman's new assertiveness carried the "promise and po-
tency of a new and truer womanhood."[9] Flappers, glorying in their
femininity and giving "free course to its native impulses," might, he
concluded, be the leaders in the complete emancipation of woman from
the standards man had set for her.

Other new women had been long at that task. The feminist had been
in the lists long before the flapper. She existed in all the bewildering
varieties of the new woman. Historians and contemporaries described
social feminists, radical, pragmatic, and even "general" feminists. They
cut across generations. In the 1920s, feminist Lorine Pruette divided
them into three generational groups: the old pioneers who had borne
the brunt of the fight and never lost their bitterness toward men; the
middle generation who were less bitter because they had borne less of
the battle; and the third, younger group who were "frankly amazed at
all the feminist pother and likely to be bored when the subject comes
up." In the October 1927 issue of *Harper's*, Dorothy Bromley made a

further distinction between "Feminist—New Style" and the feminist old-style. The latter wore flat heels, disliked men, and, accepting that women could not have both a career and marriage, opted for the career. The new-style feminist was a "good dresser" and a "pal" to men, and fully expected to have marriage, children, and a career, too. She expected, in brief, to have it all.[10] All these generations of feminists co-existed in the twenties. All joined, as one of the middle generation expressed it, in "consciously experimenting . . . to find out how women can best live."[11]

It was a question that at its deepest level concerned the nature of woman. The first generation of feminists in the twentieth century saw that nature in different terms. Most numerous were the social feminists, activists who accepted and built on woman's difference, arguing that the talents, skills, and virtues so valuable in the home were needed to clean up the larger households of community and nation. Their counterparts, the radical feminists, argued from their research that there was little distinction between man and woman in mind or psyche and that woman's full equal rights must be won. Their positions could be most graphically illustrated in the lively interaction of two institutions: Hull House and the University of Chicago.

Hull House was the lengthened shadow of Jane Addams, the leading exemplar of social feminism. Growing up in a household with strong roots in the abolitionist movement, she attended Rockford Seminary, "the Mount Holyoke of the West." Graduating at the head of her class, she planned a life of service as a doctor ministering to the poor. When ill health forced her to leave the Philadelphia Women's Medical College, she drifted in the comfortable life of the upper middle class. Traveling in Europe with her stepmother, she visited the famous Oxford University settlement, Toynbee Hall, on London's East Side. The poverty she observed and the opportunity the settlement afforded for educated men and women to help and to learn led her, with her friend Ellen Gates Starr, to found Hull House in the Chicago ghetto. It became the most famous of the hundreds of settlement houses founded in the 1880s and 1890s, a bridge for college-educated women to the public sphere. The settlement house was an outlet, Addams observed, for their "desire for action, the wish to right wrong and alleviate suffering."[12]

For women, the settlement house was an opportunity for service that found widespread approval. It did not disturb the cult of domesticity unduly, because women were merely moving into a larger home, extending their nurturing. In her first years at Hull House, Addams consistently observed that marriage was "the highest gift which life can offer to a woman." Indeed, as one historian observed, she spent much of her life working for the right of other women to stay home. Supported by tradition, the settlement house also seemed affirmed by science. It responded to the observations of Darwin and Herbert Spencer that as humanity evolved there was increasing refinement of function and difference. Women's special skills were needed to complement male aggression and capitalist excesses, to bring a spirit of cooperation to an overly competitive world. Hull House women Florence Kelley, Julia Lathrop, Alice Hamilton, and Grace and Edith Abbott spearheaded reforms throughout the Progressive Era from child labor laws to factory inspection. They joined in the common cause for suffrage to win the power to clean up America. Social feminism was serviceable and safe. Jane Addams, in 1910, was the first woman awarded an honorary degree by Yale; in a 1913 poll listing outstanding Americans, Addams finished ahead of Andrew Carnegie and second only to Thomas Edison. When Addams's *Twenty Years at Hull House* was published, the *Baltimore Sun* hailed it as the most important book of the year. She was St. Jane. All of this was imperiled, however, by her principled stand for peace. The first president of the Women's Peace party in 1915, Addams was expelled by the Daughters of the American Revolution when she spoke out against America's participation in the war.

Yet Addams and the social feminists continued their unfinished business in the cleanup of the American "household" in the twenties. They provided leadership and work in the trenches and were signally important in retaining some momentum from the Progressive Era. Yet their insistence on their special experience and talents as women, on women's complementarity rather than their commonality with men, not only limited the range of their reform efforts but reinforced the conviction that women's preeminent place was in the home.[13]

The University of Chicago was the seed-ground for the theories undergirding radical feminism. Founded in 1892 three years after Hull House opened, the university, backed by Rockefeller money and the strong leadership of President William Rainey Harper, attracted a distinguished faculty including John Dewey, James Rowland Angell, Henry Hollingworth, and George Herbert Mead. In their skepticism and scientific rigor, they made Chicago a center of the "revolt against formalism" of reform Darwinism. They challenged the Victorian verities that had wrought such a division between rich and poor. All had been educated in coeducational colleges and universities; all had married college women; all stood ready to encourage their women graduate students in their research challenging gender stereotypes.

The University of Chicago attracted and enrolled the largest number of women graduate students in the social sciences in the 1890s and the first decade of the twentieth century. They had the encouragement of one another, their professors, and the dean of women, Marion Talbot. Talbot had embarked on her own college career at Boston University in the wake of the furor over Dr. Edward Clarke's *Sex in Education; or a Fair Chance for the Girls.* Clarke, promulgating the closed energy system of Spencer, argued that the body allocated its energy resources according to priorities set by gender. In men, the brain and heart dominated, in women, the reproductive organs. To educate women with the same rigor as men would divert needed energy from the uterus. The "over stimulated brain," asserted Clarke, "would become morbidly introspective." Neurasthenia, hysteria, or insanity could result; the ovaries might shrivel or become cancerous. (Similarly, young men who overstimulated their reproductive organs, might weaken their brains and hurt their careers in business.)[14] Talbot not only survived with her health intact, but dared further study at MIT. She founded the Association of Collegiate Alumnae and through its membership began to gather the statistics to refute Dr. Clarke. Offered a position at Wellesley, she opted instead for the deanship at Chicago, for "the opportunity to overcome the restrictive conception of women's physical and mental capabilities" appeared to be greater at a major research university.[15]

One of the first to challenge the stereotypes of duality in gender was Chicago graduate student Helen Thompson. Surveying University of Chicago undergraduates, she found only slight differences in mental abilities. In her dissertation "The Mental Traits of Sex," she concluded that it was training and social expectation that accounted for the differences that did emerge. Two other graduate students from Chicago, Jessie Taft and Virginia Robinson, researched psychological factors. In 1912, they accepted the invitation of Katherine B. Davis to interview women criminals in the New York City prison system to aid in their classification. Taft and Robinson concluded, as had Thompson, that women dealt with emotional signals differently from men, but that their responses were culturally conditioned, related to the expectations of society.

In 1918, supported by Rockefeller funds, Dr. Katharine B. Davis undertook a massive study of the sexual activities of normal women. Helen Thompson, now Helen Thompson Woolley, and Jessie Taft were two of a prestigious board of consultants. The twenty-two hundred respondents not only filled out the long questionnaire but sent long explanatory letters. The study clearly indicated that women were "more highly sexed" than most believed. Sex, the researchers concluded, was "physically necessary to the woman as well as the man."[16]

At Columbia, which also had a large number of women graduate students in the social sciences, and at Stanford University, women in psychology and the other social sciences built on these early studies. Clelia Mosher, working with Stanford undergraduates, undercut a Darwinian thesis that men were more variable in their mental abilities than women and thus were the more highly evolved. Women, at least at Stanford, showed the same range of abilities.

Her Stanford colleague Mary Roberts Coolidge investigated the cross-fertilization of psychic traits. Men and women proved, of course, both rational and emotional; there was more variance within each gender than there was difference between them. This, concluded Coolidge, promised a healthier society. She explained: "Feeling less social pressure to achieve a rigidly prescribed set of psychic qualities, men and women could afford to be more relaxed than they formerly had been in the way they behaved sexually. Because society no longer viewed women's sexual functions as their 'only useful contribution,' women could accept sexuality more easily."[17] It was a conclusion echoed in the research on the family by Columbia-trained sociologist Elsie Clews Parsons. The rising divorce rate in the first decade of the century, she argued, was the result of sex differentiation and the tensions between the overcultivated leisure-class wife and the undercultivated and overworked husband, unresponsive to anything but business.[18]

By 1920, American psychologists had, as Rosalind Rosenberg pointed out, "buried the doctrine of female uniqueness propounded by their Victorian mothers."[19] With scientific research pointing to the equality of women, winning the vote was only the first step for the radical feminists in the march to full equal rights.

By 1920, however, the feminists' debate on nature and function was carried on and augmented by the theories of Sigmund Freud. The British sexologist Havelock Ellis hailed his impact. "Of old," Ellis explained, "even men of science felt unable to touch sexual matters save with a finger tip, slightly and hesitatingly, with many apologies and excuses." Freud had "taught the world that the sexual impulse—as it exists . . . in our civilization, has even wider and deeper implications than have usually been suspected."[20]

By the end of World War I, a first generation of anthropologists had provided a comparative base for the study of sexual relations. Bronislaw Malinowski's prolonged ethnographic study in the Trobriand Islands and his descriptions and pictures depicting remote tribesmen and women enviably at home within the contours of their own bodies and casual and natural in their relations with one another, children, and kinsmen found a fascinated readership in Europe and America. The simplicity of the primitive, the absence of melancholy, hysteria, and neurasthenic symptoms, suggested a world that Western industrialized civilization had left at a considerable price.

Psychologists and psychiatrists clinically analyzed the cost to the individual and developed standards of health and normality and advice on how to achieve them. None was more prominent in the 1920s than Havelock Ellis and Sigmund Freud. Ellis devoured and digested the outpouring of reports of sexual custom in the British Empire and the islands of the Pacific. Through his interviews with patients, he documented the painful fears and sadistic preoccupations (a kind of English public school syndrome) perpetuated by men in a cycle of repression of sexual feeling and exploitation of younger and weaker persons, including women. At his best, Ellis was an eloquent spokesman for sexual openness. He passionately defended women's social, economic, and what he termed erotic rights. He saw clearly that economic dependence, subordination in the family and society at large, psychological repression, and erotic timidity or immaturity were all interrelated and mutually reinforcing. He believed that women's inferior position was damaging not only to individual women but to society at large and was reflected in unhappy interpersonal relations, especially between man and wife and between mother and child.[21]

While Havelock Ellis brought his research and passion to the struggle to free men and women from the stranglehold of Victorian convention and conditioning, Freud, who also worked to free women from "sexual bondage," far outdistanced him in theory, method, and impact. Accepting that "throughout history people have knocked their heads" against "the riddle of the nature of femininity," Freud did not pretend that psychoanalysis could "describe what a woman is." It set "about enquiring how she comes into being."[22]

Freud epitomized the nineteenth-century doctor; his clinical practice was also his research laboratory. His tools were those of the nineteenth-century diagnostician: a meticulous ear for his patients' complaints, careful observation of their behavior and symptoms, and cautious follow-up after completion of treatment. Thus it should come as no surprise that his theories and propositions about sexuality and its relation to neurosis were intimately bound up with the particulars of his own social and cultural milieu. Likewise Freud's work, which has been continually interpreted since the 1893 publication with Joseph Breuer, "On the Psychical Mechanism of Hysterical Phenomena: A Preliminary Communication," has been variously interpreted and commented on depending on the social and cultural milieus in which it was received.

Freud's theories struck a responsive chord in America. His dynamic view of personality—the libido as a great energy field in which superego and id, Eros and Thanatos, generative and destructive forces, vie for control—was a microcosmic reflection of the tensions facing industrial America at the turn of the century. In enlarging enterprises, personal lines of authority involving close interaction between supervisor and employee based on cooperation and respect were no longer feasible. Freud's theory—postulating a superego and id struggling for supremacy mediated and controlled by ego—could be interpreted as an ideological formulation of bourgeois social relations and as a formulation that was conservative and oriented towards social control. Health in the individual and in the body politic was achieved through a successful balancing act—keeping too much from being repressed and preventing too much from being expressed[23]

In the 1920s, Freud's dream analysis, his studies of the unconscious, his writings on the shortcomings, indeed dishonesty, of the parent culture in imposing restraints, and his theories on sexuality were seized on by young Americans disillusioned by great causes of the past and turning inward to find themselves and a way to live in a rapidly changing present. His impact was summed up by Sherwood Anderson in *Dark Laughter*: "If there is anything you do not understand in human life consult the works of Dr. Freud."[24] Freud's research and work with patients convinced him that neuroses were of sexual origin. His major American interpreter in the 1920s, A. A. Brill, explained: "There was [a] fundamental thing that very forcibly impressed Freud, as he continued treating and studying his patients. He found that when they began to dwell on their intimate personal experiences, they practically all would invariably bring up matters appertaining to sex. He was so impressed with this fact that he asserted that in the normal sex life no neurosis is possible."[25]

His view of woman's normal sexual life was one of passivity and acquiescence. One critic concluded that it might be fair to describe Freud's attitude toward female sexuality as "old-fashioned," that their main function was "to be ministering angels to the needs and comforts of men." Freud acknowledged that his view was "certainly incomplete and fragmentary." He asserted: "If you want to know more about femininity, enquire from your own experiences of life, or turn to the poets, or wait until science can give you deeper and more coherent information."[26]

Freud's emphasis on health and home was paralleled by a commercial campaign to keep women at home. In "Women and 'Their' Magazines," a writer in *New Republic* complained that the women's magazines were nothing more than trade journals. Advertisers were "afraid of women getting too progressive and spending less time on housework." Ads portrayed women at stoves and furnaces, pushing carpet sweepers, serving food, always with "sweet, seraphic smiles on their faces. As if they never had, or wanted another thought."[27]

The short stories early in the 1920s' version of the feminine mystique also emphasized happiness in the home. In *Good Housekeeping* in September 1920, Kathleen Norris's "Young Mrs. Jim M." cried: "I'd die without Jimmy—he knows I would." Finally, he arrived: "He looked so tired, so loving, so glad to find Amy, he took possession of her with such weary content!" Harriet Abbott, in the April 1920 *Ladies' Home Journal* explored "What the Newest Woman Is." She depicted two women who had worked and then chose marriage because no vocation demanded more. Abbott ended with a credo: "I believe in woman's rights; but I believe in woman's sacrifice also. I believe in woman's freedom; but I believe it should be within the restrictions of the Ten Commandments. I believe in woman's suffrage, but I believe many other things are vastly more important. I believe in woman's brains; but I believe still more in her emotions. I believe in woman's assertion of self; but I believe in her obligation of service to her family, her neighbors, her nation, and her God."

The questions of who women were and "what do women want?" raged through the decade. In the March 1929 issue of *Harper's*, Syracuse psychologist Floyd H. Allport summarized the recurring responses. In his opening paragraph, he made it clear that nothing had been resolved:

That the nature of woman involves an essential mystery has become one of the aphorisms of the human race. Practically everything that masculine ingenuity can think of concerning women has, at one time or another, been said. And almost every utterance has been challenged by a statement as sweeping and vehement upon the opposite side. Poets and mystics, viewing women through an erotic halo, have endowed them with some vital and cosmic principle. Dour philosophers have seen in them only irrationality, frailty, and evil. The man on the street has his stock of generalizations, or stereotypes . . . through which he explains feminine conduct as complacently as he discusses changes of politics or of the weather. No matter if his stereotypes sometimes go wrong; he will never revise them. When female behavior defies the traditional categories he has in reserve a final pigeon hole: "After all, you can never tell *for certain* what a woman is going to do."[28]

The mystery endured, fed by the assumption that since there were differences in anatomy, there must be mental differences. Men were the measuring rod; their traits were "merely natural or standard human traits." The burden of difference lay with women. Allport summed up the stereotype: "1) Men and women in their inherited natures are fundamentally different. 2) But it is not so much the men who are different, as the women. 3) The sexual functions in women have a potent influence in shaping all their natural tendencies."

Ranging through the literature on difference in intelligence, character, and temperament, Allport found the old prejudices alive and well; woman was dominated by feeling, man by reason. None of the stereotypes stood the test of science, according to Allport, but they had a profound influence. By training, and "not through nature," he asserted, women became a reflection of the feminine image "men carry around in their heads. . . . Men may fail to see women as they are; but women tend to become as men see them."[29]

Yet these old notions, while they assigned women to a false position, at least assigned them some position. It might be better, Allport observed, "to have a warped social image as the pattern for one's personality than to have no pattern at all." As the old social personality was destroyed a new one must be found. The women, he concluded, must solve the riddle themselves. "Given time and freedom from biased assumptions, they will discover themselves, and will so remake their surroundings that their lives, no longer lived at cross purposes, will express the nature that is really theirs."[30]

Throughout the decade editors did ask women to write of their success in remaking their surroundings and their lives, and their perception of how generally the new women were coping with the tensions between old values and new ways. The most sweeping and scholarly, but also the most impersonal, was the collection of decade-ending assessments in the May 1929 issue of the *Annals of the American Academy of Political Science*. Earlier, in October 1927, the editors of *Current History* had dedicated an issue to the new woman, leading off with two historical overviews of progress by veteran campaigners Carrie Chapman Catt and Charlotte Perkins Gilman. Surveying past and present, they agreed that the womens' movement was rolling forward, but, as Catt observed, only time and many small skirmishes would finally win equality of opportunity.[31]

The most ambitious of these magazine assessments was the series "These Modern Women," conceived by *Nation* editor Freda Kirchway. The editors introduced the first installment on 1 December 1926, explaining: "Our object is to discover the origin of their modern point of view toward men, marriage, children, and jobs. Do spiritual ancestors explain their rebellion? Or is it due to thwarted ambition or distaste for domestic drudgery?"[32] The seventeen respondents, whose articles were published anonymously, ranged from suffragist Inez Haynes Irwin to poet Genevieve Taggard. Their average age was forty. They were Lorine Pruette's middle generation of feminists. Most had grown up in small towns and migrated to eastern cities. All had grappled with the question of marriage and career. Three had chosen to remain single. Lawyer Sue Shelton White, in "Mother's Daughter," explained her decision: "Marriage is too much of a compromise; it lops off a woman's life as an individual. Yet the renunciation too is a lopping off. We choose between the frying-pan and the fire—both very uncomfortable."[33] Most fit the pattern described by Crystal Eastman: She is "not altogether satisfied with love, marriage, and a purely domestic career. She wants money of her own. She wants some means of self-expression, perhaps, some way of satisfying her personal ambitions. But she wants a husband, home and children too. How to reconcile these two desires in real life? That is the question."[34] The majority of the seventeen managed to reconcile work and marriage, but only five were mothers. Together they presented a picture of determination and commitment to a struggle "without glamour or recognition waged by each woman alone in her home or office."[35]

Concluding the series, Kirchway asked three experts, two psychologists and a neurologist, to comment on the lives and adjustments revealed in the series. Psychologist Beatrice Hinkle, the only woman of the three, was the most sympathetic. But she did note that "in not one of these cases is the feminism of the women based on principle but in each instance it was born directly from the necessities of their personal life." Hinkle heralded their effort, for "behind their stridency and revolt lies the great inner meaning of women's struggle with the forces of convention and inertia." She concluded: "This is nothing less than the psychological development of themselves as individuals, in contradistinction to the collective destiny that has exclusively dominated their lives. . . . If they have individually failed to achieve their full destiny, their attitude is part of a great rolling tide which is bringing to birth a new woman."[36]

Several of the series contributors were not so sanguine about their accomplishments or their legacy for the next generation, sharing Lorine Pruette's concern about the next generation of women that seemed "frankly amazed at all the feminist pother." Psychologist Phyllis Blanchard later agreed, observing in her *New Girls for Old*, "The modern girl, who has seen the loneliness of older unmarried friends is beginning to discount the rewards of a materialist success that must be accomplished at the expense of love."[37]

Black clubwomen were surveyed on "Negro Womanhood's Greatest Needs" by A. Philip Randolph's magazine the *Messenger* in the spring of 1923. In the eleven letters printed in the April, May, and June issues, education, solidarity, and vision were cited, but there was a repeated stress on "home life." "Woman is by nature a homebuilder," insisted Miss Hallie Q. Brown of Wilberforce, Ohio; the "greatest need of our womanhood of today," echoed Mrs. Ella Stewart of Toledo, "is to train them to make intelligent and efficient homemakers." She must "never forget her tender womanly and great motherly heritage" and must "cling to the home," agreed Mrs. Bonnie Bogle of Portland, Oregon. Mrs. Ethel Gavin of Chicago urged that the younger women, while their minds were "yet tender," be presented with the lives of great women living and dead to help them in the struggles ahead.[38]

The young generation did not lack for models. While Henry Ford, Bruce Barton, and Babe Ruth were changing the ground rules for success Horatio-Alger style, the women of the twenties were cutting down the cult of true womanhood. The true woman would never be the same.

The stereotype of the weak and shrinking violet was challenged by a cadre of athletic champions. Tennis star Hazel Wightman, "the queen of the volley" and originator of the Wightman cup matches, was the mother of five children when she won Olympic gold medals in doubles and mixed doubles and the Wimbledon double championship in 1924.

Three years later at forty-one she was national squash champion. She was surpassed by the "queen of the courts," Helen Wills, three times winner of the U.S. singles championship and eight times winner of the Wimbledon singles. Between 1927 and 1932 she did not lose a set in her singles matches.[39]

Tennis stars, however, were no new phenomenon. In 1926, nineteen-year-old Gertrude Ederle became the "Champion Extraordinary" of her sex, as the first woman to swim the English Channel. Only five men had accomplished that feat, and Ederle's time of fourteen hours and thirty-one minutes was the fastest. Carrie Chapman Catt claimed a feminist victory, and Ederle agreed that "all the women of the world will celebrate, too." Columnist Uncle Dudley of the Boston *Daily Globe* asserted that Ederle's success gave women "new physical dignity." The *Literary Digest* surveyed the press response, observing, "No hero of all antiquity was more worthy of laurels than the German-American butcher's daughter and none ever received anything approaching the multitudinous homage that is now being paid to her."[40] Ederle had been smashing records since 1922. An Olympic star in 1924, she held eighteen world records that year, from fifty yards to a half mile. She had made her first run at the channel in 1925, spurred on by her family and coach and a jazz band on the accompanying tugboat. In 1926, there was no jazz band, but father, sister, coach, and supporters spurred her on by singing "The Star-Spangled Banner" and, at a dark moment when the giant swells were preventing forward progress, "Yes, We Have No Bananas."

The day after her victory, the morning dispatches hailed "the bob-haired, nineteen-year-old daughter of the Jazz Age," and carried the analysis of a swimming coach at Northwestern University: "A woman could not possibly have accomplished this same feat thirty years ago, for corsets and other ridiculously unnecessary clothing hampered her physical condition and deprived her of the muscular effort so necessary in the development of a good swimmer. Physical education has brought about an evolution of common sense that has wrought a complete turn-over, not only in woman's physical condition but in her whole mental attitude." "The American girl," concluded the *Washington Star*, "is all right."[41]

Two years later, in the summer of 1928, Ederle's headlines of the channel crossing were eclipsed by the press excitement over "Lady Lindy," as Amelia Earhart became the first woman to fly the Atlantic. Though a skilled pilot, Earhart's responsibilities on the flight of the

Fokker F. VII *Friendship* had been restricted to keeping the log. Embarrassed by the furor, she disclaimed the feat, reporting that she had felt "like a sack of potatoes." Her modesty and shyness only spurred on the encomiums and the comparisons to Lucky Lindy. Four years later she earned those comparisons, piloting a Lockheed Vega on a flight from Newfoundland to Ireland, becoming the first woman to solo across the Atlantic and the first person to fly the Atlantic twice.[42]

Earhart's feat continued the erosion of the lingering true-woman stereotype. Throughout the decade, however, many continued to insist that it was not only physically impossible for women to fly but socially inappropriate. At the end of World War I, there were few qualified women pilots. The aviation industry had an oversupply of planes and returning army pilots and an undersupply of business. Women like Earhart found that barnstorming was often the only entry to a career in aviation. Frequently, women pilots doubled as wing-walkers and parachutists. They hung upside-down from rope ladders; they danced the Charleston to music from a radio clamped to the wing at their feet; they skillfully grabbed ropes while being plucked from a speeding automobile or motorboat and climbed up into the cockpit of the plane above. Some made enough money to start their own barnstorming circuses; others established flight schools. Commercial aviation found them useful in winning the confidence of a nervous public. If women could fly as pilot or passenger, it must be a safe enterprise. By 1928, Earhart was only one of the women ready to challenge the oceans.[43]

Her life through the 1920s was a mixture of traditional pursuits to pay for new ventures. During World War I, while visiting her sister in Toronto, Earhart, six months out of high school, served as a volunteer aide at a military hospital and became fascinated by the tales of the pilots of the Royal Flying Corps. Returning to the United States, first to Northampton, Massachusetts, where her sister was about to enter Smith, Earhart took a course in engine mechanics. In 1919, she determined to be a physician and enrolled in the premedical program at Columbia University. The next year she joined her parents in Los Angeles, trying to help save their marriage and supporting herself through a job with the telephone company. She had her first airline ride at Glendale and, after lessons from pioneer pilot Neta Snook, soloed in June 1921. Through pawning belongings and patching together her savings, she bought her first plane on her twenty-fifth birthday, a Kinner Canary, and became part of the barnstorming stunt circuit of southern California. In 1924, Earhart, with her mother and sister, now a teacher, settled in Medford, Massachusetts. She taught English to immigrants in a University of Massachusetts extension program and then became a social worker at Denison House, the settlement house in Boston's Italian community. She kept up her flying, demonstrating Kinner planes. Once, in a perfect illustration of her mix of traditional and pioneering occupations, she dropped leaflets from the Kinner announcing a Denison street fair.

Earhart's opportunity to fly the Atlantic came from her own aviation experience and the frustrations of another woman pilot. Amy Phipps Guest, who had purchased a Fokker plane intending to be the first woman to fly the Atlantic, faced the adamant opposition of her family and friends. Yielding, she asked American publisher George Palmer Putnam to choose another woman. With the advice of explorer and aviator Richard E. Byrd, Putnam, a keen publicist, offered Earhart a place on the flight. He was struck by her talent, charm, and, because of her height and short blond hair, uncanny resemblance to Lindbergh. Earhart was ready, exclaiming: "How could I refuse such a shining adventure!"[44]

Returning to a ticker tape parade, Earhart became vice president of Ludington Airways, aviation editor of *Cosmopolitan*, and an indefatigable promoter of aviation. She helped found the Ninety-Nines in 1929, an international organization of women pilots, and helped launch and flew in the first Women's Air Derby from Santa Monica to Cleveland. Her book about the 1928 transatlantic flight, *20 Hrs. 40 Min.*, was even more modestly titled than Lindbergh's *We*. Earhart's demeanor would not have shocked the "steel-engraving lady", but her daring and deeds and those of the other women pilots were well beyond the ken of the "true woman."[45]

While Ederle and the athletes and Earhart and the professionals fleshed out the categories of the new woman and challenged the rigid divisions of male-female physical and occupational worlds, young Margaret Mead, with her 1928 best-seller, *Coming of Age in Samoa*, challenged intellectual and cultural stereotypes. Mead's autobiography, *Blackberry Winter: My Earlier Years*, provides an anthropologist-psychologist-sociologist's description of the factors making a new woman of the 1920s. "The two women I knew best," she related, "were mothers and had professional training." Her grandmother, who had gone to college, married, had a child, and, after being widowed, became a teacher and principal, had "no sense at all of ever having been handicapped by being a woman." Her mother, Emily Fogg, who met Margaret's father,

Edward Mead, while a graduate student in sociology at the University of Chicago, did not complete her degree work and found little opportunity to use her education beyond her home and five children. It had an obvious impact on Mead, who reported: "The content of my conscience came from my mother's concern for other people and the state of the world and from my father's insistence [a professor at the Wharton School in Philadelphia] that the only thing worth doing is to add to the store of exactly known facts; and the strength of my conscience came from Grandma, who meant what she said."[46] At eighteen, she enrolled as a freshman in her father's college, DePauw in Indiana, expecting, as she observed, "to take part in an intellectual feast" and "in some way . . . to become a person." Frustrated in both expectations, she transferred to Barnard and found the "kind of student life that matched my earlier dreams." At the end of three years, she wrote, "I knew what I could do in life."[47]

She had a rich student experience whether participating in mass meetings for Sacco and Vanzetti during their 1921 trial, visiting the museums, or tramping in Greenwich Village. "We knew about Freud," she wrote. "We knew that repression was a bad thing . . . and one of our friends described how she and her fiance had made up a set of topics to talk about on dates so that they would not be frustrated. When she heard that I had been engaged for two years and did not intend to get married for three years more, she exclaimed, 'No wonder your arm hurts!' " At Barnard, Mead learned "loyalty to women, pleasure in conversation with women, and the enjoyment of the way in which we complemented one another in terms of our differences in temperament, which we found as interesting as the complementarity that is produced by the difference of sex."[48]

Married after her graduation in 1923, Mead through a fellowship and an assistantship to sociologist William Ogburn continued as a graduate student in psychology. Well launched on her master's essay, but still grappling with whether she should pursue psychology, sociology, or anthropology, she talked with Ruth Benedict, Franz Boas's assistant, who had impressed her as an undergraduate. Benedict stated simply, "Professor Boas and I have nothing to offer but an opportunity to do work that matters." Mead had found her vocation. "Anthropology," she asserted, "had to be done *now*. Other things could wait." She finished her master's thesis and her doctorate in anthropology in 1925 and began her campaign, aided by Ruth Benedict, to win Boas's approval and support for her fieldwork in the South Pacific. Worried about her gender and her health, Boas insisted that she choose a location accessible by steamer at least every three weeks. Mead arrived in Pago Pago, Samoa, in 1925. She explained her early determination: "If you set a course and bend your sails to every wind to further the journey always trusting that the course is right, it will, in fact, be right even though the ship itself may go down at any time during the voyage."[49] Ruth Benedict, who became Mead's friend as well as teacher, explained that Mead expected to combine vocational achievements with love, marriage, and children, and there was no reason why she shouldn't.[50] She hoped, as the new women of the twenties, to have it all.

In *Blackberry Winter*, Margaret Mead began: "I have spent most of my life studying the lives of other peoples, faraway peoples, so that Americans might better understand themselves."[51] In *Coming of Age in Samoa*, Mead drew the contrasts between growing up in Samoa and in the United States. Her last chapter, "Education for Choice," set the challenge and the problems for the generations of the 1920s in a world of choice: "The children must be taught how to think, not what to think. And because old errors die slowly, they must be taught tolerance. . . . They must be taught that many ways are open to them, no one sanctioned above its alternative, and that upon them and upon them alone lies the burden of choice. Unhampered by prejudices, unvexed by too early conditioning to any one standard, they must come clear-eyed to the choices which lie before them."[52]

The new women, across the generations, entered the 1920s with high expectations, ready for challenge and for choice. They began the decade with victory in the suffrage fight. They had won the right to express their political choice. They must now decide how they would use it.

Clockwise from top left: Advertisement for Camel cigarettes featuring a woman smoking at a political convention. Investigators and field workers of the Women's Bureau display posters and positions. Lobbyists for the Sheppard-Towner Act (left to right, first row): Mary Stewart, Lenna Yost, Maud Wood Park, Jeannette Rankin, Florence Kelley, Lida Hafford.

CHAPTER THREE

Beyond Suffrage:
The Struggle for Reform

The world expects millions of women voters to take their appropriate place in political work, to have opinions on the great questions of the day, and to conduct themselves like "freemen."

Carrie Chapman Catt, May 1919

A woman runs for office and there is more interest in the fact that she is a woman than in her qualifications for the job she seeks. It is then she learns how tenacious the tag woman is—how palpably she is a woman, how completely shackled by her sex.

Ruth Baker Pratt, May 1928[1]

The 1920s began in the heat of the final state campaigns for ratification of the Susan B. Anthony amendment. Nearly a century of dogged petitioning, tireless lobbying in the halls of legislatures and Congress, and repeated campaigning to overcome the entrenched liquor interests, the fears of machine politicians, and the drag of prejudice and tradition finally came to an end in the steamy, tumultuous special session of the Tennessee legislature in August 1920. In Knoxville for the last battle, Carrie Chapman Catt, the leader of the National American Women's Suffrage Association (NAWSA), reported her troops in almost "helpless despair" as the opposition used money, liquor, appeals to racism, and "every other cave man's prejudice" to forestall approval of women's suffrage by the thirty-sixth state. When the amendment finally reached the floor of the house on 18 August, the women won two crucial votes: one through the arm-twisting of the Democratic governor pleading loyalty for the national Democratic cause in November, the other through a vote cast by the youngest member of the House who rose to his mother's admonition, "Hurrah! And vote for suffrage."[2] Final certification of the Nineteenth Amendment was signed 26 August 1920. Twenty-six million women were enfranchised. Never had women been so united and so effectively organized. The great cause was won.

Within six months the remarkable coalition that had forged the victory began to unravel. Middle-class clubwomen, settlement workers, trade union organizers, Prohibitionists, pacifists, and militant feminists of the fledgling National Woman's party had worked for the vote not only as a right but as a way of forwarding their own agendas. By 1923, Frances Kellor, a writer and veteran of many battles for reform in the Progressive Era, surveyed the demobilization and the determined marching to new, different drummers and reported: "The American woman's movement, and her interest in great moral and social questions, is splintered into a hundred fragments under as many warring leaders."[3] By the end of the decade, divisions and new directions were clearer. Essentially, women active in the suffrage struggle chose three paths of political action and reform in the 1920s. The largest, best organized group fought to continue and expand the reforms of the Progressive Era. Veterans like Florence Kelley and Jane Addams, joined by a second generation of middle-class, college-educated young women, had worked to protect women and children in the workplace and the home, to rid America of the curse of the saloon, and to end, once and for all, the destructiveness of war. Now they were ready to extend women's role in cleaning up the American "household." The smallest, most militant group, led by the dynamic Alice Paul and her eight-thousand-member National Woman's party, saw the suffrage victory as only the first step in the fight to win full equality for women. The third group used the vote to gain access to the party structure and worked for positions in the legislature and in executive offices as the most practical way to reform the system. Their unity had won constitutional victories in the Eighteenth and Nineteenth amendments at the beginning of the 1920s; the constitutional defeats in the child labor and equal rights amendments graphically underscored their divisions at the mid-point of the decade.

The major strategist of the suffrage victory, Carrie Chapman Catt, led the effort to retain the organization, the energy, and the commitment to extend the reforms of the Progressive Era. When Catt presided over the final convention of the NAWSA in 1920, she had already helped to found its successor, the National League of Women Voters (NLWV) in 1919. Her able lieutenant, Maud Wood Park, reluctantly agreed to serve as the first president of the new nonpartisan organization. The immediate challenge was to get out the vote in November; the long-range crusade was to build an electorate that was "intelligent and clean."[4]

Organized on the state and local levels like NAWSA, the league established citizenship schools, carried its education campaigns to college campuses, invited political science lecturers to speak at its meetings, and generally sought to mobilize the new voters. In its first campaign, the league women targeted old enemies. They were defeated in their major efforts to defeat suffrage foes, senators James Wadsworth of New York and Frank Brandegee of Connecticut. Their get-out-the-vote campaign had mixed results. Women cast an estimated one-third of the vote in the 1920 presidential contest. Though the Democratic platform included twelve of fifteen NLWV proposals, the majority of the women, like the men, seemed to have voted for Republican Warren Gamaliel Harding. Prodded by Ohio suffragist and incoming vice chairman of the Republican National Committee, Harriet Taylor Upton, Harding went well beyond the Republican platform in his support of issues women had long supported. He spoke out for equal pay for equal work, extension of the Children's Bureau, an end to child labor, enforcement of Prohibition, prevention of lynching, maternity and infancy protection, and the appointment of women to state and federal positions. It was an impressive litany. As one correspondent summarized in the *Woman Citizen*: "Women unite on a humanitarian basis . . . where the home and children are concerned, women will stand side by side in spite of creed or caste. We have also learned that home does not mean house, nor children . . . it includes worldwide welfare."[5]

The major women's organizations that had mobilized their members for the vote as a tool for reform now prepared to use it to complete the unfinished business of progressivism. These social feminists formed an impressive army. In numbers, the General Federation of Women's Clubs (GFWC) was a clear leader. More than 2,800,000 members headed by Executive Director Lida Hafford, pressed for legislation to improve the conditions of children and of working women. They were joined by the National Consumers' League (NCL). Forty thousand members, led by Florence Kelley, fought for minimum wage bills, making up in energy and lobbying skills what they lacked in numbers. The Women's Trade Union League (WTUL), led by well-to-do reformer Margaret Dreier Robins, worked to organize working women into trade unions to win conditions "necessary for healthful and efficient work." The 600,000-member Young Women's Christian Association (YWCA) worked for "the temporal, moral and religious welfare of young women who are dependent on their own exertions for support." The Girls Friendly Society, formed by Protestant Episcopal women, offered "friendly assistance to the problems of growing girls," the National Council of Jewish Women addressed the concerns of immigrants, and the National Council of Catholic Women, founded in 1920, focused on the welfare of women in industry.[6]

In 1920, eight women's organizations founded the Women's Joint Congressional Committee (WJCC) to serve as a clearinghouse for the federal legislation advocated by their members. By 1922, the WJCC was described by the *Ladies' Home Journal* and the *Journal of the American Medical Association* as the most powerful and highly organized lobby in Washington.[7] Maud Wood Park of the League of Women Voters served as chairman; Florence V. Watkins of the National Congress of Mothers and Parent-Teachers Associations was secretary. Annual dues for organizations were a modest ten dollars. A subcommittee of the WJCC formed when three organizations agreed to support or oppose a bill. A standing lookout committee tracked the legislative progress of bills. The agenda set by the WJCC founders in 1921 featured six Ps: Prohibition, public schools, protection of infants, physical education in the public schools, peace through international arms reduction, and protection of women in industry. They overwhelmingly agreed to make their primary objective the protection of infants.[8]

In 1918 the United States stood eleventh among twenty nations in infant mortality and seventeenth in maternal mortality. One of Florence Kelley's NCL colleagues reported her dismay: "We had taken for granted American superiority in sanitation and health. American plumbing was the sign and symbol . . . of our national pre-eminence in physical care." Children's Bureau studies presented a "very different and horrifying situation."[9] Appropriately, the first congresswoman, Jeannette Rankin (Dem., Montana) introduced a "baby act" in July 1918. When the Sixty-fifth Congress failed to act, Senator Morris Sheppard of Texas, who had successfully steered the Prohibition amendment through Congress, joined Congressman Horace Towner (Rep., Iowa) to reintroduce the measure in the Sixty-sixth Congress. Two hundred thousand infants under the age of one and eighteen thousand new mothers were dying annually; only tuberculosis was a greater killer of American mothers. Though Sheppard cited statistics and inveighed against the shameful record as "an accusation of the Republic and an indictment of the flag," Congress again did not act.[10]

The enfranchisement of women brought not only new hope but a firm endorsement by President Harding for the Sheppard-Towner Act. The WJCC lobby easily moved the bill through the Senate in a special session of the Sixty-seventh Congress only to have the measure languish in the House Rules Committee. Florence Kelley asked passionately, "Will Congress let Christmas come and go and New Year's come and go and the legislatures come and adjourn" without action to save the lives of children? Reintroduced in the Sixty-seventh Congress, the measure faced the opposition of old suffrage foe Senator James Reed (Dem., Missouri). He attacked the women lobbyists and the Children's Bureau with the assertion, "It seems to be the established doctrine of this bureau that the only people capable of caring for babies and mothers of babies are ladies who have not had babies." Senator William Kenyon (Rep., Iowa) fired back a warning: "The Senator . . . has erected a woman, an old-maid woman, and he has led that old maid woman in a merry chase around this chamber. . . . I would not blame the old maids for having a little resentment, and the old maids are voting now."[11] Unrepentant, Reed offered a final amendment to change the title of the Sheppard-Towner bill to "A Bill to organize a Board of Spinsters to Teach Mothers How to Raise Babies." His complaint was ironically echoed in the House by the lone congresswoman, Alice Robertson (Dem., Oklahoma), who criticized clubwomen who "sit at ease in comfortable homes, worrying about other people's children, and get a thrill over teacups by passing resolutions designed to bring about a new order in governmental affairs."[12]

While thirty-five governors, the American Federation of Labor, and the National Catholic Welfare Conference supported the Sheppard-Towner measure, the WJCC was by far "the most powerful lobby."[13] Its organizations drafted letters and their members deluged Congress. Florence Kelley, in the NCL's letter, reminded Congress that while it delayed action, America had dropped to the bottom of the list of nations ranked according to their care for the lives of mothers and children. Women were asking, she concluded, "why does Congress wish mothers and children to die?" Congressional responses were tabulated by legislative committees and sent to WJCC secretary Florence Watkins. Wearily she wrote to the YWCA Law Reporting Service, "Is it not great sport to read the letters which the members of Congress write when they wish to be noncommittal?"[14]

The opposition also increased the pressure. The National Association Opposed to Woman's Suffrage and the Woman Patriots condemned the measure as Communist-inspired. The American Medical Association's House of Delegates decried the act as a "socialistic scheme." But the women won the day and "An Act for the promotion of the welfare and hygiene of maternity and infancy, and for other purposes" passed in July 1921. The *Journal of the American Medical Association* analyzed the victory: "Women had just been given the vote. No one knew how they would use it. Nearly every Congressman had a distinct sense of faintness at the thought of having all the women in his district against him. Male opposition he was used to. But the women's vote! Awful thought."[15]

The Sheppard-Towner Act was the first major federal welfare measure. Appropriations of five thousand dollars went to each state with an additional five thousand dollars to states on a matching fund basis to provide for education, child-care conferences, and visiting nurses. The Children's Bureau was the administrating agency. At the end of five years, all the states except Connecticut, Massachusetts, and Illinois established programs. To win passage, however, the supporters had accepted a major compromise. The legislation and appropriations lasted only until June 1927. A grim struggle for renewal won only an additional two years before termination.

Yet flushed with success after the Sheppard-Towner victory, the WJCC worked to win the second of the six Ps on its agenda, a federal prison for women. While the Children's Bureau under Grace Abbott provided the statistics and the federal spearhead for the maternity and infancy legislation, the major catalyst in the drive for prison legislation was the highest ranking woman in the federal bureaucracy, Mabel Walker Willebrandt, assistant attorney general in charge of Prohibition, income tax cases, and prisons.

In 1921, the federal prison system faced a crisis in numbers and direction. The Harrison Act of 1914 and the Volstead Act were flooding the federal dockets with drug and alcohol cases. Only three federal penitentiaries, Leavenworth, Atlanta, and McNeil Island, were available to house a burgeoning male population. To complicate prison administration further, public and professional attitudes toward crime and punishment were changing. The progressive penologists' emphasis on prevention and rehabilitation was replaced by a drive to protect society from the violence and contamination of criminals and misfits.[16] Public attitudes toward the "fallen woman" also changed. Woman as victim of environment or economics was replaced by woman as threat and pariah. During World War I, the federal Commission on Training Camp Activities had rounded up prostitutes to safeguard soldiers from the "greatest destroyer of manpower."[17]

Once arrested and convicted, federal women prisoners were boarded in state and county jails. Supervision, food, and medical treatment varied from good to intolerable. Only one federal inspector monitored conditions. By 1923, the per capita cost of the best local facilities exceeded the payment allowed by the federal government. Only California and New Jersey institutions still admitted federal women prisoners. In January 1923, Willebrandt and superintendent of Prisons, Heber Votaw, brother-in-law of President Harding, found a possible prison site at Mount Weather in Virginia. Willebrandt's division drafted legislation, and she rallied the WJCC for the fray.[18]

Armed with the dates of national women's conventions, Willebrandt encouraged her staff, writing, "This is fine—go at it systematically and send literature and ask for endorsements and check them off when they come in."[19] Lida Hafford, executive director of the GFWC, distributed pertinent copies of the *Congressional Record* to club members. Harriet Taylor Upton interceded with Harding, pointing out the dismal party showing in 1922 and the need for female support in 1924. Mrs. Harding also pressed her brother's prison project.[20]

When the intense lobbying of the women and modest presidential persuasion failed to win congressional approval, Willebrandt, working with Julia Jaffray, head of the GFWC's Committee on Institutional Relations organized a meeting of the leaders of twenty-one national groups for 21 September at the GFWC's new Washington headquarters. The women were there in force. Representatives from the American Association of University Women, the Women's Christian Temperance Union (WCTU), the Daughters of the American Revolution, National Council of Women, National Congress of Mothers and Parent-Teachers Associations, and National Federation of Business and Professional Women's Clubs joined leaders from the American Prison Association, the Democratic and Republican national committees, the National Committee on Prisons and Prison Labor, the National Committee on Mental Hygiene, the American Home Economics Association and others.[21]

Willebrandt opened the session with a strong statement on the priorities of the federal prison system; she was followed by a distinguished panel of state prison administrators, Katherine B. Davis, Jessie Hodder, Florence Monahan, and H. Crittenden Hawes. All stressed the urgent need for an institution for federal women prisoners. By the end of the day a blueprint emerged. The prison envisioned would have a minimum of seven hundred prisoners housed in structures based on the cottage plan. The superintendent was to be a woman. Unanimously approving the proposal, the conference leaders pledged they would muster their organizational support.[22] Willebrandt's division at the Department of Justice drafted the new legislation.

The heavy artillery was clearly deployed. Maud Wood Park and Lida Hafford tirelessly visited congressional offices; representatives of women's organizations were highly visible at the hearings. Resolutions from the executive boards of the organizations were forwarded to key committee members. Willebrandt apprised the congressmen of the growing crisis, reporting that almost six hundred women were housed in jails "absolutely inadequate to care for their health and comfort." One federal judge refused to sentence any more women until the Justice Department could assure adequate quarters.[23] In June 1924, the prison legislation won approval.

Six months later, after steady lobbying, Alderson, West Virginia, was selected as the site. President Coolidge approved an appropriation of $909,100 to start construction in March 1925. Within three weeks, Dr. Mary Belle Harris, former superintendent of the New Jersey State Home for Girls and a leader in the prison self-government movement, became the first superintendent.

The first inmates were admitted to Alderson in April 1927. That this institution was different was obvious the first night. Prisoners entering the dining room found tablecloths and napkins; some wept. There were no walls, no guards with guns in turrets. From the outside, Alderson could be mistaken for a college campus. Two quadrangles of brick cottages were anchored by administration and educational buildings. Harris immediately established a scientific classification system to set the right work and training for each inmate to prepare her to return to society. Each cottage developed an organization for self-government. The entire cost of the handsome red brick plant, Harris pointed out, was little more than that required to build conventional cell blocks.[24]

After the major legislative victories in the Sheppard-Towner Act and the establishment of the first federal prison for women, the WJCC and its member organizations continued to work for appropriations for the Children's Bureau and the Women's Bureau. In 1922 they secured passage of the Cable Act achieving a reform in the citizenship status of American women who married foreigners. They won backing for the teaching of physical education in the public schools, though they failed to win approval for a federal Department of Education. However, their major frustration in the first half of the decade was failure to enact a child labor amendment. One legislator, the father of five, summarized the increasing congressional resistance to reform, particularly through a constitutional amendment: "They have taken our women away from us by constitutional amendment; they have taken our liquor away from us, and now they want to take our children."[25] Yet to many, a federal amendment seemed the only hope to end the evil.

In this fight the WJCC joined forces with the National Child Labor Committee (NCLC). The NCLC, the NCL, and other organizations had won passage of federal child labor legislation in the Keating-Owen Act in 1916, only to have it struck down by the Supreme Court in *Hammer* v. *Dagenhart* in 1918 as an unwarranted exercise of the commerce power. The next year Congress attempted to end the injustice through taxation, setting a 10 percent tax on the net profits of mills and factories employing child labor. The law was promptly challenged and finally declared unconstitutional in a 8–1 Supreme Court decision in the *Bailey* v. *Drexel Furniture Co.* case in May 1922. The court ruled that the tax was "a penalty to coerce people of a State to act as Congress wishes" in a matter that was completely the business of the state government.[26]

The NCLC and other organizations regrouped. By January 1923, a child labor amendment was introduced in Congress. The WJCC, the American Federation of Labor, the League of Women Voters, and the YWCA testified at the hearings and distributed pamphlets to the members of their organizations. Initially unsuccessful, they worked and won reintroduction of the amendment in December 1923. At the hearings in the spring of 1924, they met the entrenched opposition of National Association of Manufacturers leaders David Clark and James A. Emery and representatives of the Sentinels of the Republic and the Woman Patriots. In March, when Henry Ford reprinted the controversial "spider web chart" in his *Dearborn Independent*, the WJCC leaders faced charges of their communist connections, allegations that had first surfaced in the Chemical Warfare Service's attempt to discredit the Women's Peace party. The WTUL led the defense on the Red charge, while Florence Kelley, chairing the child labor subcommittee of the WJCC, went on the offensive urging the NCL membership to deluge Congress with letters. She warned, "This is a rush order hurry call to help save the federal child labor amendment, which is attacked on all sides by the Deadly Disease Delay."[27] Senator James Reed, again a determined opponent, asserted the amendment "would not receive a vote in this body were there not so many individuals looking over their shoulders toward the ballot boxes of November."[28] The measure passed the House handily in April and the Senate in June.

Though the Republican and Democratic parties and the Progressive ticket of Robert La Follette and Burton K. Wheeler endorsed ratification in the 1924 campaign, Florence Kelley realistically saw that "the opposition to ratification is so fiendish that I dare not slip one stitch." After the Coolidge victory in 1924, the immediate task was to win the votes of legislators convening in January. Kelley urged the women's magazines to carry supportive articles, tried to influence Walter Lippmann to stop the *New York World* from "going wrong editorially," and debated with Senator Reed before the National Republican Club of New York City.[29] At the same time the NCLC and twenty other organizations formed Organizations Associated for Ratification of the Child Labor Amendment. They distributed almost a half million pamphlets.

It was all in vain. In Massachusetts the combined and well-organized opposition of the National Association of Manufacturers, the Woman Patriot Publishing Company, Irish political leader James M. Curley, the Catholic diocesan paper the *Pilot*, President A. Lawrence Lowell of Harvard, and Moorfield Storey won a resounding rejection in a state referendum arguing against unwarranted state intrusion into the family and interference with traditions on the family farm. Only four states, Arkansas, Arizona, California, and Wisconsin, ratified the amendment. Reviewing the rejection in May 1925, the NCLC board resolved that, while still advancing the federal amendment, the best hope of success was in new state legislation. Sociologist Sophonisba Breckinridge later commented on the overwhelming defeat "of this most cherished and most conspicuous of women's measures," concluding "it was clear that the winter of discontent in politics had come for women."[30]

Their frustration was widely shared. The farm bloc after winning some victories early in the decade saw its major legislative attempts at parity vetoed by Coolidge; organized labor never recovered from the hysteria of the Red Scare, the determined open-shop campaigns of management, and the adverse rulings of the Supreme Court; and black Americans' fight for civil rights met the resurgence of the Ku Klux Klan. In a "calamitous split" the Socialists fragmented into two Communist organizations, and the Socialist party was "reduced to a shadow." Once prominent Socialist women, with some notable exceptions like Elizabeth Gurley Flynn, Rose Paster Stokes, and Ella Reeve Bloor, spent their remaining years "as political ghosts." When the liberal magazine *Survey* raised the question, "Where Are the Prewar Radicals?" editor William Allen White described the dilemma of the "old reformer in the new order." Injustices were not so obvious in Coolidge prosperity. The average man, he observed, "puts his hand to his mouth, yawns and walks off."[31]

For women the conservative political tide that helped to defeat the child labor amendment also blunted the drive for the equal rights amendment. The two constitutional failures at mid-decade mark the end of the reform impetus from the Progressive years and graphically illustrate the division in the women's organizations.

The National Woman's party had always been a fractious ally of the NAWSA in the suffrage struggle. Founded in 1916, the organization in its strategy and tactics reflected the experience and the character of its leader, Alice Paul. Variously described as "the only charismatic figure generated by the feminist movement," "a revolutionist," and a "fiend," Alice Paul, all agreed, was "something special." She first entered the fight for suffrage while studying abroad in 1907, learning her tactics from the rough, tumultuous contests of the British suffragists. Returning to the United States, she joined the American movement while earning her Ph.D. at the University of Pennsylvania. By 1912, she was chairing the Congressional Committee of the NAWSA. Increasingly frustrated by the slow progress of the simultaneous state-by-state and federal approaches Paul argued that the organization should concentrate its energy and effort on the fight for a constitutional amendment. Unable to convince her NAWSA colleagues, she founded the Congressional Union with her friend Lucy Burns. In 1916, preparing for the presidential and congressional contests, Paul and Burns organized the Woman's party following the British strategy of "holding the party in power responsible" and campaigning to defeat the Democrats. Their tactics, also growing out of Paul's British experience, included picketing, chaining themselves to the White House fence, and launching hunger strikes. When the United States entered the war in 1917, the National Woman's party, reflecting the Quaker background of Paul and many of the other most active members, refused to divert their energies to the war effort. Instead they increased their picketing and fashioned banners asserting that "Democracy Should Begin at Home." In the heated patriotism of the war, they met with taunts, violence, and arrest, but the combination of their militance and Catt's moderate, broadgauged "winning plan" did carry the day.[32]

After the suffrage victory, the National Woman's party (NWP), like the NAWSA, considered its future. Through the fall and winter of 1920, the National Executive Committee prepared resolutions. In February 1921, ready to set an agenda for the 1920s, the NWP hosted a convention in Washington for the representatives of fifty women's organizations. Socialist and peace advocate Crystal Eastman grumbled that "all doubtful subjects, like birth control and the rights of Negro women, were hushed up, ruled out, or postponed," but there were broad discussions on a variety of topics from peace to lynching. All agreed to work to remove the remaining legal disabilities of women. The NWP and the NLWV pledged to work for specific bills for specific ills. But although Maud Wood Park declared that women "as a sex are content to advance a little at a time,"[33] Alice Paul and the eight-thousand-member NWP characteristically determined to go faster and farther.

Paul traced their primary objective to the Declaration of Rights at Seneca Falls, explaining, "We didn't add to or subtract from 1848." What the Woman's party proposed was to eradicate with one sweeping measure all the legal barriers faced by women through a blanket equal rights amendment (ERA) and, as an interim measure, state blanket bills. Crystal Eastman explained that an ERA would "blot out of every law book in the land, . . . sweep out of every dusty court-room, . . . erase from every judge's mind that centuries-old precedent as to women's inferiority and dependence and need for protection; [and] substitute for it at one blow the simple new precedent of equality." This "battle for 'equal rights,' " Eastman asserted, "must be fought and it will be fought by a free-handed, nonpartisan minority of energetic feminists to whom politics in general, even 'reform' politics, will continue to be a matter of indifference so long as women are classed with children and minors in industrial legislation."[34]

Eastman had succinctly expressed the dividing line between the radical feminists of the NWP and the social feminists. After decades of struggle to win protection for women and children in the workplace, the social feminists were not ready to endorse any campaign that would erase these hard-won gains. But in the spring of 1921, NWP lobbyist Maud Younger, still hoping to win allies in the struggle for the ERA, began a spirited correspondence with Florence Kelley and the leaders of other organizations of the WJCC. She sent drafts of the blanket measure and asked for revisions or approval. Alice Paul and Younger followed up the correspondence with a visit to Kelley to discuss her concerns on any dangers posed to the hard-won protective legislation for working and married women. Kelley remained unpersuaded of the wisdom of the blanket bills, writing to NCL colleague Newton Baker, "There is at this moment an insanity prevalent among women where we would least expect it. This insanity expresses itself in eager demands for identical treatment with that accorded to men. The slogans of the insane are 'A fair field and no favor—Equal rights for women, nothing more—we ask no privileges now that we have the vote.' "[35] To Kelley and the social feminists, the differences between men and women could not be ignored, but they insisted that men's and women's opportunities could be different but equal.

The argument left the realm of abstraction as the National Woman's party recorded its first triumph in Wisconsin in June 1921. In that state's blanket bill, women were accorded "the same rights and privileges under the law as men," but they were to maintain "the special privileges" they enjoyed "for the general welfare." Buoyed up by the victory, the Woman's party leaders sent a draft of a federal amendment modeled on the Wisconsin measure to its state chairwomen, asking for any recommendations or modifications by October.[36] Meanwhile, they worked to win legal support and advice for specific wording for the equal rights amendment.

The NCL and the WTUL spearheaded a counterdrive to line up lawyers who agreed that an ERA would imperil protection for women workers. Felix Frankfurter, Roscoe Pound, and Earnest Freund signed on as staunch allies. Ethel Smith, WTUL lobbyist, wrote to Florence Kelley, "Alice Paul herself is fundamentally opposed to special legislation for women." She tried to galvanize the NLWV and the WJCC and wrote to her membership that "whatever the purpose, however sincere the women who proposed this amendment, they would be offering themselves as an instrument to the exploiters of working women."[37]

In spite of the outpouring of legal opinions and energetic lobbying by the WJCC organizations and by Harriet Taylor Upton, Senator Charles Curtis (Rep., Kansas) and Representative Simeon Fess (Rep., Ohio) agreed to introduce the constitutional amendment. Florence Kelley wrote bluntly to Curtis, warning him of the dangers of "this miserable amendment" and rallied her forces with the cry, "Blanket amendments to the U.S. Constitution are monstrosities. Blanket laws affecting industry in the states are atrocities." The NCL launched a postcard campaign warning, "Danger Ahead! The Blanket Bill!" and citing the danger to wife desertion laws, prenatal care, mothers' pensions, and protective legislation for working women.[38]

In December 1921, the antagonists met in Washington. Maud Wood Park, Lida Hafford, Lenna Yost of the WCTU, Ethel Smith, and Florence Kelley conferred with Alice Paul and Maud Younger. Three times Park asked Paul if she was in favor of protective legislation for wage-earning women and three times Paul responded that the amendment would not affect those laws. They were amply covered under the police powers. Paul and Younger asked instead for recommendations for changes in the wording that might meet the objections and pledged to wait for these suggestions before submitting the final draft to Curtis and Fess.[39]

None was forthcoming. Instead, Kelley drafted four pages of questions on how the proposed amendment might affect current laws on child support, desertion, pensions, penalties for rape and seduction, illegitimacy, and finally, protective legislation for working women. The NCL recruited a formidable committee of influential women to lend their names and their money to the fight on the state and federal levels: Mrs. Borden Harriman, Mrs. Medill McCormick, Mrs. Gifford Pinchot, Mrs. Willard D. Straight, Mrs. Charles Dana Gibson, Mrs. William K. Vanderbilt, Sr., Mrs. Whitelaw Reid, and Mrs. Felix Warburg. This influential array was augmented by a mass meeting led by the NLWV, the WTUL, and the New York City Club in March 1922 in a successful fight to stop the blanket bill in New York. A similar effort stymied a Louisiana blanket bill.[40]

The NWP was undaunted. When delegates convened at their 1923 annual meeting at Seneca Falls, they reiterated the Declaration of Rights and launched their drive for the Lucretia Mott amendment. Alice Paul drafted the final version: "Men and women shall have equal rights throughout the United States and every place subject to its jurisdiction." A film of the convention, pageants, plays, and articles in their journal *Equal Rights* were utilized in a concerted campaign to win public and congressional support. In all their materials and arguments, the NWP stressed that the amendment would not remove protection. Their goal was to work for the equal protection of men and women. Should an immigrant male working in a sweated industry have the freedom to contract for his labor while the woman worker did not? Should a woman lawyer have her ability to compete with men or women be limited in her freedom to contract for her labor?[41]

In December 1923, Senator Curtis introduced the equal rights amendment, writing to Florence Kelley that he believed "more good than bad would come of it."[42] It never did. The dedicated opposition of the organizations of the WJCC combined with the anxieties of conservatives over the impact on the family and women's place doomed it to defeat. The National Woman's party tirelessly worked and won the introduction of the ERA in the House and Senate in 1924, 1925, and 1929. Their members testified at hearings against the equally tireless opponents from the NLWV, WTUL, and the NCL. The ERA was never favorably reported out of committee. In 1928, the Woman's party supported the Republican ticket out of loyalty to Curtis and in response to Hoover's statement endorsing equality for all. It was a serious strategic error, alienating their Democratic members and further weakening the drive for an ERA. In 1930, the National Federation of Business and Professional Women joined the NWP in the fight. It was a case of too little too late for an ERA in the 1920s[43]

While carrying on the fight for the ERA at home, the NWP simultaneously committed its time and its resources in the struggle for equality abroad. As one party leader summarized, "The whole sex must cast aside its bondage in order to secure equal opportunity for any woman anywhere."[44] Doris Stevens, the chairwoman of the Committee on International Action, spearheaded the drive at international conferences and through international organizations for an equal rights treaty and an equal nationality treaty. In 1926, the NWP, applying for membership in the International Alliance of Women, was defeated by the fierce opposition of the NLWV, again concerned that the blanket campaign would jeopardize protection already achieved. Carrie Chapman Catt branded the Woman's party "the cuckoo" which "laid its eggs in nests that had cost much to build" and threatened to cut off any NLWV financial support.[45] The NLWV's victory led to a major schism in the alliance and the withdrawal of European equal rights activists.

Balked in this international initiative, the National Woman's party did win a significant breakthrough on an equal rights treaty at the Sixth Pan American Congress in 1928. Doris Stevens led a committee of United States and Latin American women to present the demand that the countries in the Pan American Union, by treaty, accord women equal rights with men. The delegates responded by appointing an Inter-American Commission to prepare juridical information for consideration at the seventh Congress. Chaired by Alice Paul, the Inter-American Commission analyzed the nationality laws and found glaring discrimination.[46] The commission drew up a draft agreement that there "shall be no distinction based on sex" in laws and practices "relating to nationality" and fought to win inclusion of the principle of equality in the convention of nationalities drafted by the Hague Conference in 1928. "The real problem at stake," Paul asserted, "is not the problem of whether or not a certain number of married women shall suffer the indignity and hardship of having a nationality forced upon them; the real trouble lies in the fact that the effort is being made to launch a World Code of Law . . . upon a basis of sex inequality."[47] When The Hague delegates proved deaf to Paul and the Inter-American Commission, the NWP girded for another fight, this time to win defeat of The Hague proposals by the Pan American Congress.

They were joined in this struggle by the Women's International League for Peace and Freedom, which agreed early in the 1920s to support equality over protection in its international priorities. Its first priority remained an unswerving commitment to work for peace. It was a commitment that cut through the differences of the major women's organizations. On the issue of peace, the NWP and the NLWV were allies. Maud Wood Park observed that in the first two years after the suffrage victory, the NLWV members were "interested in peace almost to the exclusion of any other topic."[48] At the NWP 1921 convention, the most heated debate had been over the resolution on disarmament.

Although women in their own organizations and in the peace movements in the Protestant churches provided the most significant numbers in the quest for peace, they also reflected the major divisions over the means to achieve an end to war. Women worked for peace through American membership in the League of Nations and the World Court, for peace through disarmament, for peace through international law and the outlawry of war. In the 1920 election, Daisy Borden Harriman and other New York women formed the Woman's Pro-League Council, a nonpartisan group funded by Thomas Lamont and Bernard Baruch, organized on the premise "that the leisured New York matrons who had triumphed in the suffrage cause could successfully transfer their reform techniques into the making of peace."[49]

In 1921, the NLWV, the WTUL, the GFWC, and the Women's Committee on World Disarmament joined in backing Senator William Borah's call for a conference on arms reduction. Though unable to win any significant participation in the conference, this "aroused womanhood" challenging "the gods of war" did contribute to the pressure resulting in the Washington Conference for the Limitation of Armaments in November.[50] The conference produced the only major arms reductions in the 1920s; yet the women remained frustrated by the limited results. *Collier's* columnist Anna Steese Richardson complained, "Nero has twenty million imitators in America . . . women who are fiddling feeble tunes while the flames of greed, hatred and war creep upon civilization." Women needed a leader with "the divine spark to set ablaze the crusading spirit, who would rather be right than president of her organization, who would build a non-partisan campaign of women for world peace."[51]

Certainly the women did not falter in their efforts. In 1922, the GFWC, NLWV, YWCA, and WTUL all joined in a campaign to outlaw war through international law. Seventeen organizations led by Maud Wood Park formed the Women's World Court Committee and worked through the WJCC for passage of legislation in the Harding and Coolidge administrations. The Women's International League for Peace and Freedom, headed by Jane Addams and Emily Green Balch, sent committees to danger spots including China, the Balkans, Mexico, and Haiti to study situations that imperiled peace. In 1924, the Women's Peace Union of the Western Hemisphere, fought unsuccessfully for a constitutional amendment that would end the war-making power of Congress. Carrie Chapman Catt launched the National Committee on the Cause and Cure of War as a clearinghouse for peace initiatives. In 1925, 463 delegates attended its first national conference to study the causes of war. The National Federation of Business and Professional Women joined in the campaign for the 1925 Harmony Plan, which called for not only congressional approval of American membership in the World Court but a commitment from the court membership for an international declaration outlawing war. Though successful in winning the requisite Senate votes, Harmony Plan backers were not strong enough to prevent a series of such stringent American reservations that the World Court rejected American membership.[52]

The high point in the efforts to outlaw war was reached during the election campaign of 1928. At fourteen thousand meetings resolutions were passed supporting the Kellogg-Briand Peace Pact and the renunciation of war as an instrument of foreign policy. Catt addressed the 1928 convention of the American Academy of Political and Social Science urging that the State Department become an active power for peace and recommending that it "receive a part of the 82 cents per tax dollar now going to the War Department" to set up "as lively a publicity section for arbitration as there is for a big navy."[53] She rallied the

NLWV. The Women's International League for Peace and Freedom garnered thirty thousand signatures on petitions of support for the Kellogg-Briand proposal. When the United States joined sixty-two nations in signing the pact, Catt cheered this "mighty stride toward peace."[54] Ohio Supreme Court judge Florence Allen, a dedicated peace advocate, gave the credit to the women, asserting, "I think it is not too much to say that the Kellogg Pact would not have been ratified in this country if women had not been voting." Only three weeks after American ratification, however, the Senate approved a measure expanding the navy. Frustrated, Emily Green Balch exclaimed that there was "no country in which militarism appears to me to be on the increase in the way it is here."[55]

Reviewing the efforts of a decade, peace activist and leader of the National Council for the Prevention of War Frederick Libby estimated that women constituted two-thirds of the American peace movement.[56] His colleague Laura Puffer Morgan saw that as quite natural since "women are instinctively more interested than men in humanitarian projects and in matters of the common welfare because they have more leisure for study and activity, because they have fewer financial entanglements, and as a result a more objective viewpoint and greater moral courage—in other words, because they are freer."[57] It was perhaps because women were expected to be peacemakers that their impact was diminished. Peace was for women, war and power for men.

Surveying the diverse campaigns of women reformers, Francis Kellor had argued early in the decade that more would have been accomplished if "responsible women" concentrated on seeking public office and helping administer the "affairs that concern women as well as men."[58] Two seasoned veterans of the suffrage struggle pioneered in the early efforts to use the victory of the vote to gain access to the party structure and political office in order to win a power base for future reform. Republican Harriet Taylor Upton, daughter of a congressman, had headed the Ohio Woman's Suffrage Association for eighteen years. Her friendship with Harding and her experience won her election as the first vice chairwoman of the Republican National Committee in 1920. On the Democratic side, Emily Newell Blair, a writer, who began her suffrage career handling the publicity for the Missouri Equal Suffrage Association and had helped launch the NLWV in 1920, became convinced that nonpartisanship was not an effective use of the vote. By 1924, she had won election as vice chairwoman of the Democratic National Committee. Both Upton and Blair were tireless in trying to organize women's clubs in the parties; each developed a network of women ready to press for appointments and opportunities. They formed the vanguard of "practical feminists."[59]

A Republican delegate to the 1920 national convention, Elizabeth Fraser, issued a challenge to the parties in a *Good Housekeeping* article, "Here We Are—Use Us." A new woman, she observed, was entering politics. Now the suffragist—"hard as granite, aggressive, antagonistic to men, intensely individualistic and clamoring loudly and continuously for her rights—was being joined by a new type—womanly, tolerant, "not afraid to be charming, who works with, not against men."[60] The major parties adopted the 50–50 plan of national committee representation. Each party in each state elected a national committeeman and committeewoman. Though some chafed and argued that they should run as citizens, not as women, they acknowledged that "as a practicality the men held the citadel."[61] The better part was to accept the system. Gradually, women argued, men would become accustomed to them and women would work up through the party to positions of power.

The number of women participants in the major party conventions rose throughout the decade. In 1920, there were 96 women delegates at the Democratic National Convention (9 percent) and 26 at the Republican National Convention (2 percent). In the 1928 national conventions, 156 delegates, or 14 percent of the Democrats, were women and 70 delegates, or 6 percent of the Republicans, were women.[62] Women headed the Credentials Committee at the Democratic National Convention in 1924 and at the Republican National Convention four years later. Reviewing the increased visibility of women at the 1928 conventions, a writer in *Outlook* concluded "The Woman Politician Arrives."[63] Democratic national vice chairwoman Emily Newell Blair was not so sanguine. In 1920, she noted, a list of those who served on national committees read like a "Who's Who" of American women. By 1929, men had eliminated most of the women who had learned to fight. Most men still saw politics as a "man's game," and when a woman sought the alliances necessary for power, men closed ranks. A woman might be a politician, but she could never forget that she was a "woman politician."[64]

Women running for elective office faced formidable barriers. The Democratic and Republican parties seldom nominated women for posts if there was a good chance of election. In 1924, when launching a women for Congress campaign, Alice Paul argued that the National

Woman's party should support all women who were qualified to sit in Congress and who supported an ERA and a general feminist program. Ten women were nominated that year. Four of the five Democrats were candidates in traditionally Republican districts; the lone Republican nominee was in the South; four ran on the Socialist ticket, and one was a candidate of the Prohibition party. The only successful candidate was Mary T. Norton, who was backed by the muscle of the Jersey City Hague machine.[65]

The major route to Congress for women in the 1920s was being the widow or daughter of an incumbent politician. In "Madame Arrives in Politics," a *North American Review* commentator observed that the women had controverted "the jeremiads of generations of anti-suffragists" since "wifely devotion and the solidarity of the home" were the shortest road to feminine political preferment. Only one woman entered the Senate; Rebecca Latimer Felton was appointed to serve one token day by the governor of Georgia. Of the eleven women who served in the House of Representatives, four—Mae Ella Nolan (Rep., California), Florence Prag Kahn (Rep., California), Edith Nourse Rogers (Rep., Massachusetts), and Pearl P. Oldfield (Dem., Arkansas)—were widows of incumbents; one—Katherine Langley (Rep., Kentucky)—was elected to fill the seat of her husband who had been convicted of Prohibition violations. Ruth Hanna McCormick (Rep., Illinois) was not only the daughter of Senator Mark Hanna but the wife of Senator Medill McCormick; Ruth Bryan Owen (Dem., Florida) was the daughter of William Jennings Bryan; Winifred Sprague Mason Huck (Rep., Illinois) was elected to the seat of her deceased father. Mary Norton (Dem., New Jersey) was neither a widow nor a daughter but the protégée of Mayor Frank Hague. The only unmarried congresswoman, Alice M. Robertson (Rep., Oklahoma), an antisuffragist, won election in 1920 at sixty-six. Defeated in 1922, primarily because of her vote against the soldiers' bonus, she retired, denouncing politics as "too unclean" for a woman.[66] Yet if name recognition or sympathy were helpful entrées for most of these congresswomen, a few proved that given an opportunity they could become highly effective politicians. Florence Kahn served for five terms; Edith Rogers won election from 1926 through 1958; Mary Norton represented her district from 1925 to 1951. Although not surprisingly women legislators were mostly appointed to committees dealing with education, Indian and veterans' affairs, and the District of Columbia, Kahn nevertheless won appointment to the Military Affairs Committee, and Pratt to Money and

Banking, and Norton eventually chaired the Committee on Labor.[67] While they represented both parties, the congresswomen ranged from conservative to progressive, suffragist and antisuffragist, wet and dry; five had college degrees and most had worked or were active in civic affairs.

On the state level, the two women governors during the decade, Democrats Nellie Tayloe Ross of Wyoming and Miriam "Ma" Ferguson of Texas, succeeded their husbands. In the states, as in Congress, the numbers of women officeholders continued to grow. In 1928, the high point of women's representation in Congress, the 7 elected congresswomen were joined on the state level by 119 elected representatives, 12 state senators, 2 state treasurers, a reelected state auditor, 3 superintendents of public schools, and 1 state railroad commissioner. In Ohio, Judge Florence E. Allen won a second term on the Ohio Supreme Court by 352,245 votes.[68]

Women's success in winning office increased in geometric proportion at the county and local levels. As one contemporary noted, "Competition for power is not so great in that dark continent of American politics."[69] Where money and power were involved, a man generally won the post. Two analysts reported in *Current History*, "Where there is dignity of office but little else, or where there is routine work, little glory, and low pay, men prove willing to admit women to an equal share in the spoils of office."[70] Women were placed in "ornamental" positions; or in "a favorite trick" women who would "take orders blindly" were appointed.[71]

In appointed positions as in elections women did make gains through the decade. By 1930, there were thirteen significant presidential appointments. Several of these were in traditional areas of women's concern: Dr. Louise Stanley, chief of the Bureau of Home Economics; Grace Abbott, director of the Children's Bureau; and Mary Anderson, director of the Women's Bureau of the Department of Labor. Yet appointments to the Board of Tax Appeals, the Justice Department, the Civil Service Commission, and the Internal Revenue Service indicated that some women professionals were achieving recognition.[72]

Women's status within the party structure, their effectiveness as political candidates, and their impact as lobbyists all depended on their use of the ballot. By mid-decade analysts concluded that not only was there no women's bloc but that "women have not utilized the ballot to the same extent as men." Illinois, which kept a record of ballots cast by gender, provided statistics indicating that men voted up to 74 percent and women up to 46 percent of their potential. A survey of women in Chicago after the 1923 mayoralty election reported that one-third of the women who did not go to the polls gave "lack of interest" as their reason. Immigrant women noted language difficulties. By far the greatest number, however, stated their "disbelief in women's voting."[73] Reformer-muckraker Charles Edward Russell questioned "Is Woman Suffrage a Failure?" and concluded, "If political regeneration and the more intelligent conduct of public affairs were the main considerations on which we fought for woman suffrage, it would be absurd to contend that the present results constitute success."[74]

Following the relatively low voter turnouts in the presidential elections in 1924, Republican and Democratic leaders were unprepared "for the enthusiasm and even hysteria" generated by the presidential candidacies of Herbert Hoover and Alfred E. Smith in 1928. To women, reported Anna Steese Richardson in the *Woman's Home Companion*, this election was the "first exciting event since the war."[75] For the first time since its founding in 1874, the WCTU endorsed a candidate for president. Viewing the campaign as "a clear-cut, Wet-Dry contest," WCTU president Ella Boole promised to work for southern women's votes for Hoover if he spoke for Prohibition.[76] Frustrated by flagrant violations of the Eighteenth Amendment and inadequate appropriations for enforcement, and challenged by the emergence of a powerful lobby, the Association for the Repeal of the Prohibition Amendment, and its female counterpart, the Woman's Committee for Repeal of the Eighteenth Amendment, the WCTU and other dry forces saw the nomination of Al Smith as a direct threat to the noble experiment.

In addition to the perceived dampness of Smith, the drys were concerned about his Tammany Hall origins and his religion. What emerged was one of the hardest fought American presidential contests. Wet and dry, urban and rural, Catholic and Protestant, newer Americans and old-stock Americans were deeply divided. In both the Democratic and Republican campaigns, women were more active and important than ever before.[77]

The panoply of women signing on for the Hoover campaign was prodigious. Ella Boole of the WCTU spoke to the Southern Baptist Women's Missionary Society, the Methodist Episcopal General Conference, and the General Assembly of the Presbyterian Church. Margaret Dreier Robins worked for the votes of women in industry, and other social feminists—Carrie Chapman Catt, Jane Addams, Julia Lathrop, and Maud Wood Park—worked with their organizations. Alice Ames Winter, former president of GFWC, directed the Homemaker Division of the campaign. Black women leaders Mary Church Terrell, Mary McLeod Bethune, and Ida Wells Barnett campaigned among black women voters. The NWP, loyal to vice presidential nominee Charles Curtis and adamantly opposed to Smith's determined support for protective legislation, backed the Hoover ticket with its usual energy.[78] The *Ladies' Home Journal* endorsed Hoover; *Good Housekeeping* was more oblique in issuing a plea for enforcement of the Volstead Act.

Through its Women's Speakers Bureau and Women's Publicity Bureau, the Republicans stressed the issue of the *home*. A Republican ad insisted: "Hoover's cause is the cause of the home. Every woman should feel the deepest pride that her vote can help make this great man the leader of our country."[79] Republicans distributed thimbles inscribed "Hoover, Home and Happiness" and enlisted "Hoover hostesses" to gather women to listen to Hoover broadcasts. Mrs. Alvin T. Hert, vice chairwoman of the Republican National Committee, asserted, "No woman can afford to oppose the election of Herbert Hoover."[80]

The home issue, though it could be tied to the prosperity and stability themes of the Republicans, was connected most directly to the Prohibition cause. Nellie Hall Root, a leader of the Woman's Hoover Independent League, charged in *Tammany and Womanhood* that Tammany was built on the "unruly appetite of unprincipled males for liquor and for woman flesh."[81] But the leader in the fight of the dry forces for Hoover was Assistant Attorney General Mabel Walker Willebrandt. An accomplished speaker who was active on the chautauqua circuit on the subject of law enforcement, Willebrandt effectively chaired the Credentials Committee at the 1928 Republican National Convention, bringing in a majority report upholding the Hoover contested delegates. In August she appeared with Eleanor Roosevelt on the NBC / NLWV series of broadcasts, speaking on Prohibition to an estimated 20 million listeners. In September, the Republicans dispatched her to speak for Hoover in the Midwest and in the border states. By the end of the campaign, *Collier's* concluded that "No woman had ever had such an impact on a Presidential election."[82]

At Springfield, Ohio, Willebrandt spoke to a conference of two thousand Methodist ministers. Reviewing the long, successful campaign of the Methodists for the Eighteenth Amendment, she cited the areas where the law was ignored. The worst was New York City, ruled by Tammany and its underworld connections. As Tammany's governor, Smith had signed the law repealing state enforcement of Prohibition.

Would he defend and protect the Constitution? Methodists, by electing Hoover, could prove that "obedience to law can be secured." She sent the pastors forth with the plea: "You have in your churches more than six hundred thousand members of the Methodist church in Ohio, alone. That is enough to swing the election."[83] It was a thundering challenge and a sharp attack. Not once did Willebrandt mention Smith's religion. But for the Methodist audience, the plea for action forged the religious connection.

The speech was reported fully in the *New York Times*, but it was not until two weeks later that Smith, angered by a growing "whispering campaign" against his religion and stung by the presence of burning crosses as he approached Oklahoma City for a major address, determined to face the religious issue directly. Against the advice of his managers and before a tense local audience, he made a nationwide broadcast appeal to "look at the record" and excoriated the introduction of religion into politics. He cited the vicious bigotry of the pamphlets distributed by the Ku Klux Klan's Fellowship Forum and the whispered stories of his drunken driving. The use of religion had been denounced by the Republican National Committee, but, he noted, no one had disclaimed responsibility for Willebrandt's exhortation to the Methodists. No Catholic, he concluded, should vote for him because of his religion; but if anyone believed he were better qualified and voted against him because of his Catholicism, "he is not a real, pure, genuine American."[84]

Willebrandt spurred the Methodists on in the dry fight; Smith urged his audience to reject religion in politics. Together the two speeches made the linkage that formed the major cultural divisions of the campaign. Catholic, wet, Tammany, urban Smith versus Protestant, dry, rural Hoover.[85] Willebrandt's position in the Republican administration and Smith's nationwide address brought the religious issue into the open. Smith believed the gauntlet had been hurled; he responded with his own challenge.

An old Tammany adage warned that one should never be put on the defensive in political campaigns. Smith battled back. He had a remarkable group of strong and dedicated Democratic women supporters. Belle Moskowitz, the most influential woman in the Smith campaign, directed his publicity. Former governor of Wyoming Nellie Tayloe Ross worked unstintingly in her role as Democratic National Committee vice chairwoman. Molly Dewson, settlement worker Lillian Wald, and former Women's Bureau chief Mary Van Kleeck organized social workers and peace activists. Frances Perkins toured the South, trying to hold on to the women workers' votes for the party. New York City alderman and congressional candidate Ruth Baker Pratt, Barnard College dean Virginia Gildersleeve, actresses Helen Hayes and Fanny Brice, and novelist Gertrude Atherton wrote and spoke for Smith. Eleanor Roosevelt, busy with the campaign of her husband for governor of New York, loyally rallied her growing network of women for the presidential ticket.[86]

In its November issue, *McCall's* presented "A Woman's Guide to Intelligent Voting." Mrs. Henry Morgenthau and Mabel Walker Willebrandt listed the reasons to vote for the Democratic and Republican candidates. Willebrandt began with an image from nature that immediately linked the issues: "Spiritual and material fields in America lie fallow, awaiting a wise husbandman." She cited the Hoover stands on Prohibition, the tariff, agriculture, and inland waterways, and his role in bringing the current booming prosperity. Pointing to his international experience and the need for peace, she concluded: "The spiritual undertone of Mr. Hoover's acceptance reveals that he would receive the nation's highest office with a deep sense of consecration. He was the trustworthy candidate."

On election day the issues of Prohibition, religion, prosperity, agriculture, race, waterways, government organization, and the character of the candidate, and party loyalty produced a Hoover victory. In an impressive 70 percent voter turnout, Smith won 15,016,000 votes, more in a losing cause than any other previous challenger, but well short of Hoover's 21,302,000 total and 444 electoral votes. Analyzing women's role in the campaign and election, Sophonisba Breckinridge concluded, "The women of America may reasonably be depended upon in future presidential campaigns to do their part in elections"[87]

In 1928 women participated more fully and effectively than in any previous presidential contest. Yet there were some unsettling harbingers for the future. The Prohibition issue was a fight from the past rather than a cause for the future. For women who had won the vote eight years earlier, the collision between middle-class, old-stock, rural Americans and the emergent voting power of urban, ethnic, wet America represented only one part of the changing of the guard. Leaders of the NLWV, the Socialists, and the NWP reported an inability at the end of the 1920s to interest both their own and the young generation in their organizations or their causes. The indifference of the next generation to rights and reform was most troubling. Veteran reformer Mary Heaton Vorse, returning from Europe in 1928, reprovingly surveyed the flappers and noted that whereas she had spent her youth marching, they spent theirs dancing. Her generation had "willed freedom" for the next: "Well, here it is. Look at them." Young Lillian Hellman acknowledged, "My generation didn't think much about the position of women."[88] This indifference was also a powerful index to the success of the political struggles for fuller citizenship and of the reforms of the early 1920s. The new generation was free to move on to new issues and new challenges.

NEW JOBS FOR WOMEN

Everyone is getting used to
overalled women in machine shops

Women have made good as
Street Car Conductors and Elevator Operators

Clerical Work
quite a new job for Negro Girls

Slav, Italian and Negro Women
making bed springs

The war brought us
Women Traffic Cops and Mail Carriers

Laundry and domestic work didn't
pay so they entered the garment trade

"New Jobs for Women" poster of the Women in Industry Service.

CHAPTER FOUR

On the Job: Still Separate Spheres

What has become of the useful maiden aunt?
Anno Domini 1900
She isn't darning anybody's stockings . . . not even her own. She
is a draftsman or an author, a photographer or a real estate agent.
She is the new phenomenon in everyday life.

Robert S. and Helen Lynd, Middletown

The "new economic woman" was greeted with some of the same fan-
fare, skepticism, and heated debate that heralded the "new woman" in
politics. Yet here the experience of the past offered at least some guide-
posts for the future. Women *had* always worked, but the nature of the
work and the work site had radically shifted with the emergent demands of industrial expansion and specialization and the erosion of
women's traditional tasks as purveyor and provider of food and clothing. The censuses of 1900, 1910, and 1920 tracked the increased march
of women into jobs and careers outside the home and the changing
patterns away from agriculture and domestic service and into manufacturing and clerical positions. World War I quickened the pace as
women patriotically responded both to Uncle Sam's call to form "the
second line of defense" and to the reality of new opportunities and
higher wages. After investigating the jobs and working conditions of
women workers in heavy industry, the YWCA's War Work Council reported a major change in the character of women's work. They now
had access to the "master machines and the key occupations" leading to
the high wages of the machine shop and tool rooms. This expansion in
the factories was paralleled by an acceleration of women entering clerical jobs and careers. By 1920, women composed 23.6 percent of the
labor force.[1] *Main Street's* Carol Kennicott was joined by battalions of

young women who came to Washington to do their part in staffing government offices.

At the war's end the perennial query "what do women want?" was joined by the economic question of what women would do or be allowed to do. In the March 1919 issue of *Ladies' Home Journal*, Emily Newell Blair speculated on "Where Are We Women Going?" Some, she concluded, who had signed on only for the duration would happily return to husband and home; others, "having done a man's work and received a man's wages," would balk at returning to women's work and women's wages. Factory workers faced replacement by returning veterans; those who sought to reclaim domestic or laundry jobs would encounter war widows and black women ready to accept lower wages. It was an uncertain future, but Blair believed that new industries would open new opportunities for women.[2] Her confidence was shared by former president William Howard Taft in "As I See the Future of Women" in the same issue of the *Journal*. Not only had the war opened new opportunities for women, but it had raised the consciousness of the nation to both the competence and the number of working women.[3]

The most enduring legacy of women's war work and the most effective instrument in continuing to emphasize women's competence and women's problems in the workplace was the Women's Bureau in the Department of Labor. Social workers Jane Addams and Mary McDowell and the WTUL had long agitated for such a division. With the onset of the war, their lobbying effort was joined by the General Federation of Women's Clubs, the National Consumers' League, and the YWCA. Their first victory was the creation of the Women in Industry Service (WIS) in the Labor Department in 1918. Mary Van Kleeck of the Russell Sage Foundation was appointed the director of the new service; she brought as her assistant Mary Anderson of the WTUL, who had served with her in the Women in Ordnance Division of the War Department. Charged with determining policies for women workers, and observing and interpreting tendencies in women's employment that might have permanent social effects, the WIS had a hectic beginning. Anderson and Van Kleeck not only evaluated managements' requests for women workers on night shifts or in hazardous jobs but worked successfully for the inclusion in all war contracts of the protective measures for women workers already won in the states. Their major defeat was failure to win inclusion of the principle of equal pay for equal work in federal contracts. Anderson wearily reported questioning one munitions plant manager on the differential in his starting wage of twenty-five cents an hour for women and forty cents an hour for men. He cited the family responsibilities of the men. When reminded of the same burdens of his widowed workers, he admitted: "If I paid them the same, there would be a revolution. There is a tacit understanding that women should not make over twenty-five cents an hour."[4]

Their investigations and battles with other government agencies convinced Van Kleeck and Anderson that their most important mission was to regulate the conditions of work for all workers; the most important legacy of the WIS was the approval of the "Standards Recommended for the Employment of Women." The standards were a compendium of protective legislation won on the state level by the persistent efforts of the Progressive reformers. They included the eight-hour day, forty-eight-hour maximum week, three-quarters of an hour for meals, and a ten-minute rest period in the middle of each work unit. The principle of equal pay for equal work was affirmed, as was the recommended prohibition of night work between 10:00 P.M. and 6:00 A.M. To Anderson, the approval of these standards by the Department of Labor was the most important contribution of the WIS. It was a first step. Looking toward the problems of peacetime, and readjustment in industry, Van Kleeck saw the problem as finding "new means of enforcement of standards which have received such authoritative sanction of the nation at war." The continued leadership of federal agencies, she concluded, was a necessity.[5]

This necessity produced WIS's successor, the Women's Bureau. Van Kleeck drafted the legislation in the spring of 1920. Almost every women's organization lobbied for it; the bill introduced in the House by Representative Philip Campbell (Rep., Kansas) and the Senate by William Kenyon (Rep., Iowa) faced no opposition in the joint hearings. When the measure passed in June 1920, Mary Anderson wrote happily, "At last it was a matter of public record that women in industry were an important asset to the nation and the federal government was ready to assume responsibility for their well being."[6]

The legislative charge to the Women's Bureau was to "formulate standards and policies which shall promote the welfare of wage-earning women, improve their working conditions, increase their efficiency and advance their opportunities for profitable employment." Harriet Taylor Upton, the head of the Women's Committee of the National Republican party, and Theodore Roosevelt's sister, Mrs. Douglas Robinson, convinced Harding and his advisers to forgo politics and appoint Mary Anderson as the first director.[7] Her appointment ensured two crucial linkages: the continuation of the work and standards of the WIS and the close connection between the federal agency and the WTUL.

The difficulties in winning acceptance of the WIS/Women's Bureau standards were graphically stated by WTUL organizer and historian Alice Henry in an enumeration of "The Facts":

1. Women are in industry in large numbers and are entering new trades.
2. They work too often under inhuman conditions.
3. For the most part they are unorganized and have only just acquired the power of the vote. Colored women in many of the southern states are still practically voteless.
4. Not only do they suffer from overwork and underpay but working under such disadvantages, they necessarily become underbidders to men, and seriously weaken what ought to be the solid front of organized labor.
5. As the mothers of the race, they are being injured in regard to this function.[8]

To Henry, the obvious solution was to organize; the equally obvious problem was the American Federation of Labor. Never overly enthusiastic in welcoming or energetic in organizing women workers, the AFL faced changes in the 1920s that were "too swift for the mental comprehension of those workers who had created an organization to cope with a different economic world geared to a slower speed."[9] It was no match for the challenges of a triple revolution.

The technological revolution in industry that had so awed Henry Adams at the turn of the century intensified under the impetus of high wartime wages and a shortage of manpower. In the ten years between 1919 and 1929 new machines increased the horsepower per wage earner by 50 percent; but they also replaced the labor of 3,272,000 workers. A British observer reported that "in the big plants no man is allowed to do work which can be done by a machine." Skilled or unskilled, a worker could be reasonably certain that although he might escape technological unemployment, a machine would almost certainly change the nature of his job.[10]

The political revolution that rocked Europe in the wake of the Bolshevik victory and the Red Scare that emerged in the United States in 1919, kept the conservative AFL on the defensive during much of the decade, fighting radical rivals for leadership within the unions and striving for public recognition of its allegiance to American values. When Boston police struck in September for the right to organize and join the AFL, the *Wall Street Journal* asserted: "Lenin and Trotsky are on their way." When the United Mine Workers struck in the midst of the steel strike, the *New York Tribune* described the miners as "red-soaked in the doctrines of Bolshevism." On the defensive, the AFL organ, the *American Federationist*, warned against those who would plunge labor into turmoil and bloodshed, asserting that the chief barrier against Bolshevism was the AFL.[11]

The third revolution threatening organized labor was the massive exodus of agricultural workers from the land. The surge to the cities of the 1890s was dwarfed by the march from the farm in the 1920s. It brought an army of 19,436,000 into the factories, replacing the flow of immigrant labor interrupted by the war and increasingly restricted by legislation. This influx was joined by black workers who remained in the labor market in the northern cities following their migration during the war.[12]

Women felt the impact and played a role in the technological, political, and demographic revolutions. In 1920, 8.3 million women over fifteen worked outside the home, making up 23.6 percent of the work force; by 1930 this figure increased to 10.6 million, a rise of 27 percent. Much of this expansion came in response to the new jobs created through technological innovations in office machines and communication. Some women became airplane pilots or radio operators, but 86 percent of the women employed toiled in only ten occupations. Twenty percent still worked as domestics; more than a third were in personal service; three of every ten were in factories. Throughout the 1920s, the world of work was largely determined by gender. Management was sensitive to the "social differentiation of the sexes" in their hiring, and both men and women, as Julie Matthaei has argued, asserted their sexual identities in "work reserved for their sex alone." Women's work primarily remained women's work.[13]

As in the Progressive Era, women found that if they wanted something done they had better do it themselves. The Women's Bureau and the WTUL led the fight to win better conditions for women in industry. Challenged by the National Woman's party charge that the hard-won protective legislation of the prewar years was a barrier to women's equality of opportunity in the job market and that equity would be won only through the equal rights amendment, the Women's Bureau launched a series of investigations to study the necessity and efficacy of protection.

One of the first major successes of the earlier fight of the WTUL and the National Consumers' League to improve the conditions of women in the workplace had been the limitation of hours. Capped in the 1908 decision of *Muller v. Oregon* upholding the ten-hour day, the organizations' drive continued in other state legislatures. By the 1920s only Florida, Alabama, North Carolina, West Virginia, and Indiana had failed to act. Surveying the hours worked of 233,288 women in 2,608 plants, the Women's Bureau reported, not surprisingly, that the greatest number of women worked excessive hours in the states where the lowest legal standards existed. In Alabama more than 63 percent and in Georgia more than 68 percent of the women studied worked more than fifty-four hours a week.[14] A Virginia mother, deserted by her husband, reported her typical day in a tobacco factory. Rising at 5:30 A.M., she cooked breakfast, dressed the children, took them to a day nursery, and was at the factory by 7:30 A.M. When the factory closed at 6:00 P.M., she picked up the children and arrived home at 7:00 P.M. to cook dinner, do the housework, and sew the children's clothes, usually going to bed at midnight. Women's Bureau chief Mary Anderson concluded: "Ten hours in the factory and the double duty at home was bad not only for the woman's health but bad for family life."[15]

Surveying the impact of limiting the number of hours women could work in eleven states, the Women's Bureau, after interviewing employers and employees and examining payrolls, found only two isolated instances where men had been substituted for women when women could not work more than nine hours. Employers hired women for work because they wanted women. Generally, the Women's Bureau concluded that women did not lose their jobs because of limitations; instead limited hours increased the number of jobs for women.[16]

Prohibition or limitation of night work produced a different result. The Women's Bureau surveyed the status of night work in Kansas, Ohio, and New Jersey; in the five southern textile states of South Carolina, Georgia, Alabama, Mississippi, and Tennessee; in one tobacco state, Virginia; and in three largely agricultural areas, Iowa, Kentucky, and Oklahoma. Investigators discovered that a preponderance of young women "at the height of their reproductive capacity" and married workers were attracted to the allegedly higher night wages. They collected testimony on the adverse physical effects of night work, citing a reversal of natural rhythms, loss of sleep, and deprivation of sunlight. They detailed the schedule of a working mother who hurried home from the night shift to fix the family breakfast, get the children to school, do the cleaning and washing, snatch a few hours sleep, and prepare the family supper, and then, "still weary and unrefreshed," started her night work. While Rhode Island mill managers argued that the women made up for lost sleep on the weekends, the Women's Bureau observers disagreed. They found the night workers worn and pale, hollow-eyed and listless with "lines of exhaustion around the mouth" and "feverish movements." Mothers were high-strung and irritable. Children were "nagged and buffeted, and some left to fend for themselves like alley cats." Ironically, the investigators reported, women frequently took night work not only so they might make higher wages but so they could be with their children. The single worker, although she lacked such a heavy double burden of home and job, faced insults, dangers, "or worse" as she returned home on dark streets with long waits for a streetcar.[17]

The Women's Bureau found that often there was no night work because of "an astonishingly strong feeling among employers against night work for women."[18] It was a feeling shared by the majority of the Supreme Court. In a key decision upholding the constitutionality of a New York law prohibiting employment of waitresses at night in first- and second-class New York cities, (*Radice* v. *New York* [264 U.S. 295]), Justice George Sutherland concluded that "night work so seriously affected the health of women, so threatened and impaired their peculiar and maternal functions and so exposed them to the dangers and menaces incident to night life, that the state was well within its rights." National Consumers' League director Florence Kelley, who had been so instrumental in the pioneering *Muller* v. *Oregon* case, agreed that "every study of effects demonstrates that women in industry need not less labor legislation but vastly more."[19]

Yet Women's Bureau studies also demonstrated that sixty thousand women had lost their jobs through such legislation. The damage was restricted to a small number of special occupations or semiprofessional work, but these were frequently at the cutting edge of job opportunities. One cause célèbre involved the women printers of New York. Restricted to a fifty-four-hour week and prohibited from night work by a 1919 law, the women lobbied to lift the limitation, arguing that there were more morning papers and hence more job opportunities at night and that there were higher wages and shorter hours on the night shifts. Their efforts won repeal of the law in 1921, and the number of women printers on night shifts increased markedly. In another New York City instance, three thousand women streetcar conductors were not so fortunate, losing their wartime jobs to a combination of legislation, returning servicemen, the seniority system, and prejudice.[20]

Other Women's Bureau studies tracked the working conditions of women, the threats to health, and the incidence of industrial accidents. Dr. Alice Hamilton investigated chemicals used in the rubber industry, wood alcohol in the manufacture of varnishes and shellac, and solvent for dyes in the production of flour. In each area, she found that women workers were more susceptible to poisons than men and that the evidence of poisoning of offspring was serious.[21] Another study found that although in absolute terms more men than women were injured on the job, a much higher proportion of young women than men were injured, further indicating the dangers for the next generation from the work experience of their mothers.[22]

The major fight led by the bureau and its allies in the WTUL and National Consumers' League was for equal pay for equal work and for a minimum wage for all workers. In a mid-decade survey of Ohio women workers, the Women's Bureau reported median weekly earnings of $13.80, while the Ohio Council of Women in Industry estimated the minimum income needed was somewhere between $15 for the smaller communities and $20 for the cities. The council drew up a budget estimate for a single woman worker:

Board and lodging	$ 5.50
Clothing	4.50
Laundry	.75
Carfares	1.00
Doctor and dentist	.38
Church	.13
Newspapers and magazines	.12
Vacation	.37
Recreation	1.50
Savings for reserve	1.50
Incidentals	.75
Organization dues and benefit associations	.13
Insurance	.37
Self-improvement	.25
	$17.25

In studying actual expenses, the council reported that of those women who earned less than $15, 54 percent omitted any sum for self-improvement, 32 percent provided no money for laundry, 27 percent had no funds for vacation, 43 percent paid no organizational dues, 20 percent did not buy newspapers or magazines, 17 percent did not budget for medical or dental expenses, and 12 percent had no money for recreation.[23]

The reasons for the wage differential between men and women workers (women's median wage was generally 52 to 55 percent of men's) were many and complex. Nelle Swartz, a WTUL leader and the director of the Bureau of Women in Industry of New York cited the law of supply and demand, women's own view of work as temporary and bridging the gap between school and marriage, the long prejudice against women working, and the jealousy and fear of men over female competition. Everyday phrases abounded like "a very good wage for a girl" or "she does good work for a woman."[24] The most pernicious and persistent of the reasons, Mary Anderson argued, was the pin-money theory. Women did not need to work; they just wanted money for extras. Anderson wryly noted that there wasn't much fun in a ten-hour day in the factory.[25] What women's wages signaled to women was their inferiority outside the confines of the home, the need for male protection, and the realization that independence and mobility were not seen as goals appropriate for them. The ultimate effect of low wages for women was to reinforce "the docility, the perverse sense of marginality, that kept most women immobile, poverty-wage workers."[26]

The drive for a minimum wage for women workers won legislation in twelve states before World War I. By the early 1920s additional victories were recorded in Washington, Oregon, California, Colorado, Utah, Arizona, Kansas, Minnesota, Wisconsin, Texas, and North and South Dakota. Only Massachusetts and the District of Columbia passed mandatory minimum wage laws. Most of the legislatures had established commissions for setting the minimum. All this progress was brought to a jolting halt by the 1923 Supreme Court decision in *Adkins v. Childrens' Hospital* overturning the minimum wage law in the District of Columbia. In a 5–3 decision, Justice Sutherland and President Harding's other new appointment, Pierce Butler, carried the day. Sidestepping the decision in *Muller* v. *Oregon*, Sutherland argued that the Nineteenth Amendment and "other revolutionary changes" since 1908 had virtually obliterated the inequality of the sexes. Women were now on almost equal terms with men in contracting the terms of their labor. Both Chief Justice Taft and Justice Oliver Wendell Holmes submitted vigorous dissents. Taft, citing *Muller* v. *Oregon*, questioned how limitation of hours was permitted and regulation of wages was not. Holmes, noting that minimum wage legislation was already broadly accepted in other nations, also cited the Oregon case and rejected the changed relation of the sexes between 1908 and 1923, concluding, "It will need more than the Nineteenth Amendment to convince me that there are no differences between men and women."[27] In a domino effect, state laws toppled so rapidly that only the Massachusetts statute survived in the Adkins decision aftermath, and it had no mandatory enforcement clause. In spite of a chorus of protest, a call by the WTUL for a plan of action by twenty-eight organizations, a spate of critical articles in legal journals, and a 1925 *New Republic* review of the Supreme Court and minimum wage decisions that found a "degree of poignancy not to be discovered in adverse comment upon any decision," the *Adkins* judgment stood.[28]

Throughout the 1920s, while the Women's Bureau labored to report the conditions of women in industry, the WTUL lobbied to retain and extend protective legislation, to educate and train women workers, and to organize them for the AFL. From 1907 to 1922 the WTUL was led by Margaret Dreier Robins. Her one-time lieutenant Mary Anderson asserted: "Almost everything we undertook to do was at her inspiration. . . . Sometimes we were aghast at what she thought we could do, but finally it was unfolded before our eyes and it was done."[29] Married to social work reformer Raymond Robins, she "knew everybody" and worked with Jane Addams, Julia Lathrop, Florence Kelley, Sophonisba Breckinridge, Dr. Alice Hamilton, and Grace and Edith Abbott. She contributed her money, energy, drive, and a crucial middle-class liaison for working women to church and civic groups.

Robins led the WTUL pioneering efforts in training women organizers. In 1914 the Chicago Training School for Active Workers in the Labor Movement accepted its first three students: Fannia Cohn, Myrtle Whitehead, and Louisa Mittlestadt. All became effective organizers. In the next twelve years, forty-four women in seventeen trades had completed the curriculum of economics, typing, bookkeeping, and contracts through programs at either Northwestern University in the School of Civics and Philanthropy or the University of Chicago. Thirty-two became active organizers, but by 1926 in spite of the success rate, expenses and the emergence of other labor colleges led to the demise of the Chicago experiment.[30]

Meanwhile, Bryn Mawr's powerful president, M. Carey Thomas, responded to the challenge of Mrs. Robins that women's colleges should open summer schools for women in industry. Consulting with Felix Frankfurter and working out the curriculum with Bryn Mawr professor Susan Kingsbury, Thomas's venture outmatched the WTUL Chicago effort in scale, ambition, and problems. Launched in 1921, the Bryn Mawr program was established for seventy-five women. Expenses would be paid, but the students would lose their salaries for the two-month summer session. An eighth-grade education was the standard admission requirement, but that was lowered or waived for some southern delegates. Unions were pressed into recruitment except in the South where the YWCA recommended candidates. For the next ten years, the Bryn Mawr summer school was a model effort, meshing academic training, union-organizing skills, and participatory democracy. The WTUL contributed its leaders Alice Henry, Agnes Nester, and Matilda Lindsey to work in the summer sessions and Robins's considerable fund-raising skills.[31] Mrs. Robins registered her fatigue in 1921, writing, "I feel as if I were nothing but a money machine."[32]

Her work for the league and the Bryn Mawr experiment was further extended by her efforts to raise money for WTUL participation in international conferences. During the postwar deliberations at Versailles, the WTUL dispatched vice president Rose Schneiderman and Mary Anderson to Paris to present standards for women workers to the labor commission, which was organizing an international labor conference of the League of Nations. At the June 1919 WTUL convention, the reports of Schneiderman and Anderson and the resolution of British leader Margaret Bondfield led to WTUL sponsorship of a women's international conference to meet in Washington in the autumn concurrently with the League of Nation's International Labor Conference. Delegations from eleven nations responded to the WTUL call. Representing the WTUL were Robins, Leonara O'Reilly, Rose Schneiderman, Mary Anderson, Fannia Cohn, Elizabeth Christman, Agnes Nestor, Julia O'Connor, and Maud Swartz. The agenda was a compendium of WTUL objectives. Delegates were asked to study the question of the eight-hour day, child labor, unemployment, and maternity care. Resolutions urged the International Labor Organization of the League of Nations to demand an eight-hour day and forty-four-hour week for all workers, to prohibit night work for women, to allow no child labor under sixteen, and to regulate conditions in hazardous trades. Branching into politics, the women asked for the lifting of the blockade of Russia and, most idealistically, pressed the League of Nations to name a committee to plan for the equal distribution of raw materials throughout the world. Finally, the conference named officers and made arrangements to establish its headquarters in Washington. Mrs. Robins was president and Maud Swartz was secretary-treasurer. Other officers were from

Britain, Norway, Czechoslovakia, and France, with one reserved for the Central Powers who had no delegates to this first convention.[33]

The second conference met in Geneva, Switzerland, in October 1921 in the midst of a recession. Members discussed the conditions of unemployment and agreed on a name, the International Federation of Working Women, and set priorities to promote trade union organization among women, to develop international policies for women and children, and to win representation for women on the boards of the League of Nations. Robins was reelected president, but the secretariat of the federation was moved to London. A major debate on the federation's future erupted at Geneva and continued into the 1923 conference at Vienna. British and French delegates urged the young federation to affiliate with the International Federation of Trade Unions headquartered in Amsterdam. Robins and Mary Anderson vehemently opposed the move. Anderson argued that it would be "the same old idea of putting women on the side, forming a committee at which they could talk, and then not paying any more attention to them." Women would be included seriously only on women's problems, and, Anderson concluded, "the person who decides what is a woman's problem is usually a man who does not want to bother with it." European women who were more integrated into the labor movement were incapable of realizing "how much on the fringe" American working women were and how powerless they were to act independently of the AFL.[34] The basic problem was that the AFL was not affiliated with the International Labor Organization.

At Vienna the American delegates succeeded in winning a resolution on the outlawry of war, urged revision of the peace treaties and cancelation of the inter-Allied debts, and condemned the French occupation of the Ruhr, but they lost the major organizational issue when the delegates agreed to open negotiations with the International Federation of Trade Unions to develop a women's department at Amsterdam and to organize an International Women's Advisory Committee. Robins, who had refused to stand for reelection as president of the WTUL in 1922, now refused reelection as president of the international federation.[35]

Disappointed in its efforts to forge an international coalition, the WTUL under Robins and her successor Maud Swartz faced major frustrations in their organizational drives at home. From its inception, the WTUL had sought the approbation and the support of the AFL; it was an uneasy and uneven alliance. A report in the June 1921 WTUL journal

Life and Labor from an organizer in Grand Rapids, Michigan, exemplified the problem. When she attempted to bring women furniture workers into the union, the men in the shops tried to have the women fired, belittled the volume and quality of their work, and made them feel they were interlopers. When the women tried to organize separately, the AFL refused them a charter.[36]

Undaunted, the WTUL member delegates to the AFL convention in 1922 introduced a resolution calling for the Executive Council to issue charters to women's unions when they were refused admittance by the existing male unit. All that the Executive Council did promise was to discuss the question with those "few unions who, due largely to the nature of their work," excluded women. When women barbers in Seattle were refused membership in the AFL affiliate, they asked for and received a charter only to have it quickly rescinded when the International Barber's Union protested.[37]

Stung by the *Adkins* decision in 1923, the AFL did launch an organizational drive. Gompers, asserting that the WTUL was academic and inadequate to the task of organizing, suggested that the AFL create a separate Women's Bureau under his supervision. He tactfully sent his secretary to sound out Mary Anderson if the WTUL could be persuaded to "go out of business." The ever-accommodating league promised cooperation if and when the AFL Women's Bureau was organized. They need not have worried. Gompers's call to forty-five unions to send representatives to Washington for a strategy session to plan for the bureau and the organizational effort was answered by only thirteen unions. Meanwhile, the United Brotherhood of Carpenters and Joiners and the International Molders' Union adamantly refused to admit women. Mary Anderson observed that the "men did not seem anxious to get women organized because they had all they could do to attend to their own grievances."[38]

The organization of women in trade unions did not accelerate under the new AFL leadership of William Green after the death of Gompers in 1925. Elizabeth Christman, WTUL executive secretary, noted that only two of the twelve WTUL chapters had organizers in the field. Finances had always been a problem. If the WTUL was successful in its organizing efforts, the dues of the new union members went to the AFL. The WTUL had to depend on ongoing support from the trade unions. By 1926, WTUL resources were so slender, it agreed to hold triennial rather then biennial conventions and intensified its efforts to wring support from the AFL.[39]

Three years later when the WTUL celebrated its twenty-fifth anniversary, its convention featured William Green, Frances Perkins, Grace Abbott, and representatives from the southern textile mills. The August 1929 issue of the *American Federationist* was dedicated to women in the unions. An editorial, flanked by a picture of four women welders, noted that all the articles were written by women in positions of responsibility, demonstrating that they had "been accepted upon their ability to do things." Together, the articles provided a picture of "what women are doing to improve conditions for those who work. It is an inspiring record which will bring pride in work well done."[40]

In spite of this brave assertion, women in the AFL faced the same bleak conditions as their male comrades during the 1920s. The 1930 census underscored the problem. Of nearly 11 million working women, only 250,000 were organized in trade unions. Half of them were in the garment industry. Nationwide, one in nine male workers were in unions, one in thirty-four females.[41]

In industries where women were unionized, losses in membership were particularly sharp. Prohibition decimated the ranks of brewery workers, and technological innovations led to massive layoffs of cigar and tobacco workers; but nowhere were the challenges to organized women greater than in the textile and needle trades. Rocked by competition from new synthetic fabrics and faced with changing styles, the industry shifted operations and jobs southward for the well-advertised nonunion, docile, white labor. In the northern cities, unscrupulous jobbers moved into a chaotic market and pushed down labor costs. Radical factions, inspired by the Bolshevik Revolution and frustrated by the conservatives' poor record of organizing blacks, the unskilled, and women, launched a campaign for control that led to bloody fratricidal strife. As Left and Right vied for power and membership in a declining industry, there was "a perfect carnival of violence and unrestraint."[42]

Rivalry for members and control was frequently waged through the struggles for benefits and the strikes that followed. In 1924, the leftist leadership of Chicago locals of the International Ladies Garment Workers Union (ILGWU) led a strike for collective bargaining, a 10 percent wage increase, and a forty-hour week. Three thousand strikers, 90 percent of them women, braved an injunction limiting picketing; five hundred were arrested. Arriving to exhort the "girl strikers" on, Mother Jones, exclaiming that it was "a damned real war," urged, "Picket, strike, fight." It was to no avail. Though the Chicago Federation of Labor belatedly entered the struggle, the strike ended in defeat for the

ILGWU. A year later, the ILGWU cloakmakers, urged on by their leadership on the Left, pressed for limitation of jobbers, higher wages, and a shorter week. Forty thousand struck in July and did win compromises on wages and hours; however, the economic decline in the industry continued. Between 1920 and 1927, union memberships in the clothing industry dropped more than a third, from 172,700 to 101,409. By 1929, union membership was down by 30,000. Only 7 percent of the shops of cloakmakers were fully organized.[43]

Women textile workers faced the same bleak outlook and the same division in the organizational fights and struggles for benefits. When the United Textile Workers (UTW) of the AFL led a walkout in 1924 in Paterson, New Jersey, in protest over a stretch-out, they were defeated by management's importation of French Canadian strikebreakers. Two years later when management at the Passaic woolen mills announced 10 percent wage cuts in plants where Women's Bureau investigators had previously reported poor working conditions and night work, the Communist Trade Union Educational League assumed the leadership of the 15,200 strikers. Women marching on picket lines, helping in the food kitchens, attending mass meetings and classes to learn English so they could communicate with one another provided an "epoch-making example" of the ability of women workers to organize and fight.[44] Four-fifths of the women were married and they dispatched their children to picket the homes of scabs. Forming a Council of Working Class Housewives, they won donations from store owners. The struggle attracted visits and valuable publicity from national leaders Norman Thomas, Mary Heaton Vorse, Jeanette Rankin, and Elizabeth Gurley Flynn. When management agreed to negotiate, but balked at bargaining with Communists, the leadership stepped aside and the United Textile Workers union stepped in to win union recognition and the right to bargain collectively.[45]

In 1928 when cotton manufacturers in New Bedford and Fall River, Massachusetts, announced a 10 percent wage cut, the UTW led the strike of six thousand workers. Angry that the UTW was not organizing the unskilled, Gus Deak and others of the Textile Mill Committee of New York launched a new, rival union, the National Textile Workers Union. They won a 5.5 percent increase in the Massachusetts fight, but now instead of rival factions there were rival textile unions.[46] Each struggle, although it demonstrated the commitment and effectiveness of women workers, underscored the plight of the industry and accelerated the migration of plant operations to the South. For unions on the Right and the Left, the logical action and the desperate need was to mount an organizing drive for these new southern workers.

In 1926 while the average New England textile worker earned $21.49 for a forty-eight-hour week, the average worker in the South earned $15.81 for a fifty-five-hour week. The family was the unit of work, as it had been on the farms they had abandoned. Novelist Sinclair Lewis reported from Marion, North Carolina: "It is difficult to imagine which prospect was more disheartening for the mother of a large family: to start a long shift in such a mill or to end it exhausted and then begin the cooking and household chores for her family."[47]

The AFL mounted efforts in education and organization late in the decade. In 1927, the North Carolina Federation of Labor sponsored a Southern Summer School for Women Workers at Booneville. The next year representatives from six state federations met in Chattanooga to plan an organizing drive for coal and textile workers. At the AFL convention, southern delegates won adoption of a resolution to map strategy for a major southern organizational drive.[48]

The first challenge to this resolve was the "first of the great strikes" at Elizabethton, Tennessee, in March 1929. Angered at the demotion of a popular leader, Margaret Brown, when she had asked for a pay raise for her workers, five hundred women walked out of the American Bemberg and Glanzstoff plants. Matilda Lindsay, WTUL southern field representative, arrived and helped to organize a UTW local. Faced with a sweeping injunction against picketing, representatives of the UTW and Tennessee Federation of Labor met with local management, Tennessee National Guard leadership, and the sheriff and negotiated a settlement calling for an end to the injunction, a wage increase, the recognition of shop committees, and the rehiring of striking workers. When this oral agreement was not ratified by management, workers began to drift back to their jobs. In April, the UTW local called a second strike. Vice president Edward McGrady and UTW organizer Alfred Hoffmann arrived to negotiate. Both were unceremoniously muscled over the state line and warned not to return. When the arrests of pickets reached over twelve hundred, the Labor Department sent Anna Weinstock to negotiate with management in Elizabethton, Washington, and New York. She won a rehiring agreement to be monitored by a new plant manager, E. T. Willson from Passaic. His efforts were dedicated instead to development of a company union. His weapon was the blacklist; his carrot was a welfare program. The result of the UTW intervention in Elizabethton was a "staggering defeat" for labor.[49]

While the AFL was balked in Tennessee, the rival Communist National Textile Workers sent veteran organizer Fred E. Beal with Ellen Dawson to organize the workers in Gastonia, North Carolina, the South's "City of Spindles." In April 1929, the same month of the Elizabethton strike, two thousand workers at Loray, the largest of the 570 Gastonia mills, struck over wage cuts, working conditions, and the dismissal of union workers. They asked for a five-day, forty-hour week, elimination of piecework and the stretch-out, a minimum wage of twenty dollars a week, equal pay for equal work for women and children, and reductions in the rent and light charges in the mill houses. The company's response was to apply pressure gradually evicting the workers. The Communists sent representatives from the Young Communist League, the Workers International Relief, and the International Labor Defense. Twenty-nine-year-old Ella May Wiggins arrived to encourage the workers by ballad and example. A tent city blossomed to house the homeless strikers. In June, in the wake of the destruction of union headquarters, a police unit led by Chief O. F. Aderholt arrived to serve a warrant on the union leaders in their new headquarters in the tent city. In the tension shots rang out. The chief was killed and three deputies wounded. Sixteen organizers and strikers, three of them women, were indicted for murder. In the ensuing months vigilantes raided the union headquarters, attacked strikers on their way to a rally, blasted a pickup truck, and killed, among others, Ella May Wiggins. Gastonia remained in the national headlines. The first trial of the union leaders ended in a mistrial when the prosecution brought the bloody effigy of the slain chief into the courtroom. Before the second trial opened, Fred Beal jumped bail and fled to Russia, thus affirming for conservative southerners their worst suspicions that labor equaled Red.[50] The conservative UTW efforts in North Carolina and Virginia in 1930 had no chance of success in this climate and in the broadening grip of a nationwide depression. They did keep the focus on conditions in the South and the determination and courage of women workers.

The struggles in the textile mills were fought primarily by white women. Their black sisters also labored in the southern mills, but they were scrubbing floors and cleaning lint and cotton from the machines. Generally, unless only black workers were employed, they had no hope of moving into skilled operations. In the tobacco industry, when one manager tried to open opportunities in cigar making for black women, he was overruled by the central office and the Tobacco Manufacturers Union, even though "they made the prettiest, most perfect segars you

ever saw."[51] A 1920 Women's Bureau study of 11,802 black women
workers in 150 plants found that in industry after industry black
women held the unpleasant heavy jobs from dragging peanut bags to
working on the stockyard floor. Not only was the work heavier, but
the wages were lower. The inequity was most glaring when segregated
white and black women did the same work in different buildings.
There was little security or predictability for the black worker; as one
stated, "You never know what you are going to get; you just take what
they give you."[52] In 1929 a second Women's Bureau survey of black
workers found that the largest number, as in 1920, were in the tobacco
industry, followed by those in slaughtering and meatpacking, textiles,
and nuts. Only 13.6 percent worked eight hours or less; 40 percent
worked ten hours or more. More than 56 percent were pieceworkers.
There was little job stability. Seventy-one percent remained at the same
job less than five years; 22 percent lasted less than one year. Though
the Women's Bureau optimistically predicted in 1920 that black women
were gaining "a footing, however slippery" which would make them an
increasingly important factor, WTUL historian Alice Henry was more
sanguine in her assertion that "unless black men and women found
justice, they would continue to drag down the standards of white workers to their wage level and be available as desperate strikebreakers in
the future."[53]

While studying the barriers of race faced by the black worker, the
Women's Bureau also examined the problems of language, education,
and tradition of the immigrant woman. The Women's Bureau found
that of fifteen hundred women in clothing, hosiery, office cleaning, and
cigar making in Philadelphia more than a third of those in the United
States ten or more years could not speak English and two-thirds could
not write it. One in six could not read or write in any language.[54] However, a 1929 study of the conditions in industrial home work presented
the bleakest picture of working conditions for immigrant women. The
age-old problems of long hours, low pay, irregular employment, and
child labor continued and posed an actual and potential menace to the
health of workers and the public. New York attempted to regulate this
work and reported conditions throughout the decade. In 1926–27, the
state found 21,500 home workers: 11,000 Italian and 4,800 Jewish.
Eighteen thousand worked in the clothing trade. The U.S. Children's
Bureau, studying home workers in New Jersey in mid-decade, described the great majority of the workers at "very near the border line

of economic independence." Women restricted by language, skill, or experience and wanting to be with their children (even though it frequently meant working with their children) worked for one-third of the earnings of those in the textile factories. Philadelphia investigators found violations of the child labor law in 1,140 of the families visited. Clearly, the sweatshop, as the Women's Bureau concluded, cried out for regulation.[55]

While women struggled to improve their working conditions in industry during the decade, the major expansion of women in the work force was into the offices. From 1910 to 1920, the feminization of the clerical sector quickened. By 1930, women filled over 52 percent of the clerical positions. It was a rare instance of a shift from man's to woman's work. A combination of good working conditions, regular (though not high) earnings, paid vacations, the belief in an opportunity to advance, the "ancient stigma" attached to manual work, and the higher status of any occupation "supposedly mental" helped produce the revolution. Also significant was the rapid expansion in the 1920s of service industries. Banks, real estate and insurance offices, publishing houses, and trade and transportation industries all needed armies of clerks to handle the mounting paperwork required by the demands of modern business and federal taxes and regulation. There was a fresh supply of young high school–educated women workers from the middle and working classes ready to meet the challenge of the technological changes in the nature of office work. By 1920 the typewriter and telephone were joined by dictating and adding machines and other devices that not only raised output but radically reorganized tasks and transformed the work processes.[56] The stereotype of the woman worker fit the new compartmentalization in the office. Women were "tolerant of routine, careful, and manually dextrous." Docile and less ambitious, they seemed born to be file clerks or stenographers. Early in the decade they also fit the stereotype of the woman who took a job only as a way station to marriage. An article in *Delineator* in November 1919 addressed to "Those Who Spin in Offices" warned:

A girl in an office must have distinction without being distinguishable, she must have brains that are disciplined; . . . she must have enough force of character to lead a double life and not let its halves interfere with each other; be feminine enough to make the man . . . love her and want to marry her, and yet masculine enough to be impersonal and to concentrate on what she's doing.

She could add charm and beauty to an office through her personal appearance
and flowers on her desk. Certainly she could fight "down on the upper lip or
liver spots."[57]

The job was in the eye of the beholder. For the working-class
woman, it was a way up, an escape from the manual labor of the factory
to clean white-collar respectability. For those in the middle class the
steno pool was sometimes faced with the horror of Booth Tarkington's
Alice Adams who passed the forbidding entrance of the grim doorway
of the business college that spelled the "end of youth and the end of
hope." Yet as she took the fatal first step toward the doorway, she too
found hope in a future in the office:

> How often she had gone by here, hating the dreary obscurity of that stair-
> way; how often she had thought of this obscurity as something lying in wait
> to obliterate the footsteps of any girl who should ascend into the smoky dark-
> ness above! Never had she passed without those ominous imaginings of hers;
> pretty girls turning into old maids "taking dictation"—old maids of a dozen
> different types, yet all looking a little like herself.
> Well, she was here at last! . . . She went bravely in, under the sign, and
> began to climb the wooden steps. Half-way up the shadows were heaviest, but
> after that the place began to seem brighter. There was an open window over-
> head somewhere, she found, and the steps at the top were gay with sunshine.[58]

While some young single women might enter the office with one eye
on respectability and possible advancement and the other on marriage,
their employers early in the decade not only preferred single women
but frequently dismissed women when they married. Yet increasingly,
pressed by the desire for a stable work force, they began to retain and
to welcome married women in their firms. Though the clerical work
force was still 82 percent single women, the number of their married
counterparts doubled by 1930.[59]

Married or single, the women clustered in the most mechanical and
routine positions. In 1930 95 percent of the typists and stenographers
were women. A secretarial position was hard-won, usually reserved for
college graduates and at the upper echelons frequently reserved for
men. Josephine Stricker, Theodore Roosevelt's confidential secretary,
wrote in "A Woman's Road to Success" in *Delineator*, October 1919, of
the enormous obstacles facing a woman whose ambition was to be a
first-class secretary. She described "how few and bitterly won are the
lifts up the long road that leads to a woman's secretarial success." To

succeed in the hard, cold business world, a woman must adapt and see life as a man sees it. Women who did not take their work seriously or worked only in the hope of romance contributed to their employer's tendency to stereotype all women as flighty, undependable, and temporary workers. One employer noted that "a pretty stenographer is just as demoralizing to a crew of young men as a Bolshevik delegate is to a crew of workmen." Business, Striker warned, did harden women. It made them predatory and selfish if they competed. It caused even those who loved children to put off having them until they were nervous and set in their habits—not, she concluded, the best qualifications for motherhood. Was it all worth it? Yes, responded Stricker, as long as one worked with a purpose and remembered that "your first and greatest loyalty is to yourself as a woman."[60]

Therein lay the central problem of the woman at work—society's perception and frequently her own confusion and ambivalence about where her loyalty as a woman lay. One contemporary observed that the qualities of a good wife and secretary were complementary, for a secretary "thinks *with* her employer, thinks *for* her employer, thinks *of* her employer."[61] Yet the meshing of woman and work and the tension in meeting old responsibilities and new opportunities and obligations was a continuing subject for analysis, advice, and debate throughout the 1920s.

To some, having a job (much less a career or a profession) lessened the chances for marriage. Ernest R. Groves, author of *The Marriage Crisis*, cited the passionate concern of one business manager. Pointing to a roomful of young women bending over their desks, he asked, "What would these young women do to us, if they understood what we were taking from them?" He provided his own answer: "They would rend the flesh from our bones if they knew that for our weekly wage and the promise of a slight advancement we were taking from them their legitimate right to be married and to have children. They think they are selling their time and labor. Actually they are surrendering their biological rights."[62] Groves worried more about the threat to future marriage posed by rigid routines, exhaustion, concentration by sex on the job, and perhaps most of all that a woman would be "coarsened or hard-boiled" by her business experience and develop qualities that would frequently repel rather than attract a mate.[63]

Should she find a mate she might find herself returning to the work force. Whereas only one in four women employed outside the home was married, by the end of the decade 11 percent of the native white,

10.2 percent of the foreign born, and 37.5 percent of the black married women were working.[64] The increasing employment of married women was a major development and a major concern. Union leader William Green lamented the "regrettable tendency" of newly married women to continue in employment, asking rhetorically, "Can we make ourselves believe that such homes raise the level of national life and bring a deeper satisfaction to the individual?"[65] Investigator Mary N. Winslow in her 1924 Women's Bureau study of "Married Women in Industry" concluded that everyone had an opinion. One argued that it was good for a mother to work since she could do so much for her children; others contended the children would be better off if she remained at home and took care of them and her husband. An unemployed single woman, sick with worrying how she could support her dependent mother, might assert that the married woman with a husband to support her had no right to be working. Finally, Winslow cited a British magazine's portrait of the perfect wife, devoted mother, and ideal working woman—Queen Victoria![66]

To approach the question more scientifically, Winslow cited three factors for consideration: the economic needs of industry, the social needs of the family, and the human needs of the individual. She concluded that women obviously met the economic needs of industry. Employment of women had risen 40 percent since 1914. Women frequently worked for low pay and in undesirable occupations. In surveying the contribution of married women's work to the social needs of the family, she concluded that their earnings either provided necessities or raised the family standard of living. Ninety-five percent of these working women contributed all their earnings to the family. Finally, in trying to assess how working met the human needs of the individual, Winslow observed that married women who worked frequently lost health, vitality, opportunities for education, and participation in community life. What they won varied from the economic survival of the family to a chance for their children to have an education.[67]

Throughout the decade, studies of the married women workers emphasized the continuing prejudice against married women working and the reality that they worked because they had to. A survey of 728 Philadelphia working mothers reported 29 percent were on the job "because my husband wasn't making enough"; another 22 percent were widows; 14 percent had husbands who were ill; another 23 percent worked because of desertion or because the husband "wouldn't support me." Only 11 percent asserted "I'd rather work."[68] In her massive research of working women in the 1920s, Sophonisba P. Breckinridge concluded simply that in factory, store, or laundry there was no question whether the married woman preferred housework to work in the factory. She must do both.[69] Mary Winslow hailed her effort: "Because of the work she is doing, because of the individual sacrifices she is making, because of the high ideal she is striving to fulfill, the married woman in industry is the greatest social worker of us all."[70]

Clockwise from top left: Illustration for Eureka Vacuum Cleaner Co. Margaret Sanger and Dr. Charles Drysdale at the opening of the Sixth International Birth Control Conference in New York, 25 March 1925. The family of Mayor Ole Hanson of Seattle.

CHAPTER FIVE

Marriage and the Family:
New and Old Responsibilities

The American people as a whole has retained to the present a
remarkable proneness to marriage.[1]

Arthur W. Calhoun,
A Social History of the American Family

As women entered choppy and uncharted waters in politics and on
the job, the old havens of marriage and family proved even more challenging and turbulent. Wooed and wed, the wife and mother faced an
array of expectations, responsibilities, choices, and roles. She was to
be wife-companion, consumer-in-chief, scientific homemaker, childbearer, and sensitive and educated child rearer in a nation excited by
the ideas of Freud, Margaret Sanger, and James Watson—all while rac-
ing to keep up with the Joneses. Small wonder that family sociologists
Ernest R. Groves and William F. Ogburn surveying their data in 1928
issued the sober understatement that it was apparent that old attitudes
were "disintegrating more rapidly" than new ones were being formed.[2]

The tension between old and new was graphically illustrated in dis-
courses on romance and true love. Couples in Middletown reassured
their children that love still made the world go around and that they
would know when the "right one" came along. At Rotary meetings
fathers sang "It Had to Be You," while sons and daughters hummed the
more inelegant hit "I Wanna Be Loved by You." But the rules were
changing. Movie ads depicted a world of "brilliant men, beautiful jazz
babies, champagne baths, midnight raids, petting parties in the purple
dawn." The new freedom afforded by the automobile, scored by one
judge as "a house of prostitution" on wheels, the vogue of titillating

true confession magazines, the lure of the illicit speakeasies, the wail of the crooner and "the barbaric saxophone," and the syncopated rhythms on the dance floor all set a new pace for courtship. *Harper's* editor and contemporary historian Frederick Lewis Allen recorded the generational change, observing that "none of the Victorian mothers—and most of the mothers were Victorian—had any idea how casually their daughters were accustomed to be kissed."[3] More poignant was the lament of a young college graduate: "I want to do just one thing . . . I want to get married . . . and can't do it because I haven't anyone to marry. I don't know how to pet." It was a complaint echoed forcefully in an *Atlantic Monthly* article "No Courtship at All" by "Another Spinster."[4]

Poet Edgar A. Guest, popular with the parental generation, tried to inject some reality into the headlong romancing, warning "that pretty little face across the street is not always pretty . . . out of that curving little mouth may come the bitterest of speech." While hundreds plunged into marriage, their friends merely smiled indulgently, saying "Poor little fools! They have a lot to learn." That, to Guest, was the peril: "Too many people set sail upon the sea of matrimony without the slightest knowledge of what to do when the hurricane blows."[5]

The 1920 census recorded that Americans did retain "a remarkable proneness to marriage." Sixty percent of American women over the age of fifteen were married. Groves and Ogburn, analyzing the age, ethnic, and racial factors, and rural and urban rates of marriage from 1890 to 1920, demonstrated that in all groups and areas marriage had increased; 80 percent of American women in their thirties were married in 1920. With the heavy migration of rural and black women to the cities during the decade and the high incidence of the daughters of immigrants living and working in the cities, the percentage of city marriages lagged somewhat behind that in the country. Adjustment, economic pressures, a shifting male-female ratio, and in the case of the immigrants' daughters, a generation coming of age tended to delay decisions to marry for many city women.[6]

Those who chose marriage did not lack for advice. Popular magazines bulged with articles and happily-ever-after stories. Groves and Ogburn, scientifically analyzing the changing functions of the family, particularly the erosion of the economic function, concluded that the distinguishing factor of the modern family of the 1920s was affection. Love and sexuality provided the cohesive force. Patriarchy was yielding to a more democratic marriage model. Where formerly, a writer in the staid *Atlantic Monthly* explained, there had been "only one melody in the household of the trembling wife; the melody of the master's voice," marriage was now marked by "polyphonic harmony." Margaret Sanger in her *Happiness in Marriage* insisted that "The nuptial relation must be kept romantic. . . . Do not be afraid to take the brakes off your heart, to surrender yourself to love. Unclamp this emotion; let it have full, healthy exercise."[7]

Sanger, the sociologists, and, less explicitly, the popular magazines emphasized the necessity of good and satisfying sex for both partners. A husband who had reveled in the high spirits and independence of his fiancée might find his admiration changing to annoyance when facing the reality of the "democratic trend of the home." He also, warned Groves and Ogburn, might not be ready for the testing of his sexuality when his wife insisted that sex be satisfying to her and refused to have her "sex exploited." Sex, they concluded, could change from an asset to a family liability for the unwary male.[8]

In a major pioneering study, Katharine B. Davis, general secretary of the Bureau of Social Hygiene, working with a committee of eleven women, psychologists, physicians, and sociologists, investigated the "Sex Life of Normal Married Women" in 1922. Their goal was to help bring about a "more satisfactory adjustment of the sex relationship"; their departure point was that "except on the pathological side, sex is scientifically an unexplored country." Five thousand letters were sent to married women "of respectable standing in the community," and when this resulted in only 436 returned questionnaires, another 5,000 women culled from the lists of college alumnae and members of women's clubs were approached. A total of 1,000 women finally responded to the committee's central question: "Is your married life a happy one? If not, why?" Davis cautioned that the respondents were not a cross section of American wives and mothers; they were middle class, 69 percent were college graduates, and more than 60 percent had worked before marriage. Nevertheless, the findings, cross tabulated for age; occupation, health, number of children, age at the time of marriage, and sex experiences, provide one of the most significant insights into American marriages in the 1920s. Of the group responding, only 116 reported they were unhappy. The major reasons given were "incompatibility of temperament or interest" and "difficulties of adjustment of sexual life." The committee searched the sample for 116 happy wives with a similar profile and then tested variables matching the unhappy with the total 872 and the sample 116. The unhappy were on average forty-two years of age, five years older than their happy counterparts; they lagged slightly behind in education, tended to work and not to be happy in their work, experienced poor health before marriage, married earlier, and had fewer or no children.

There is a striking frankness in the discussion of their sexual experiences by both the happy and unhappy respondents. Davis and the committee, testing for differences in the age of the partners, summarized the sexual experiences of a small sample of happy and unhappy respondents who had husbands more than ten years older then they and of another group of wives who were more than three years older than their husbands. The categories the committee charted in testing for happiness included sex feeling and practices in childhood, sex practices from fourteen years to marriage, spooning (broken down into hugging, kissing, fondling, and intercourse), and general sex instruction. There were negligible differences between the happy and unhappy respondents in their sex feeling and practices in childhood; nearly 40 percent reported some sexual experience and almost 25 percent of the total masturbated. In comparing the sex experiences from fourteen years of age to marriage, there were no major differences between the unhappy or happy respondents to questions of masturbation and emotional and/or physical relations with other women, but the unhappy reported a markedly higher incidence of spooning and intercourse. There was a similar difference in the fuller sex education of the happy respondents.[9]

The committee also tested the sexual experience in the marriages of their thousand respondents. There was an appreciable difference in the response to the question, "Were you attracted or repelled by the manner in which married sex relations came into your experience?" Almost 50 percent of the happy group and only 25 percent of the unhappy reported being attracted; 37 percent of the unhappy group indicated they were repelled. Similarly 60 percent of those happy in their marriages and only 15 percent of the unhappy responded that their marriage relations were pleasurable throughout their married life. The happier group generally perceived their husbands' "sex impulses and satisfactions, in degree or intensity, as the same or greater than their own"; in the unhappy group of 116, 12 percent found their intensity greater than their husbands.[10]

Summarizing the findings, Davis and the committee concluded that the profile of the happier wives showed that they were healthier before marriage, had general sex instruction in physical and emotional aspects before marriage, satisfactory sexual relations in marriage, stable health after marriage, and children. No differences were apparent in "recollection of sex feeling in childhood, sex practiced during childhood, masturbation in girlhood, strong sex feeling for other women with or without physical expression, and occupation before marriage."[11] The conclusions, in spite of the modern frankness of the questions, affirmed that happiness came through a combination of health, education, children, and the old morality.

While the husband grappled with more broadly defined responsibilities as lover, companion, and breadwinner, the wife faced the challenge of being beautiful and interesting. Ads containing Listerine's warnings on the perils of halitosis, Ivory soap's claim to purity, and Jergen Lotion's promise to provide a creamy hand for that engagement ring regularly filled the pages of *Good Housekeeping*, *Ladies' Home Journal*, and *Woman's Home Companion*. Beauty parlors proliferated to provide hair cutting, styling, and dying, manicures, and facials. Women spent more than $1.8 billion annually on the beauty quest; another tabulation estimated a pound of face powder and eight rouge compacts sold for every adult woman and enough lipstick that, if placed end to end, would reach from New York to Reno. Columnist Dorothy Dix succinctly phrased it, "Good looks are a girl's trump card."[12]

The glamour had to be more than skin deep. Marriages failed, a woman's college official insisted, not because of slovenly housekeeping or inept child rearing but because of uninteresting wives. The thrifty, industrious "domestic drudge" was a hindrance. The wife in the middle class who cultivated the right people, belonged to clubs, played bridge and outdoor sports, and made herself agreeable was the best helpmate to her husband. Groves and Ogburn agreed: "The modern wife needs to carry a heavy insurance in social interests . . . if she is tempted to concentrate unduly on either her household or parenthood duties, the family loses from her rapid narrowing and the effect of this upon the husband, even when he is himself most responsible"[13]

The expanding role of the wife was paralleled by her added responsibilities as a homemaker. As the economic functions of the wife yielded to factory and grocery store, her work as producer gave way to her responsibilities as consumer. Women spent more than two-thirds of the $47 billion annually expended on consumer goods. In a May 1929 article, a professor of household economics, hailing "The Home Woman as Buyer and Controller of Consumption," concluded that the typical family lived in a world "built for it by the woman who spends." As a purchasing agent she was central to social progress. Domestic science leader Anna E. Richardson also emphasized the "grave responsibility of the homemaker as purchaser." The wife-homemaker was barraged by ads designed to change the thrift and scarcity psychology to abundance psychology. As the emphasis changed from making a living to "buying a living," columns in women's magazines gave tips on managing budgets that would enable the prudent to plan and paradoxically scrimp and save in pursuit of the rising American standard of living. The siren songs were sometimes so tempting and the pressures of individual family members on the mother-purchaser so great that sociologists perceived an erosion of the "strong sense of family spirit."[14]

The consumer's choices were dazzling. Technology and new industries spewed out automobiles, refrigerators, vacuum cleaners, and radios. The burgeoning advertising industry ensured tantalizing packaging. Purchases were made easier through installment buying. Ads for automobiles led in volume, as the car became a purchase second only to the family home, and some would dispute that ranking. By 1929, there was one car for every 1.3 families. The car expanded the options for buying a home. It took the wife to grocery store, school, and clubs. It brought freedom, status, and even adventure and stood as a symbol of the new values and the heightened American standard of living.[15]

The anchor of the family and the old values remained the home. The three most notable words in the English language, concluded a Middletown women's club speaker in 1924, were "mother, home, and heaven." In Middletown, as elsewhere, owning a home was "a mark of independence, of respectability, of belonging." Cities trying to lure new businesses cited the percentages of home owners. In Middletown 86 percent of the thirty-eight thousand citizens lived in one-family homes. The homes, like every other phase of Middletown life, were differentiated graphically by class. A poor working man returned home to a frequently unpaved street and turned in to "a bare yard littered with a rusty velocipede or worn-out automobile tires." From the living room the entire house was visible: "the kitchen with table and floor swarming with flies and lumps of coal and wood; the bedrooms with soiled, heavy quilts falling off the beds. . . . The whole interior is musty with stale odors of food, clothing, and tobacco."[16] A more comfortable working-class home might feature a tidy yard with geraniums in front of a neat bungalow or cottage. The living room was brightened with a rug bought on the installment plan, oak furniture, and embroidered pillows. Piano, phonograph, sewing machine, knicknacks, magazines, and pictures of the children adorned the living or dining room. In the more spacious homes of the business or middle class, "everything from the bittersweet in the flower-holder by the front door to the modern mahogany smoking table by the over-stuffed davenport bespeaks correctness." From the poorest to the wealthiest home owners, the Middletown researchers estimated that a family had to sacrifice more than its entire annual income to own a home. This strain on the budget and the continuing migration to the cities took its toll on home owning. For many, a home remained an unfulfilled dream. Analyzing the building permits issued in the United States in 1928, sociologist Ogburn noted that two-thirds of the families occupying the new units would be living in apartments or flats; only one-third would buy a single family house.[17]

By the end of the decade, 17 million middle- and working-class homes and modern apartments were wired for electricity, forming a market for the new home appliances. Women bought 15.3 million electric irons, 6.8 million vacuum cleaners, 5 million washing machines, and a smaller volume of toasters and sewing machines. A 1928 study estimated the percentages of the American budget spent for goods and services:

Goods and Services	Percentage
Food	27%
Clothing	13
Shelter	12
Fuel and light	04
Sundries	
Furniture and furnishings	02
Tobacco, candy, soft drinks, gum	05
Education and reading	01
Health	02
Automobile	05
Other recreations (theater, ball games)	03
Miscellaneous (cosmetics, streetcar fares, writing materials)	04
Savings and insurance	12
Taxes	10
Total	100%[18]

While the wife and mother sought to keep up to the all-American standard through her buying for home and family, her role as household administrator was expanded and challenged by experts from the growing American Home Economics Association and the Bureau of Home Economics in the Department of Agriculture. Congress, recognizing that 6 million women still were primarily housewives and responding to lobbyists, supported new research in home management in the Purnell Act in 1925. An outpouring of textbooks, new home economics courses in colleges and high schools, and advice columns in *Ladies' Home Journal, Good Housekeeping,* and *Woman's Home Companion* armed the wife and mother with tips on how to be efficient and economical. Housekeeping, while a challenge and a profession, could also be a guilt trap. As one observer concluded, "Neglect of housecleaning was tantamount to child abuse."[19]

Time-and-motion experts invaded the home management industry. The Bureau of Home Economics reported in one study that rural, town, and city homemakers averaged over fifty-one hours a week in housework. Anna E. Richardson of the American Home Economics Association, surveying the amassed data on American homemakers in 1929, observed: "If this be part-time work what may one ask would be considered full-time? Homemaking still ranks first as the occupation employing the largest number of persons, expending the longest hours in labor."[20] Columnist Dorothy Dix was more dramatic, asserting: "Marriage brings a woman a life sentence of hard labor in her home. Her work is the most monotonous in the world and she has no escape from it."[21]

Studies revealed that child care, purchasing, and planning averaged only six and three-quarter hours a week. The routine housekeeping jobs, cooking, cleaning, sewing, and mending absorbed the most time and energy. The new electric appliances did not lessen the tasks. Indeed, the machines provided "a silent imperative to *work.*" An article in *Ladies' Home Journal,* "Selling Mrs. Consumer," reported: "Because we housewives of today have the tools to reach it, we dig every day after the dust that grandmother left to a spring cataclysm. . . . If our consciences don't prick us over vacant pie shelves or empty cookie jars, they do over meals in which a vitamin may be omitted or a calorie lacking."[22] The full-time homemaker prodded by experts and surrounded by equipment probably spent more time on her tasks than her mother or grandmother.[23]

The emphasis on domestic science challenged the old category "just a housewife." Home economists, reflecting the hoped-for status for home administrators, tried to establish the market value of housework. Hildegarde Kneeland of the Bureau of Home Economics estimated the weekly value of housewives' work based on the full and part-time wages that cooks, laundresses, waitresses, or nursemaids earned. Surveying the work habits of a thousand housewives, she estimated the upper limit would be about sixty dollars a week or three thousand dollars a year. The question was, who would pay? Kneeland, rejecting the solution that the husband might give the wife more than half of his income, observed: "Such voluntary martyrdom is perhaps too much to expect, even of that model of generosity, the American husband."[24] What she tried to make clear was the double source of the family support: the cash income of the husband and the housekeeping services of the wife. Yet the twin problems of money and status would not disappear. Anna Richardson lamented that though the "mother's service is praised in song and story, her success in homemaking is seldom recognized." She cited the case of one weary and unsung homemaker who announced her need for rehabilitation: "I have carried on this job without recognition or remuneration for 20 years. I think it time I learned to do something else."[25]

Married women who did try "something else" by working outside the home did so for a variety of reasons: the emphasis on the new woman and new career options; the escalating standard of living which called for two salaries; the desire to make a jump to the middle class, and, most urgently, the need to contribute to the family food and shelter. Generally all reasons were included under the umbrella of "necessity." The 1920 census recorded that one in four wage-earning women was married and one in eleven of all married women was employed. By the end of the decade an analysis of the Women's Bureau studies of 169,255 working women indicated more than 46 percent were or had been married. They faced public opinion that regarded the working wife and mother as "socially disturbing" or worse, an "ethical problem."[26] Wives who did not work complained that married women displaced men, lowered wages, avoided childbearing, and through their contacts on the job, encouraged divorce. Husbands with working wives felt branded as poor providers. Overwhelmingly, those who worked were from the working class. Their necessity was economic; the wages were for the family.[27]

Nevertheless, surveys proliferated on why married women worked outside the home. In a Philadelphia study of seven hundred working mothers, 89 percent reported inadequate support by the husband. While the disasters of death, illness, and desertion were all factors, 29 percent observed that their husbands were simply not making enough for the family. The average minimum wage to maintain a decent family standard of living varied from $1,500 to $1,800 from state to state. A 1927 National Industrial Conference Board study demonstrated that unskilled men in twenty-five industries generally earned 49 cents an hour and averaged $1,200 annually; skilled and semiskilled workers averaged 65 cents an hour, but would have to work fifty-two weeks to reach the minimum standard.[28]

Still, there was remarkable variety in why and where married women worked. Ethnicity, family size, generation, job experience, and opportunities were all factors. A study of Philadelphia women working outside the home from 1910 to 1930 found that Italian women were the least likely to do so. The first-generation Italian woman, hampered by barriers in language, tradition, and geographic location, worked at home at low-paying piecework on materials frequently brought by the padrone. While 40 percent of second-generation Italian women entered the work force by 1929, 70 percent left their jobs after marriage. Polish women, although more literate than the Italians, still rarely spoke English. Their husbands tended to be in Philadelphia neighborhoods close to the mills where "female" jobs were not plentiful. Since the women were in a distinct minority, many found work cleaning their compatriots' homes or taking in boarders. The Irish women, who had the advantage of language, a culture that expected women to work, and a tradition of late marriages, clustered in domestic service. In 1920, 24 percent of them were domestics, but increasingly second-generation women were going into white-collar jobs as telephone operators, clerical workers, nurses, or teachers. By 1925, the percentage of Irish domestics declined to 14 percent. With a similar language advantage, 83 percent of the black women in Philadelphia worked in 1920. Encouraged to move to northern cities during and after the war by employment agencies, they found themselves, even though their education and training were frequently equal or better that their white counterparts, increasingly squeezed out of all but the lowest jobs in factories and office buildings. Black women were cleaners, strippers in cigar work, pressers in clothing manufacture, laundresses, but more and more they were forced into what remained—domestic work. Jewish women had to live in walking distance of the synagogue. Like the Italians, family and tradition were central. They worked in the shops of relatives and friends and, as their capital grew, helped their husbands start up small businesses. Finally, the Philadelphia study showed that native-born whites earned the highest wages; by the 1920s, however, they had moved up to the middle class and had almost retired from the work force.[29]

Increasingly large numbers of married women chose part-time work. Agencies in New York and Philadelphia reported that high school and college graduates were finding jobs in department stores, tea rooms, or offices, or were typing or sewing in their homes. Lorine Pruette, a perceptive and anxious observer of the American home, concluded that, given the demands of home and children, the part-time job could be the solution and sometimes the salvation for the married woman. It eased the tension of "the nervous housewife," increased the funds available for home and family needs or wants, saved the child from too much mothering, recognized that there was no guarantee of security in domesticity, and protected the wife against being tossed into the job market at middle age trained for nothing except the home. Whether working full or part time, however, most married women saw outside work not as an assertion of autonomy but as a way to serve their families.[30]

While the roles of wife, consumer, and homemaker were fully scrutinized and shaped by experts, the responsibility of motherhood—childbearing, and child rearing—was the most subject to advice from professionals. Increasingly, middle-class women chose to have their babies in hospitals. Advertisers stressed the germ-free safer environment. The hospitals provided not only rooms that were "white gems of purity and up-to-date models on sanitation" but X-ray machines, and blood banks, and doctors and nurses were in attendance day and night. New hospitals featured a blend of the efficient and the homey in their design. Most important, women were attracted by the new hospital-based techniques for painless birth. Twilight sleep, a technique imported from Germany, was increasingly utilized in the 1920s. "Streamlined maternity's miracle," twilight sleep was described in promotional material: "Two yellow capsules, a jab in the arm, swiftly blot out the scene, time, knowledge, and feeling for the woman. . . . When she is not aware, sunlight pierces the drapery. And one of the amiable nurses chirps 'It's all over. You've got your baby.' "[31] The rising costs for delivery and the emphasis on consumerism and status affected the declining birthrate, a decline found in both middle-class and black families and in city and country.

The Lynds concluded from their interviews in Middletown that although childbearing remained a "moral obligation," the emphasis had shifted somewhat to child rearing. Voluntary parenthood and the grow-

ing respectability of the birth control movement were major phenomena of the 1920s. To one analyst, contraception was "at once the crux
of the new morality, the opening wedge of economic independence and
the most crucial change in women's lives in the decade." Sociologists
Groves and Ogburn concluded soberly, "No invention seems destined
to have a greater influence upon family life."[32]

Certainly the most enduring and effective advocate for birth control
was Margaret Higgins Sanger. Born the sixth of eleven children, Sanger believed that her mother's killer was not tuberculosis but the debil-
itation of bearing too many children. Reared by a socialist father and
trained as a nurse, Sanger, to whom "the thought of marriage was akin
to suicide," married young William Sanger and, after a brief suburban
sojourn, moved to New York, returning to nursing on the lower East
Side and joining in the excitement of Greenwich Village life and socialist causes. In her autobiography, Sanger told of the anguish and
death of Sadie Sachs, who had pleaded in vain for help in avoiding
another pregnancy. It was her conversion experience. She was haunted
by a vision, "a moving picture with photographic clearness, women
writhing in travail to bring forth little babies; the babies themselves
naked and hungry, wrapped in newspapers to keep them from the cold;
six-year-old children with pinched, pale, wrinkled faces, old in concentrated wretchedness . . . their small scrawny hands scuttling through
rags, making lamp shades, artificial flowers, white coffins, black coffins, coffins, coffins, interminably passing in never-ending succession
the scenes piled one upon another. I could bear it no longer."[33]

Sanger had her cause; she joined a fight already launched. Emma
Goldman, Sanger's major tutor in radicalism, demonstrated for her
how economic-justice issues and the feminist demand for the right of
women to control their bodies might be merged. Becoming an organizer
of the Women's Commission of the Socialist party, Sanger wrote on
venereal disease and hygiene for the Socialist newspaper the *Call*,
achieving her greatest notoriety for a column "What Every Girl Should
Know," which was banned from the mails. Frustrated at the low priority given birth control in the pantheon of Socialist issues, Sanger began
the independent course that marked her crusades. She briefly published the *Woman Rebel*, successfully printing seven issues before it was
repressed. Her pamphlet on family limitation was distributed at meetings of the Industrial Workers of the World. Traveling and studying in
Holland, France, and England in 1914 and 1915, she gathered information on the use of the diaphragm and honed her sexual radicalism

with the advice and encouragement of the English leader for sexual revolution, Havelock Ellis. Returning in 1916 to an environment in America increasingly hostile to radical causes, she lectured and, defying the Comstock laws which treated contraceptive devices and discussion as pornography, opened a birth control clinic in the Brownsville section of New York, earning a jail sentence of thirty days. Within two years she derived renewed hope from a New York Court of Appeals ruling that licensed physicians could prescribe or provide contraceptives to their patients to prevent or cure disease. As a nurse, Sanger was open to the medical model; her challenge was to stretch this small legal opening as far as possible.[34]

Sanger's strategy throughout the 1920s was twofold: she continued her writing and lecturing, but she concentrated more fully on building an organization and respectability for the birth control movement. Her *Woman and the New Race* in 1920 and *The Pivot of Civilization* in 1922 preached birth control as the source of freedom for women. Women with a knowledge of contraceptives were not "compelled to make the choice between a maternal experience and a married love life . . . not forced to balance motherhood against social and spiritual values." On the other hand, women's ignorance not only kept them chained to their place in society but hurt the race. "War, famine, poverty, and oppression of the workers," Sanger argued, "would end only when women limited reproduction and made life too precious to waste." "Can," she asked, "a mother who would 'rather die' than bear more children serve society by bearing still others?"[35] Given the knowledge of birth control, free women could turn their thoughts to "the new race." Such women, Sanger lyricized, would "bring forth a Plato who will be understood, a Socrates who will drink no hemlock, and a Jesus who will not die upon the cross." America and the world could be saved. In the deluge of five thousand letters Sanger received, she was further confirmed in her cause. They were overwhelmingly from working-class women, of whom 80 percent had married before twenty; they averaged five children.[36]

In the midst of writing these two major works asserting the necessity for birth control, Sanger organized the first American Birth Control Conference in New York in November 1921. The American Birth Control League (ABCL) was formed to carry forward the cause, but this development was almost obscured in the rash of headlines greeting the tumultuous final session at Town Hall. As Sanger rose to speak on "Birth Control: Is It Moral?" the New York police, responding to the urging of Roman Catholic Archbishop Patrick J. Hayes strode down the aisle and removed Sanger and the other speakers from the platform while the audience defiantly sang "My Country 'Tis of Thee." Sanger, escorted by the police and followed by supporters, then led a parade up Eighth Avenue to the station house to hear the charges. The *New Republic* castigated Hayes's "undercover" intrigue and his use of the police as the "puppets" of the Catholic church. But Hayes and the National Catholic Welfare Council remained inveterate foes of Sanger and the movement. Acknowledging that "contraceptive propaganda" had not only "played havoc" in non-Catholic families but was also "making headway" among Catholics, the Welfare Council, describing itself as "the only strong organized power" struggling against the birth control propagandists, believed it stood against "the degradation of the moral life of the entire social body."[37]

Sanger, who reveled in a good fight, was not without religious allies. Protestant clergy, particularly those who ministered to prosperous congregations, frequently endorsed birth control in their emphasis on the importance of good sexual relations within marriage. They did not so much challenge convention as seek to save middle-class marriages. In the wake of the ABCL Town Hall furor, W. R. Inge, the dean of St. Paul's Cathedral, warned in *Nation* magazine that attempts to suppress birth control information only brought a greater evil. Comstock's laws, he asserted, had "achieved nothing except to substitute a crime for a practice which many good people regard as innocent." The United States, with an estimated million illegal abortions annually, had become "the classic land of abortion."[38]

While winning some church backers, the birth control movement's most significant advocates proved to be the medical professionals. In 1920, Dr. Robert Latou Dickinson, president of the American Gynecological Society, urged his colleagues to seize the lead in the birth control movement. Three years later, Dickinson established the Committee on Maternal Health to undertake research on contraception, sterilization, and a broad range of issues of "conjugal hygiene." The gynecologists' practices no longer centered on middle-class wives weak from the vapors; the emphasis on health and the new woman now produced a patient who typically was "a pretty, well-educated girl of good social status, usually coming for a pre-marital examination, marrying her first love, intending to learn the physical mechanics of coitus and to control fertility."[39]

By mid-decade, Sanger sought to join forces with the medical profession. Writing in 1924 in the *Woman Citizen*, she explained: "The American Birth Control League desires that the instruction in Birth Control should be given by the medical profession. Only through individual care and treatment can a woman be given the best and safest means of controlling her offspring. We do not favor the indiscriminate diffusion of unreliable and unsafe Birth Control advice."[40] At the 1925 International Birth Control Conference in New York organized by Sanger, she won the lukewarm endorsement of the cause from William A. Pusey, head of the American Medical Association. In that same year she asked the Committee on Maternal Health to take over control of the ABCL clinic she had opened in New York. Though headed by a physician, the clinic had not been licensed by the state. It had, however, treated 1,655 patients and had valuable records needed for the research of the Committee on Maternal Health. Dickinson accepted her offer with the proviso that the ABCL drop all propaganda through the clinic. In the final analysis, however, Dickinson was not successful in gaining either the license or support from much of the medical community. Some physicians, believing that fear of conception kept many unmarried girls "straight," were reluctant to approve dissemination of information that might imperil traditional values. Others agreed with the editor of the *Journal of the American Medical Association* who asserted in 1925 that there were no safe or effective birth control methods.[41] Nor did the medical profession mass behind the lobbying efforts of Sanger, the ABCL, and Dickinson in their efforts to win passage of "doctors only" bills in the New York, Connecticut, Pennsylvania, Massachusetts, New Jersey, and California legislatures and the federal Congress. In the face of division within the medical profession, the alert and powerful opposition of the Catholic church, and the strong pull of traditional values, there was little chance for success.

Still, the birth control movement gained increasing allies throughout the 1920s. The most numerous group and perhaps most influential in winning conservative backing were the eugenicists. Their alarm that the wrong people were breeding had escalated throughout the prewar Progressive decade. In 1924, Progressive sociologist Edward A. Ross wrote of the "Slow Suicide among Our Native Stock." "We fill two cradles for one coffin, and the cradle margin is growing. What we have to worry about is *quality*. The most fruitful fourth of a people will produce well nigh as many children as the remaining three-fourths," he warned. "What if this fateful fourth should include most of the pinheads and oafs!"[42] The *Literary Digest* also questioned, "How long will it be before the original ancestral stock of this country gives way to the later racial stocks that now predominate in the birth-rate records?"[43]

Sanger, who frightened some physicians with her radical past and heated rhetoric, found increasing compatibility with the eugenicists. In her 1922 *The Pivot of Civilization*, she lamented "the lack of balance between the birthrate of the unfit and the fit." Two years later in "The Case for Birth Control" in *Woman Citizen*, she observed, "We see that those parents who are least fit to reproduce the race are having the largest number of children; while people of wealth, leisure and education are having small families." In her *Autobiography*, Sanger saw "eugenics without birth control" as a house built on sand. The eugenicists, she explained, sought more children from the rich rather than fewer children from the poor. The ABCL "sought first to stop the multiplication of the unfit." In joining the eugenicists, Sanger's Sadie Sachs and the poor, were transformed into the "unfit."[44]

Sanger aggressively wooed the eugenicists as she had the physicians. Prominent eugenicists were invited to the organizational conference of the American Birth Control League in 1921. Lothrop Stoddard, author of the popular racist study *The Rising Tide of Color against the White World*, served on the board of directors of the ABCL. Eugenicists brought the mantle of scientific respectability and the monetary support that Sanger and the ABCL had never had from the Left. Yet the eugenicists' emphasis on woman as breeder was a distant remove from Sanger's early arguments for freedom and romance.

While Sanger garnered professional support by accepting the medical model of "doctors only," a rival birth control organization, led by suffrage champion Mary Ware Dennett, sought to keep the argument focused on the individual rights of women. Dennett had founded a New York–based, short-lived National Birth Control League in 1915; four years later with the Nineteenth Amendment a reality, she organized the Voluntary Parenthood League. Disapproving of Sanger's doctors-only approach and her confrontational tactics, Dennett lobbied in the legislatures and supported arguments in the courts to remove birth control and abortion from the category of laws against indecency. She was backed by the American Civil Liberties Union and some physicians who worried that Sanger would revert to her radical ways. Like Sanger, Dennett wrote to disseminate birth control information, publishing *The Sex Side of Life*. Writing to a Dennett supporter, however, Sanger worried that the "more ignorant classes" were so liable to misunderstand written instruction that it was perilous to distribute "unauthoritative literature."[45] She found Dennett's twin attack on birth control and abortion laws ill conceived. Many might accept birth control, but linking that issue with abortion was not only unrealistic but highly dangerous. By 1927, the Voluntary Parenthood League had yielded the field to the ABCL. With fifty-five clinics in twelve states, thirty-seven thousand dues-paying members, and a national staff, the ABCL had a more immediate response for those in need than the long-range legal arguments of the Voluntary Parenthood League.[46]

In 1929, New York police again raided a Sanger clinic. This time, as a partial sign of the times, the case was thrown out of court. Emblematic of the other changes in the birth control movement, Margaret Sanger lost control of the ABCL and the *Birth Control Review*. Her conservative backers shifted the movement from its early vision of birth control in transforming women's rights or of fashioning a possible link between feminist and socialist causes. Birth control, solidly in the hands of the physicians, became a class issue. The middle class used contraceptives and took birth control, reported the Middletown reseachers, "for granted." In the 1922 study, conducted by the Bureau of Social Hygiene Committee, of the sexual relations of one thousand married women, almost 75 percent approved voluntary parenthood; all but a few of these middle-class respondents had used contraceptive methods. Ninety-three of the respondents, or 9.3 percent, had had an abortion, many when contraceptive measures had failed. The working class surveyed in Middletown was either ignorant of methods or resistant owing to religious traditions. As a movement birth control had moved from the political Left to the Right, from a social revolution to a charity cause.[47]

While physicians took over the birth control clinics and home economists advised the homes, nowhere was a mother's role more scrutinized or her domain more fully invaded than in the area of child rearing. In 1909 Ellen Key, announcing *The Century of the Child*, asserted the centrality of the mother's role: "The transformation of society begins with the unborn child." It was a transformation requiring a new conception of the vocation of mother. Only, Key insisted, by a "total focus on children for several generations could women hope to bring forth the completed man." Two years later, Jane Addams in *Youth and the City Streets* emphasized the problems of "raising a healthy child in urban industrial America, raising an American child in the ghetto." Psychologist G. Stanley Hall emphasized that child rearing could, with research, become a science. It was too complex, too important to leave to mothers. Mothers were affirmed as the "major agents of child development but also as the major obstacles to it."[48]

The women's magazines of the 1920s deluged mothers with advice on raising their children. In January 1922, William Emerson, M.D., asked the readers of *Woman's Home Companion*, "Are You a 100% Mother?" and provided a chart for mothers to rate themselves.

How to Find Your Rating

I.   25 points if your child is "free to gain"

Deduct five if you do not know whether he is underweight;
Deduct ten if he is underweight and has not had a complete physical-growth examination;
Deduct ten if the physical examination showed physical defects and you have not had them corrected.

II.   25 points for home control

Deduct ten if your child has not been trained to obey;
Deduct five if you interfere with his proper discipline by others;
Deduct five if you have not trained him to have a sense of responsibility;
Deduct five if you allow your feelings to prevail over your judgment.

III. 25 points for a good daily program

Deduct five if you do not know the causes of overfatigue in his school program or his outside activities;
Deduct five if you do not know whether he has proper food habits;
Deduct five if you do not know whether he has good health habits;
Deduct ten if you have not made the necessary adjustments in his program, and if you have not brought him up to average weight for his height.

IV.   25 points for training in ideals

Mark yourself as liberally as your conscience will allow. (There are many 100 percent mothers.) Give yourself honest credit for all that you can claim.

Emerson urged mothers to put physical care first. The wise mother, having met her responsibilities there, would know that the first moral training to impart would be the duty of obedience. Emerson stated simply, "If you have been spoiling your child, stop it." The 100 percent mother would make a forty-eight-hour list of the child's activities to learn the reasons for his fatigue. Finally, he asked, "What are you doing to help your child develop high ideals, which are the basis for character building?" As encouragement, Emerson concluded, "The ambition of the normal woman to be an ideal mother is the greatest influence for good that we have."

Another physician, Dr. Frank Crane, admonished in an article in *American Magazine*, "Don't be a Door Mat." "The mistaken door-mat mother," he observed, "rubs off her fingernails on the washboard in order that Daughter Suzy may play the piano and feed records to the phonograph. She ruins her eyes darning socks as she sits up till midnight to wait for Suzy to come home from the jazz party. She is too busy baking and mending and slaving to read any books or improve her mind. . . . She gladly ruins her health, flattens her chest, wrinkles her skin, and incites tuberculosis so that Suzy's cheeks may be rosy and her ankles trim."[49]

Such florid warnings were balanced by more sober suggestions. Throughout the 1920s, the Laura Spelman Rockefeller Foundation expended $7 million to support seventy-five major organizations devoted to research on child rearing. In the midst of this broad effort to improve American motherhood and the end product, the child-citizen, there was no more powerful influence than psychologist John B. Watson. The leading American behaviorist, Watson wrote frequently for *Parent's Magazine*, *Collier's*, and *Harpers*. Watson's ideas formed the basis for the advice presented in the U.S. Department of Labor's best-selling twenty-five-cent booklet *Infant and Child Care*.[50]

Watson dedicated his 1928 study *Psychological Care of Infant and Child* "To the first mother who brings up a happy child." Watson believed that such a mother might one day be found but only if she followed his strictures to the letter. Even though, as Watson observed, "no one today knows enough to raise a child," there was some hope. The modern mother was "beginning to find that the rearing of children is the most difficult of all professions."[51]

Beginning at the beginning, Watson cautioned that the decision to have a child should be "a carefully thought-out operation. It was a *conditio sine qua non* that each child have a separate room for the first two years of infancy." Watson believed that when 25 million homes accepted that childhood right to privacy and adequate psychological care there would be fewer children born. "Not more babies," he asserted, "but better brought up babies will be our slogan."[52]

Watson laid the theoretical basis for the many "first impressions" and "as the twig is bent" articles in the popular magazines. He insisted there was "nothing from within to develop." Parents, starting with a "healthy body and the right number of fingers and toes, and eyes, did not need any other raw material to make a man, or the kind of man desired— gentleman, rowdy, or thug."[53] The fashioning began in the child's first day of life, for at the age of three, the child's emotional life plan was established, his emotional disposition set. Having raised the challenges and possibilities for parents, Watson also presented a nightmare, relating an automobile journey with two boys, aged four and two, their mother and grandmother and nurse. For two hours, he writhed as one of the boys was kissed thirty-two times. Children, cautioned Watson, should be treated as adults: "Dress them, bathe them with care and circumspection. . . . Never hug and kiss them, never let them sit in your lap. If you must, kiss them once on the forehead when they say good night. Shake hands with them in the morning. Give them a pat on the head if they have made an extraordinarily good job of a difficult task." Coddled children became mother's boys. "Let the child learn as quickly as possible," urged Watson, "to do everything for itself." Build a routine for him to prepare him to go out into the world at two. Parents had to be constantly on the alert, for "in the majority of American homes there was invalidism in the making." On the other hand, if parents would follow his recommendations, they would find how easy it would be to be kind, effective, and objective with the child.[54]

In stressing the psychological pitfalls, Watson was joined by the followers of Freud in their warnings of excessive and possibly incapacitating parental influence. If children identified with or reacted against their parents, they could be severely victimized. The family, the state, and outside institutions could all retard the full development of individuals. Both Watson and the Freudians set as the goal rearing the free individual, armed against the "assault of other personalities," unencumbered by other selves. Regularity, routine, reason, and the absence of repression would ensure the autonomous, adjusted child.[55]

In the writings of Watson and the Freudians, the advice fell most heavily on the mother. She was in "a terrible trap." Too much devotion to the child could warp his growth; ignoring the child would lead to similar disaster. But she was not alone. There was an army at her disposal: the psychologist, the pediatrician, the child guidance clinic, and the nursery school. Elizabeth Frazer, in "Changing Johnny's Behavior" in a 1926 issue of the *Saturday Evening Post* presented a classic tale of how, why and what to do when Johnny developed a "limp" morally or mentally. In his destructive or antisocial behavior, he was "wigwagging to all and sundry that something has gone wrong in his obscure little insides." In dealing with Johnny, sympathy without science and science without sympathy were doomed. Yet scientific treatment would put Johnny "under the microscope," scrutinized by the "cool, calm, searching eye of science, which seeks, first, causations, then remedies, in precisely the same fashion as if Johnny were a typhoid case." Johnny was taken to a child guidance clinic for examination by physicians, psychologists, psychiatrists, and social workers. Johnny did not have to survive "amateurish, superficial, or pseudo-scientific claptrap."[56] He had probably gotten his "limp" through parental shortcoming or influence. Frazer, citing statistics from a Los Angeles child guidance clinic, observed that 96 percent of the cases resulted from poor parental training. As another writer in *Ladies' Home Journal* concluded: "Our children are as we mothers make them. . . . If each and every one of us did our duty, not just the material duty of seeing that the money our husbands earn is turned into food and clothes and pleasure for our children, but in that more difficult matter of child training . . . there would be less fear for this new generation."[57]

When interviewing middle- and working-class parents in Middletown, the Lynds found them eager for the guidance of experts. Their reliance on physical advice from the old bellwether Dr. L. Emmett Holt's *The Care and Feeding of Children* (1894) was expanded in their "eagerness" to seize every available resource for help in raising their children. Yet weaving a path between routine and order and freedom, affection and firmness, the parents of the 1920s were beset by advice but wracked with insecurity. One Middletown businessman, helplessly sputtering at the antics of teenagers, exploded: "These kids aren't pulling wool over their parents' eye as much as you think. The parents are wise to a lot that goes on, but they just don't know what to do, and try to turn their backs on it."[58]

The ultimate challenge to marriage and the family was, of course, its survival. The emergence of "mass divorce" in the Progressive Era had launched a heated discussion in the bastions of middle-class manners and morals, the *Atlantic Monthly* and *Century Magazine*, as well as in religious periodicals. In 1909, James Cardinal Gibbons, warning that divorce was "descending like the plague in Roman times," inveighed against the "reckless facility" with which one was obtained. There were, he asserted, more divorces in America than in the rest of the Christian world.[59] While Catholic and Protestant clergy defended the permanence and sanctity of marriage, psychologists and sociologists asserted that divorce would be beneficial for the individuals and for the institution. If marriage made "a mockery of connubial ideals," divorce could end this charade.

The numbers of divorces that had so troubled the Progressive generation shuddered forward during the pressures of World War I and continued to escalate in the 1920s. In 1922, there were 131 divorces for each 1,000 marriages; by 1928, there were 166 per 1,000. In a lecture tour that same year, Judge Ben B. Lindsey, the reformer and veteran of the Denver Domestic Relations Court, made headlines with his allegation that American marriage had "lamentably" failed, basing his assessment on the grim Denver statistic that for every two marriage licenses issued there was one divorce suit filed. And as one worried analyst observed, it was Americans and the Americanized who were "divorcing all over the place," not the immigrant Catholics and Jews, nor the blacks. The reasons given for the dissolution of marriages perceptibly changed. Neglect and failure to provide had been the most frequently cited reasons for divorce at the end of the nineteenth century. *Nation* magazine in an 1891 issue listed further causes: mobility, decline in the belief in life after death, general resort to legal remedies, and greater opportunities for self-support for women.[60] In 1920, an *Atlantic Monthly* article "What God Hath Not Joined" added to the list, citing the mood of the age, particularly its "yeasty unrest," "enfeebled spiritual authority," shifting moral sanctions, increasing economic pressure, the emergence of new demands among women, and the impact of war. "The riot of divorce," concluded the *Atlantic* article, "has become almost an orgy."[61] Three years later another *Atlantic* writer stressed the negative impact of "the happy ever after syndrome" on marriages, the speed-up of life, the higher cost of living, the increase of luxury, the acceleration of competition, and the overinsistence of woman upon her rights. A judge of the Court of Domestic Relations in Dayton, Ohio, added a homier rationale, noting that the wife who went to the store too often for canned goods or to the delicatessen for dinner might find that "beans could be breeders of divorce."[62] A New York attorney, relating his sixteen years of dealing with legal aid clients seeking divorce, listed the "Nine Common Causes of Unhappy Marriages": incompatibility of temperament, interference from relatives or friends, jealousy, infidelity, extravagance, stinginess, slovenliness, a lack of sense of responsibility, and a difference in religious beliefs. Dorothy Dix explained that "people are demanding more of life than they used to. In former times . . . they expected to settle down to a life of hard work . . . and to putting up with each other. . . . Now, . . . we see that no good purpose is achieved by keeping two people together who have come to hate each other." More scientific analysis of the divorces granted in Los Angeles and New Jersey to white-collar families found that neglect was no longer a prominent cause, but tensions over *how* money should be spent. In blue-collar families, where mass consumption was not possible, frustrations in the midst of Coolidge prosperity, as well as basic financial insecurity, were major reasons for the breakups.[63]

The percentages of divorces varied widely from state to state depending on the law. In South Carolina there was no legal recourse for divorce; in New York only adultery was acceptable. Basically, the northeastern and middle Atlantic states had the smallest percentages, and the western states, particularly Nevada and California, and some midwestern states, because of their more liberal laws, had the highest. Throughout the 1920s there was a cry for uniform divorce laws. An *Atlantic Monthly* writer argued that laws should reflect the people's will, not "the dead hand of the past." The law in New York encouraged collusion. Conversely, while hastening to point out that Middletown "was not a Reno," the Lynds detailed how easy it was under Ohio law to obtain a divorce. In an uncontested divorce, ten dollars and ten minutes could dissolve a marriage. One citizen explained, "All you got to do is to show non-support or cruelty and it's a cinch." Cruelty was obviously open to a broad range of interpretations from unwanted pregnancies and poor sexual relations to physical abuse. Nonsupport was a frequently cited cause by working-class women. Women who worked or had worked were more frequently in divorce court. One foreman's wife with children in high school provided an explanation: "Marriage ought to be a partnership, but we started out wrong by not sharing money matters. My husband doesn't believe in telling such matters. I don't know either how much he is earning or how much we save. . . . It was because of this that I went to work. I liked having my own money and my husband hated my having it. Men are to blame for women going out to work. They haven't treated their wives fairly."[64]

The Lynds compared what Middletown accepted as the minimum

essentials for a marriage with the conditions that actually existed. The husband should support the family, but recurrent layoffs made that difficult. The wife should make a home and care for the children, but increasingly she was employed. Husband and wife should have a good sexual relationship, but they feared children. Affection should be the basis of marriage, but that seemed in the day-to-day struggle more a memory than a reality. None of the working-class wives cited her husband as a source of the "courage to go on when thoroughly discouraged." Husbands, rather, were the focus of fears: anxiety over loss of a job, fear of conception, or worry over failure. Whatever the underlying complexities, the causes translated in the courts to cruelty, nonsupport, adultery.[65]

Although the causes of divorce in middle- and working-class families varied, in both there was a growing generational divide. In a 1924 article in *Woman's Home Companion*, "I Did Not Believe in Divorce," a mother related her conversation with her daughter. Angry when her mother questioned her engagement after a whirlwind three-week courtship, the daughter finally exploded: "Even if I am making a mistake— good heavens, Mother, we're only getting married. It needn't be a life-sentence. I believe in divorce. I wouldn't put up with what you have put up with. . . .I respect marriage too much. I simply couldn't let it grow into just a dull farce—just a holding tight to a piece of property. You may think divorce is ugly, but it certainly doesn't look half so ugly to me as using marriage for a meal-ticket. Oh, Mother, if only you had had the nerve to tell Father where he got off in the first place." The stunned mother reflected she would like to tell her what she had learned, but concluded that they were both daughters of their age: "The age believes in divorce, thinks reticence old-fashioned and false, holds that getting married is 'only getting married.' "[66]

For all the battering by experts, the changes in sexual relations and expectations, home management, birth control, child rearing, working mothers, and escalating divorce ratios, the family proved both flexible and resilient. There was no doubt, as Ogburn pointed out in a 1929 *New York Times Magazine* article, that "as a social institution" the family was declining. Its economic, educational, protective, and recreational functions continued to be eroded. At the same time, many of the old ideas and values undergirding the family endured. Reviewing their survey on marriage and the family in Middleton, the Lynds observed, "For many couples . . . for whom the thought of divorce court may never figure even as a remote possibility, marriage seems to amble along at a friendly jog-trot marked by sober accommodation of each partner to his share in the joint undertaking of children, paying off the mortgages and generally 'getting on.' "[67] For American wives and mothers, marriage and family life was not a case of the more things change the more they remain the same. It was a major unrelenting challenge.

Clockwise from top: Central Colored High School, 4
July 1920. Social worker visits a home in Louisville, January
1922. Mount Holyoke College students play mah-jongg.

CHAPTER SIX

Education and the Professions: Expansion and Limits

The fundamental trouble is that men and women are different
creatures with different minds and different aptitudes and
different paths in life. . . . Why train her for a career that she is
never going to adopt? Why not give her an education that will
have a meaning and a harmony with the real life that she is to
follow?

Steven Leacock, "We Are Teaching Women All Wrong,"
Collier's Weekly, December 31, 1921

While marriage and the family were buffeted in the crosscurrents of
the old traditions and new realities of the 1920s, education, that other
traditional anchor of the Republic, also faced tumultuous pressures for
change. Schools took on functions yielded by the family. One-fourth
of the nation was either learning or teaching in its schools. Years spent
in school increased for more students from kindergarten through high
school and college. Progressive education, vocational education, psychological studies, and an emphasis on scientific measurement and
professional standards all marked the decade. But always the issue remained the same for schools, parents, and the community: education
for what? For women the question was particularly acute, and the answers hotly debated.

When Benjamin Rush, in the enthusiasm of the early Republic, had
advised that woman should be educated for her role as citizen-nurturer-
teacher-guardian of morals, the American world had two spheres: men
would lead in politics, theology, and philosophy; women would maintain hearth and home. By the middle of the nineteenth century, popular
magazines preached the cult of true womanhood. The qualities most

prized for the middle-class Victorian woman were piety, obedience, submissiveness, and domesticity. She was restricted to the home, but her influence spread outward through the character and strength of her husband and sons. An early argument for higher education for women, framed by nineteenth-century pioneers Emma Willard and Mary Lyon, was that studies would provide teachers not only for the West or for the missions but also for the home. At Oberlin, the first coeducational institution, women's duties included cooking, cleaning, and mending while they pursued their course of study. Their presence not only ensured clean socks but was seen as helpful to the mental health of their male colleagues. By the end of the century, Willard's Female Seminary at Troy, New York, and Lyon's Mt. Holyoke at South Hadley, Massachusetts, were joined by a cadre of the Eastern colleges modeled on the classical and literary curricula of Harvard and Yale. Launched in an era of industrialism, concern over immigration and urbanization, and a burgeoning campaign for women's rights, Vassar, Smith, Wellesley, Bryn Mawr, Barnard, and Radcliffe, and their counterparts like Jane Addams's alma mater, Rockford Seminary, had graduated women with a vision of their role and responsibilities in the larger home, women who became settlement workers, suffragists, and labor organizers.[1] They and their coed colleagues from the land-grant universities were integral to the Progressive reforms of the first two decades of the century.

The responsibility of the home, however, remained the central reality for women and their educators. Caroline Pratt, founder of the progressive Play School in Greenwich Village in 1915, observed:

The girls generally, in those early days of the school, clung to their domestic interests. They played mother and children, cooking, washing the baby and putting him to bed. The only way to extend their horizon was by leading them to see the connection of the home with the outside world. Despite a few rebels, woman's place in our society was still in the home. You needed only to watch the occupations chosen by our little girls to know it.[2]

While the "true woman" seemed the model of the child entering elementary school through the Progressive Era, the speculation for the 1920s was what inroads the "new woman" would make in the nation's schools.

The classroom was one arena where the reforms of the Progressive Era continued. Spurred by shortcomings revealed in the testing of young men drafted for service in the war, by the challenge to the traditional curriculum and teaching methods posed by the impact of psychological studies and educational research, by the new demands of industry and technology, and by the emphasis on professionalism and business efficiency, experts visited, studied, and prescribed for schools and systems. Typical was a survey of the Baltimore city public schools in 1920–21 by George Strayer and a team from Columbia Teachers College. Strayer reported, "In Baltimore the children's natural instinctive impulses to play are being repressed by a system of training that is artificial, unhygienic and totally unwarranted from any standpoint." The Board of School Commissioners accepted recommendations for a massive reorganization including changing to a 6–3–3 system of elementary and secondary grades, providing more for individual differences, training teachers more adequately, and improving vocational and business education.[3] It was a compendium of the issues and changes that marked the 1920s.

In the elementary schools, John Dewey's progressive ideas focused on child-centered education with both psychological and sociological dimensions. Rightly or wrongly interpreted, these ideas became increasingly pervasive. The Progressive Education Association, founded in the wake of World War I, issued its creed: "Freedom to develop naturally, interest the motive of all work, the teacher a guide, not a taskmaster, scientific study of pupil development, greater attention to all that affects the child's physical development." Throughout the decade the Office of Education supported these aims. Stressing creative self-expression, Harold Rugg and Ann Schneider's influential study, *The Child Centered School*, urged as the teachers' motto: "Try anything once and see if it works."[4]

As women dominated the teaching profession, they also shared in progressive experiments. Profiled in Dewey's 1915 *Schools of Tomorrow*, a celebration of successful progressive schools, was Marietta Pierce Johnson's Organic School in Fairhope, Alabama. The curriculum grew from the interests of the child. Students at Fairhope had no rewards, no examinations, no failures. Another progressive experiment, the Children's School in New York, was founded by Dewey's student Margaret Naumburg, who had worked with both Johnson and Maria Montessori. Writing in *The Child and the World* in 1928, Naumberg pledged to fight "all prohibitions that lead to nerve strain and repression of normal energy," and to work for "an indomitable independence of feeling, thought and action" in all her students. Speaking to the 1928 convention of the Progressive Education Association, Naumburg asserted, "Anything less than 'progressive education' is now quite out of date in America."[5]

Dewey, viewing the school as both preparation for life and an experience of life in an embryonic miniature society, saw what his followers had wrought and protested, "Baby does not know best." The teacher's task was twofold: to command and share knowledge of the disciplines and to have an awareness of the common experience of children so that she could lead her students toward understanding. Child-centered schools that eschewed adult guidance and knowledge were, he concluded, "really stupid."[6]

Professional educators grappled with Dewey's challenge to curriculum and teaching methodology. In two works, *The Curriculum* in 1918 and *How to Make a Curriculum* in 1924, Franklin Babbitt of the University of Chicago ambitiously combined a child-centered approach and the application of science to develop an activity analysis to build a curriculum. The Los Angeles school system, headed by superintendent Susan Miller Dorsey, became a testing ground for Babbitt's ideas.

Miller's career was a model of woman's path to educational leadership. Born on a dairy farm in New York, Miller, an only daughter, graduated from Vassar College in 1877 with a major in classics. After teaching at Wilson College and Vassar, she married a Baptist minister and settled in Los Angeles. She joined the WCTU and did volunteer work until deserted by her husband who took their only child with him. She taught in the public schools of Los Angeles and became a principal and, in 1913, assistant superintendent of schools. Meanwhile, she was elected president of the Southern Section of the California Teachers Association. In 1920, when named superintendent, she presided over a system of 75 teachers and 4,700 students; by the end of the decade there were 9,000 teachers and 360,000 students. In the interim she lobbied for and won a multimillion-dollar bond issue, secured higher teachers' salaries, sabbaticals, and tenure. The National Education Association hailed her in 1929 as "the greatest administrative genius in the history of American education."[7]

Miller marshaled her system to build a curriculum based on Babbitt's ideas. Teachers, organized by discipline in committees of twenty-five, worked with lists of objectives for the activity analysis drawn up by Chicago graduate students. The results were mixed. Five hundred objectives in seven groups were developed as the foundation for new curricula. Los Angeles, concluded one observer, profited more from the process than the product. It was an outcome shared by curriculum review in many systems. The Lynd's reporting on Middletown compared the subjects offered in the elementary schools in 1890 and 1924. New subjects added to reading, writing, arithmetic, language, spelling, drawing, science, and music were geography, civic training, history and civics, hygiene and health, and physical education.[8]

The major changes in curriculum, structure, and student life, however, and the major impact on the education of girls occurred in the secondary schools. Surveying the schools for Hoover's Commission on Recent Social Trends, educator Charles Judd concluded that the emergence of the junior high school and the changes in the content and character of instruction constituted "a revolution in the educational system."[9] While these changes in the first grades of secondary schools were put into place, legislation was lengthening the time required for attendance. With fewer job opportunities, girls had always attended high school in greater numbers than boys; the legal requirement of full-time attendance until sixteen and part-time attendance until eighteen narrowed the gap. In 1900, 58 percent of high school students were female; in 1930 the percentage was cut to 51 percent. By 1930, 47 percent of the 14–17-year-olds were in high schools. The average annual increase was enough to fill seven thousand classrooms of thirty students each. Still underrepresented were rural youth, who frequently had no local high school, and blacks. For the daughters of immigrants the attraction of the high school was succinctly expressed by one of their teachers in the South Philadelphia High School for Girls. "The neighbors believe," she reported, "education is the door which opens the way to that Elysian field, the modern office."[10] In Middletown, education "evoked the fervor of a religion." It was the means to salvation. The Lynds observed, "So general is the drive towards education in Middletown today that, instead of explaining why those who continue in high school or even go on to college do so, as would have been appropriate a generation ago, it is simpler today to ask why those who do not continue their education fail to do so."[11]

The National Education Association's Commission on the Reorganization of Secondary Education had issued clear guidelines in 1918 in their Cardinal Principles of Secondary Education. Their goal was the development of the comprehensive high school; their seven curricular aims were health, command of fundamental processes, citizenship, vocation, worthy use of leisure, worthy home membership, and ethical character. The impact of the principles was tangibly seen in the response of state school systems and legislation. A 1924 Texas Education Survey, appalled at the high registrations in algebra, Latin, and ancient history, concluded, "In the matter of the high school curriculum Texas needs an awakening."[12] There were more than 131 new legislative prescriptions on what to teach in the schools. The number of subjects escalated from twenty-three in 1910 to forty-eight in 1928. Ancient history was joined by American, English, and medieval history in many schools; courses in physical education were mandated by most state legislatures.

The major curricular expansion, supported by appropriations from the Smith-Hughes Act of 1918, was in the vocational area, in manual and industrial arts, home economics, and agriculture. Enrollments also increased in business.[13] The president of the school board in Middletown reflected: "For a long time all boys were trained to be President. Then for a while we trained them all to be professional men. Now we are training boys to get jobs."[14] It was a sentiment more broadly and elegantly phrased by Professor Thomas Briggs of Columbia Teachers College who argued that free public education was a wise investment for the nation since the school "just as truly as a manufacturing plant . . . must work up all its raw material so as to make it maximally useful."[15] Girls were increasingly part of that raw material to be trained for use.

Eighty-six percent of the Middletown high school girls reported they expected to work after graduation. Although high school plainly was the path for women from low-paying blue-collar jobs to white-collar futures in teaching or the office, the high school curriculum clearly reflected that the long-term vocation for the woman graduate was still that of homemaker. The expansion of domestic science in the classroom came from two contradictory sources: the culture of professionalism with the emergence of home economics as a field and the growing statistics of working blue- and white-collar mothers. Home management was learned not at mother's knee but in the junior and senior high school. Matrimony courses were introduced to enable a "daughter to hold a husband after catching him." Beauty culture courses were introduced because "the making of a beautiful face has become as technical a performance as the manufacture of a fine silk dress." Future mothers practiced in the classroom on dolls and borrowed babies rather than on younger sisters and brothers.[16]

School was no longer a place to which "children go from their homes for a few hours daily but a place from which they go home to eat and sleep." Students struggled for acceptance and to keep up with the Joneses. In Middletown, dropouts testified, "If you don't dress right, you haven't any friends." One girl, trying to explain eligibility for membership in a prestigious club, reported: "The chief thing is the boys like you and you get them for the dances. . . . Good looks and clothes don't necessarily get you in, and being good in your studies doesn't necessarily keep you out unless you are a grind."[17] "It's not much good to belong to a Y.W. club," another reported, "*any one* can belong to them."[18]

The drop in popularity of the YWCA was a harbinger of the increasing incursion of "flapperdom" from the colleges and the excitement of the jazz age. The *Educational Journal* warned that Indiana students were being "jazzed to death." Movies like *Smooth as Silk*, *Unguarded Women*, *A Perfect Flapper*, and *A Gilded Butterfly* and confession magazines with their "literature of lust" were eroding youthful morals. Administrators, sometimes supported by students, girded to protect the schools. In Lynn, Massachusetts, the high school principal, averring that "bridge is responsible for wrecking homes," banned it as a lunchtime recreation. Girls at a Denver high school passed resolutions to keep the vamp at bay by forbidding the use of eyebrow pencils, lipstick, heavy face powder, fancy hose, and dresses with low necklines. In Hackensack, New Jersey, girls could not attend class unless they were wearing stockings. In Knoxville, administrators faced the problem of new and perhaps dangerous styles by mandating uniforms.[19] While the emanations from the "revolution in manners and morals" were clearly rocking the high school, it was equally clear that high school girls more than boys had the major responsibility for upholding propriety and safeguarding tradition.

It was in the colleges and universities that their older sisters met the major intellectual and social challenges of the decade. There the surge in enrollment was extraordinary. In 1900, 85,000 women were in college; in 1920, the number increased to 283,000; by 1930, 481,000 were enrolled, 43.7 percent of the total college population. They remained an elite group, however; in 1930, only 10 percent of American women in the 18—21 cohort were in college.[20] Those who did continue formal study past high school could choose from a "strikingly heterogeneous array of acceptable and praiseworthy institutions: from normal schools, land-grant universities, elite Eastern women's colleges, and Catholic and Negro colleges." President William Allan Neilson of Smith, reflecting on the pioneers, observed that those "adventurous souls with a burning thirst for knowledge" had "blazed a path that had become a highway." Surveying an incoming class, he observed that those "who throng it are no longer exceptional spirits but merely the run of our brighter youth."[21] Historian Barbara Solomon divided the generations of educated women into "those who hungered for education, those who fought for it, and those who took it for granted."[22]

The college woman, particularly at the women's college in the East, remained primarily the daughter of the middle-class American. A survey of Vassar fathers in 1919–22 indicated half were manufacturers, merchants, lawyers, bankers, brokers, or doctors. Most Vassar undergraduates were Episcopalians. Two percent of the students were Roman Catholic; Jewish students could be counted on one hand. The median family income of $5,140 of the student in the private nonsectarian women's colleges was considerably higher than the family income of $3349 of the coed in a state university. While Bryn Mawr regretted that only 15 percent of its students came from public high schools, there was increasing democratization in higher education throughout the 1920s. In socially mobile immigrant families, the college-educated son was being followed by the daughter. Black college women remained "the exception of exceptions." In 1929, the median family income of the black women at Howard University was $1,560.[23] Financial aid for women was modest. Stanford, an early leader in coeducation, allotted only three fellowships to women in 1919; the presidents of the major eastern women's colleges campaigned for contributions to their endowment funds, citing the imbalance of support for men's and women's education.[24]

In the swirl of change the "education for what?" question was particularly difficult; for women, of almost equal complexity was the question "where to seek that education?" In December 1921, McGill University professor Stephen Leacock deliberately roiled the waters in an article in *Collier's Weekly*, "We Are Teaching Women All Wrong." He began with the premise that the fundamental trouble was that "men and women are different creatures with different minds and different aptitudes and different paths in life." Why, he questioned, train woman for a career she will never follow? Currently, he concluded provocatively, a woman could be ill taught in two environments. At McGill, the coed, obviously awed by her male colleagues, "sat for four years as silent as a frog full of shot." She would do better at Bryn Mawr and Wellesley, "where there isn't a man allowed within the three-mile limit."

Leacock's tongue-in-cheek endorsement of the flagship women's colleges reflected the good press they had won in the first years of the century as American magazines discovered the college girl. During the war, students at Mt. Holyoke, Wellesley, Vassar, and Barnard earned plaudits for their efforts as farmerettes, Red Cross volunteers, and nurses. For the women's colleges, however, World War I signaled the end of an era. [25] Paradoxically, while they were deluged with applications and forced to set new admissions criteria, they were forced to evaluate and defend their mission and to lobby for financial support. [26]

The reputations of the prestigious Seven Sisters—Mt. Holyoke, Vassar, Smith, Wellesley, Bryn Mawr, Radcliffe, and Barnard—were built on their scholarship, on their fierce determination to prove in their classical and liberal arts curricula their conviction that women were the intellectual equals of men. Smith's president observed of the first graduating class that "more restraints were needed for the diligent than coercive stimulants for the indolent." By the 1920s their reputation for brain power was so well known that an aunt of young Catherine Drinker, gazing at her high forehead, asserted that she ought to go to Bryn Mawr and write a book. The future biographer responded heatedly, "Never to Bryn Mawr! Never to any of their stuffy colleges." By 1926, the seven college presidents confidently asserted, "There is in general an understanding between the women's college and the student that she has come to work seriously at a long and arduous task which is important to her as an individual, but also important because she is to be later a member of a community to which she must make a serious contribution." [27]

Though all were committed to the life of the intellect, by 1920 the ideas of the founders, the leadership of strong presidents, and differing environments produced variations in their graduates. In November 1920, Helen Bennett, in a *Woman's Home Companion* article "Seven Colleges—Seven Types," related a standard joke:

If you give a piece of work to graduates of the women's colleges, the Vassar girl will sit down and talk about it, the Bryn Mawr girl will philosophize over it, Mt. Holyoke will pray over it, Wellesley will go down into the library and read all about it, and Smith will go out and do it.

Bennett fleshed out the stereotype: "Smith College turns out the doer; Wellesley, the student; Vassar, the adventurer; Bryn Mawr, the social philosopher; Mt. Holyoke, the conservative; University of Chicago, the enterprising; and the state universities, in general, the practical girl."

The Smith graduate was an efficient participant in community affairs. Wellesley tended "to produce the Henry Adams quality of mentality," which did "not always make connections with the mechanical technic of a modern world." Images were legion: Smith students and graduates were athletic, Barnard's sophisticated, Wellesley's blond and literary, Vassar's radical, and Mt. Holyoke's "refreshingly wholesome." All had a sincere desire for service.[28]

In the press for vocational education, the emergence of home economics as a profession, the proliferation of business courses, and the perceived opportunities for women, the Seven Sisters reevaluated their curricula. As early as 1917, President M. Carey Thomas of Bryn Mawr, the most determined defender of the traditional liberal arts curriculum, complained: "Japanese Geisha schools are springing up on all sides. Practical vocational courses are to be given. . . . Now is the time for us to fight for our lives, for our educational convictions, and save, if we can, at least the girls of the East by refusing to give up our present college curriculum. It is our highest duty as educated women to pass on unimpaired . . . this precious intellectual heritage."[29]

The curriculum at each woman's college tended, as it always had, to reflect the programs of their male Ivy League neighbors. The general education programs were strengthened in the first year; honors programs were developed for upperclassmen. Requirements in English, history, philosophy, mathematics, science, Latin or Greek, and modern languages remained at each of the seven colleges. Courses were rarely dropped, and many were added. Psychology and the social sciences, particularly political science, economics, and sociology were popular majors and electives. Chemistry departments added work in food analysis. Although the faculty and administration generally held firm, one waggish Smith alumna expressed the creative student's enduring ability to meet her needs in a curriculum: "We took Latin so that we could read and translate the best parts of Havelock Ellis. We also took chemistry and wasted a great deal of time trying to distill pure alcohol."[30]

The presumed dual life of the graduate in career and marriage led to expanded course offerings in health, hygiene, physiology, and psychology. Only at Vassar, the alma mater of home economics pioneer Ellen Swallow Richards, was a major program installed in that field. Fostered by a $550,000 gift from Minnie Blodgett and supported by beleaguered president Henry Noble MacCracken trying to survive an assault from conservative trustees, an extensive program in euthenics, "the scientific study of the home," was developed at Vassar. Housed in a new complex of buildings, the interdisciplinary program combined research in the chemistry lab, practice in interior decorating, and the study of children in the nursery school.[31]

While the learning environment modestly expanded to meet the practical aspirations of students, the living environment was radically transformed. The close campus community characterized by the home environment of the Smith cottages, the suites at Bryn Mawr, and close relationships among women professors and fellow students was challenged by the sexual attitudes of the age of Freud and the easier acceptance of men on the campuses. Wellesley professor Vida Scudder, who had joined with students in strikes and settlement house work, missed the easy friendships and described the 1920s, in terms of student interests and connections, as the bleakest in her life.[32] Earlier studies indicating the low marriage rates of women's college graduates were reviewed. Articles in conservative and women's magazines questioned the "natural environment" and the impact on marriages of sex-segregated education. A writer in *Harper's*, after scoring the four-year segregation as "biologically unnatural," admitted that no conscious effort was being made to close the minds of the students to marriage. However, she observed, "this is what is happening." She worried that "cut off from healthy male companions," the students might turn to each other. "Intense homosexual friendships form a problem," she concluded, "that is admittedly disturbing some of our best women's colleges."[33] Writing in *Forum* magazine, Dr. W. Beram Wolfe echoed these concerns. Psychiatrists, he insisted, viewed "women's colleges as important contributors to the mental disquietude of modern life." Rather than training their women for living, they offered "the sickly pabulum of archaeology and art appreciation instead of the robust material of human cooperation."[34]

Worried about charges that their education led to a degree of "spinster of art," Vassar and the other colleges included statistics on the marriage rate of their graduates in a 1925 series in *Ladies' Home Journal*. Sixty-five percent of Vassar women married within ten years of graduation. Bryn Mawr reported that of 906 married graduates, 734 devoted all their time to homemaking, a rather bitter pill for M. Carey Thomas who had once declared, "Our failures only marry." The largest number had married lawyers, followed by physicians, professors, engineers, clergymen, and the military.[35]

New dormitories at the Seven Sisters reflected these concerns. Suites and cottages were joined by new dormitories with spartan single rooms. The public areas were warm and welcoming as Victorian gates opened to admit an invasion of males on campus. While students pleased with the prestige and the programs of the colleges generally did not transfer to become coeds, they did chafe at restrictions and worked to bring the walls tumbling down.[36]

Their efforts were partially reflected in the comments of administrators. Mt. Holyoke's veteran president, Mary E. Woolley, reviewing "The College Girl Today and Yesterday" for *Woman's Home Companion*, noted that words like *social responsibility* and *duty* fell on deaf ears. She concluded, "Withall, the student life is still in a state of transition." Barnard's Virginia Gildersleeve was not as sanguine, describing her students as blasé, indifferent, self-indulgent, and irresponsible. A more relaxed Henry MacCracken at Vassar observed, "The trouble with us is that we're too attractive. We give them too good a time."[37] Vassar professor Hallie Flanagan, arriving in 1925 to work with theater majors, agreed, describing her majors with dangling marquis earrings, velvet headbands, and embroidered shawls à la Isadora Duncan. Explained one alumna, "We all wanted to be vivid."[38]

Students organized not for suffrage or community action but for themselves. As one rather harshly declared, "We're not going to suffer over how the other half lives."[39] Newspaper editors of the colleges met in 1923 and complained that they could not reach their readers. All they found "was a languid tolerance for any idea." "Modern students," they concluded, "cannot be shocked or won. They are pleasantly aloof from the bitter interests that tear the world." Leaders in student government found their cause in attacking the "Castle Adamant" image and the concept of in loco parentis. Curfews were fought. Barnard and Vassar yielded on compulsory chapel attendance. Bryn Mawr accepted the reality of smoking on campus, while Mt. Holyoke and Wellesley stood firm. In South Hadley students turned the college cemetery into a "four-acre ashtray," and Wellesley students repaired to a stone wall at the edge of town to perch and puff. Wellesley's House of Representatives won the right for students to attend movies unchaperoned and to go for automobile drives on Sundays and early in the evening. One 1922 graduate remembered: "We were not supposed to drive after dark but that was nonsense. It was wonderfully easy to run out of gas in those days, and we used to dazzle the college with stories about spark plugs, radiator cracks and blowouts."[40] Smith and Mt. Holyoke students journeyed to tea dances at Amherst fraternities and drank bootleg whiskey from teacups decorously disguised with a floating lemon slice. There was a weekend flight for football stadiums, ski slopes, or New

York or Boston, as students "usually chose not to spend one unnecessary moment in each others' company."[41] Men came to campus for parties, teas, and tennis. Bryn Mawr, the last holdout, had its first tea dance in 1929.[42]

While the Seven Sisters remained the flagship women's colleges, three new women's colleges were formed in the 1920s, each reflecting the crosscurrents in learning and life faced by women. The first, Sarah Lawrence, proved a study in paradox. Launched as a junior college, it reflected the founder Matthew Lawrence's view that woman should be educated for her separate sphere. She would marry; what she needed was the cultivation and training to be a skilled homemaker, an interesting wife, a knowledgeable child rearer. He wanted the daughters of the best families and deliberately set a high tuition rate. The two-year program, the focus on marriage, and seeming exclusivity brought a flood of applications. Lawrence's mentor was Vassar president MacCracken. His advice, the Vassar connection, and the leadership of President Marion Coats transformed Sarah Lawrence. The combination of no requirements, an insistence on tutorials and small enrollment courses, and a creative faculty made Sarah Lawrence a leader in innovation and experiment in the arts, language, and literature.

In Vermont, Congregational minister Vincent Ravi Booth, working with New York backers and Barnard advisers, created Bennington College, with living modeled on the democratic New England village and learning related to preparation for careers. On the west coast, Scripps College was founded as a female neighbor to Claremont. Its carefully crafted curriculum was built on women's attributes and perceived strengths in human relationships. Freshmen and sophomores took a required course in domestic science. In the final two years, courses and majors provided grounding for married life and child rearing and traditional "nurturing" careers in public health, child growth and development, and social research. All were practical; all reflected the decade's expectation of their graduates—if they entered a profession, they would also return to the home.[43]

Although the founding of Sarah Lawrence, Bennington, and Scripps and the vitality of the Seven Sisters attested to a still healthy market for women's colleges, by far the greatest numbers of seventeen-year-olds were choosing coeducation. The major expansion in the decade was at the state colleges and universities. While some contemporaries doubted the merit of sex-segregated colleges, others argued about the impact of coeducation on undergraduates. Jessica B. Peixotto, a Berke-

ley professor, succinctly argued "The Case for Coeducation" in a 1923
Forum article. "Faith in coeducation," she explained, "is based on two
propositions. The first is a belief that in its main lines, university life
should be a pattern of the society which the student proposes to enter."
She concluded idealistically that when trained together "the old Adam
and Eve are likely to find a new paradise wherein they may perhaps
stay because neither blames the other and both have learned to work
together, even it may be to seek the apple of knowledge together without the fatalities of the past."[44]

Women may have entered the garden, but other analysts contended
they were not Adam's equal. Olivia H. Dunbar, answering Peixotto in
Forum, observed that the term *coed* applied only to girls. The boy is
educated; the girl is coeducated. Indeed, she insisted, women's position
in state universities had yet to be "legitimized." Women were taught by
male instructors, watched men's football games on Saturday with an
"appalling passivity," and slept in a dormitory under curfew rules that
men would never tolerate. Her complaints were echoed by a Colorado
college instructor who asserted that coeducational colleges had honed
their "neglect" of women students to a fine art. Dr. W. Beram Wolfe,
who had so criticized women's colleges, charged that coed institutions
barely tolerated their young women.[45]

Ancient debates that the coed was a temptress-distractor or a man-
tamer were muted. But there was more discussion of the coed's impact
on the classroom and curriculum. Olivia Dunbar reported a typical
scene: "To the front rows drift the exponents of the conforming and
receptive sex, who are, so to speak, on parade. Their hair arrangements
are intricate and laborious, they are soft of eye and of voice, their ef-
fervescence is charmingly subdued." "Behind them," she continued,
"lounge the boys, rough-shirted, unkempt, taciturn," keeping their
"crude masculine pose." Young English professor Bernard De Voto described the front row of his class as looking "like a hosiery window at
a spring opening." De Voto, however, appreciated the brains behind
the facade. The coeds were the "chief hope" of preserving the values of
liberal education. His literary colleague Rollo Walter Brown, on the
other hand, argued that as women crowded into the humanities, literature, and language, men fled. He was supported in his complaint by
the report of one registrar at a state university that there was only one
man in the senior class in the field of literature or language. Subjects
were divided into those that were "useful full-blooded, and manly and
those which were ornamental, dilettantish and feminine."[46]

Choices of fields, others insisted, were not gender based, but reflected the uses that could be made of them. President Neilson of Smith observed that since women had won the franchise, courses in political science and sociology had risen in popularity. Home economics was a popular field for rural and city women from Cornell to Berkeley. Literature courses were effectively integrated into Cornell's home economics curriculum to ensure culture as well as efficiency in the home. At Michigan, President Clarence C. Little, in a rationale that was echoed by Scripps College, stated that the curriculum for women students should be built on women's supremacy in the field of human relations. Michigan women should study human biology, anatomy, physiology, genetics, hygiene, and nutrition. They should elect fine arts, drama, literature, history, business, and international relations. The graduate would be a cultured woman, skilled in creating a cultured home.[47]

The uneven integration of women into academic life was matched by inequities in student life. At the University of North Carolina, women had an assembly room on campus, but no gym or tennis courts. They were on their own in locating housing in Chapel Hill. In 1922–23, in spite of the vociferous objections of alumni and male students and the clamor that North Carolina should remain a man's university, the Student Council of the Women's Association successfully campaigned for a dormitory on campus. The coed victory was short-lived. In 1924, the university announced that except in special programs not available elsewhere in the state, it would henceforth admit women only to the upper classes.[48]

When living on campus, women students at state universities lobbied for freedom and equality. At the University of Wisconsin, women held a mass protest against chaperone requirements; at Maryland, students waged a winning campaign against a rule requiring them to be locked in their rooms each evening at dark.[49] Reporters for the *Ohio State Lantern* surveyed the sign-out sheets at the women's dormitory and discovered that the average coed went on dates four nights a week and the most popular had a date every night. The reporter concluded, "Ohio State girls are no stay-at-home, play-at-home, eight o'clock, sleepy-time girls."[50]

Extracurricular activities flourished. The *Daily Illinois* reported, "We are clubbed to death." Amory Blaine's Princeton ambition in F. Scott Fitzgerald's *This Side of Paradise* was only the most romanticized version of the student quest to belong, to make the right sorority, club, or team. The YWCAs continued, and the Catholic Clubs and Menorah Societies were organized, but they lacked the prestige of the exclusive. As at the women's college, chapel attendance, never required, declined. One contemporary, asserting that the college woman was not irreligious, but merely unsettled and "going through a phase," urged the colleges to bring challenging men and women to their pulpits rather than "worn-out clergymen who have had their day."[51]

University administrators worried about the student life-style celebrated in the cheeky anthem: "Collegiate. Collegiate. Yes, We are Collegiate." In previous decades the student body had been "small, select, and closely watched." No longer. Size, heterogeneity, and mobility precluded close scrutiny. Administrators at the University of Kansas and at Michigan were unsuccessful in their attempts to restrict the use and number of automobiles.[52] Students set their own standards in working out acceptable dress and behavior. For women, long the accepted guardians of morals in the larger community, there was a particularly taut tightrope to walk. As they sought freedom and equality in classroom and dormitory, their simultaneous challenge was to win, if not the dominant voice afforded by the larger society, at least an equal role in charting new paths on the murky ground of collegiate manners and morals. The rules for petting, smoking, and dancing were worked out campus by campus. On each, coeds were determined to be heard.

The fight against bans on coed smoking was particularly central and symbolic; it merged the fight for equality with a moral and generational issue. Phyllis Blanchard and Carol Manasses, surveying coeds and parents, found that 80 percent of the daughters approved of smoking for young women. Only 26 percent of the parents agreed. An editor of the Louisiana State University paper argued that if there was nothing inherently wrong or degrading in cigarette smoking, then there should be no difference in men or women doing it. Yet, *Literary Digest* in an article "Women and the Weed" cited an Associated Press survey of campuses in the wake of President Marian Edwards Park's 1925 capitulation at Bryn Mawr. Midwest campuses reported smoking "simply isn't done by college girls"; it remained taboo in the South. At Wesleyan Teachers College in Nebraska, women who smoked were refused certificates of teaching. At Illinois, sorority women requested rooms on the fire escape to circumvent the rule against smoking in the house.[53] While coeds continued their agitation, it was obvious that on many campuses they also continued their smoking.

There were also efforts to curb drinking. This was a matter of upholding the law of the land as well as safeguarding student morals.

Administrators worked with fraternities at the University of Chicago, Michigan, and elsewhere to try to keep liquor out. At the end of the decade, however, witnesses at a congressional hearing testified that drinkers on campus outnumbered teetotalers two to one. The *Cornell Sun* simply reported, "Liquor violation is in the category of an indoor sport."[54]

While drinking and smoking challenged law and custom, dancing, the favorite fun of the coed and her partner, posed problems also. In *The Damned and the Beautiful*, Paula Fass summarized, "The dancers were close, the steps were fast, and the music was jazz."[55] Dancers enthusiastically learned the Charleston, the black bottom, and the tango. At the University of Kansas women students pressed the chancellor to forbid indecent dancing. Their counterparts at Minnesota went further. At dances sponsored by the Women's Self-Government Association, coeds handed cards to offending students which read: "We do not dance cheek to check, shimmy, or dance other extreme dances. You must not. A second notice will cause your public removal from the hall. Help keep up the Minnesota standard."[56] It was impossible, however, to monitor the dancing at roadhouses clustered near the campuses.

At parties on and off campus, there was petting. Fraternities featured discussions on girls who pet. One investigator reported that 92 percent of the coeds surveyed reported petting at one time. A visitor to the University of Wisconsin concluded, "So-called petting parties are neither more nor less serious in the coeducational university than elsewhere." Surveyors Blanchard and Manasses concluded that "very many girls draw a distinct line between the exploratory activities of the petting party and complete yielding of sexual favors to men." There was a wide tolerance, a respect for privacy and the right to make one's own decision. Petting was the means "to be safe and yet not sorry." At Wisconsin, eight of three thousand coeds were dismissed for poor moral conduct, leading one contemporary observer to conclude, "The number who go to smash morally is amazingly small."[57]

An incident at the University of Maryland provides a case study of a campus code and the pitfalls of monitoring it. In the fall of 1922 all the campus sororities refused bids to a group of coeds with a reputation for being too "fast." Some of the rejected reacted by an even more energetic flaunting of convention. In March 1923, President Albert Woods suspended two of the leading "troublemakers" for smoking; the Washington and Baltimore newspapers picked up the dismissal story and suggested that there was more immoral conduct involved. On campus Vivian Simpson, not one of the dismissed or rejected, took up their cause as a case of women's rights. A midwestern attorney, Mary Love-Collins, representing the national Chi Omega sorority, arrived at College Park to establish a chapter and invite the rejected and the rebels to be the founding members. Though the sorority was organized in violation of university regulations, Woods hesitated to institute massive suspensions.

Chi Omega members and others went on the attack, collecting affidavits of administrators' seduction of coeds at petting parties at night swimming-pool capers. They implied that perhaps even the upright President Woods was involved. The charges formed the lead story of the *Washington Post* on 23 April 1923. The campus newspaper and the students at a mass meeting rallied behind the president and urged the administration to stand firm against the "attempts of any 'Amazon-hued' sorority to gain recognition." When Woods and his staff ferreted out those responsible for the affidavits, he informed Vivian Simpson and one other student that they would not be readmitted in the fall. On Simpson's appeal, he relented if she would give up membership in Chi Omega. Simpson took the university to court. While facing this court challenge, Woods was simultaneously locked in deadly budget combat with the governor who threatened the future of the university. Legislators entering the state house to vote on the continued existence of the University of Maryland were handed pamphlets by Chi Omega members accusing university officials of moral turpitude. Meanwhile, Woods hesitated to press slander charges against the *Washington Post* because he feared that some officials might indeed have been involved. In the final outcome, the legislature supported the university; the state court of appeals ruled that the university had to have the discretion to select students for the general welfare; and President Woods resigned soon after.[58] Authority, rights, and responsibilities were all tested in this evolution of manners and morals at Maryland.

There were clearer guidelines for undergraduate behavior at the Catholic colleges for women, which like the state universities expanded throughout the decade. The pioneers in Catholic women's higher education were launched in the 1890s against a background of nativism, the need for teachers in the parochial schools mandated by bishops in the Third Plenary Council of Baltimore in 1884, and the decision of the Catholic University of America to admit men only. The College of Notre Dame of Maryland, evolving from an academy to a college, awarded the first baccalaureate degrees in 1899; one year later Trinity

College in Washington, D.C., was the first institution founded as a four-year Catholic women's college. Both were established with the encouragement of the rector of Catholic University of America. In the first decade of the century, women's Catholic colleges proliferated. Like their eastern, elite, secular counterparts, these early colleges produced an army of teachers, religious and lay. Bishop Charles McDonald, with the Ursulines' College of New Rochelle already in his diocese, welcomed the Sacred Heart order's establishment of Manhattanville since he was "fully cognizant of the dangers threatening the spiritual welfare of the Catholic young women" who entered secular colleges. In the Midwest, Catholic colleges usually evolved from academies. Frequently, they established an affiliation with a neighboring men's college or university. In Indiana, St. Mary's College worked with Notre Dame; Loretto College, Fontbonne, and Maryville College all cooperated with St. Louis University. In the West, the founding of St. Mary of the Wasatch near Salt Lake City was typical. The local bishop, wanting a college for women in his diocese, invited the Sisters of Holy Cross to establish it. The order dispatched young Sister M. Madeleva, with a fresh doctorate in literature from Berkeley in 1926, to join a handful of her sisters to set up a college in the wilderness. She described the experience: "We had often been cold, sometimes hungry; coyotes had cried under our windows at night. Water shortages had left us parched and unwashed during all but unbearable months in summer." Yet there was, she concluded, splendid scenery. In a few years they had a small but flourishing operation and were bringing in eastern scholars to lecture at the tiny outpost.[59]

By 1921, there were thirty-eight four-year colleges; eleven years later, reflecting the Catholic share of the burgeoning enrollments of the decade, there were seventy-three colleges, with enrollments of 13,496. Most remained small; in 1929, forty-seven had enrollments of less than 200. There were few Catholic coed colleges: DePaul admitted women to all its courses in 1914, and Marquette followed. In New Orleans, Xavier College was the only coed Catholic black college. The Catholic decision not to mix the sexes in the classroom beyond the elementary grades was strongly reiterated by Pope Pius XI in 1929: "False . . . and harmful to Christian education is the so-called method of 'co-education.'"[60]

The curriculum at Catholic women's colleges was rooted in the liberal arts tradition with a bent to the practical, mindful of their frequently ethnic student body and reflecting the 1920s emphasis on vocational education. Theology and philosophy were central, but otherwise the general education requirements could have been taken from the Seven Sisters' catalogs. The mission statements, however, were quite different. St. Mary's College, Indiana, stated its goal of developing "a disciplined mind and a cultivated soul." St. Mary's wanted to "produce women who understood the cooperative values of life and followed the teachings of Christ." Its graduates should "inculcate the principles of justice in society." Finally, the college sought "to instill the right attitude toward home life and to train the homemaker for her duties."[61]

There were also differences in student life on the Catholic campuses. At Marygrove College in Detroit, the day began with mass (optional) at six o'clock and ended with curfew at ten. The 1923–24 catalog at the College of Notre Dame of Maryland set prescriptions on dress. Students were to wear a blue or black frock with a white collar and the hem ten inches from the floor. Sweaters, sleeveless dresses, or low-cut gowns were forbidden. Exposed bare shoulders on the dance floor were discreetly covered with a nun's shawl before the culprit was banished from the festivities. Young women could have male visitors on Saturday or Sunday if they had given a week's notice. Some institutions required parental permission. Yet there were Sunday teas, class entertainments, and hikes. Their size, mission, and rules promoted a strong sense of community. Life, concluded one observer, was neither dull nor gay.[62]

While the Catholic colleges were founded to educate in the faith, the pioneer Negro colleges were launched in the idealism of the years immediately following the Civil War. They sought to educate the new citizens and to meet the need for black teachers of black youth. Howard, Fisk, Atlanta, and Shaw universities and Straight College and Tugaloo all accepted students in the 1860s. By 1910, there were one hundred black colleges including the women's colleges of Spelman in Atlanta and Barber-Scotia in North Carolina.

The dynamic and charismatic Mary McLeod Bethune, an ardent negotiator for equal rights, provided forceful leadership for the education of black women. Her school for black girls, founded in Daytona Beach, Florida, in 1904 with $1.50, six students (five girls and her son Albert), and a spirit of determined optimism, by 1923 had a twenty-acre campus and a student body of three hundred in elementary, secondary, and teacher training divisions. In this year, eager to gain collegiate status, Bethune agreed to merge her Daytona Normal and Industrial Institute with Cookman Institute of Jacksonville. This new coed institution became Bethune-Cookman College in 1929 and received junior college accreditation three years later.[63]

Unlike the Catholic pattern, in black colleges and universities, co-education was dominant. One study of black institutions in 1915 found the education "deplorable." By 1928, only one college received an "A" rating, and Howard University was the only black institution accredited by the Middle States Association. Reflecting slow growth and the need for additional resources, many private black colleges became part of state systems in the 1920s[64]

For black women, perhaps more than for black men who were even more rigidly segregated in jobs, college or normal school was a path to the middle class. In 1920, an overwhelming majority of black women were still segregated in domestic or rural work; in the South and in the North as the wartime demands eased, black women were generally excluded from service occupations or the expanding fields in communication for telephone operators. A position in teaching brought respect and a decent salary.[65]

In their academic programs, black colleges always included a major emphasis on the practical, but in the 1920s some expended their liberal arts offerings. As Lucy Slowe, dean of women at Howard explained, the new course work was aimed at lessening the cultural isolation of the black college-educated woman. In the area of student life, the black woman undergraduate lived with in loco parentis under regimens that in some institutions were so strict that W. E. B. Du Bois compared them with prison discipline.[66]

In white coeducational institutions black women faced a double fight. Oberlin, the first institution to admit blacks, was typical in its struggle to maintain its traditions. Black students were welcomed, but there was an anxiety that too many might enroll. Housing for blacks was problematic. Oberlin usually housed no more than two black students in any one residence hall. The acting dean of women wrote a frank note to the president of her concern if a lottery system for room assignments was endorsed by the Women's Senate, explaining: "But they do not really *believe* that it is best for either race to live in the same dormitory. . . . I do not know a girl who would be willing to have any purely scholastic opportunity closed to colored students; . . . But they do not want social relations with the colored race, and they do not find it to be a duty."[67] The social interactions between men and women were particularly troublesome to the dean who insisted she "would swiftly put a stop to the slightest intimacy between white girls and colored men." The white men, she added, found the presence of colored girls in a social group especially "embarrassing."[68]

In 1923, Oberlin's racial situation was graphically underscored on and off campus. Throughout the country alumni heading fund-raising committees faced the question of how and when to include their black alumni and alumnae. Some answered it by having separate dinners for white and black, some by ignoring the black alumnae in their midst. Meanwhile, Oberlin received a $60,000 bequest for black scholarship funds. When President Ernest Hatch Wilkins took office in mid-decade, he was asked if Negroes were welcome in large numbers at Oberlin. No, he responded. It was not in the best interest of Oberlin or the black students. Trying to keep alive the Oberlin tradition, Professor Kemper Fullerton urged the college to award honorary degrees and to add black faculty and courses on black history and culture since "colored people should be made to feel that we are really interested in them."[69]

Black college women could find a receptive environment at Radcliffe or Barnard. Marita Bonner, a talented writer and Radcliffe graduate, related her attempt to carry out the tradition of service of the Seven Sisters. Accepting a teaching position at Armstrong High School in Washington, she explained, "All your life you have heard of of the debt you owe 'Your People' because you have managed to have the things they have not largely had." She looked at the lives of her students and their parents in the ghetto: "Cut off, flung together, shoved aside in a bundle because of color and with not more in common. . . . Milling around like live fish in a basket. Those at the bottom crushed into a sort of stupid apathy by the weight of those on the top. Those on top leaping, leaping, leaping to the sides; to get out." White friends, "who have never had to draw a breath in a Jim-Crow train or had petty putrid insult dragged over them—drawing blood," urged her "not to grow bitter." Bonner determined not to live with a chip on her shoulder, "for chips make you bend your body to balance them." She concluded with an image of Buddha, "brown like I am, sitting motionless and knowing":

So . . . too. Still; quiet; with a smile, ever so slight, at the eyes so that Life will flow into and not by you. And you can gather, as it passes, the essences, the overtones, the tints, the shadows; draw understanding to your self.

And then you can, when Time is ripe, swoop to your feet—at your full height—at a single gesture.

Ready to go where?
Why . . . Wherever God motions.[70]

Bonner, with the heritage of family and Radcliffe, had the strength to survive in the traditional path of service of the woman college graduate. She had yet to confront the central dilemma of the educated woman: how to live up to the promise of her education and at the same time fulfill her female role.

The Smith College *Weekly* of December 1919 underscored the hope and the challenge of the educated woman of the 1920s, insisting, "There must be a way out, and it is the problem of our generation to find a way."[71] In the area of education and career, generation—as it had in attitudes toward marriage and family and political causes—proved to be the dividing line. Educated pioneers like Jane Addams still led organizations and marshaled hopes. A middle generation coming of age in the excitement of Progressive battles and wartime opportunities, established careers and professions and built networks to help one another and encourage the next generation. The pioneers generally had chosen: marriage *or* career. The middle generation hoped to have both. The young generation had "to find a way."

Graduates of the 1920s did not lack for advice. Conservative writers, particularly, worried that like the pioneers they would choose to be a spinster of arts. Henry R. Carey, in two extravagant articles in the *North American Review*, asserted that eugenicists and sociologists had long been aware that something was "desperately wrong with the wifehood and motherhood of college women." In a survey of seventeen hundred Radcliffe graduates, he reported, only 15 percent had placed marriage and the family as the "most important service of women to the world." Citing the lament of an ex-feminist in an *Outlook* article, "The Harm My Education Did Me," that "you can't educate a girl's mind without educating her heart," he argued that personal ambition, "the friend of efficient fatherhood" was the enemy of "efficient motherhood."[72] Carey's concerns were joined by those of William S. Sadler, M.D., who sounded the alarm of race suicide. Writing in *Ladies' Home Journal*, Sadler, rehearsing the statistics showing Mt. Holyoke graduates' failure to reproduce, thundered, "Motherhood should be taught in season and out of season in our educational system." A writer in *Harper's* updated the numbers showing that Barnard and Smith graduates produced only 1.2 to 1.5 children.[73]

On the defensive, President Henry MacCracken, cited Vassar's course on the family and its new program in euthenics. He observed that two-thirds of college women were marrying in the 1920s. It was a growing trend. Seventy-five percent. of the Vassar graduates of the classes of 1912–21, 67 percent of Bryn Mawr graduates of 1909–18, 46 percent of the Radcliffe classes of 1911–20, and 60 percent of Michigan graduates of 1909–18 married.[74] To discover "Why They Failed to Marry," Katharine Bement Davis surveyed twelve hundred college graduates still unmarried five years after graduation. They reported being in good health (77.1 percent), happy (78.3 percent), and success-ful (55.1 percent). The predominant reason for not marrying was never having met the "right man." One-third had been engaged. Slightly more than half regretted not marrying and two-thirds indicated they would if the right man did come along. Only one out of twenty had never had a proposal of marriage. Davis, who agreed that it would be better for "the race" if more college women married, observed, "One of my college professors, a woman, used to say that a girl could not grad-uate from Vassar and be a complete fool unless she had a perfect genius for it." She "ought to be able to adjust herself to the requirements of homemaking, to getting on with her husband, and to learning the latest on the subject of child hygiene."[75] Certainly, Davis's sample of unmar-ried graduates belied the stereotype of the unattractive old maid.

For most college women, there was pressure to use their education. M. Carey Thomas of Bryn Mawr had been particularly forceful. Her successor, President Marian Edwards Park, was more temperate, urg-ing the 1926 graduates to "put yourself to the t' st of earning your living for around a year at least." A not untypical a' cle in *Century* magazine asked, "Why should not a woman round out her life, as does a man, with many interests and with many activities, each of which contrib-utes to the fulness and richness of her experience?"[76] The norm was employment for at least a time. Davis found that only 4.4 percent in her survey had never worked. Approximately 90 percent of Wellesley's graduates were employed. A survey of Smith alumnae and two AAUP studies also found that most college women did work, a good many continuing after marriage until they had children. Surveying a hundred successful career women in New York City, Virginia MacCracken con-cluded, "Happiness is the chief result from this extra-activity of women; happiness for herself and hence happiness for those she loves and cherishes."[77]

The college graduate faced a seemingly bewildering array of career and professional choices. Catherine Filene in a 1920 survey *Careers for Women* asked 175 women, leaders in their fields, to describe the work, the training needed, the receptivity and experience of women in it. Occupations ranged from public accountant through factory inspector and physicist. Geraldine Farrar described the career opportunities in opera, Florence E. Allen the experience of an attorney. Throughout the decade, articles appeared on women in "odd and unusual" positions from steeplejacks to deep sea divers. Sociologist Sophonisba Breckinridge, analyzing the numbers of women in the professions reported their proportions: 1910: 429 of 1,000; 1920: 468 of 1,000; 1930: 469 of 1,000. In sheer numbers, women, though not leaping forward, obviously held their own.[78] Yet, while women made advances, the professions remained largely gender divided. Women continued to dominate in the traditional nurturing and service professions. Within the "learned professions," although the doors were partially ajar, they proved by no means open. Vassar economist Mabel Newcomer graphically presented the percentage of women in selected professions in 1930 and the percentage of degree recipients in these fields:

	Occupational Groups	*Degree Recipients*
Engineers	0.05%	0.02%
Dentists	1.8%	2.1%
Lawyers	2.1%	4.8%
Architects	1.7%	1.3%
Clergy	2.2%	5.6%
Physicians	4.6%	4.6%
Social workers	78.7%	98.3%
Teachers	81.0%	67.6%
Librarians	91.4%	93.3%
Nursing	98.1%	100%[79]

When women did become professionals in medicine or science or law, they frequently were in "feminized" areas—pediatrics, home economics, or aspects of family law.

An overwhelming number of college-educated women continued to elect teaching. In 1900, forty-three thousand of the sixty-one thousand women in coeducational schools were in teacher training programs; in the 1920s teachers represented 57 percent of the women professionals. Eighty-eight percent of elementary and 62 percent of secondary teachers were women. On her inauguration as Bryn Mawr president, Marian Edwards Park affirmed the "business" of the women's college "to call out and encourage the students who show that combination of intelli-

gence and imagination for the good teacher and direct her there."[80] But
at the Seven Sisters, while one-third of the students still indicated an
interest in teaching, the number electing teaching in the secondary and
elementary schools continued to decline. The upwardly mobile daughters of the middle class, the Irish, the Jewish, the Italian, and the blacks
increasingly swelled the programs in normal schools and the new state
teachers' colleges. The *Chicago Tribune* worried about the impact on
future citizenry taught by an army of women "unaccustomed to thinking politically." An article in *School and Society*, echoing a lament of the
National Education Association (NEA) that education was not attracting
enough good people, cited the low salaries and the low public esteem,
commenting, "A sort of social stigma seems to cling to the teacher."[81]
The teachers' response was primarily threefold: to fight through the
NEA and the fledgling American Federation of Teachers for better salaries, pensions, and conditions in the classroom; to work for higher
professional standards in the field; and to lobby, unsuccessfully, for the
establishment of a Department of Education to address the plight of
teacher and student.

Perhaps none of the "semiprofessions," or female fields, changed
more significantly than social work. In 1917, Mary Richmond, director
of the Russell Sage Foundation, using her wealth of experience in the
field in Boston, Baltimore, and Philadelphia, published *Social Diagnosis*,
a blueprint of the nature of social evidence and ways to utilize it in
treating the individual and the family.[82] In the 1920s, leaders continued
Richmond's fight for professional training and credentials in an area
that was grappling with the proliferation of child guidance clinics, the
expanding field for social workers in the public schools, the burgeoning
growth of central agencies, and, most significantly, the impact of
Freudian theory.

Whereas Richmond had not mentioned Freud in her *Social Diagnosis*
or *What Is Social Case Work?* the 1920s were marked by a "growing conviction that insight into emotions and psychic life was the key to skilled
casework." One social worker recalled colleagues peering "anxiously
into the faces of their comrades with the unspoken question: have you
been psychoanalyzed?"[83] As Mary Richmond had influenced the field
through her funding position as director of the Russell Sage Foundation, so the Commonwealth Fund influenced the development of child
guidance clinics where the psychiatric social worker demonstrated that
social casework was a form of therapy. Young Charlotte Towle, ready

to apply her training from the University of Chicago, understood the need to "meet the basic emotional needs of the individual."[84]

The Commonwealth Fund and the White-Williams Foundation spurred the movement of the social worker into the schools as a visiting teacher. White-Williams director Anna Beach Pratt worked in the Philadelphia schools to educate the public and teachers about the pressures of mass education on the child and the role of the visiting teacher to help the classroom teacher address not only academic performance but the student's health, home, social environment, and emotional needs. In 1929, Pratt achieved even more leverage by winning appointment to the Philadelphia school board.

Throughout the profession, in hospitals and in family agencies, social workers adopted the therapeutic mode of diagnosis. The major champion of the psychiatric approach, Virginia Robinson, summarized her conclusions in her 1930 *A Changing Psychology in Social Case Work*. To Robinson, social work came of age when interest shifted from the environment to the "meaning of experience within the individual psyche."[85] Robinson's close friend, Jessie Taft, from her position in the Department of Welfare and the Children's Aid Society of Pennsylvania, led in applying Otto Rank's theories in casework and in carrying on the lively debate in school and agency between the Freudian and Rankian approaches—the "psychology of cure" versus the "psychology of helping."[86]

In an attempt to bring more coherence and professionalism to the field, 750 social workers formed the American Association of Social Workers (AASW) in 1921. By 1930, membership had expanded to more than five thousand. Working with the more specialized associations—the American Association of Hospital Social Workers, American Association of Visiting Teachers, and American Association of Psychiatric Social Workers—the AASW set educational standards for those entering the profession of at least two years of college and three years of technical training and employment in the field.

There were major advances and increased professionalism in the related areas of social service in prison and police work. Miriam Van Waters utilized her doctoral study at Clark University in psychology and anthropology in establishing an experimental home for delinquent girls, El Retiro in Los Angeles. She related her approach in introducing self-government and vocational training in *When Girls Do Right* in 1922. Prison wardens and reformers Katharine B. Davis in New York, Jessie

Hodder in Massachusetts, and Mary Belle Harris at the new federal prison for women at Alderson, West Virginia, developed a system of scientific classification of prisoners to ensure better vocational training (though there remained an emphasis on home economics and women's work). Policewomen, through the new International Association of Policewomen, set up entry standards in education, training, and experience.[87]

Like teaching and social work, the librarians' profession was also largely feminized by the 1920s. Women's representation in the profession increased from 88.4 to 91.3 percent during the decade. The librarians sought to improve professional standards and expanded into new areas. Sarah Boyle as assistant secretary of the American Library Association upgraded standards, while Jessie M. Flexner through her *Circulation Work in Public Libraries* pressed librarians to develop strong outreach into the community. She demonstrated her words through her work in the New York Public Library, building model programs in adult education and counseling for adult readers. At the other end of the readership, Anne Carroll Moore, supervisor of children's work at the New York Public Library, initiated her highly successful and widely copied storytelling hours. In Cleveland, Laura A. Eastman, the first woman to head a major metropolitan library system, instituted the divisional plan in shelving books, a policy of open shelving, and a county extension service.[88]

Of all the professions or semiprofessions, nursing was the most feminized. Women comprised 96 percent of the nurses in 1920 and 98 percent in 1930, so that the profession represented an "actual monopoly of women." Like teaching, nursing seemed the quintessential woman's work; as one contemporary observed, "women had been the nurses of mankind throughout all time." Also like teaching, it was a profession that seemed to promise security, a decent salary, and access to the middle class. World War I, the epidemic of pneumonia in 1917, and the pandemic influenza of 1918 and 1919 which took 500,000 lives graphically demonstrated the need for nurses.[89] Yet in 1923, the Goldmark report, *Nursing Education in the United States*, financed by the Rockefeller Foundation, concluded that nurses' training was in some instances mired in an apprenticeship "earn-while-you-learn system." Nursing still served "two masters: the care of the sick in the hospital and the education of the nurse." In a contest between the two, care of the sick always was the first priority. The Goldmark report cited poor preparation and the practice of immediately adding a new student when one left the program during the academic year; it underscored the need to reorganize educational programs and to secure stronger financial support.[90]

Spurred by the report and building on Adelaide Nutting's long and continuing work to raise professional standards, nurse-educators reviewed curricula and developed stronger programs. In 1923 the Yale University School of Nursing was founded. Its first dean, Annie W. Goodrich, brought a varied experience to the task of building a strong program and educational leadership, particularly in public health. With a degree from Columbia Teachers College, Goodrich had been joint director of the Henry Street Visiting Nurses Service in New York City and dean of the Army School of Nursing. The Yale curriculum she developed required a college diploma for admission, two years of course work, and clinical experience in obstetrical, public health, and pediatric nursing. The first independent university school of nursing to give a bachelor's degree, Yale's success was recognized by a million-dollar endowment from the Rockefeller Foundation in 1929.[91] By the end of the decade, 60 colleges and 2,155 nursing schools had reviewed and revised their programs.

Nurses did not lack for organizations to carry their fight for better standards and higher salaries and benefits. The American Nurses' Association had a membership of seventy-six thousand in the 1920s. It held its biennial meetings jointly with the National League of Nursing Education and the National Organization for Public Health Nursing.[92] Lobbying within their place in the medical model and with the low leverage of an almost all female constituency, nurses had made substantial professional progress.

While women continued to choose the traditional women's professions and worked to upgrade their status and professionalism, it was obvious that their choice was not always their own. Surveying the curricula and the career choices of graduates of the Seven Sisters colleges, Muriel Robinson observed the clustering of graduates in a few fields and questioned whether they were in a field because it suited their talents. New vocations and opportunities did exist, but would not "open automatically."[93]

The segregation of professions by sex was graphically illustrated in higher education. The number of women earning doctorates continued to rise in the 1920s. But the path to the Ph.D. was seldom easy. The American Association of University Women reported that 70 percent of the degree holders surveyed had had some fellowship assistance, but that it usually was not enough to cover expenses. Sophonisba Breckinridge noted that the doctorate was not won by scholarship alone; in most cases the first prerequisite was "a steadfast courage." On achieving their degrees the new Ph.D.s usually found that American universities were more willing to educate than to employ them. Historian Angie Debo, who completed her master's degree with straight As at the University of Chicago and published her thesis, found that, though she was encouraged to continue for her doctorate by male professors at Chicago, "she was virtually unemployable." Debo related her experience: "The university stood so high that even a master's degree was important enough so that colleges and universities over the country were contacting the history department for some of their people who were receiving master's degrees. . . . There were thirty institutional contacts. . . . Twenty-nine of them said they wouldn't take a woman under any circumstances. One of them said they preferred a man."[94]

The success of women in achieving faculty positions varied by type of institution. A 1921 survey of 176 institutions by the American Association of University Professors (AAUP) revealed that in twenty-nine men's colleges and universities, there were only two women among 2,000 faculty members. One of those was Alice Hamilton, internationally renowned for her work in industrial toxicology, who joined the Harvard Medical School faculty in 1919 as an assistant professor at age fifty. One of the conditions of her hiring was that she agree not to join her male colleagues in academic processions. In coeducational institutions the women provided 13 percent or 1,646 of the faculty. In women's colleges, more than 25 percent of the 989 faculty members were male.

In 1924 the AAUW surveyed department chairmen on their attitudes toward hiring women faculty. Overwhelmingly, the responses asserted that although they were not prejudiced against women, they were concerned about "quality" and feared the "feminization" of the profession. Though there were some outstanding full professors, Jessica Peixotta at Berkeley and Louise Pound at Nebraska, most women remained clustered in the lower ranks of assistant professor and instructor. In all ranks, they did not earn equal pay for equal work. The 1921 AAUP survey found 73 percent of the women's colleges and 53 percent of the coeducational institutions paid lower salaries to the female faculty.

In 1927–28 at the land-grant universities, the median salary for women faculty was $860 less than that of the men. Explanations for the discrepancy in staff and salary included the need to keep men in teaching, the need of the male faculty to support their families, and the law of supply and demand.[95] Partially, the salary differential reflected the congregation in field and specialty of the women in the humanities and social sciences. A study by Marion Hawthorne of 1,600 women faculty found the largest number in English and modern languages. In the sciences, men received the highest number of degrees in chemistry, medical science, and engineering; women's fields were the biological and social fields of botany, zoology, and psychology.[96] When they did teach, women frequently were shunted into home economics or related fields.

Like their colleagues in the elementary schools and social work, women college faculty had image trouble. Three-fourths of those surveyed by Hawthorne were single, divorced, or separated. Only one-tenth combined marriage and a career. Eugenicists worried about the impact of "unattractive and desiccated teachers" as role models. Hawthorne's respondents had developed, she observed, "a defensive attitude bordering on martyrdom, and complained, waxed bitter, and voiced resentment toward the conditions of which they were victims."[97]

Yet there were some grounds for hope. Although the women's colleges, facing a barrage of criticism of their single-sex environment and reflecting in some instances, as at Mt. Holyoke, the replacement of a female with a male president, tended to augment their faculties with male scholars, the variety of institutions of higher education did broaden the opportunities for women. The land-grant institutions increased their appointments to women. A study of the numbers and ranks of sixteen prestigious colleges, including California, Cornell, Wisconsin, Minnesota, Illinois, Stanford, and Ohio State, showed an increase in women faculty, even though they remained clustered in feminized disciplines.[98] In spite of these signs and in spite of the fact that the number of women earning doctorates continued to rise in the 1920s (though the percentage receiving the Ph.D. declined) Hawthorne concluded her 1929 report, "It would appear that the field of college teaching holds comparatively little promise for women."[99]

The situation was bleaker in medicine. Women were actually moving backward during the decade. From 6 percent of the physicians in 1910, women totaled only 4.4 percent in 1930. In absolute numbers the drop was from 9,015 in 1910 to 6,825 in 1930. In Boston where women physicians had achieved the most success, their percentage fell from 18.2 percent in 1910 to 9.7 percent in 1920. The American Medical Association, stung by a report on professional training by Abraham

Flexner and vigorously attacking homeopathic medicine, set new curricula and standards. The acceptance of women into every medical school except Harvard and the advances in medical technology eroded both the need for the women's medical colleges and the ability of the generally small underendowed institutions to continue to compete for students. With the homeopathic schools and women's colleges in decline, two important routes of women to medicine were closing. By 1925, women faced a 5 percent admissions quota in the major medical schools. For those who were admitted and completed their programs, there was the further barrier of an internship. In 1921, 482 hospitals reported only forty women interns. Hospitals explained that they faced housing problems with female physicians, a difficulty they did not encounter with their nursing staffs. Outside the profession, the environment was no more welcoming. Dr. Alice Hamilton observed that it was easier to become a physician and begin a practice when the "woman doctor could count on the loyalty of dedicated feminists who would choose a woman doctor because she was a woman." Dr. Lilian Welsh, reflecting on the previous three decades in medicine, concluded in 1927 that the demand for women physicians had become "as keen as that for a horse and buggy.[100] Women did band together in the American Medical Women's Association (AMWA) and held meetings in conjunction with the AMA, which it required its members to join. The AMWA sent out speakers trying to interest young women in the field, but realists would have to struggle to find many words of encouragement.

Conversely, the number of woman lawyers increased appreciably during the 1920s. In 1920 the census recorded 1,738; ten years later the total of women in law had almost doubled to 3,385. They comprised only 2.1 percent of the nation's lawyers, however. While the healing skills of the doctor could be construed as possible woman's work, the law had traditionally been reserved for men. The American Bar Association's emphasis on professional standards in the 1920s, by hastening the trend away from access through reading the law in an office to three years of study at a law school, had helped women enter the profession. Though there were some holdouts, particularly Columbia and Georgetown, only Harvard refused to admit women by 1929. As in medicine, it was one thing to earn a degree, another to gain admittance to the bar and to establish a practice. A 1911 graduate of the School of Law of the University of Southern California, after "innocently" opening an office, found one of her first clients expected her to charge only half the regular fee because she was a woman. She and her colleagues from the university formed the legal fraternity Phi Delta Delta and began to build a network of support. By the end of the 1920s, there were forty-one Phi Delta chapters.[101] They were joined by another fraternity, Kappa Beta Pi, and the more encompassing Women Lawyers Association.

The careers of the two most famous women lawyers of the 1920s provide case studies of roads to legal success. Mabel Walker Willebrandt received her LL.B. from the University of Southern California in 1916. She had been a part-time student for most of the program, earning her way as an elementary school principal while helping put her husband through the School of Law. With her marriage breaking up, she set up an office with two male colleagues from USC and, through another USC contact, was appointed the first assistant public defender in Los Angeles, defending in the next year over two thousand women, primarily prostitutes. A member of Phi Delta Delta, she also helped found the Women Lawyers Association of Los Angeles to set up a network of women in the face of the old-boy system in the courts. Active in women's organizations and the Republican party, Willebrandt was appointed an assistant attorney general of the United States in 1921. She was thirty-two. In Washington, she continued to support women in the profession. She brought women into her division in the Justice Department, and on department business in St. Louis or Chicago, she was always armed with a roster of Phi Delta members. Serving as international president of Phi Delta Delta from 1924 to 1926, Willebrandt helped establish its professional advisory committee to assist law school graduates getting started in the profession. She was continually balked, however, in her own aspiration to be appointed to a federal judgeship. Political divisions in California, the conviction of President Coolidge that the country was not yet ready, and her own controversial involvement in Republican politics in 1928 frustrated that hope.[102]

In 1918, as secretary of the Los Angeles Women Lawyers Association, Willebrandt corresponded with a young county prosecutor in Cleveland, Florence E. Allen, urging her to share her experiences to inspire young women of the West with the possibilities of a life in the law. Allen, after postgraduate study in Germany, had taught school in Cleveland, worked with the Henry Street Settlement in New York, and then served as an assistant to Maud Wood Park in her campaign to win college students and alumnae for the suffrage cause. With her LL.B. from New York University, she returned to Cleveland, represented the suffragists in their legal battles, and stumped the state for the cause. In 1920 a coalition of women won her election as a judge of the Court of Common Pleas; two years later her record, her strong campaigning, and the continued backing of women allies secured her election to the Ohio Superior Court. Reelected on her record in 1928, she was the highest woman jurist in America.[103]

When women were appointed judges, it was frequently to a juvenile or woman's court. *Good Housekeeping* in an April 1920 article asserted the "mother instinct of judges made women more humane. Women tend to hold life more dear because they bear children; thus they strive harder to reclaim those who might otherwise be lost."[104] In Los Angeles, juvenile court judge Orfa Jean Shontz, a Phi Delta Delta founder, working with Miriam Van Waters provided a model of Progressive reform and reclamation. Another California Phi Delta Delta Georgia Bullock became a judge of the Women's Court of Los Angeles in 1924. The "discerning woman judge," it was believed, would bring a special sensitivity and skill to women's cases. Compiling a remarkable record of only one appeal made on her twenty-five thousand decisions, Bullock won appointment to the Los Angeles Superior Court. Overall, however, the number of women judges remained minuscule. The number of women lawyers led one contemporary to conclude, "Apparently the legal profession does not prove strongly attractive to women."[105]

The ranks of the clergy remained almost totally closed to women. In 1926, a senior at New Jersey College for women sent a list of questions to the directors of eighty-two schools of theology on their admissions policies and their advice to her. The answers were "not very encouraging." Although 70 percent of the respondents admitted or would admit women should they apply and be qualified, two-thirds advised her against seeking a career in the ministry. One Lutheran minister responded that woman's ordination was "opposed to the word of God." Most suggested alternative church service. Sophonisba Breckinridge concluded that for women the educational path to the ministry was "not very smooth." Yet the 1920s did produce the "world's most pulchritudinous" evangelist, Aimee Semple McPherson, founder of the highly successful International Church of the Foursquare Gospel in Los Angeles.[106]

Beyond pulpit, court, and ivory tower, educated women increasingly applied their knowledge. At the beginning of the decade, the Women's Joint Congressional Committee discovered that 60 percent of the civil service examinations were closed to women. They and Civil Service

Commissioner Helen Gardener successfully ended that discrimination. They also won legislation to reclassify positions in the effort to win salary equity. Neither reform was fully realized as the veterans' preference policy and the discretion of the appointing officer was retained and as women's positions were frequently reclassified downward and their salaries maintained at a lower level. When appointed, women scientists tended to be clustered in the Department of Agriculture, the Bureau of Home Economics under bureau chief Louise Stanley, or the Bureau of Plant Industry or the Hygienic Laboratory of the U.S. Public Health Service. Grace Abbott brought women into the Children's Bureau as did Mary Anderson in the Women's Bureau at the Department of Labor. Again, it was a case of women helping women where they could in an environment of sex-segregated work.[107]

At the beginning of the decade, the most euphoric expectations were for the future of the educated woman in the business world. Magazine stories proliferated on the "new business woman" and her new frontiers. The women's colleges established the Bureau of Vocational Information in 1915 to sponsor lectures and symposia on careers and worked to find positions for women graduates.[108] Study in home economics, which had won success for some to higher education and laboratories, was hailed as an entry to business. A *Saturday Evening Post* article, "Getting on in the World: Business Wants Housekeepers," asserted: "Banks, department stores, chain stores, factories, life-insurance companies, public utilities, advertising agencies—all these and many more have discovered that the woman who has made a specialty of things feminine had a definite mission in the modern business organization. . . . Scarcely a bank today is without its home service department."[109] In the *Ladies' Home Journal*, Alice A. Winter, president of the General Federation of Women's Clubs, discussed "Business Plus," and concluded that "the woman in business has come to stay. . . . But there are differences between man and woman in their activities and their points of view. Women in public life are asking everywhere this question about our institutions, our education, our industry, our government: What is the human side of it, how does it touch life?"[110]

In the expanding fashion and cosmetic industries, Hattie Carnegie, Madame C. J. Walker, Helena Rubinstein, and Elizabeth Arden all built multimillion-dollar empires. Carnegie and Walker provide classic rags-to-riches stories. Carnegie (Harriet Konigeiser) grew up on the lower East Side of New York, where her father, an Austrian immigrant, worked in the garment industry. She left school at thirteen and worked briefly at Macy's. Encouraged by a seamstress, Rose Roth, she opened her first business, Carnegie—Ladies Hatter, in 1909. Four years later, with Roth as a partner, she opened a shop near fashionable Riverside Drive. By 1929, Carnegie-designed clothes, the "Carnegie Look," brought sales of $3.5 million. In the cosmetics field, Madame C. J. Walker was an early pioneer. Born on a Louisiana farm, orphaned at five, married at fourteen, and widowed at twenty, Madame Walker worked eighteen years as a washerwoman to support herself and her daughter. In 1905, she reported dreaming of a formula to improve the appearance of the hair of black women, and developed the Walker System of shampoo, pomade, brushing, and heated iron combs. Selling it door to door, she soon had Walker agents carrying her products throughout the United States and Latin America. At her death in 1919, the *Crisis* declared that she had "revolutionized the personal habits and appearance of millions of human beings." She left two-thirds of her multimillion-dollar estate to charity and stipulated that only a woman should run her enterprises. In the 1920s, Josephine Baker made her treatment famous in Paris.[111]

In spite of these successes, women were still having to prove their skills, staying power, and mettle in business. Three topics that appeared with some frequency were women's efficiency on the job, the necessity of women having the right attitude on the job, and the question of whether women were receiving a "square deal." Efficiency expert Lillian M. Gilbreth insisted in a May 1929 article that investigation over a quarter of a century in her field indicated that "the safest method is to grant unlimited opportunity for all, regardless of sex." But women, she insisted, must bring the right attitude and philosophy to their work.[112] She was echoed by a litany of questions in a *Delineator* article "What Kind of Business Woman Am I?":

Am I working for my pay?
Or am I being paid for my work?
In other words, which interests me more, the next pair of shoes, or whether I am making good on my job? . . .
Have I any right to crab when the men my own age outstrip me, or are they really steadier and more full of vision and purpose than I?[113]

Answering the question "Does Business Give Women a Square Deal?" in *American Magazine*, Helen C. Bennett cited the career of Mary Dillon, president of the Brooklyn Borough Gas Company, the first woman to head a major public utility company. Dillon believed that business gave women a square deal, but cautioned they must work harder than men. She began her career at the gas company as an office clerk and moved up in three years to office manager, promising her employer she would not marry. For thirteen years she was office manager, serving for five of those as general manager without title or recognition. In 1924, she was named general manager and vice president and married. To Dillon, her career reflected the "general change in attitudes toward women in industry."[114] Answering the same question in *Atlantic*, Anne W. Armstrong, reviewing the problem of the educated woman in business, observed, "Speaking generally, the business man's secretary today is more often a college graduate than he is himself." Women who had been successful in more advanced positions were still receiving from half to a third of their male colleagues' salaries. The only reason, she noted, that women's resentment did not boil over was that "business women do not feel themselves strong enough yet, as a class, to force the issue."[15]

Businesswomen did not lack for organization, however, In 1920, the year-old National Federation of Business and Professional Women's Clubs had twenty-six thousand members and 217 clubs; by the end of the decade they were sixty thousand strong. They pressed for higher educational standards for the businesswoman, recommending at least a high school education for every woman entering any business career, and encouraged their membership through the journal the *Independent Woman*.[116]

Throughout the decade educated women worked out ways to integrate their education with their decisions for career and home. The pioneers in many instances remained pioneers, a small minority in their chosen fields. The middle generation in their thirties and forties had established themselves professionally and built networks to enlarge opportunities for themselves and the next generation. These national professional networks were connected to other local clubs and organizations. The New York Woman's City Club, for example, continued to build on the associations and friendships forged in earlier and ongoing reform battles. Young Eleanor Roosevelt knew and worked with Frances Perkins, Katharine B. Davis, and Lillian Wald. In Washington, veteran Helen Gardener was a focus for gatherings of lawyers and young professionals in the government. For women professionals it was still a time, when, as one Phi Delta Delta president explained, "we all knew one another."[117]

Yet the next generation, which had so frustrated suffragists and reformers, was displaying what one contemporary researcher described as "the first signs of disillusionment with the New Freedom." Concerned at the loneliness of older, unmarried professionals, they were beginning to discount the "rewards from a material success that must be accomplished at the expense of love."[118] The younger generation wanted economic independence and satisfying work, but if forced to choose might give up the law book for the cookbook. The work of the pioneers and the middle generation had won each new college graduate the pleasure and pain of her own decision.[119]

Poster of the Interchurch World Movement.

CHAPTER SEVEN

Religion and the Challenge of the Revolution in Manners and Morals

> In retrospect it becomes clear that the decade of the twenties marked a crucial transition in American religious history.[1]

> If the family was in trouble, the church was in ruins, and the more the churches adjusted, the less they seemed to matter. . . . the young had simply "thrown religion overboard."[2]

> Society is not only undergoing a revolution, it is experiencing a devil-ution. Not only is it undergoing, but it is going under.[3]

Traditionally perceived as the guardians of American morals, women faced daunting challenges in the 1920s. The onslaught of the automobile, jazz, movies, and confession magazines, and the impact of Freud in theater and home led to the alarming conclusion from pulpit and hearth that America was undergoing a "revolution in manners and morals." Seen as both cause and cure, women were called to reform, to save, and to battle by church leaders. Women of all faiths exhorted their daughters to lead a life of greater probity. Protestant women marshaled to win Prohibition and, in some instances, to support husbands and brothers in the Ku Klux Klan. As they loyally answered the call from the pulpits with their energy, organization, and money, they explored how their role, so changed in other institutions, might find expanded service and power within the church.

The churches emerged from their efforts in war service and relief filled with Wilsonian idealism. In December 1918 Protestant leaders formed the Interchurch World Movement as a "religious counterpart of the League of Nations." It sought to join the agencies of American Protestantism in a cooperative effort at spiritual revival. By 1920, these hopes, like those for the league were considerably diminished. Over-expectation, high budgets, the perceived dominance of liberals (partic-ularly evident in their mediation of the 1919 steel strike), and the resurgence of denominational loyalty left the Interchurch World Move-ment shattered, "a victim of its dreams and overhead."[4]

The decade was increasingly marked by clerical expressions of a re-ligious depression. Charles Fiske, Episcopal bishop of central New York, claimed he had "evidence of a sad disintegration of American Protestantism." A Unitarian writer described "Our Spiritual Destitu-tion" and scored religion as "timorous, unimaginative." Young Reinhold Niebuhr asserted that "a psychology of defeat . . . gripped the forces of religion."[5]

The symptoms and causes were myriad and graphic. C. Luther Fry, writing for the President's Research Council on Recent Social Trends, reflected that an American returning after a twenty-year absence would notice that "church buildings now appear trivial and unimportant in contrast with the enormous skyscrapers of commerce and finance." He "might raise the question whether this development is a symbol of the recent tendency of the secular to overshadow religious interests." Church attendance declined as did the numbers of clergymen and new converts; income for the missions dropped; volunteers for missionary work were scarce. The increasing competition for the congregation's time by the automobile, radio, motion picture, and golf and tennis was palpable. Most serious, though impossible to quantify, was "a pervasive thinning out of evangelical substance, a tendency to identify religion with the business-oriented values of the American life."[6] Bruce Barton's best-seller in 1925, *The Man Nobody Knows*, depicting Christ as master salesman, contained the epigraph, "Wist ye not that I must be about my Father's business?" Bishop Charles Fiske, writing as a "puzzled par-son" in 1929, complained that "America has become almost hopelessly enamored of a religion that is little more than a sanctified commercial-ism. . . . Efficiency has become the greatest of Christian virtues. . . . Protestantism, in America, seems to be degenerating into a sort of Bab-sonian cult, which cannot distinguish between what is offered to God and what is accomplished for the glory of America and the furtherance of business enterprise."[7]

Beyond the challenge of commercialism, the other "isms"—scien-tism, behaviorism, and humanism—posed significant threats. Darwin-ian battles of the turn of the century were renewed and intensified in the challenge to Scripture by the new biblical criticism and science. Prominent Baptist clergyman Dr. Harry Emerson Fosdick asked in *Harper's* "Will Science Replace God?" and concluded it was hard to find solace in "science is my Shepherd. I shall not want." Yet he worriedly reported: "The men of faith might claim for their positions ancient tradition, practical usefulness, and spiritual desirability, but one query could prick all such bubbles. Is it scientific?"[8] The religion-science controversy was most visible in the highly publicized Scopes, or monkey trial over the teaching of evolution in the Tennessee public schools.

Fosdick, author of a 1922 article, "Shall the Fundamentalists Win?" became the center of the wrenching struggle between the fundamentalists and modernists that characterized the 1920s. Serving as guest preacher in the First Presbyterian Church in New York, Fosdick was the target of an effort to purge pulpit and seminaries of liberals or those who would not make a formal declaration of their adherence to the inerrancy of Scripture, the virgin birth of Christ, his physical Resurrection, his substitutionary Atonement, and his miracles. Fosdick left for another post, but fundamentalists were defeated in the struggle for control of the prestigious Princeton Seminary. Liberals in fighting off the frontal attack of the fundamentalists were challenged by humanists and naturalists in their formulations for living in the modern world.[9]

The religious debate generated an outpouring of books and articles. Ominously, one survey showed that by 1930, 67 percent of them were critical of the churches. Contemporary historian Frederick Lewis Allen asserted that the discussion itself was a sign that for millions religion had become a debatable subject. In Middletown, the Lynds found that although "in theory" religious beliefs dominated all others, the actuality was different. Religion was little debated and little discussed by the business class. Ministers were more highly esteemed by women than by men; religious services were more valued by the working class than the business class. Rev. Charles Stelzle, writing in *World's Work*, reported a weakening of loyalty to the church by the young and an undeniable vagueness about what it offered. The church was declining, he asserted, largely because "those who are identified with it do not actually believe in it."[10]

Since there was a traditional identification of denominational Protestantism with Americanism and the American way of life, an erosion of Protestant values could be construed as a challenge to the Republic. In Middletown the Lynds reported that civic loyalty was emerging as civic religion. To many, being a Christian was synonymous with being civilized or being a good citizen. Magic Middletown was the religion that appeared to have the "greatest drawing power" for some citizens. Meanwhile, the churches were extending activities into the community, developing basketball and recreational programs for youth and theatrical evenings for adults, further blurring the line between things civic and things spiritual.[11]

Although women did not formally participate in the theological debates between fundamentalists and modernists, they formed an increasing majority in the congregations. Luther Fry reported five women for every four men in Protestant congregations; 73 percent of black women and 62 percent of white women were church members. Many churchmen looked to the commitment and witness of these women; at the same time, many women were ready for a larger role in the church.[12]

Traditionally, women had made their greatest contribution in the institutional church in the home and foreign missions. In the 1920s, the mission fields provided another index of religious decline. A postwar burst of enthusiasm had sent the number of Protestant missionaries to a high of 13,098 in 1923. Three years later the Foreign Missions Conference of North America cited the apathy of local churches and the declining income for mission work. Overall contributions to the six major mission boards dropped $6 million. More serious was the decline in volunteers for service. In 1920, 2,700 students had volunteered for foreign service; in 1928, only 252 stepped forward. Conversely, the American Roman Catholics, previously occupied with an expanding immigrant church, accelerated their foreign missionary work. In 1929, Maryknoll, the most active missionary religious order, had 550 members in East Asia. Catholic contributions to the Society for the Propagation of the Faith increased. An officer of the Protestant Home Mission Council reported that almost all the major Protestant denominations faced a period of financial stringency in their work.[13] The decline came, paradoxically, as American responsibility in support of Protestant missions worldwide grew. American's accounted for two-thirds of the support; in 1923, their contribution was $45 million out of the $69 million expended on missionary activity.[14]

The challenge to Protestant Christianity at home was echoed in the mission field. World War I destroyed the optimistic belief in progress and the onward march of Western civilization. Nordic arrogance and the concepts of Nordic superiority were attacked. W. S. Maugham's *Rain*, a 1922 Broadway hit, was only one attack on the missionary as "a long-faced, sour-tempered, narrow-minded killjoy" who either in yielding to the flesh and the devil or in being eaten by cannibals got what he deserved. As the new biblical criticism shook Protestant belief in the infallibility of Scripture, the new missionary developed a new respect for Eastern religions and Eastern culture. As one Methodist missionary testified, he had found good teachings in these religions and a warmer appreciation for other faiths. The new missionary worked with people rather than for them. One wrote home of the questioning of these potential postwar converts: "Picture young pagans heckling a missionary to explain to them the mysteries of the Virgin Birth and the atonement, to reconcile Christianity with Western business methods, and to explain how the oil scandal could occur in a Christian country."[15]

Yet the new missionary also faced some old problems. A Methodist wrote home of the daily sights of misery and suffering, the assault on the nostrils of dirt and filth, and the loneliness. One wife, noting that she was merely an asterisk on the missionary roll next to her husband's name, listed the practical difficulties of service. Her family budget was $1,700 a year, with $100 to $250 for each child. With tithing and insurance deducted, she had an average monthly income of $113.33 and average monthly expenses of $111.14. Her husband was wearing shoes he had bought in 1912. When their daughter went to college, she would have to return with her to America to reduce expenses.

While these concerns were aired at home, home problems traveled abroad. The fundamentalist-modernist fights exploded in China as the fundamentalists tried to carry out their purge of liberals overseas. At the same time, one East Asia expert complained that Protestant liberalism was giving out an "uncertain sound" and that "men and women do not stake their lives in an alien land in an attempt to propagate a question."[16]

The challenges to the missions particularly challenged women's contributions to the church. As early as 1811 Presbyterian women had organized in Cent Societies to send their pennies for the cause. The minutes of the General Assembly hailed their support, noting, "Benevolence is always attractive, but when dressed in a female form, possesses peculiar charms." By 1870, there were forty-two women's societies supporting the home and foreign missions. Wives served in the mission fields, but since they were also "the light and solace" of Christian homes, they were joined by single women. By 1893, women comprised more than 60 percent of the missionary force; in 1900 women's societies supported 389 wives and 856 single women missionaries. Realizing that in Asia as in America women were the custodians of morals and religion in the family, the Protestants accepted the importance of a woman-to-woman approach. By 1920, there were forty women's boards with an income of $6 million. Women made up 69 percent of the missionary force; 48 percent were single.[17]

More than a century of women's work and a half-century of organization fell, as the churches decided to emulate business and rationalize and streamline their organizations. Presbyterians, Baptists, Methodist Episcopal, Congregationalists, and Mennonites reorganized and consolidated their home and foreign operations. The Presbyterian experience provides the most graphic case study of the erosion of women's role and responsibility.

In 1921, the General Assembly of the Presbyterian church in the U.S.A. appointed a Committee on the Reorganization and Consolidation of the Boards and Agencies. The Women's Board of Home Missions issued a brief history of its work and sent three representatives to try to persuade the committee to retain their separate board. The women operated missions from Alaska to the Caribbean, administering a million-dollar annual budget. Mrs. Charles Roys, secretary of the Board of Foreign Missions, explained that the women liked to raise their own funds and worried that "any missionary program for the Church which casts aside this wonder-working system of distinctive financial responsibility of women is doomed to failure." The churchmen were not persuaded. In 1923, they formed a consolidated Board of National Missions with a membership of one-third ministers, one-third laymen, one-third women. Two years later, there was a drop of 48 percent in women's contributions to the missions, and the disaffection was so marked that the church elders asked Katherine Bennett and Margaret Hodge, two leaders of the Women's Board of Foreign Missions, to investigate the "Causes of Unrest among the Women of the Church."

Their report in 1927 was devastating. They asserted that among "thinking women there arose a serious question as to whether their place of service could longer be found in the church when a great organization which they had built could be autocratically destroyed by vote of male members of the church." Churchmen who in their "benevolent paternalism" had thought it "pleasant" for women to organize and raise funds had failed to see that a new force had been unleashed. The report concluded that what women wished was "the removal of inhibitions which constantly remind them that they are not considered intellectually or spiritually equal to responsibilities within the church.

Most ask for no one thing, only that artificial inhibitions that savor of another century having been removed, they may take their place wherever and however their abilities and the need of the church may call."[18]

In the Mennonite church, women, traditionally silent partners, had founded the Mennonite Women's Missionary Society in 1912. By the 1920s they supported women in India and South America through sewing circles and provided half of the missionary force at home and abroad. On station in India they could manage their own affairs, or as one put it, "run amok." In the United States, they were severely circumscribed by the Mennonites' scriptural view of the role of women. One of the founders, Clara Steiner, expressed her ideas on women's role but was told by a male board member to "go home and raise my children, that was *all* the Lord required of me. . . . I went home and pondered and had some dark hours because of it." Missionary Mary Berkhard observed, "One does feel like telling what one thinks but on second thought when I remember what church leaders think of women's thoughts, I feel what's the use, they won't take it from us anyhow." In 1928, the churchmen took over the women's group. Ruth Yoder complained, "I think the Board had made themselves quite busy with taking over what we have." Memberships in the sewing circles and other missionary groups dropped from 8,629 to 3,000; contributions were markedly down.[19]

The leader of the Woman's American Baptist Missionary Society, Lucy W. Peabody, also fought incorporation of the women's organization into a new board. She urged church leaders to imagine the YMCA and YWCA "being able to work as effectively in a joint way as they had separately." After the merger, she observed, "Our place and contribution seem to be changing." In 1927, she expanded her concerns in a report on the Conference on Church Unity in Lausanne, Switzerland. There the seven women among the more than four hundred delegates questioned why, since women were in the majority in membership and were the major supporters of the churches, only a negligible number were invited to the conference and none was permitted to speak.[20]

In each instance of consolidation, Mennonite, Baptist, and Presbyterian women urged the churches to find an opportunity for service for their young educated women. Louise Blinn, who had been active in Presbyterian home mission work for twenty years, asserted to a committee of the General Assembly in 1929 that she would advise her college-educated daughter to look outside the church for an outlet for her considerable talent and energy. Blinn and others who saw their organizations subsumed into amalgamated boards in the name of efficiency and economy called for new roles of leadership and service. The Bennett and Hodge report had concluded that not many Presbyterian women wanted to preach; yet there were some women in the pulpits in other denominations. Presbyterian foreign mission executive Mrs. Charles Roys reviewed the status of women in the church in 1924. The Nazarenes had 350 women preachers, followed by the Cumberland Presbyterians with 25, Congregationalists with 20, Unitarians with 14, the Brethren with 10, and the Baptists–North with 5. There were also women ministers in the Universalist, United Evangelicals, Christian Scientist, and Christian churches. The Methodist Episcopal church approved the ordination of women as local preachers in 1924.[21]

The call for leadership or at least equality was perhaps most consistent and frustrating in the Presbyterian church. Four decades earlier Frances Willard had wryly commented on "the slow-moving Presbyterians." When their minister left his pulpit in 1918 to serve as a chaplain in World War I, the elders of the North Church in Elmira, New York, asked one of their well-qualified members, Mrs. Lillian Herrick Chapman, to serve. They were immediately challenged for "irregularity" and the Synod and General Assembly were asked to rule. In 1919, the Synod's judicial commission agreed that the procedure was irregular. In the same year, however, the General Assembly, approached by three presbyteries to examine women's status in the church, appointed a commission to study ways to enlarge opportunities for women. The Special Commission on the Official Relation of Women in the Church surveyed one hundred ministers and forty prominent women. The commission examined three questions: (1) what do Scriptures say? (2) what is the practice of other denominations? and (3) what are the results of the survey? They concluded that there was no scriptural barrier, noted that other denominations accepted women to any position except the ministry, and found that half of the ministers surveyed favored the ordination of women as ruling elders, giving them voice and vote in the decisions of the church. More than half of the women surveyed favored ordaining women as ministers and as elders. Yet instead of making specific recommendations, the commission asked that the presbyteries be sent an Overture: "Shall the Constitution of the Presbyterian Church in the U.S.A. be so amended as to admit properly qualified and educated women to ordination as Ruling Elders?" In 1921, the vote of the presbyteries was 13 shy of the requisite majority of 152.[22]

Three years later, Louise Blinn, president of the Women's Missionary Society of Cincinnati, angered over the reorganization of the mission boards, asserted that women were tired of acting only as a collection agency and were drifting into other work. She petitioned for the removal of sexual discrimination in all ordinations. Involved in the fundamentalist-modernist controversy, the General Assembly referred the matter to the General Council charging it to report the next year. The council advised no action since the matter had been decided so recently in 1921.

Two events moved the question forward in 1927: the thoughtful and troubling report of Bennett and Hodge on the causes of unrest among Presbyterian women and a study of the Federal Council of the Churches of Christ in America and the Federation of Women's Boards of Foreign Missions of North America. The report of their joint committee showed that of twenty-two denominations, only seven recognized women and men equally as clergy and laymen. There were 95 Congregationalist women ministers and 150 ordained by the Disciples of Christ. Fourteen did not ordain women at all; among those were the Southern Baptists, the United Lutherans, the Protestant Episcopal, and all the Reformed and Presbyterian churches. This record, the joint committee observed, existed in spite of the fact that women were the majority in congregations and meetings and provided most of the Sunday school teachers and missionaries. Their report asserted that "the whole work of the church should be planned by men and women working together." Then the church might be a "church of men and women, for men and women, by men and women."[23]

In 1929, responding to the evidence of the Bennett-Hodge report and the continuing exhortation of women at conferences in May and November, a Special Committee on the Status of Women (Bennett and Hodge were members) recommended that the General Council adopt an inclusive proposal for the removal "from the Government of any form of speech which is inconsistent with the recognition of the complete equality of men and women in the life and work of the church." Some of the testimony had been stinging; one convert from the Congregational church remarked that Presbyterians "put a premium on dumbness. You weren't to have opinions on this or that—opinions were not asked for." The council forwarded the recommendation to the General Assembly. It repeated the procedure of 1921 and polled the presbyteries not with the council's inclusive recommendation but with three Overtures: Overture A called for the full ordination of women; Overture B approved ordination of women as elders only; Overture C permitted the presbyteries to license women as local evangelists for one year. Katherine Bennett fumed at the retreat from the council's full recommendation, arguing that if it was right that women have an equal place, it should be given fully to them, and if were not, then they should have no halfway ordination as elders. The debate raged in the Presbyterian journals. With the full weight of tradition mustered by the well-organized opposition, Overtures A and C were defeated. Overture B was narrowly approved 158–118. The first five women elected to the General Assembly took their places in 1931. Disappointed but loyal, Bennett noted that her mind continued to rebel even if her heart kept her quiet.[24]

Within Reform Judaism, there were also the stirrings of change. In 1919, seventeen-year-old Martha Neumark, a student at Hebrew Union College (HUC) and the daughter of an HUC professor asked to lead the services for the High Holy Days if a pulpit were available. The faculty considered the request and divided evenly on its appropriateness. The president stated that if a congregation would accept her he would approve. But he also formed a joint faculty/Board of Governors committee to consider the larger question of rabbinic ordination. The committee voted 4–2 that there was no logical reason women should not be entitled to receive a rabbinical degree, but owing to practical considerations, committee members stated that women could not be admitted to HUC with the hope of ordination. The board then asked the Central Conference of American Rabbis whether Jewish law prohibited the ordination of women. The majority concluded that they could not logically and consistently refuse ordination, but the HUC board armed with that advice still decided in 1923 that "no change should be made in the present practice of limiting to males the right to matriculate for the purpose of entering the rabbinate." Neumark continued to study at HUC until 1924 when she earned the first certificate of Sunday school superintendentship issued by the new HUC School of Teachers. Like Bennett, Neumark was loyal but not content, asserting that since there were more women then men in the congregations and since women experienced a similar spiritual life, women should be ordained.[25]

There was no request for or consideration of ordination for women in the Roman Catholic church; yet women were called to religious life in the many and expanding orders of nuns. It was a life that offered "institutional space to women's spiritual gifts." As historian Mary Ewens observed, "Catholic nuns, though they belonged to an extremely patriarchal church whose male hierarchy defined female roles according to medieval notions that women were irresponsible, soft brained and incapable of logical thought, were in some ways the most liberated women in the nineteenth century." They supported themselves, owned property, exercised leadership, and were sustained by friendships "based on common interests and a sharing of the deepest aspirations of the human soul." By the 1890s, women in Catholic religious life outnumbered men two to one, a ratio that continued to rise in the twentieth century. Although the cloistered orders attracted only small numbers, American Catholic women in religion served as teachers, nurses, and social workers—in brief, in all the professions attracting their lay contemporaries.

As their Protestant counterparts had faced restrictions on their service and leadership in the missions, Catholic nuns encountered the 1917 changes in canon law, the first in more than six hundred years. New and highly detailed regulations for living a religious life were promulgated. Nuns might be given permission to sing in the choir of a parish church, but they were to stand where they would not be visible to the public. As at the women's colleges, the nuns faced increasing worry about particular friendships. Every five years, the heads of congregations forwarded a questionnaire to Rome as a review of how well the sisters were adhering to the new prescriptions. Nuns were, as Mary Ewens observed, "pushed back behind their cloister walls." Yet where there was a need, there was a way. In Brookline, Massachusetts, when St. Mary's parish opened a coed high school, the Sisters of St. Joseph were called in to replace the Sisters of Notre Dame de Namur, whose rule forbade the teaching of boys. The practical details of survival could be discouraging even with a vow of poverty. One community appealed for a salary of at least three hundred dollars for the sisters in 1924 since "they can hardly live on the present one." The local pastor who was building a school refused. Overall, the salaries paid to the women religious were only half that paid to the priests, who had to hire housekeepers and faced heavier living expenses.[26]

While women sought service and leadership in the mainline churches, several founded their own sects, achieving power not through ecclesiastical authority but, as women traditionally had done, through personal charisma.

The most famous preacher of the 1920s was Aimee Semple McPherson, the world's "most pulchritudinous evangelist," the "Mary Pickford of revivalism," the "Barnum of religion." Born in Canada, Aimee had early helped her mother in Salvation Army work. Converted in a Pentecostal revival, she had subsequently married Scotch evangelist Robert Semple, joining him at his revival meetings and becoming a preacher of the Pentecostal Full Gospel Assembly in 1909. She traveled to China with Semple on a brief preaching tour that ended abruptly with his sudden death, just before the birth of their first child. Returning to the United States, Aimee lectured and helped her mother in Salvation Army work before she remarried and moved to Providence, Rhode Island. Bearing another child, but increasingly restless in her marriage, she interpreted a long illness as a sign that God wanted her to preach. In 1915, she conducted a revival service and began to practice faith healing. For the next few years, she toured the East Coast in her "gospel auto," pitching her tent and giving revivals. In 1918, she ended a gospel tour in Los Angeles and made it her headquarters. She continued to tour, ranging from Montreal to Sydney, Australia, usually accompanied by her mother. In Denver her revivals in 1921 and 1922 filled the coliseum with a crowd of twelve thousand every evening for a month. In 1921 she began construction of the Angelus Temple in Los Angeles. By 1923 she had completed this $1.5 million building, amassed a following of thirty thousand, and founded her own sect, the Four Square Gospel. The temple, according to one contemporary, had "a brass band bigger and louder than Sousa's, an organ worthy of any movie cathedral, a female choir bigger and more beautiful than the Metropolitan chorus, a costume wardrobe comparable to Ziegfeld's." By the end of the decade, she owned a broadcasting station and had founded a university that graduated five hundred evangelists in 1928. She had everything but "Swedish baths and a half-mile track."

The occasionally raucous press coverage always mentioned her appearance. She weighed about 145 pounds and had large wrists and ankles, wide hips, broad shoulders, and a mass of dark red hair. Her smile was wide and friendly, her voice the "husky vibrant contralto of the midway." Observers cited her "electric quality" and "animal magnetism" and concluded that "she has It, and plenty of it."[27]

Sister Aimee preached every night and three times on Sunday to congregations of five thousand. One night there was a healing service, another a prayer night, and another a night for baptism by immersion. Volunteers manned a prayer tower in two-hour shifts; telephone counselors stood by to help with spiritual or earthly concerns. The temple offered a free employment bureau, Bible study groups, and summer camps. Food brought to the commissary as well as funds from the collection box were shared with the poor.

Her followers were described by a writer in the *Nation* as poor, undernourished, and maladjusted. A *New Republic* critic described them as "the moronic, the bucolic, the sick, the aged—and a whole army of former back-East Christians, who . . . mellowed in the warm sunshine of Paradise." On Sundays, they filled the temple an hour before the service; latecomers lined up for blocks. Her message was one of hope and salvation, not hellfire and damnation.

The service began with the blare of trumpets playing "The Stars and Stripes." The women's chorus dressed in blue sailors' jackets sang "Throw Out the Lifeline" in front of the structure of the Gospel Lighthouse. A dozen maidens clung to the Rock of Ages awaiting salvation. Sister Aimee preached in white gown with blue robe bathed in a spotlight. Critics railed against the content and the theatrical background. "No national evangelist," complained an *Outlook* writer, had ever performed with such "insufficient mental ballast." Her sermon was, complained another, "utterly devoid of sound thinking, loose and unsubstantial in its construction, preposterously inadequate in its social implications." It was also admittedly "amazingly successful." Others decried the "supernatural whoopee" and "the sensuous debauch served up in the name of religion."

At the height of her success and service, in May 1926, Aimee disappeared while swimming in the Pacific. Her followers kept an anxious vigil along the shoreline. She reappeared a month later, wandering up to a cabin in Mexico with an account of kidnapping. Her abductors were never found; the press launched an orgy of speculation on where she had been. Had she "gone off" with Kenneth Ormiston, a former member of her staff? Had she, overwrought and overworked, sought to disappear and leave her pulpit? Had she really been abducted? The questions were dragged out when she was indicted for obstruction of justice, a charge later dropped for lack of evidence. She returned to the Angelus Temple with even more followers attracted to her in her hour of need. She remained, as the California magazine *Sunset* pointed out, "shepherdess of one of the world's great religious revivals."[28]

Two other remarkable preachers and leaders founded their own churches in the expansion of Pentecostal and Holiness groups in the 1920s, Bishop Alma White and Elder Lucy Smith. White, the seventh of eleven children, worked in her father's Kentucky tannery as a young girl and, determined to escape that drudgery, won enough schooling to become a frontier schoolteacher in Montana. Though she longed to be a preacher, she was advised that the only way to even approach the pulpit was to marry a minister. She took that advice, wed Methodist missionary Kent White, and led hymns and sometimes did the readings at White's services. By 1893, she was convinced that she should preach. She led highly successful revival meetings, never writing out her sermons, but waiting for the "heavenly dynamite." When the explosion came, she was able to move her listeners to jump, skip, and shout in the joy of conversion. The Methodist church, which had once welcomed her to the pulpit but was distressed at the physical excitement, forbade her to preach in 1901. Undaunted, White formed her own sect, the Methodist Pentecostal Union, renamed in 1917 the Pillar of Fire Church. She moved her headquarters and built her major church in Zaraphath, New Jersey. Her congregation expanded over the next thirty years to more than four thousand. The first woman bishop of any Christian church in America, the indefatigable Alma White preached three or four times a day at revival meetings. She crossed the Atlantic fifty-eight times; in one year she traveled fifty thousand miles on the railroad. Like Sister Aimee, Bishop White owned radio stations, one in Denver, the other in New Jersey. She edited seven magazines and established seven schools. In 1921 she started the Alma White College in New Jersey. Author of more than two hundred hymns, she published seven volumes of poetry.

Elder Lucy Smith left Atlanta in 1909 and became part of the black migration to Chicago. Reared a Baptist, she joined a white Pentecostal group at Stone Church where she received her calling of "divine healing." She began prayer sessions and healing in her home. Described as a "black puritan preaching holiness," Smith conducted services that, like White's, were interrupted by shouting, rolling, and speaking in tongues. Blacks and whites were welcome at her services. She urged, "Come to my Church more often and witness how many hundreds of men and women I heal." Her success in the laying on of hands won her a wide following, but she asserted her converts came for other reasons, explaining: "I started with giving advice to folks in my neighborhood. This made me realize how much a good talking does to many people." Like Sister Aimee, her message was "not about sad things, but always about being saved." She stated, "The singing in my church has 'swing' to it, because I want my people to swing out of themselves all the mis'ry and troubles that is heavy on their hearts." The contributions of her large following enabled her to establish the All Nations Pentecostal Church in the 1930s.[29]

Sister Aimee, Bishop White, and Elder Smith echoed the leaders of the mainline churches in crying for Christian witness in dangerous times. Though rarely summoned to the pulpit, women were called to action to help stem the tide of revolution in morals and manners challenging Protestantism and Americanism. The disillusion with Versailles, the success of Godless communism in Russia which threatened to spill over its borders into Hungary, Germany, and even the United States, the economic strains of the postwar boom and bust, the lingering depression on the farm coupled with apprehension of the growth of power and population in the cities—all combined to begin the decade with the Red Scare and the wartime cry for 100 percent Americanism. Protestant, Catholic, and Jewish women could rally to the familiar charge to do battle against crime and immorality; it was harder to keep their unity in defense of the old American way.[30]

In the search for causes and scapegoats for the erosion of American morals, the churches focused on youth and women. A writer in the *Literary Digest* detailed "The Case against the Younger Generation" in 1922:

There is such a thing as Bolshevism in the moral and spiritual spheres. . . . We are suffering from its effects at the present time. A spirit of libertinism is abroad among our young. There is little or no respect for parents and superiors in many of our homes and schools and churches. There is an ominous lack of reverence for things sacred of noble ambition and earnest moral purpose, and a bold and brazen defiance of decency and modesty in dress and speech and conduct. Women paint and powder and drink and smoke, and become an easy prey to a certain class of well-groomed and well-fed high livers whose chief business is to pluck the blush of innocency from off the cheek of maidenhood and put a blister there.[31]

The religious press raised the loudest cry of anguish. The Presbyterian magazine *Mississippi Visitor* warned of a "very decided break in the moral levee." The Jesuit publication *America* thundered, "We have gotten into a spiritual mess that demands immediate remedial measures." For multitudes, the *Christian Advocate* announced, "life is nothing but a giggle." The *Lutheran* urged parents in the home and preachers in the pulpit to "burn with holy wrath against the evils of the day" in a society that was "Pleasure-Wild and Enjoyment-Crazy." The *Baptist* asserted "Butterfly life is in the ascendance and everywhere conspicuous." The Episcopalian periodical the *Living Church* complained that not all the butterflies were young. The new life-style was spreading: "Grandma bobs her hair and puts rouge on her face. Grandpa puts away the pipe of dignity for the cigaret of impudence."[32]

The trendsetter was the flapper. Willard Thorp, writing in the sober *Forum*, decried the "Flapper Age"; the dean of the Graduate School of the University of Southern California bemoaned the "pernicious near-cult of what might be called flapperolatry." *America* inveighed against the flapper who depended "daily on a row of pots of paints and pomades," whose lips imitated "a gash hastily inflicted by an unskilled surgeon," who sat in bondage to "a parcel of barbers who put mud on her face and pull out her eyebrows." The *Presbyterian Banner* agreed that it was "pitiful to see the face painted and overlaid with all manner of these artificial enhancements that are not even skin deep and will wash off like whitewash, while the deeper face of the soul is unadorned and marred with an unhappy disposition and evil spirit."[33]

The clerical concern for painted faces was matched by distress at thinly clothed limbs. In Philadelphia a Dress Reform Committee sent a questionnaire to one thousand clergymen in fifteen denominations, asking for a description of proper dress. From the responses the committee devised a loose-fitting gown with sleeves below the elbows and a hem seven and a half inches from the floor. In New York City, staunch Episcopal churchwomen, led by Mrs. J. Pierpont Morgan, Mrs. Borden Harriman, and Mrs. Henry Phipps, proposed organizing against the excess of nudity in fashions. From Rome, Pope Pius XI launched a crusade against increased immodesty in 1927 and urged Catholic husbands, fathers, and brothers to check the ugly "ruinous catastrophical tendency." The National Council of Catholic Women (NCCW) sent out pledge cards to their 700,000 members, urging the signers to "observe in private and public life the standards of Catholic teaching, particularly with regard to dress, reading, and entertainments." The head of the Catholic Big Sisters of Brooklyn asserted that the clothes had become so extreme that it was "not a question of decency" but simply a matter of being "esthetic." Mrs. Michael Gavin, the president of the NCCW, modeled a dress deemed modest by the organizations. Sleeves, though transparent, reached to the hand; the loose-flowing gown stopped just short of the ankles. Yet skirts rose to the knee by 1927 and remained there until the end of the decade; young, middle-aged, and even some elderly women continued to shed petticoats and corsets.[34]

The flapper who smoked also concerned the churchmen. The *Presbyterian* warned that a man was ill advised to choose a wife "who habitually fills the circumambient atmosphere with ill-smelling exhalations." The Methodists pleaded with women: "Crush the habit! Be merciless. . . . And America's manhood will rise up and call you blessed." At the end of the decade, they added a health warning to the admonitions against a habit so "foreign to the ideal of womanly decency" by noting that many physicians worried about the children of mothers who were nicotine addicts.[35]

The half-dressed, fast-stepping female on the dance floor was even more alarming. The *Lutheran* observed: "It is not difficult to guess why boys do not care to dance with 'old ironsides,' and why some girls like that particular style of dance which bans corsets." The *Lutheran Witness* went further, asserting that modern dance was "undeniably indulgence in fleshly lust," a "training school for fornicating." The *Lutheran* denounced the "close-grip dance" and the "white heat sex stimulation" of "the dance of death." Methodists refused to admit dancing teachers to church membership unless they repented of "teaching lasciviousness and adultery and of ruining homes and youth." The dance marathons carried all these evils to extremes; they were, asserted the *Lutheran Witness*, a "symptom of mental breakdown, the result of over-indulgence in that hideous shuffling and squirming of men and women locked in close embrace."[36]

A whole range of other amusements presented difficulties. The automobile exemplified the obsession with "speeditis" in society. The *Lutheran* asked, "Need we wonder that nerves are being rocked and that the most prevalent and stubborn diseases that physicians have to deal with are nervous diseases?" A Methodist writer agreed that Americans were "going nowhere at the rate of sixty miles an hour." Yet worse than what people were doing to one another *with* cars—casualties at the rate of one every forty-two seconds in 1927—was what they were doing *in* them. The *Baptist* pleaded for more motorized police to check the "carnival of lust."[37]

The movies presented another technological intrusion into the old ways. The storm of criticism of the portrayal of sex and morality had led to Hollywood's circling of the wagons and the appointment of Will Hays, President Harding's former post master-general, to clean up Gomorrah. Charles McMahan, who regularly reported on the movies in the *National Catholic Welfare Conference Bulletin*, ticked off a litany of cinema evils in 1921: "unwholesome sex appeals, adultery, unfaithfulness, moral laxity, indecent dressing and undressing, crime, disrespect for law, for religion, and for plain morality." All were "shamefully portrayed under the guise of 'art' in a large percentage of the film factories." Catholics were ready to fight. The National Catholic Welfare Confer-

ence through the National Council of Catholic Men and the National
Council of Catholic Women (NCCW) pledged 20 million Catholics to an
"unrelenting fight against immoral and unwholesome motion pictures."
The NCCW promised to discourage attendance at theaters showing ob-
jectionable films. By 1924, the *Lutheran* believed there had been some
progress. The "terrible sex slush" and "brazen immoral suggestiveness"
no longer appeared. The *Presbyterian Banner* was not convinced, however, asserting that the movie business was "about as demoralizing as
the old time drinking saloons and disreputable houses."[38]

Bathing beauty contests were also deplored. The *Presbyterian Banner*
protested women parading in front of "ogling eyes," concluding that
"the whole thing is vulgar and debasing." The NCCW passed a sweeping
resolution at its 1927 convention: "against those violations of womanly
dignity known as beauty contests, against the moving pictures, the
magazines, the books that lower the dignity of the Christian girl and
the Christian mother." The NCCW urged all Catholic women to "work
for the fuller restoration of the divine-given dignity" of womanhood.[39]

Although Protestant, Catholic, and Jewish women could unite in
their concern over the inroads of "jazzocracy," the affront of Atlantic
City Miss America pageants, and Theda Bara's vamping, their community of interest dissolved when the values and the morality to be
defended were translated into an American way of life, which was
understood by Protestants to be theirs, born in New England and nur-
tured on the frontier and the broad countryside. The growing ascendancy of the city in population and the ethnic mix of that population
led to fears that "newer Americans" would dominate the culture and
set the values. Old-stock, Protestant, rural Americans seemed to be
losing. H. L. Mencken, ready to cheer their discomfort, observed,
"Every day a new Catholic church goes up; and every day another
Methodist or Presbyterian church is turned into a garage." "Protestantism," he concluded, "is down with a wasting disease." There was a read-
iness then, among some Protestants struggling for economic survival
on the farm or those who collided with Italian or Jewish Americans in
the city, to support the slogan of the Ku Klux Klan: "America is Protestant and so it must remain."[40]

The "old-time religion" was pervasive in Klan rhetoric and leadership. The architect of the Klan's renewal in 1915, Colonel William J.
Simmons, had once been a preacher. The Stone Mountain, Georgia,

meeting that launched the new Klan was illuminated with a fiery cross; members were initiated before a flag-draped altar. Simmons had written up the Klan ritual in the Kloran. Each Klan had a chaplain, or kludd. The kloxology was read at each initiation. Protestant hymns were adapted to Klan words. Protestant ministers were given free memberships, and Klan lectureships proved attractive to some underpaid ministers. Frequently, Klan members in full regalia appeared at the rear of Methodist or Baptist services and contributed twenty-five dollars ostentatiously into the collection boxes.

Though the initial concerns of the Klan were "uppity Negroes" and wartime slackers, and though the largest number of physical attacks by Klansmen were perpetrated on white Protestants, by 1921, Catholics were perceived as the major enemy. In the summer of that year, a Klansman and Methodist minister shot a Catholic priest on his doorstep; in Illinois, Klansmen torched a Catholic church after an initiation ceremony. The governor of Alabama instituted convent inspections to ensure that no women were being kept against their wills. In Indiana Klansmen agreed not to patronize Catholic or Jewish stores. Pledging their allegiance to the Bible and the flag, Klansmen saw themselves allied with the churches in the struggle for righteousness.[41]

Denominationally, most of the support for the Klan came from the Baptist, Methodists, and Disciples of Christ, though many Methodist bishops were hostile to the Klan. Presbyterians, Episcopalians, Lutherans, Universalists, and Congregationalist leaders were generally opposed to the Klan. The only church group formally supporting it was Bishop Alma White's Pillar of Fire Church.[42]

White wrote three books supporting the Klan. In *The Ku Klux Klan and Prophecy* in 1925, she examined biblical passages to establish that the Klan was approved by God. The apostles and the good samaritan were Klansmen, she asserted. One year later her *Klansmen: Guardians of Liberty* began with an introduction by the Grand Dragon, Realm of New Jersey, and the assertion that she was revealing the true program of the Roman Catholic hierarchy "to control the minds of men and to take from them their own desire for liberty and freedom." In her own text, White thundered: "Roman Catholicism is paganism, and cannot be called Christian in any sense. The worship of the Virgin Mary sprang from the old pagan custom of worshipping some goddess." Three presidents had been shot by men raised as Roman Catholics. She called for inspection of the "prisons" of convents, monasteries, and the House of Good Shepherd homes for wayward girls. Two years later, in *Heroes of the Fiery Cross*, she asserted that neither Judaism nor Roman Catholicism had any use for the Christian church.[43]

Americans who followed Alma White's exhortations in support of the Klan did so for a variety of reasons. A *Baltimore Sun* reporter described Klan members on Maryland's Eastern Shore as "mainly perfectly good, kindly people, generally without anything to occupy their minds when they quit work, looking for novelties, attracted by the idea of something mysterious, perhaps a little thrilled at the suggestion that they are members of a band pledged to support 'Americanism.'" Kansas editor William Allen White urged readers to "look at their shoes," depicting them as potential Horatio Algers who had been left at the post in the race for success in consumer America. Historian John Higham placed them in the recurrent nativist context, defenders of the old way of life against the incursions of "strangers in the land." All would agree that the union of the Bible and the flag in Klan rhetoric was a powerful recruitment device. Initiated before cross and altar, a new Klansman could feel both moral and patriotic.[44]

Women were recruited into auxiliary units by the national and local leadership. Few rose to positions of influence, and when they did so, it was usually as the wife of the local Kleagle or Goblin. One exception on the national level was Elizabeth Tyler who, with Edward A. Clark, joined Colonel Simmons in 1920 and brought business and public relations expertise to his fledgling operation. It was Clark and Tyler who helped set the membership fees and the percentage of the initiation fee that stayed with the local Kleagle or flowed to national headquarters in Atlanta. They helped establish the Gate City manufacturing company that produced the white robes. Their contribution was commercial, however, not moral.

There were two efforts to organize Klanswomen on the national level in 1923. Colonel Simmons issued a call for women to form the Kamelias in April, but that invitation quickly became embroiled in internecine squabbling at the national office. The incoming Imperial Wizard Hiram Wesley Evans forbade Klanswomen to join the Simmons group. However, there was a two-day Kamelia convention in Tulsa, Oklahoma. Several hundred representatives showed their allegiance by marching through the central business district. A more enduring organization began in Little Rock. Encouraged by Grand Dragon Judge James Conner, the women were led by Robbie Gill, who later married the judge who "called the tune." In 1927, the Gill-Conner organization, the Women of the Ku Klux Klan, held the First Imperial Klonvocation at St. Louis and issued a Konstitution. It was a compendium of God and country rhetoric:

We the Order of the Women of the Ku Klux Klan reverently acknowledge the majesty and supremacy of almighty God and recognize His goodness and providence through Jesus Christ, our Lord.

We shall ever be devoted to the sublime principles of a pure Americanism and reliant in the defence of its ideals and institution.

We avow the distinction between the races of mankind as decreed by the Creator, and we shall ever be true to the maintenance of white supremacy.[45]

Klanswomen were active on the state level. They were "indispensable elements in hooded political success" in campaigns in Denver, Portland, Indianapolis, Chicago, and Dallas. In Memphis and Maryland, they unsuccessfully fought Boss Crump and "wet" Governor Ritchie. In the 1924 "bonnet or hood" contest, they battled Miriam Amanda "Ma" Ferguson, supporting her opponent with his campaign against the "Jew, Jug, and Jesuit." The Klan promised to see that "the young man who induces a young girl to get drunk" would be punished. A Klan broadside summed up the issues: "Every criminal, every thug, every libertine, every gambler, every home wrecker, every wife beater, every dope peddler, every moonshiner, every crooked politician, every pagan Papist priest, every shyster lawyer, every K. of C., every white slaver, every brothel madam, every Rome controlled newspaper, every black spider—is fighting the Klan. Think it over, which side are you on?" "Ma," helped mightily by her husband's campaign style and his focus on Klan violence and lambasting of "longhorn Texas Ku Koos," carried the day.[46]

The position of the women was, however, subsidiary. In Pennsylvania, the Philadelphia Klan leader removed the head of the women's KKK arbitrarily; the men swindled funds collected by the women and were deaf to protests of immoral conduct of a local leader with two Klanswomen. The Philadelphia and Chester women were driven to rebellion and quit.[47]

In Indiana, immoral conduct brought down D. C. Stephenson, state Klan boss and hopeful candidate for Hiram Wesley Evans's Imperial Wizard post. Stephenson took staff member Madge Oberholtzer on a weekend trip to Chicago. On the train, Stephenson, who was drunk and out of control, allegedly attacked Oberholtzer. She arrived in Chicago badly bruised and proceeded to take poison. Frightened, Stephenson reportedly refused to take her to a hospital unless she agreed to marry him. She steadfastly refused. Medical help in Indiana was administered too late and Oberholtzer died. Stephenson, indicted and convicted of second-degree murder, was angry that the Klansmen whom he had put into state offices were not able to save him from prison, and he made his records available to press and public.[48]

Klan political power peaked by mid-decade. Antimasking laws from Illinois to Maryland proved major deterrents to parades and demonstrations. In the cities and in the Northeast and Midwest, the Klan was increasingly beleaguered. When a Klan recruiter spoke at Alma White's Pillar of Fire Church, irate neighbors surrounded the building and hurled stones at the congregation huddled inside. In Perth Amboy, New Jersey, an angry crowd of six thousand, led by Jews and Catholics, did battle with five hundred Klansmen. In Steubenville, Ohio, three thousand attacked a hundred Klansmen after an initiation ceremony.[49]

Primarily, however, Jews and Roman Catholics, on the defensive, reacted to Klan rhetoric and organization by rhetoric and organization of their own, stressing their patriotism and contributions to America. A half-page ad in the Baltimore *Catholic Review* stated, "The Best Answer is Cardinal Gibbons, Churchman and Citizen." The *Catholic Review*'s emphasis on good citizenship was echoed throughout the decade in the resolutions of the National Catholic Welfare Conference (NCWC), which issued a call in September 1921 to Catholic women to organize. Women, the NCWC urged, "who have been the leaven of the parishes must now come to a realization that America is their parish and help to leaven the whole national life."[50]

The size of the undertaking and the initial enthusiasm were evident in an organizational meeting in January 1921 at the 48th Street Theater in New York City. A thousand women, unable to gain entry into the jammed theater, stood in the street to hear an address by Archbishop Patrick J. Hayes. The new national president of the NCCW, Mrs. Michael Gavin, hailed the gathering as evidence "that the great national movement inaugurated by the Hierarchy to unify and coordinate the strength and activities of the splendid Catholic womanhood of America is really epoch-making in its significance." Aided by NCCW executive secretary Agnes Regan, the organization set its goal for a million members in 1922. The New York City meeting was paralleled by mass meetings in Chicago, Pittsburgh, Milwaukee, Boston, San Francisco, and Hartford. The NCCW worked with immigrants, supported the new National Catholic School of Social Service, worked against birth control "propaganda" and eugenics, fought the ERA and aid to public education, and rejoiced as the Supreme Court overturned the Oregon school law that would have prohibited parochial schools in that state. Its purpose, consistently reiterated, was "the preservation of the integrity of the home; the bringing of women's conduct and decency into the determination of great questions of public policy; and the exercise of the influence usually imposed by the presence and companionship of pure womanhood."[51]

Jewish women organized in the National Council of Jewish Women, the National Federation of Temple Sisterhoods, the Women's League of the United Synagogues of America, and the Women's Branch of the Union of Orthodox Jewish Congregations of America. Although divided by ethnic and class background and by religious practices as Reformed or Orthodox, Jewish women were stirred by the strong Zionism after World War I. Hadassah was the largest Zionist group in the United States by 1930. The Junior Hadassah was organized in the 1920s with the slogan "Every member of Junior Hadassah is an American, a Jew and a Zionist. She is not one time one, another time another, she is all three in one." Jewish women, cherishing their Jewishness, saw full assimilation into a hostile gentile society as a threat to their heritage and identity. They, more than Jewish men, married within the faith and sought to return to the study of Hebrew and the sources of Jewish culture.[52]

Earnestly avowing their faith, their patriotism, and their own commitment to moral values, most Roman Catholics and Jews never actually confronted a Klansman. Their lives and their culture were more immediately touched by Prohibition, the final great crusade of rural Protestant America to sustain the "old moral order" of town and countryside in an increasingly urban, sophisticated, and pluralist society. Demon rum was the bond that united Klansmen and churchmen in a "kind of Protestant revival." Columnist Walter Lippmann described the Eighteenth Amendment as "the rock on which the evangelical church militant is founded." It stood for "a whole way of life and an ancient tradition."[53]

The major denominational support for Prohibition came from the Methodists, Baptists, Presbyterians, Congregationalists, Mormons, Christian Scientists, and Disciples of Christ. Leading all the rest in the length and intensity of its commitment was Methodism, called by one observer "Christianity in earnest." The two major organizations carrying the battle were closely linked to these churches. The first in the field was the Women's Christian Temperance Union (WCTU). Founded in the 1870s, the WCTU grew rapidly under the effective leadership of Frances Willard. She drafted their pledge: "I hereby solemnly promise, God helping me, to abstain from all Alcoholic Liquors . . . , from opium in all its forms and to employ all proper means to discourage the use of and traffic in the same." The early proper methods were prayer meetings. The women then walked singing in a group to a saloon and, if permitted to enter, petitioned the bartender to shut down. A historian of these early years saw the WCTU appeal to women in its connection to "the Protestant churches, practical support of the nurturent home, and implicit acceptance of the moral superiority of women." The WCTU joined other women in the Progressive movement and honed its political skills and power in a broad range of causes to protect the home. In 1893, its temperance efforts were joined by the new Anti-Saloon League. Calling itself the "Protestant church in action," the Anti-Saloon League, with thirty thousand affiliated churches, muscled Prohibition through state legislatures and the Congress in a masterful lobbying campaign.[54]

The rhetoric in the campaign and in the aftermath of victory linked Prohibition with Americanism and morality. Methodist bishop James Cannon asserted, "It cannot be too strongly emphasized that the Prohibition movement in the United States has been Christian in its inspiration." Anna Gordon, former secretary to Frances Willard, national president of the WCTU from 1914 to 1925 and president of the World WCTU from 1922 to 1933, stated, "We are co-workers with God to bring about world sobriety, world morality, and world peace." Her successor, Ella Boole, who had served as a national administrator for the Women's Home Missionary Societies of the Presbyterian church, declared her love of country in 1928: "As my forefathers worked and struggled to build it, so will I work and struggle to maintain it unsullied by foreign influences, uncontaminated by vices and poison. Its people are my people, its institutions are my institutions, its strength is my strength, its traditions are my traditions, its enemies are my enemies and its enemies shall not prevail."[55]

The WCTU issued a call for a million members by 1924, but by that year, that organization, the Anti-Saloon League, and their Klan allies in the dry crusade were increasingly on the defensive. The migration of millions fleeing the lean yields of the countryside for city jobs and opportunities weakened their political power. Frustratingly apparent were the weak, inept, and underfunded enforcement efforts, the burgeoning crime wave (most notorious in Chicago gunfights between Al Capone and rival bootleg factions), and the flagrant violations in major cities from San Francisco to New York. Speaking to the state WCTU convention in December 1923, Pennsylvania governor Gifford Pinchot reported that at one saloon patrons were standing forty-one deep around the bar. Crowds walked in and out while a policeman stood at the door. It was obvious that urban Americans were breaking the law, stubbornly clinging to their wet ways.[56]

The wet coalition brought together the wealth and cultural sophistication represented in the organization of the American Association against the Prohibition Amendment (AAPA) and the ethnic, primarily Catholic, working class. Led by William Stayton, the Du Ponts, and industrial magnate and Democratic power John J. Raskob, the AAPA started its uphill battle on the high ground of individual rights and liberties and the appalling breakdown in the social fabric. It organized Molly Pitcher Clubs in New York and Pennsylvania, women's auxiliaries to join in lobbying Congress for repeal. In 1929, however, the women, led by Pauline Morton Sabin, launched their own effort, the Women's Organization for National Prohibition Repeal (WONPR). Sabin, the wife of Charles Hamilton Sabin, AAPA member and chairman of the board of Guaranty Trust, served on the Republican National Committee and was a delegate to the Republican National Conventions in 1924 and 1928. She originally supported Prohibition, attracted by "a world without liquor" as a world in which to raise her sons. But she became increasingly concerned that her children and others were growing up with a total lack of respect for the Constitution and for the law. In 1928, when she listened to Ella Boole claim before a congressional committee, "I represent the women of America," Sabin said to herself, "Well, lady, here's one woman you don't represent." She loyally supported Hoover in the presidential campaign and then resigned her post on the Republican National Committee. She testified before the House Judiciary Committee, "Today in any speakeasy in the United States you can find boys and girls in their teens drinking liquor." At least in the past, saloon keepers who sold to minors lost their licenses. Now there was no check. Sabin devoted her considerable organizational skills to the WONPR. She tapped her friends, Mrs. Casper Whitney, Mrs. Cortland Nicoll, and Mrs. Coffin Van Rensselaer of New York, Mrs. William Lowell Putnam of Boston, Mrs. Pierre S. Du Pont of

Delaware, and other wealthy and socially prominent women for contributions. By 1931, the WONPR claimed 300,000 members in thirty-
three states. It was the largest anti-Prohibition organization in America,
thrice the size of the AAPA.[57] Two years later, a victim of organized
opposition, flagrant violation, and, most significantly, the economic
depression, the Eighteenth Amendment was repealed. The AAPA and
WONPR had achieved their goal.

Walter Lippmann described the changing of the guard: "The evil
which the old-fashioned preachers ascribe to the Pope, to atheists, and
to the devil is simply the new urban civilization with its irresistible
scientific and economic and mass power. The Pope, the devil, jazz, the
bootleggers are a mythology which expresses symbolically the impact
of a vast and dreaded social change." Half a century later, historian
Sidney Ahlstrom agreed that "the debacle of Prohibition functioned
both as evidence and the cause of the churches' loss of authority in a
culture where urban values became primary."[58]

Women were at the center of the struggle. Some were the miscreants
and flappers challenging the old ways; others mounted the battlements
in their defense. As the traditional guardians of morality, women had
been securely anchored in the church and home and family. These
moorings seemed increasingly tenuous. The emerging dominance of
the city, the technology and commercialism of the decade, the postwar
letdown of idealism paired with postwar paranoia—all posed challenges
to long held values. In the 1920s old America faced newer Americans,
the countryside faced the city, Protestant faced Catholic and Jew, rich
and poor faced the middle class, old faced young. Called to action by
their churches, Roman Catholic and Jewish women made some organizational gains; within the mainline Protestant denominations, women
experienced the generational pattern they had met in education and in
the professions. Hard-won advances of the older generation were reversed or barely sustained by the middle generation. The young generation, to the distress of grandmothers and mothers, cared little for
the battle or the cause.

Clara Bow, the "It" Girl.

CHAPTER EIGHT

The Cultural Landscape

> Did other generations ever laugh so hard together, drink and
> dance so hard, or do crazier things just for the hell of it? Perhaps
> some did—most certainly they did—but they did not leave
> behind such vivid records of their crazy parties and their
> mornings after. . . . They had taken more liberties than other
> people, and in return they had accepted the duty of portraying
> their new world honestly, in all its exultation and heartbreak.
>
> *Malcolm Cowley, A Second Flowering*[1]

The cultural ferment of the 1920s, so troubling to institutions and so
challenging to individuals, produced an artistic explosion. A dazzling
array of artists cut across generations and gender. In 1920, F. Scott
Fitzgerald's *This Side of Paradise*, Sinclair Lewis's *Main Street*, Willa
Cather's *A Lost Lady*, Edith Wharton's *The Age of Innocence*, and Edna
St. Vincent Millay's *A Few Figs from Thistles* amply heralded Cather's
later pronouncement that the "world broke in two in 1922 or thereabouts." Reeling from the cataclysm of war, the erosion of tradition,
and the commercialism of Coolidge prosperity, writers and artists grappled with the central questions of civilization and survival. How to find
the words and forms to describe a world seemingly devoid of anchor
or lodestar? How to capture in their lives and formulate in their art the
sense of wonder, the cluster of values that would bring integrity, dignity, and hope?

In the rejection of tradition and the quest for new forms and values,
the young men, scarred and wounded from the war, claimed special
insights and knowledge and rushed their experience into print. They
were and they created the "lost generation." Generation was the key
word. Literary historian Frederick Hoffman found it an essential distinction. The "old gang" of Sinclair Lewis, Theodore Dreiser, H. L.

Mencken, and Sherwood Anderson, he observed, reflected on the abuses and shortcomings of tradition; the new generation, armed with a "useful innocence," assumed the task of renewing the culture, of finding new principles. Poet Ezra Pound set the division more trenchantly, finding "an anemia of guts on one side and anemia of education on the other."[2] Malcom Cowley, one of the young generation, saw additional divisions in gender and ethnicity. The "admired writers of the generation were men in the great majority," white Protestant men, he asserted. The greatest women poets and storytellers were of an earlier or later time; the Jewish and black writers would emerge in the 1930s. Yet if gender, not generation, is taken as the prism, the creative landscape of the 1920s is dramatically changed. The decade brought a rich outpouring of women writers and artists that transcended generation and race. In their living and in their writing, in the matter of values and survival, women, too, had a special knowledge to share.

Edmund Wilson pointed out the special way stations on the artists' pilgrimage through the decade, explaining: "When you're in Galesburg, Illinois, you want to get to Chicago; then when you get to Chicago, you want to make good in New York. Then when you do put it over in New York, what in God's name have you got? The thoroughly depressing companionship of a lot of other poor smalltowners like yourself who don't know what the hell to do with themselves either! . . . You think it would be better in Paris, but then when you get to Paris, you find the same old fizzled-out people."[3] From Paris the journey wound home through New York and, for some, on to the southwest to Taos or Hollywood. Paths crisscrossed in Greenwich Village, Harlem, Montparnasse; groups gathered in salons, studios, and at the Algonquin Round Table. They roved in bands, Cowley observed, finally retiring "from the herd like old rogue bull elephants."[4] In each location and in each group, women were important contributors, companions, midwives.

With Chicago as a starting point, the career of Margaret Anderson provides an example of midwife, the interaction of life and art, and the eastward journey from Chicago to Paris. Born into a comfortable middle-class family in Indianapolis, Anderson, after teaching herself to type and completing some course work in a small college, persuaded her father in 1908 to let her and her younger sister strike out on their own in Chicago. She wrote reviews for a religious weekly, worked as a clerk in a bookstore, and then joined the staff of the *Dial* and wrote reviews for the *Evening Post*. By 1913, she was reviewing over a hundred books a week, enjoying concerts of the Chicago Symphony, and joining the literary gatherings at the apartment of Floyd Dell and Margaret Curry. At twenty-one, tired and somewhat bored, she saw that it was "time to confer upon life that inspiration without which life is meaningless."

She conceived of the *Little Review* with a series of precise thoughts: "First precise thought: I know why I'm depressed—nothing inspired is going on. Second: I demand that life be inspired every moment. Third: the only way to guarantee this is to have inspired conversation every moment. Fourth: most people never get so far as conversation; they haven't the stamina, and there is no time. Fifth: if I had a magazine I could spend my time filling it up with the best conversation the world has to offer. Sixth: marvelous idea—salvation. Seventh: decision to do it. Deep sleep."[5] Personally pounding the pavements for subscriptions and contributions, Anderson launched the *Little Review* in March 1914. The first issue carried articles on feminism, Nietzsche, and psychoanalysis. Articles by Emma Goldman, Ezra Pound, Amy Lowell, Hamlin Garland, Hilda Doolittle, Hart Crane, and Gertrude Stein followed. Serving as foreign editor, Ezra Pound observed that "no editor in America, save Margaret Anderson, ever felt the need of or responsibility for, getting the best writers concentrated . . . brought together in an American periodical." To save expenses in one particularly lean summer, Anderson, accompanied by her sister's family and two friends, pitched five tents and squatted by the lake north of Chicago. Her only disappointment was her inability to arrange delivery of her grand piano to the beach.

Joined in 1916 by Jane Heap as coeditor and housemate, Anderson and the *Little Review* moved to New York in 1917. Their apartment became a gathering place for poets, artists, and characters. The most dazzling poet-character was Baroness Elsa von Freytag-Loringhoven. Disillusioned when William Carlos Williams's present to her of peaches did not signify his undying love, the baroness shaved her head, lacquered it a high vermilion, made a dress from a crepe stolen from the door of a house of mourning, and arrived at the Anderson-Heap apartment. Anderson reported: "First she exhibited the head at all angles, amazing against our black walls. Then she jerked off the crepe with one movement. 'It's better when I'm nude,' she said. It was very good. But we were just as glad that some of our more conservative friends didn't choose that moment to drop in." In 1918, the *Little Review* began to

publish installments of James Joyce's *Ulysses*. Four issues were confis-
cated by the postal authorities as obscene. In December 1920, Anderson and Heap were indicted and subsequently fined a hundred dollars.
In 1922 Anderson left for Paris, and Heap continued to edit the *Little
Review*. The final issue fittingly was in 1929. It had been, concluded
one critic, "an extremely honest, naive, and audacious representation
of a many-sided and tumultuous period."[6]

Anderson was only the most flamboyant of a remarkable cluster of
significant woman editors in Chicago and New York promoting and
fostering the creative outpouring of the 1920s. From 1925 to 1929, poet
Marianne Moore was acting editor of the *Dial*. Early in the decade,
poet Elinor Wylie was literary editor of *Vanity Fair*. Irita Van Doren
served as literary editor of the *Nation* from 1923 to 1926 and as book
review editor of the *New York Herald Tribune*. Jessie R. Fauset, literary
editor of the *Crisis*, made that journal a showcase for young writers of
the Harlem Renaissance. She was, according to Langston Hughes, one
of those "who midwifed the so-called New Negro literature into
being."[7]

In Paris, Margaret Anderson met three other midwives, women who
anchored the network of American artists in their salons and shops.
The closest to Anderson in temperament and life-style was Natalie
Barney. "Born with every advantage—not only wealth but beauty, talent, intelligence, and an extraordinary magnetism," Barney like Anderson was from the Midwest, the daughter of wealthy parents of Dayton,
Ohio. Like Anderson, too, she believed in making her life a work of
art. Described as "the most daring and candid lesbian of her time,"
Barney and her love affairs were the subject of several novels. She began her own writing career in 1900 with *Quelques portraits—sonnets des
femmes*. Before World War I she moved to 20 rue Jacob and made that
address an international salon and "literary landmark" for the next sixty
years. Her weekly receptions brought Gertrude Stein, Colette, Edith
Sitwell, Ford Madox Ford, Djuna Barnes, T. S. Eliot, André Gide,
and Ezra Pound together. Her *Pensées d'une Amazone*, a collection of
epigrams, captures some of the wit of the discussions at the salon. Late
in the 1920s, she established an Academie des Femmes, giving women
writers an opportunity to read their work. For over forty years she
shared her life with artist Romaine Brooks.[8]

Another American who served as midwife and go-between was Sylvia Beach. The daughter of a Presbyterian minister, Beach had spent
her teens in Paris where her father served as assistant pastor of the

American Church. Though the family returned to the United States in 1906, they regularly visited France. Beach, accompanied by her younger sister, returned in 1917 to study and assist in Red Cross efforts. Her studies took her to the bookshop–gathering place of Adrienne Monnier. Monnier became her friend and professional colleague and helped Beach, backed by her mother's life savings, establish an English-language bookstore, Shakespeare and Company. When she moved the shop to rue de l'Odeon across the street from Monnier, the street became, in T. S. Eliot's view, the center of "the Franco-Anglo-American literary world of Paris." Beach's customers and supporters quickly included Gertrude Stein, Ezra Pound, Sherwood Anderson, Robert McAlmon, Margaret Anderson, Djuna Barnes, and Katherine Anne Porter. Shakespeare and Company became an informal club, bookstore, post office. In 1922, Beach helped with the transcription and almost single-handedly arranged for the first publication of Joyce's *Ulysses*. She frequently took traveling American artists to the most prestigious of the Paris salons, the home and studio of Gertrude Stein at 27 rue de Fleurus.[9]

Gertrude Stein's home was "the place to see" and she was "a person to consult." The youngest of seven children, Stein like Beach had spent her early years traveling in Europe. She graduated from Radcliffe magna cum laude in 1897 and studied medicine at Johns Hopkins University. When she lost interest in medicine, she joined her brother Leo in Paris, and the two Steins began to amass their extraordinary collection of paintings of Cézanne, Renoir, Gauguin, and Picasso. The artists brought friends to see the paintings and the salon began. In 1907 Alice B. Toklas, who had known Stein's family in California, arrived in Paris and met Gertrude. Three years later she joined the Stein household on rue de Fleurus and remained her inseparable companion for the next thirty years. Stein described their remarkable relationship in *The Autobiography of Alice B. Toklas* in 1933, which won a large and immediate audience. Her other works were more complex. Described by critics as primitive or symbolist, one concluded that her writing was "the product of a completely systematic and sophisticated aesthetic: what one might call the psychological theories of William James grafted onto the cubist concepts of Picasso and Braque." Sherwood Anderson had been influenced by her *Three Lives* in writing *Winesburg, Ohio*, and Ernest Hemingway also acknowledged her influence. Stein was sure of her own place, observing, "Einstein was the creative philosophical mind of the century and I have been the creative literary mind of the century." As American artists streamed into Paris in the 1920s, Stein's salon became a mecca. "We were," Stein noted, ". . . constantly seeing people." Stein began her own writing after eleven at night, since that was the only time when it was certain that no one would appear at the door. Her salon was a gathering place for French and Americans, young and old, but she observed a trend early in the decade, stating: "It was not long after that that everybody was twenty-six. It became the period of being twenty-six. During the next two or three years all the young men were twenty-six years old."[10] For most of these young Americans, Paris was one stop on a longer pilgrimage.

The center of their lives and work was New York. Though poet Marianne Moore sometimes felt there were "too many captains in one boat," the steady help in "getting things launched" was amazing. Writers and artists clustered in Greenwich Village, the Algonquin Round Table, Harlem, and Broadway. In their lives and their works, they demonstrated over and over again their rejection of old values and intense search for meaning. Caroline Ware described the artists and writers who settled in the Village. They had, she asserted, "a disregard for money values and for prestige based on either income or conspicuous expenditure." They had a broad tolerance for unconventional conduct. They were neither radicals nor reformers. Few, stated Ware, "had the heart or the faith to predicate their conduct and their thought on the assumption of a new social order." These Villagers "found escape but few solutions."[11]

In a decade rich in poetry, Greenwich Village was home to important women poets. The home of Elinor Wylie and her husband, poet William Rose Benet, on Ninth Street was a popular gathering place. Though Wylie's classic lyric poetry was critically acclaimed in the 1920s, two other Greenwich Village poets received wide attention for their innovation: Edna St. Vincent Millay and Marianne Moore. Millay arrived in the Village after four restrained years at Vassar. Already a published poet, she plunged into the literary Village group and had a brief fling at the stage. At five feet, with red hair and green eyes, Millay, according to Edmund Wilson, had "an intoxicating effect on people." In 1920 *A Few Figs from Thistles* was published. Its opening poem "First Fig" became the most quoted of the decade:

> My candle burns at both ends;
>   It will not last the night;
> But ah, my foes, and oh, my friends—
>   It gives a lovely light!

Her cheeky "Thursday" demolished the "true love" poem:

> And if I loved you Wednesday,
>   Well, what is that to you?
> I do not love you Thursday—
>   So much is true.
>
> And why you come complaining
>   Is more than I can see.
> I loved you Wednesday, yes—but what
>   Is that to me?

Three years later she won the Pulitzer Prize for poetry with *The Harp-Weaver and Other Poems*. Poet Allen Tate, reviewing her sonnets, believed her sensibility helped form a generation and observed, "her diverting mixture of solemnity and levity won the enthusiasm of a time bewildered intellectually and moving unsteadily towards an emotional attitude of its own." Millay left the Village in 1923, when she married Eugen Jan Boissevain and then moved to a farm in the Berkshires. Four years later she again wrote movingly for her generation in an article on the Sacco-Vanzetti case for the *Outlook*.[12]

Marianne Moore, the daughter of a Presbyterian minister, left Kirkwood, Missouri, for Bryn Mawr in 1906. After graduating, she taught at the Carlisle Indian School and then moved to Greenwich Village with her mother in 1918. She continued to teach and then worked part-time in a library. Meanwhile, she published in *Poetry*, the *Little Review*, the *Egoist*, and the *Dial*. The "*Dial* crowd" made her one of their own. William Carlos Williams declared simply, "Everyone loved her." Her first collected work, *Observations*, in 1924 won critical accolades. Whereas Millay was hailed for her sensibility, Moore was challenging because of the "intelligence" of her poetry. She tried to be a "literalist of the imagination" and to show, as she put it in her "Poetry": "There are things that are important beyond all this fiddle. . . . one discovers that there is in it after all a place for the genuine."[13]

A third major poet could be found north of Greenwich Village at the Algonquin Hotel's famous Round Table. Primarily a masculine bastion of Robert Benchley, Robert Sherwood, Donald Ogden Stewart, Harold Ross of the *New Yorker*, and Alexander Woollcott, its most redoubtable and quoted wit was Dorothy Parker. Parker's life and writing and the promotion by her Round Table colleagues present a microcosm of artistic strength and personal trauma that so characterized the lost generation. Born Dorothy Rothschild, her early years make a poor little rich girl story. Her stepmother sent her to a convent school and then to Miss Dana's, a finishing school, where she began to write verse. She was, she later reported, "following in the exquisite footsteps of Edna St. Vincent Millay. Unhappily in my own horrible sneakers." After her father died in 1911, the family resources dwindled. Dorothy Rothschild continued to write and finally sold a poem in 1916 to *Vogue* editor, Frank Crowninshield. Encouraged, she rented a room in a boarding-house on 103rd Street and Broadway, won a job with *Vogue*, and then became drama critic for *Vanity Fair*. In 1917 she married Edwin Pond Parker II, a Wall Street broker from an old Connecticut family. Parker, young, handsome, and witty, served with the army in France and Germany for the next two years. At home, Dorothy Parker became a regular of the Round Table and a celebrity, as Franklin P. Adams published her wit in his column "The Conning Tower." Typical was the Parker response when told that Calvin Coolidge had died: "How could they tell?" She was, observed Woollcott, an odd mixture of Little Nell and Lady Macbeth. Her life reflected that sweetness and desperation. In the first five years of the decade, Parker separated from her husband, had an unhappy affair and an abortion, and attempted suicide at least twice. She wrote regularly for the humor page of the *Saturday Evening Post* and in 1926 published her first volume of poetry, *Enough Rope*. It had brisk sales. Critics compared her work to Millay; Genevieve Taggard quipped that Dorothy's poetry was "whisky straight, not champagne." The most quoted two-liner was "News Item": "Men seldom make passes / At girls who wear glasses." Love, but certainly not romantic love, was a central theme of her work. In "Unfortunate Coincidence," she wrote:

> By the time you swear you're his,
>   Shivering and sighing,
> And he vows his passion is
>   Infinite, undying—
> Lady, make a note of this;
>   One of you is lying.

and in "God Speed":

> Oh, seek, my love, your newer way;
>   I'll not be left in sorrow.
> So long as I have yesterday,
>   Go take your damned to-morrow!

Her thumb-to-nose gesture was apparent in "Observation" ending with the lines: "But I shall stay the way I am, / Because I do not give a Damn." Bitterly close to her own life was "Résumé":

> Razors pain you;
> Rivers are damp;
> Acids stain you;
> And drugs cause cramp.
> Guns aren't lawful;
> Nooses give;
> Gas smells awful;
> You might as well live.

While Parker followed with *Sunset Gun* in 1928 and *Death and Taxes* in 1931, her short stories were winning critical acclaim. In 1929, her "Big Blonde" won the O. Henry Prize. A powerful study of oppression, "Big Blonde" tells the story of thirty-five-year-old Hazel Morse, striving with decreasing success to meet the deadly male imperative for a big blonde to be "fun" and "a good sport." She drifts from flirting to marriage to a series of affairs and finally makes a failed attempt at suicide. Parker had brought her art close to home.[14]

North of Greenwich Village and the Algonquin Round Table, poets, editors, novelists, artists, musicians, and scholars were creating the Harlem Renaissance. There was creative profusion in both high culture and popular culture. Poet Langston Hughes wrote: "I can never put on paper the thrill of the underground ride to Harlem. I went up the steps and out into the bright September sunlight. Harlem! I stood there, dropped my bags, took a deep breath and felt happy again." It was the greatest Negro city in the world. The migration from the South had continued after the war, and African and West Indian blacks settled in significant numbers. Harlem, asserted Howard University Professor Alain Locke in "The New Negro," was a laboratory in a great race welding. Locke asserted: "Negro life is not only establishing new contacts and finding new centers, it is finding a new soul. There is a fresh spiritual and cultural focusing. We have, as the heralding sign, an unusual outburst of creative expression." The Negro was "spiritually coming of age."[15]

Locke, approached by the editors of *Survey Magazine* in 1925 to edit an issue on Negroes, gathered thirty-three authors. When the *Survey* issue sold thirty thousand copies, Locke brought the articles out in a book *The New Negro*. The new Negro's task, he believed, "was to discover and define his culture and his contribution to what had been thought a white civilization." Harlem had its salons, little magazines, and editor midwives. Regina Andrews, daughter of a black middle-class family in Chicago, who came as a librarian to the 135th Street branch of the New York Public Library, made that library and her apartment a gathering place for black intellectuals. Jessie Fauset, the literary editor of the *Crisis*, encouraged young black writers as an editor, as a friend in gatherings in her home, and as a talented novelist. The Urban League's magazine *Opportunity* sponsored contests in short-story writing, poetry, drama, essays, and articles on personal experiences. Zora Neale Hurston captured a second prize in the short-story competition. Georgia Douglas Johnson won the *Opportunity* prize in drama for *Plumes* in 1927. New though short-lived magazines *Fire* and *Harlem* were other outlets.

The outpouring of poetry and novels and essays and music had a biracial audience. A trip in a taxi brought New Yorkers to an enclave that seemed exotic, primitive, unrepressed. They filled the Cotton Club and Small's Paradise. Carl Van Vechten, who became "violently interested in Negroes" in 1922, brought whites and blacks together in his apartment. His novel *Nigger Heaven* celebrated the primitive. He contributed articles to *Vanity Fair* on Ethel Walters and Bessie Smith. Eugene O'Neill's *Emperor Jones* in 1921 and DuBose and Dorothy Heyward's *Porgy* in 1924 seemed to confirm that "the Negro was in."[16]

The richness of the mix of writers and artists was nowhere duplicated except perhaps in Greenwich Village. As with writers, the Village proved a powerful magnet for painters and sculptors. When the 1920s began Alfred Stieglitz from his Gallery 291 on Fifth Avenue was already a major force in discovering and encouraging new artists. He was the first to exhibit the drawings of Georgia O'Keeffe. O'Keeffe, born in a small Wisconsin town, had studied at the Chicago Art Institute and briefly studied and taught at the University of Virginia. She became the supervisor of art for the public schools of Amarillo, Texas. After a row with the school board over methods she believed were stifling creativity, she arrived in New York to study at Columbia Teachers College. After another brief teaching stint at a South Carolina college, O'Keeffe settled in Greenwich Village. With Stieglitz's encouragement she had her first major exhibit in 1922. One New York critic reported, "Her work exhibits passage upon passage comparable to . . . the powerfully resistant planes of close intricate harmony characteristic of some of the modern music." She was "one of those persons of the hour who, like Lawrence, for instance, show an insight into the facts of life of an order . . . intenser than we have now." In 1923, O'Keeffe married Stieglitz, continuing her work in New York and in the summers at Lake George. Her studies of skyscrapers at night, the barns near the lake, and blowups of flowers marked her work. But she chafed for space, saying of Lake George, "The people live such pretty little lives, and the scenery is such little, pretty scenery." In 1929, at the invitation of painter Dorothy Brett and Mabel Dodge Luhan, who had moved her Greenwich Village salon to Taos, she began to spend her summers in New Mexico.[17]

In midtown Manhattan, Katherine Sophie Dreier, the youngest sister of Margaret Dreier Robbins of the WTUL, rivaled Stieglitz in the encouragement and promotion of modern art. A painter who had exhibited in the 1913 Armory show, Dreier with Marcel Duchamp and Man Ray formed the Société Anonyme to "promote the study in America of the progressive in art." The Société's building at 19 East Forty-seventh Street exhibited more than seventy artists for the first time; it became the first museum of modern art in America. Nine blocks north on Fifty-eighth Street, Florine Stettheimer, her two sisters, and her mother presided over a salon in their elegant apartment at Alwyn Court. It was a gathering place for Carl Van Vechten, O'Keeffe, Sherwood Anderson, and H. L. Mencken. Stettheimer's paintings have been classed as camp and "rococo subversive" for their wry views of American society, particularly *Spring Sale at Bendel's*, *Asbury Park South* and the *Cathedrals of Broadway*. The apartment of Neysa McMein, a member of the Algonquin Round Table, was another gathering place. McMein, one of the most beautiful women of the lost generation had studied at the Art Institute of Chicago. Her first major sale of her work in New York was a cover for the *Saturday Evening Post*. From 1923 to 1927 she drew all the covers of *McCall's* and many for the *Woman's Home Companion*.[18]

The greatest artist-patron of the 1920s was sculptor Gertrude Vanderbilt Whitney. Committed to her art, Whitney managed to raise three children, meet a heavy round of social obligations, and convince skeptical friends and critics that she was more than a dilettante. Her studio in Greenwich Village became a gathering place for young artists; Whitney gave them studio space and encouragement. Aided by her assistant Juliana Force, she launched the Whitney Studio Club and then the Whitney Studio Galleries where new talents could show their work.

Artist Peggy Bacon, a leading member of the Whitney group before she settled in Woodstock with her husband and established yet another art colony, did an etching *Frenzied Effort* (1925), depicting a group of regulars sketching a nude in the studio. When the Metropolitan Museum of Art refused her offer to build a new wing to house modern American art, Whitney planned for and opened her own museum in 1931, the Whitney on West Eight Street.[19]

Throughout the decade the New York Art Students' League was an important center for artists' work and learning. Anne Goldthwaite, Jane Peterson, Peggy Bacon, and sculptors Anna Hyatt Huntington and Malvina Hoffman studied or taught there. For the sculptors, it was usually a way station on the way to Paris and study with Rodin. Malvina Hoffman, who developed an interest in Africa and did her finest work in the 1920s in African and Indian portrait heads, and black sculptor Meta Warrick Fuller, whose *Awakening Ethiopia* was exhibited in New York in 1922, were Rodin protégées.[20]

The lives and careers of two artists illustrate, like that of Dorothy Parker, the color, complexity, and community of the creative life in the 1920s. The first, Marguerite Thompson Zorach, grew up in a middle-class home in Fresno, California. Admitted to Stanford University, she accepted instead an invitation from her aunt, Addie Harris, to join her in Paris to study art. She visited Gertrude Stein's salon and met Picasso, but was most influenced by the work of Matisse and the bold colors and distortions of the *Fauves*, or "wild beasts." She also met and fell in love with young immigrant-American lithographer, William Zorbach. Taken away by her alarmed aunt, she returned to California by way of Egypt, China, and Japan. She exhibited her paintings in Los Angeles, where critics were impressed with her bold color, and then she married William Zorach and set up home in Greenwich Village. They both exhibited in the 1913 Armory show and joined the artists' groups in the Village and during summers at Provincetown. When the care of their two children took away the extended time she needed for painting (even though ably helped by William), Marguerite Zorach turned to needlework and created tapestries of the same brilliant colors. In the middle of the decade, she founded the New York Society of Women Artists, a center for avant-garde painters. She returned to her painting as her children grew. Her tapestries, a classic example of "women's art," were classified as crafts and rejected by the Museum of Modern Art.[21]

More bizarre was the life and distinguished career of Romaine Goddard Brooks. Brooks entitled her memoirs *No Pleasant Memories*. Her youth was one of terror and abandonment. Her father deserted the family early, and her mother, obsessed with raising her disturbed brother, left Romaine at one point with her laundress in a New York tenement house, forgetting to send the money for her support. Rescued by relatives, Romaine was boarded in schools in Pennsylvania, Switzerland, and Rome, with stints of holidays with her mother and increasingly dangerous brother. At twenty-one, she finally secured a small allowance from her mother, acquiring the independence to study art, a pursuit always forbidden at home. Her work and study on the island of Capri was interrupted by the illnesses and deaths in succession of her mother and brother. Now independently wealthy, she returned to Capri. With the advice of Charles Freer and after a brief marriage of convenience with Englishman John Brooks, she moved to Britain, working in London and in Cornwall and developing her distinctive style and use of nuances of gray. After another move to Paris in 1910, she entered the literary, artistic, and homosexual circles there, adopting a severe mannish dress. In 1915, she began her forty years' friendship with Natalie Barney and became part of the Barney salon. Her portraiture was striking, including her self-portrait. Some of her studies were so harsh that the subjects begged her not to exhibit them. In 1925 she had highly successful exhibits in Paris, London, and New York. By the end of the decade she had turned to surrealist drawings, showing, as art historian Charlotte Rubinstein observed, "the fears that haunted her subconscious world." Her *Mother Nature* depicts babies being eaten by sharks; in another drawing, she is presented wrapped in a shroud. She signed them with a wing grounded by a chain.[22]

New York from the Village to Harlem was also the mecca for American musicians. The 1920s was a period rich in the experimentation of George Antheil and Henry Cowell, the compositions of Aaron Copland, Virgil Thompson, and Charles Ives, and the jazz creations of Fats Waller and Louis Armstrong. There were also some serious women composers, Ruth Crawford-Seeger, Marion Bauer, who studied with Nadia Boulanger, and Mabel Wheeler Daniels, called by Randall Thompson "one of our finest composers" for her *Symphony Exaltate* (1929). Daniels, the music director of Simmons College in Boston, expressed frustration in interviews on her relative rarity as a woman composer: "What difference whether written by a man or a woman or a Hottentot or a Unitarian."[23]

The ranks of women concert pianists were also thin. Two who had outstanding careers during the decade were Hazel Harrison and Ethel Leginska. Harrison, the daughter of black middle-class parents in La Porte, Indiana, began her piano lessons at four with the choirmaster of her parents' church; at the age of eight she was supplementing the family income by playing for dancing parties. Discovered at one of these parties by German musician Victor Heinze, she was taught and encouraged by him, commuting to Chicago for her lessons. She won critical acclaim at a recital in Chicago and, after an earlier triumph with the Berlin Philharmonic, returned to Berlin to study with Ferruccio Busoni. During the 1920s she toured the United States and Germany, playing Strauss, Bach, Liszt, and the music of Scriabin and contemporary composers of the Soviet Union and Poland as well as unpublished black composers. She played to segregated audiences. One reviewer after a 1922 Chicago recital observed, "She is extremely talented . . . it seems too bad that the fact that she is a Negress may limit her future plans."

Ethel Leginska, the "Paderewski of women pianists," was another child prodigy. Born in England, she studied in that country and in Vienna and Berlin before marrying an American and making her debut in New York in 1913. In 1918, locked in divorce proceedings and a battle for custody of her son, she offered to give up her concert career and support herself and her child by giving piano lessons. She lost the struggle, but in the process she became a strong proponent for better support and encouragement for professional women. After a nervous breakdown in 1926, Leginska announced she was turning to a career of conducting and composing. She had already appeared as a conductor with orchestras in London, Paris, Munich, and Berlin, as well as with the New York Symphony, frequently winning contracts by agreeing to appear as a pianist also. In 1926, she founded and conducted the Boston Philharmonic Orchestra and headed the Boston Woman's Symphony Orchestra. By the end of the decade, she had established the Boston English Opera Company and taken over the directorship of the Woman's Symphony Orchestra of Chicago.[24]

Outside of these traditional areas of music, American women made other significant inroads and contributions. In opera, while Mary Garden continued her long career with the Chicago Opera Company, Geraldine Farrar, to the dismay of her fans the "Gerry-flappers," retired from the Metropolitan Opera at the end of the 1921 season. The two new stars of the 1920s arrived at the Metropolitan by way of vaudeville and the Broadway stage. Grace Moore had heard Mary Garden sing while studying in Washington and determined to become an opera singer. Facing her father's opposition to a career on the stage, Moore struck out on her own. She studied in New York and worked to support herself at a Greenwich Village nightclub. When she suddenly lost her voice, she was helped by her teacher, Dr. Mario Marafioti, to recover. He also found her roles in musical comedy. In 1920, she was a hit in the musical review *Kitchy-Koo*. Until her money ran out, she studied in Paris where she was encouraged to consider an operatic career. Back on Broadway, she starred in Irving Berlin's *Music Box Review* in 1923 and 1924 with the hit tunes "What'll I Do" and "All Alone." She continued to study with Marafioti and then returned to France to work with a coach recommended by Mary Garden and to further hone her acting skills. She finally made her operatic debut at the Metropolitan in 1928 as Mimi in *La Bohème*. In 1930 she was lured to Hollywood to make a biography of Jenny Lind and continued a remarkable career on Broadway and at the Metropolitan. Moore failed several early opera auditions, but the other new star of the 1920s, Rosa Ponselle, faced no such delays. Ponselle sang in church and on a vaudeville tour with her sister Carmella. After study with Romano Romani in New York, her extraordinary voice and skill in bel canto won her an audition with Enrico Caruso. In 1918, nineteen-year-old Ponselle sang the lead in *La forza del destino* with Caruso and was an immediate sensation. In 1927, her performance in *Norma* established her as one of the great sopranos of the century.[25]

Other singers in Harlem, New York speakeasies, and Broadway achieved greatness in singing the blues. The great blues pioneer, Gertrude "Ma" Rainey, had been touring with her husband in Negro minstrel troops and in tent shows since 1904. Her recordings in 1923 with Paramount Records made her remarkable renditions of *Traveling Blues*, *Jelly Bean Blues*, *Moonshine Blues*, and others available to a wide audience. "Ma" Rainey taught her style of country blues to Bessie Smith, the "Empress of the Blues," in the 1920s. Beginning in 1923, Smith recorded over 160 blues songs in the decade, ranging from *Careless Love* and *Empty Bed Blues* to *A Good Man Is Hard to Find*. Blues singer Bertha "Chippie" Hill recorded *Careless Love* and *Trouble in Mind* with Louis Armstrong. On Broadway, torch-blues singer Helen Morgan scored hits in *Show Boat* with "Why Was I Born" and "My Bill." Blues singer-dancer Florence Mills, at fifteen one of the leads in the all-black Eubie Blake production of *Shuffle Along* in 1920, stopped the show with her "Sometimes I'm Happy—Sometimes I'm Blue."[26]

While the 1920s was a great decade of the blues, it was a golden age for women and the dance. Ruth St. Denis, Isadora Duncan, Martha Graham, and Doris Humphreys all changed modern American dance. Duncan was the most determined pioneer. She observed, "When I was fifteen years old. . . . I realized that there was no teacher in the world who could give me any help in my desire to be a dancer because at that time the only school that existed was ballet." Duncan studied the movements in nature, the opening of flowers, the flight of the bees, and sought to emulate "the freedom and grace of movement and the dignity of pose that the flowing garments of the ancients allowed." In 1911, Duncan electrified an audience at Carnegie Hall when she leapt forward barefoot from the back of the stage, clad in light translucent silk and, as one critic noted, "nature unadorned." She danced to the music of Wagner, Beethoven, Tchaikovsky, and Gluck. Her performances were controversial but unforgettable. After one of her dances, actress Ellen Terry sprang up from the audience to address it: "Do you realize what you are looking at? Do you understand that this is the most incomparably beautiful dancing in the world?" Years later Anita Loos wrote after a Duncan performance: "When Isadora danced, she became a goddess; she was one of the few authentic geniuses I ever met. I left her performance in a spirit of humble apology." Duncan's life, marred by the tragic drowning of her two children in a freak accident, and the hysterical reaction to her dancing, teaching, and marriage in Russia during the Red Scare, ended dramatically in Nice when her long Spanish shawl caught in the spokes of a wheel of her car and broke her neck. Her friend Alexis Kisloff summarized her career: "She came with something entirely new." To simplify everything was her aim.[27]

Like Isadora Duncan, Ruth St. Denis was self-taught. Growing up on a farm in New Jersey, she too danced to the rhythm of nature. Where Duncan had emulated the Greeks, St. Denis was moved by the Egyptians and the Orient. Touring with a David Belasco production of *DuBarry*, St. Denis related seeing "The Poster" advertising Egyptian Deities, a Turkish cigarette. She was transfixed by the image of Isis, the temple, and the mystics of the Egyptian world and began conceiving of a dance drama *Egypta*. She began researching Eastern culture, particularly Indian. Her first production, backed by twenty-five New York patrons, was *Rahda*, not *Egypta*. In 1914, with successes in *The*

Yogi, *The Cobras*, *The Nautch*, and *O-mika* behind her in New York, California, and Europe, she took dancer Ted Shawn as a pupil. Within a year they were married; within two years they established Denishawn in Los Angeles, a school and permanent home for the Denishawn Company.[28] One of their early pupils was Martha Graham.

A twenty-two-year-old Californian, Graham's fierce determination, talent, and work quickly won her performances and a position as a teacher. After six years, Graham was ready to create her own works. In 1922, she left the Denishawn Company and began teaching dance at the new Eastman School at Rochester. In 1926, teamed with another former Denishawn artist, Louis Horst, Graham gave her first recital. She was thirty-two. In the next three years, working first with the Eastman dancers, and then with her own group, Graham evolved her own style—gaunt, tense, and forceful. One of her early pupils, actress Bette Davis, observed: "I worshipped her. She was all tension—lightning. Her burning dedication gave her spare body the power of ten men. . . . She was a straight line—a divining rod. . . . who would, with a single thrust of her weight, convey anguish. Then, in an anchored lift that made her ten feet tall, she became all joy. One after the other. Hatred, ecstasy, age, compassion! . . . What at first seemed 'grotesque to the eye' developed into a beautiful release for both dancer and beholder."[29]

This incredible richness in music and dance was matched by the creativity on Broadway in the 1920s. Plays by Eugene O'Neill, Thornton Wilder, Sean O'Casey, George S. Kaufman, Elmer Rice, and S. N. Behrman opened next to productions of Ibsen, Shaw, Chekhov, and Shakespeare. Women were important as promoters, performers, and playwrights. In 1919, the same year Actors' Equity rocked Broadway with a successful strike, the Theater Guild was organized. Its driving force was Theresa Helbrun. A Bryn Mawr graduate who had joined George Baker's play-writing workshop, Helbrun worked to build the subscription list of the Theater Guild to twenty-five thousand members. The Guild produced the plays of O'Neill and Shaw and the major plays of Philip Barry and S. N. Behrman with Helbrun occasionally serving as "play doctor." Helbrun's support of O'Neill was joined by that of Edith Isaacs, the editor of *Theater Arts*. Isaacs had broad-ranging interests in music, dance, art, and black culture, and excelled at discovering and promoting new talent.[30]

Of the playwrights, veteran Rachel Crothers had the longest string of Broadway hits, beginning with *Nice People* in 1921, a study of generations, and ending with *Let Us Be Gay* in 1929, a play about divorce. Edna Ferber began her Broadway collaboration with George M. Cohan in 1919 and later scored a success with George S. Kaufman in *Royal Family*. In the Village, Susan Glaspell with her husband George Cram Cook and Eugene O'Neill formed the Greenwich Village Playwrights Theater to produce original works by Americans. Glaspell's powerful *The Inheritors* in 1921 was followed by O'Neill's *The Emperor Jones*, which was such a commercial success that the idealistic Cook left with Glaspell for Greece to renew the interest in theater at its birthplace.[31]

On the Broadway stage, Maude Adams continued her long and distinguished career. Katharine Cornell was only the most acclaimed of the galaxy of new stars and leading ladies. They included Ethel Barrymore, Helen Hayes, Lynn Fontanne, Ethel Waters, Florence Mills, Abbie Mitchell, Tallulah Bankhead, Josephine Baker, Jeanne Eagels, and Fanny Brice. Cornell triumphed in Shaw's *Candida*, Michael Arlen's *The Green Hat*, and Wharton's *Age of Innocence*. She had what Mabel Dodge Luhan called "radiance." Luhan explained, "To see her in action or to talk to her at leisure is to note the perpetual presence of the indwelling, fiery guest that it is her destiny to harbor while she is on this earth." Barrymore, a heroine of the Equity strike, demonstrated, with the exception of the unsuccessful performance in *Romeo and Juliet*, her range in roles from Portia to the second Mrs. Tanqueray. Jeanne Eagels's portrayal of Sadie Thompson in Somerset Maugham's *Rain* brought forth "an emotional demonstration never exceeded in the theater of this country." Ziegfeld Follies star Fanny Brice proved that women, according to one critic, "could excel as comedians without exploiting their society or making fools of themselves or other women." Her poignant rendering of "Second-Hand Rose" and "My Man" would precede a sidesplitting takeoff on vamp Theda Bara or on the Dying Swan.

Even more versatile than Brice was Josephine Baker. Daughter of a black mother and Spanish father, Baker was raised in East St. Louis, where she witnessed the brutal and bloody race riots of 1917. At thirteen, she ran away and joined a vaudeville troupe; at sixteen she was in the cast of *Shuffle Along* on Broadway. Traveling to Paris in 1925 with *La revue Negre*, she was stranded when the French rejected the production as having "too much tap dancing." Baker won a place for a dance number with the Folies-Bergère. The audience reaction was so spirited, she put on a one-woman show, dancing, singing, and, for a finale, leaping into the air and into a banana tree. It was instant stardom. "Josephine" meant *le jazz hot* to the French. A dance critic grew lyric over this "Black Venus," who danced with such impulsive vehemence and wild splendor. On stage and off she was madcap and exotic. She lived the life of a legendary star rivaled only in Hollywood.[32]

> Hollywood is sex under the spotlight
> Hollywood is the world's illusion
> Hollywood is the font of vicarious enjoyment.[33]

Throughout the 1920s, actresses, actors, playwrights, and novelists were lured to that new outpost of culture in southern California, Hollywood. Moving out of its infancy, the industry with the exception of United Artists created by Mary Pickford, Charlie Chaplin, and Douglas Fairbanks in 1920, was increasingly dominated by the big studios, Metro-Goldwyn-Mayer, Fox, and Paramount. Each had its stable of directors, stars, and public relations men. New magazines *Photoplay* and *Motion Picture Magazine* worked to satisfy the public curiosity about the glamorous lives lived by the glamorous stars. The power was in the hands of the producers and directors, and few women were included. But women frequently provided the scenarios and scripts and glamour that translated into box-office success and gave them a degree of power. In her *From Reverence to Rape*, Molly Haskell asserts that women "have figured more prominently in film than any other art." There were plenty of opportunities. Between 1912 and 1929, producers churned out ten thousand silent films. The movies were hungry for stories and stars. By 1920, the census listed over fourteen thousand actresses (not all in Hollywood), about the same number of women who graduated from college that year. Lured by the success of Mary Pickford and others, the "movie-struck girls" flooded into Hollywood. There was always the chance of being discovered in a drugstore or called out of a crowd of extras to stardom. The trick, after discovery, was to be able to avoid the pitfall of stereotyping. Hollywood had found the marketable images for women: the orphan, the fatal woman, the actress, the millionaire's daughter. Heroines were small, blond, and vulnerable; vamps were dark and foreign. An article in *Photoplay* set out the dilemma: "If you have too much IT, you are promptly put in your place as a brazen and obvious hussy, with no ability and nothing but a lot of sex appeal. . . . If you have too little IT, you are labeled a colorless prig, with a cold heart and no emotional appeal. . . . There is no pleasing the public in the sex business."[34]

The role of the heroine-child-orphan was most fully created as a Hollywood staple by D. W. Griffith, Lillian Gish, and Mary Pickford at Biograph Studios. Griffith, one of the first Hollywood geniuses, had brought respectability (and controversy) to films with his 1915 *The Birth of a Nation*. Lillian Gish, the heroine, was, according to Anita Loos, "the personification of all the heroines D. W. ever created, so sweetly childlike, vibrant, and timorous that even her type of girl belonged to a far distant past." "From the moment Gish steps on the screen," observed one critic, "there is the feeling of inevitable doom. Too good for this world's pain, her only hope of happiness appears in death or the cloister." In *Way Down East* for Griffith in 1920, Gish wins a happy ending, but only after a mock marriage and the death of an illegitimate child. Denounced as a fallen woman, she staggers out into a raging storm to be rescued by her true love heading for a waterfall on a large slab of ice. Of Gish the person rather than Gish the actress, Loos observed she was an "irresistible siren, with an extraordinary gentle exterior, under which lies a character of stainless steel."[35]

Lillian and her sister Dorothy Gish had been introduced to Griffith by Mary Pickford, the "Biograph girl," the "girl with the curl," "America's sweetheart." Born in Toronto, Pickford had gone on stage at the age of five to help support her mother, sister, and brother. She had worked her way up on the vaudeville circuit, finally winning a role with a David Belasco company. At the end of the run in 1909, she used her last nickel to get to Griffith's Biograph Studios. Winning a part her first day, by the afternoon she was negotiating a raise. The perennial "child" star was one of Hollywood's shrewdest businesswomen. By 1917, she was earning $350,000 a year and bonuses.

Her starring roles were all sunshine. As she explained in a 1922 article in *Collier's*, she had found her philosophy in the fatigue of playing on the road: "Suddenly it occurred to me that I was engaged in what should be the greatest business in the world—the production of happiness. . . . If I could sell happiness . . . I would always exceed the supply. I would have a market as wide as the world."[36] But though she formed United Artists with Chaplin and Fairbanks and bought up all her Biograph films to keep them off the market in 1920, she never could break out of the "child-girl with the curl" mold. At twenty-four she played the lead in *Rebecca of Sunnybrook Farm*; at twenty-six she was an orphan in *Daddy Long-Legs*; at twenty-seven she played twelve-year-old Pollyanna; and at twenty-eight she portrayed both Little Lord Fauntleroy and his mother. In 1925 she tried to break the stereotype, playing the heroines in *Rosita*, directed by Ernst Lubitsch, and *Dorothy Vernon of Hadden Hall*. That same year the Mary Pickford Company sponsored a contest through *Photoplay* magazine offering fifty dollars for the most helpful letter recommending future roles. Pickford explained why she had chosen her earlier roles, stressing that she liked to give a message of hope. She did not want to do costume films or foreign themes, but "only those dealing with the problems of the average American girl." She added, "Of course, I will continue to present the sweet, wholesome type of girlhood which I have tried to play in the past." She was deluged with more than twenty thousand letters. Ninety-nine percent begged her to return to the lovable characters of youth. With a clear mandate from her public, Pickford made *Little Annie Rooney*. She was thirty-two.[37]

In real life Pickford was allowed to grow up, but was still an inhabitant of never-never land. Adela Rogers St. Johns wrote of her marriage to dashing Douglas Fairbanks as "the most successful famous marriage the world has ever known." They were "living a great-love poem." Theirs was an old-fashioned lovematch marriage. In 1928, when they returned to Hollywood from a trip to Britain, Pickford observed the changing environment: "When Doug and I sailed for Europe last spring—we hardly knew what a talking picture was. Three months later, when we came back to Hollywood and went over to Chaplin's for the first time, nobody could talk of anything else."[38]

Pickford's first talkie, *Coquette*, in 1929 won her an Academy Award. She had shed her curls and become a teenager. In a melodramatic plot, the heroine, Norma, falls in love with Michael, only to be thwarted by her father who proclaims the young man is not worthy of her. Michael goes off to earn enough money to win her; Norma whiles away the time dancing at wild parties. Michael reappears and takes Norma to his hideaway in the woods, returning her home at four in the morning. Norma is ready for marriage, promising: "I'm going to be so good to you. I'll keep house and I'll cook and scrub and I'll take care of you. I love you more than all the men, women, and houses, and everything." But in spite of her compromised virtue, her father remains adamantly opposed to her marriage. Michael argues, saying "Where do you think she spent the night? I'm just protecting her good name. You should be begging me to marry her." The enraged father thereupon kills him. At

the trial, Norma forgives her father, fights to win his acquittal, and
testifies that Michael brutally raped her. Moved by her forgiveness, the
father, after an emotional reconciliation scene, seizes exhibit A and
shoots himself. Norma is last seen walking, ruined and alone, down a
dimly lit street. Pickford had grown up. Though *Coquette* was an artistic triumph, the public did not embrace her new maturity.

While the child-woman formed one end of the Hollywood spectrum
of good and evil, the vamp was the other. She was introduced on the
screen in *A Fool There Was* in 1915 by Theda Bara (Arab spelled back-
wards) with the stirring line: "Kiss me,you fool." Born Theodosia
Goodman in Cincinnati, she changed her name to Bara in 1917. Press
agents insisted that she had been born on an oasis in the shadow of the
Sphinx and kept her from the public and from interviews. Her film
victims, in true vampire fashion, were wrecked and drained "morally,
financially, and even physically, and seemed to die from sexual excess."[39] *The Unchastened Woman* and *Madame Mystery* were two Bara ve-
hicles of the mid-twenties. She established the pattern that "bad"
women were invariably foreign. The highly talented Alla Nazimova,
"the woman from Yalta," fit this foreign, mysterious, evil model. Nazimova had studied acting with Stanislavsky. She played Ibsen on
Broadway and toured in vaudeville before arriving in Hollywood. By
1919 she was one of the top Metro stars, playing foreign roles. As one
critic asserted, even her pantomime had an accent. The stereotype was
too limiting. After her role in *Salome* in 1922, she went back to vaudeville and New York, starring in the Chekhov and Turgenev productions
of Eva Le Gallienne's Civic Repertory Company.[40]

Between the all-sweet goodness of Pickford and the devouring vamp
of Bara was the Hollyoood version of the young and the restless who
could be redeemed from their wrongheadedness or minor transgres-
sions and brought to reason and true love at home. Clara Bow, the "It"
girl, embodied a mix of flapper and femme fatale. Bow had come to
Hollywood through winning a "fame and fortune" contest sponsored in
1921 by the fan magazines *Motion Picture*, *Shadowland*, and *Motion Picture Classic*. Her photograph earned her a screen test, a silver trophy,
and then a contract for a picture. She began at fifty dollars a week with
Preferred Pictures, winning notices as the flapper in *Black Oxen*. She
played a coed in *The Plastic Age* in 1925 and another flapper in *Dancing
Mothers*. Flirtatious, warm, and virginal, Bow's charisma was simply
described by Elinor Glyn as IT. By 1928, when she starred in an early
technicolor production *Red Hair*, Bow was a top box-office draw. Like

Bara and Pickford, however, Bow was doomed to repeat her roles. She was invariably the "Northwest Mounted policeman of sex"—she got her man. The number of her roles, reflected her fortunes: fourteen in 1925, eight in 1926, six in 1927. While her on-screen persona had a heart of gold, her torrid off-screen romances made troubling headlines. Off-again, on-again engagements with Harry Richman, a suit for alienation of affections, and a messy court case hurt the Bow fortunes. In 1929, Bow like Pickford made her debut in a talkie, *The Wild Party*. Her husky voice and Brooklyn accent did not win plaudits. A *Photoplay* feature in October 1929, "Empty-Hearted," described her: "Miserable as a caged tigress. . . . On the little table by her bed stand rows of bottles of sedatives put there to lull her active, restless, undisciplined brain. . . . She strives for some far off Utopia where her mind may be lulled and her tired little body put to rest."[41]

Two of the mega stars of the 1920s did manage to hold out for variety in their roles: Greta Garbo and Gloria Swanson. Garbo was brought to Hollywood as part of a package deal worked out by Louis B. Mayer. Mayer wanted the Swedish director Maurice Stiller. Stiller insisted that Garbo join the M-G-M stable also. After two successful roles as a Spanish temptress in *Torrent* and *Temptress* in 1926, Garbo became a box-office sensation, starring with John Gilbert on and off the screen in *Flesh and the Devil*. Adela Rogers St. Johns enthused, "Gilbert and Garbo were added by movie fans to the list of immortal lovers, Romeo and Juliet, Dante and Beatrice, Anthony and Cleopatra." When she asked for a raise from $600 to $5,000 a week (Gilbert was making $10,000) and refused to make the next scheduled temptress picture, Mayer balked and suspended her. Garbo held out for seven months, finally triumphing through her sincere indifference. When she returned with a new contract, she starred with Gilbert in *Anna Karenina*, retitled *Love* for the box office. M-G-M got its money's worth. In 1928, Garbo starred in *The Mysterious Lady* and *The Divine Woman*. In 1929, she played in *A Woman of Affairs*, *Single Standard*, *The Green Hat*, and *Wild Orchids*. In 1930, she made the transition to talkies in *Anna Christie*, promoted by M-G-M with the simple line "Garbo Talks." Director Clarence Brown made audiences wait until the second reel, when a weary and worn Garbo sat down in a bar and demanded in her deep voice, "Gimme a visky . . . and don't be stingy, ba-bee." When she left Hollywood in the 1930s, it was in her own way and on her own terms.[42]

Gloria Swanson, a skilled comic, won her first role in a two-custard-pie feature at the Essanay Studio in Chicago. Though she wanted the role and the money, she walked off the set, refusing to sprawl as instructed after being struck by the second pie. Her first important role in Hollywood came in 1919 in the Cecil B. deMille film of J. M. Barrie's *The Admirable Crichton*, retitled *Male and Female* for better box office by the always commercially alert deMille. He was a master at presenting torrid passion, generally in a dream or foreign or historic sequence, while managing to uphold traditional morality. Swanson was a perfect actress for this duality. She believed that her role as a "beautiful, selfish, emancipated woman" represented a large percentage of misguided American women. She asserted in a *Photoplay* interview: "No woman in the world is ever happy with a man unless that man is her master. He may be her slave; her adorer, her devoted servant—but at the same time he must be her master." She also warned of the peril of a woman attempting to combine marriage and a profession. Her own experience provided a convenient case study. Ironically, while starring in a deMille feature *Don't Change Your Husband*, Swanson in 1925 was entering her third marriage. Her new husband was the Marquis de la Felase de la Coudraye. The editor of *Photoplay* wrote, "If there was ever a happy couple" it was the Marquis and Gloria. "The secret," he believed, "is that they play together. They are like a couple of children eagerly interested in the same things, seeing the funny side and the joyous side of life through the same eyes, having a wonderful time together in the best of all wonderful worlds."[43]

Garbo and Swanson, according to critic Lewis Jacobs, "were prototypes of the ultra-civilized, sleek and slender, knowing and disillusioned, restless, oversexed and neurotic woman who 'leads her own life.' " Hollywood exploited their glamour but rarely gave them happy endings. Sin and passion were lavishly depicted. But after the good woman had indulged in escapade and dalliance, Hollywood insisted on wrenching her back to where she had traditionally been—in the home with husband and a loving family. It was an ironic message from an industry rocked by scandal and a community where divorce was commonplace.[44]

Only in Hollywood was life so radically divorced from art. The creative women of the 1920s worked hard in their lives and their work to define a world and discover a way to live in it. They were helped in both endeavors by networks and communities that provided links and support from New York to Paris and Taos and Hollywood. The 1920s called for more than the usual courage needed by the artist. For the women artists, crafting their lives was sometimes more difficult than creating their work. If they did not always find success, they did achieve a fierce integrity. It was sometimes more obvious in their works than in their lives.

Anzia Yezierska.

CHAPTER NINE

Telling Lives: Images of Women in Fiction

> I do not admit that dish-washing is enough to satisfy all women!
> I may not have fought the good fight, but I have kept the faith.
>
> *Carol Kennicott in Main Street, by Sinclair Lewis*

> Real women . . . are much more resilient and resourceful than
> our fictional heroines have been.
>
> *Elaine Showalter, These Modern Women*[1]

In a decade rich in music, art, film, and literature, the novel remained the form that most deeply and subtly reflected the culture. When Sinclair Lewis and F. Scott Fitzgerald introduced the icons of Main Street and the flapper in 1920, it was a faint harbinger of the cultural map that was to come. Never had America had such a profusion of good novelists. The galaxy of Lewis, Fitzgerald, Ernest Hemingway, John Dos Passos, William Faulkner, and Theodore Dreiser was matched by an assemblage of women novelists. There were the best-sellers Fannie Hurst, Dorothy Canfield Fisher, Mary Roberts Rinehart, and Edna Ferber; the regionalists Ruth Suckow and Zona Gale; the still prolific "old gang" Willa Cather, Edith Wharton, and Ellen Glasgow; and the young, the ethnic, and the black novelists Anita Loos, Anzia Yezierska, Nella Larsen, and Jessie Fauset. The central concern of all their serious works was always the same—the individual's search for meaning in the face of rapid and sharp changes in tradition and institutions.

The characters they created had extended lives. The new Book-of-the-Month Club made them available to a wide readership. Their re-creation on the stage and in films brought them to a mass audience. Zona Gale's novel *Miss Lulu Bett* became a Broadway hit and a cinema box-office success in 1921. Gertrude Atherton's dramatic study of rejuvenation and generations, *Black Oxen*, was translated into a film. Eugene O'Neill's *Anna Christie* provided a starring role for Greta Garbo. Rachel Crothers's play *Mary the III* and the hits *Dancing Mothers* and *Show Boat* became Hollywood productions. Not until the 1950s and the television explosion was there such a reiteration of plot, theme, and character across the media, such a juncture of high and popular culture.

The novelists most frequently identified with the decade were male: Sinclair Lewis, F. Scott Fitzgerald, and Ernest Hemingway. Lewis, one of the "old gang," was so successful in his factual rendition of town and character in *Main Street* and *Babbitt* that he was derided on the Left Bank as nothing but a journalist. Fitzgerald introduced his readers to the flapper in *This Side of Paradise*, and in *The Great Gatsby* he wrote movingly of the vanishing of the American dream. Hemingway in *A Farewell to Arms* and *The Sun Also Rises* revealed the searing wounds of the lost generation and the integrity of their search to "find out how to live." All, as Malcolm Cowley observed, were members of the same team. They were white, Anglo-Saxon, and Protestant. They also reflected Frederick Hoffman's assertion that the generations wrote of the crisis in values from opposite poles: the older, like Lewis, examined the failures of the American tradition; the young searched for new values. These paradigms are hopelessly scrambled, however, when gender, not generation, is the dividing line. The major novels by women in the 1920s came from the "old gang"—Cather and Glasgow. The young novelists, unlike their male counterparts, were ethnically diverse. Their characters provide a markedly different view of women and their success and survival in the 1920s.

The contrast in the men's women and the women's women is visible in every setting: in the small towns created by Sinclair Lewis and Willa Cather; in the New York societies portrayed by F. Scott Fitzgerald and Edith Wharton, and the ethnic and black novelists Anzia Yezierska, Nella Larsen, and Jessie Fauset; in the expatriate worlds of Ernest Hemingway and Edith Wharton. As a group, the women novelists were older. Their novels deal more fully with conflicts in value across generations. Their heroines, unlike those created by their male counterparts, make their own decisions, forge their own survival.

Sinclair Lewis's *Main Street* (1920) might be subtitled "The New Woman Meets the Village Virus." The collision between old ways and new values is played out in the contest between Gopher Prairie and Carol Milford Kennicott. Carol, a "rebellious girl," is alive in "every cell of her body." About to graduate from Blodgett College, she rejects a proposal of marriage, exclaiming: "But I want to do something with life. I can't settle down to nothing but domesticity." She knows that she wants to help people; indeed, she hopes to inspire them, and she is excited by the possibilities in town planning. She would bring beauty and order to the towns of the Northwest, "Make 'em put in a village green, and darling cottages, and a quaint Main Street!" Instead, at graduation she chooses a more traditional path, becoming a librarian in Minneapolis.[2]

Friends introduce her to Dr. Will Kennicott. His whirlwind courtship is helped by the lure of Gopher Prairie. It is, boasts Kennicott, "mighty pretty . . . but go to it . . . make us change." Carol accepts Will and the challenge. As the train to her new home rolls by squat dull town after squat dull town, she becomes increasingly apprehensive. Gopher Prairie proves unremarkably like all the rest, "there was no dignity in it nor any hope of greatness." Its commonplaceness is reflected by its inhabitants. Lewis describes the stolid complacency, "the contentment of the quiet dead . . . dullness made God." Yet Gopher Prairie is proud of itself and important as "a village in a country which is taking pains to become altogether standardized and pure." It would not be "satisfied until the entire world also admits that the end and joyous purpose of living is to ride in flivvers, to make advertising pictures of dollar watches, and in the twilight to sit talking not of love and courage but of the convenience of safety razors."[3]

Stifling in the smugness, Carol joins the aristocracy of Gopher Prairie. Her society is bounded by the bridge playing and gossip of the Jolly Seventeen. Culture is embodied in the Thanatopsis group which is working its way through English literature at its monthly meetings, allotting ten minutes to Tennyson and Browning. No one backs her ideas for a new city hall or town beautification; no one can be induced to try anything new. The problem, explains Guy Pollack, the lawyer, is "the village virus . . . the germ which infects ambitious people who stay too long in the prairies."[4]

Halfway through her first year as the doctor's wife, Carol realizes she is a woman "with a working brain and no work." Refusing to give in, she forms an amateur theatrical group, attends chautauqua meetings, and serves as a member of the library board. She has a baby. Her frustration only deepens. "What," she asks, "is it we want—and need? Will Kennicott there would say that we need lots of children and hard work. But it isn't that. There's the same discontent in women with eight children. . . . What do we want?" She has one answer. Women want "a more conscious life." They are tired "of always deferring hope till the next generation." In her depression, she admits: "I have become a small town woman. Absolute. Typical. Modest and moral and safe. Protected from life. Genteel!"[5]

Lewis's major foil for Carol Kennicott is Vida Sherwin, senior high school teacher, leader of the Jolly Seventeen, a believer in "steadiness and democracy and opportunity." Once infatuated with Will Kennicott, she has "given him up" and finally married the unprepossessing Raymie Wutherspoon, who had the decency to become a hero in World War I. Tired of Carol's criticism of Gopher Prairie, Vida exclaims: "You're an impossibilist. And you give up too easily. . . . Just because we didn't graduate into Ibsen the very first thing. You want perfection all at once." The town will get a new high school, because others have done the necessary politicking and groundwork. Carol rejoins: "Will the teachers in the hygienic new building go on informing the children that Persia is a yellow spot on the map, and 'Caesar' the title of a book of grammatical puzzles?"[6]

Restlessly drifting into a flirtation and almost an affair, Carol flees from the edges of scandal and the dead weight of Gopher Prairie. She joins a host of women streaming into Washington to help with the war effort. After a year, Will Kennicott arrives, asking her to return, but insisting that she make up her own mind. From her Washington perspective, Gopher Prairie seems less threatening. Carol waits another five months and then goes "home." She has her second child, a girl, and speculates whether the baby will become a feminist leader or marry a socialist or both. She decides she will send her to Vassar and hopes that she will become "a bomb to blow up smugness."[7]

Lewis pounds home his message with repeated sledgehammer blows. The American heartland is in trouble. It is dull, commercial, soulless. Emblematic of the forces bringing change is Carol Kennicott, the college-educated, "want it all" new woman. Yet Lewis stacks the odds against her even more heavily than he does against Gopher Prairie. Her only family, when Will Kennicott woos and wins her, is a rather distant sister; religion is not a source of either comfort or strength. While her talents are diverse, none is towering. She has an enormous need to be accepted, but her skill in making friends or maintaining a relationship is rudimentary. Lewis arms her with beauty, eagerness, dreams, and the courage of youth. It is not enough. Her hope for life beyond domesticity is placed in the next generation. In the last of her many speeches, Carol asserts: "I do not admit that dish-washing is enough to satisfy all women. I may not have fought the good fight, but I have kept the faith." The last word is Will's and Gopher Prairie's: "Sure. You bet you have, . . . Sort of feels to me like it might snow tomorrow. Have to be thinking about putting up the storm-windows pretty soon. Say, did you notice whether the girl put that screw driver back?"[8]

While Lewis explored his version of the new woman, F. Scott Fitzgerald depicted the flapper and the urban sophisticate. Isabelle in *This Side of Paradise* is the perfect model: "her education, or rather, her sophistication, had been absorbed from the boys who had dangled on her favor: her tact was instinctive, and her capacity for love affairs was limited only by the number of the susceptible within telephone distance. *Flirt* smiled through her intense physical magnetism." The other women in *Paradise* are neurotic, untrustworthy, or mercenary. None reaches maturity: "they were lovely, they were expensive, they were nineteen."[9]

Five years later in *The Great Gatsby*, Fitzgerald's women are more fully drawn and more dangerous. Daisy Buchanan is the young beautiful sophisticate, who centers Jay Gatsby's dreamworld. A Louisville debutante, with a background similar to Zelda Fitzgerald's, Daisy has chosen money and the security promised through marriage to Tom Buchanan rather than wait for Gatsby to return from the war and improve his fortunes. The narrator, Nick Carraway, describes his first visit to the Buchanan's Long Island mansion. Two young women, both clad in white, are reclining on the sofa, talking "unobtrusively and with a bantering inconsequence that was never quite chatter, that was as cool as their white dresses and their impersonal eyes in the absence of all desire." Daisy has "the kind of voice that the ear follows up and down, as if each speech is an arrangement of notes that will never be played again. . . . there was an excitement in her voice . . . a whispered 'Listen,' a promise that she had done gay, exciting things just a while since and that there were gay exciting things hovering in the next hour." It is a voice, Gatsby later explains, that is "full of money." Daisy, as trapped in boredom as Carol Kennicott, explains to Nick, "I've been everywhere and seen everything and done everything. . . . Sophisticated—God, I'm sophisticated."[10] Unlike Kennicott, she holds little hope for her little girl, greeting her birth with disappointment: "And I hope she'll be a fool—that's the best thing a girl can be in this world, a beautiful little fool."[11]

The two other women in *Gatsby* are Jordan Baker and Myrtle Wilson.

Jordan, a golf champion, is "incurably dishonest." She "had begun dealing in subterfuges when she was very young in order to keep that cool,
insolent smile turned to the world and yet satisfy the demands of her
hard jaunty body." But, Fitzgerald concludes, "dishonesty in a woman
is a thing you never blame deeply."[12] Myrtle Wilson, married to a gas
station owner, is Tom Buchanan's mistress. A vain, grasping woman,
Myrtle "carried her surplus flesh sensuously as some women can. Her
face . . . contained no facet or gleam of beauty, but there was an immediately perceptible vitality about her as if the nerves of her body
were continually smouldering." The depth of Tom's regard is registered
in a blow that breaks her nose.[13]

Gatsby meanwhile has amassed a fortune through gambling and
bootlegging and has bought a mansion near the Buchanans. If Daisy
has been won by Tom's money, she will now be purchased by Gatsby.
Angry at Tom's philandering and flattered by Gatsby, Daisy leads him
on. Returning from a trip to New York with Gatsby, she accidentally
runs down Myrtle Wilson, who had rushed into the road. Gatsby as-
sumes the blame and the responsibility for the hit-and-run murder.
Shot by Myrtle's distraught husband, Gatsby ends his dream of Daisy
and success face down in his swimming pool. Daisy, Jordan, and Myrtle survive by taking, cheating, lying, destroying. Devoid of sensibility,
honor, or courage, they are incapable of undertaking any search for
values. They are not interested. What they scheme for is wealth and
security. Clearly Gatsby is worth more than "the whole damned bunch
put together."[14]

While Lewis depicted the women of Main Street and Fitzgerald portrayed the urban sophisticates of New York society, Hemingway explored the search for identity of the expatriates. In *The Sun Also Rises*
his heroine, Lady Brett Ashley, is alternately lover and one of the boys.
She loves and relies on Jake Barnes, though his wound from the war
frustrates consummation of that love. Brett's greeting to Jake at the
beginning of the novel captures her anguish: "Oh, darling, I've been so
miserable.—Please don't touch me. Love you? I simply turn all to jelly
when you touch me. . . . I don't want to go through that hell again."
She is in the process of getting a divorce from her titled English husband and marrying another Englishman, Mike Campbell. She loves
neither. In the interim she has a brief affair with Jake's friend, Robert
Cohn. Jake vents his anger: "To hell with women. . . . To hell with
you Brett Ashley. . . . Women make such swell friends. Awfully swell.
In the first place you had to be in love with a woman to have a basis of

friendship. I had been having Brett for a friend. I had not been thinking about her side of it. I had been getting something for nothing. That only delayed the presentation of the bill. The bill always came. That was one of the swell things you could count on. I thought I had paid for everything. Not like the woman pays and pays and pays. No idea of retribution or punishment. Just exchange of values." "Enjoying living," he concludes, "was learning to get your money's worth and knowing when you had it."[15]

Through the wounded Jake Barnes, Hemingway explores the generation's search for meaning. Jake finds peace in nature during a fishing trip in Spain; he slips briefly into a church to try to pray; he is an aficionado who has discovered in the bullfight a vital sense of ritual and order. Brett is allowed none of these. She misses a fishing trip and remains with her quarreling lovers in Pamplona. She has no solace in religion, claiming: "I'm damned bad for a religious atmosphere. I've the wrong type of face." She is not an aficionado; indeed, her affair with the young bullfighter, Romero, threatens his career. In the final sequence, when she wires Jake to rescue her from a Madrid hotel, she has left Romero, realizing that "he shouldn't be living with anyone." It is her only responsible, moral act in the novel. Riding in a taxi with Jake, she utters one of the famous lines of the 1920s, "Oh, Jake, we could have had such a damned good time together." Jake, like Will Kennicott, has the last word, "Isn't it pretty to think so?"[16]

In these novels of Lewis, Fitzgerald, and Hemingway, the men not only have the last word; they consistently hold center stage. They have perspective and values. Will Kennicott's sturdiness, Jay Gatsby's dream, and Jake Barnes's stoicism and courage are nowhere apparent in the heroines. Carol Kennicott, Daisy Buchanan, and Lady Brett Ashley are armed with neither family nor friends. Religion has no meaning in their lives; their communities are oppressive or destructive. Stripped of the usual sheltering institutions, they are devoid of humor, vision, or endurance. They prove no match for the forces arrayed against them or the traps waiting to be sprung. The women created by women are a different story.

From the best-sellers to Pulitzer Prize winners (and sometimes, as in the case of Edna Ferber's *So Big* in 1924, they were both), the women novelists illumined the struggle of women for freedom and dignity. Fannie Hurst, the highest paid woman writer of the decade, underscored in her seventeen novels the conviction that a woman's "place is not at the front door waiting for the steps of her John and fearful lest the roast be overdone. Her place is where she can give the most service and get the most out of life."[17]

These novelists wrote of women and Main Streets also. William Allen White called Dorothy Canfield Fisher's *The Brimming Cup* in 1921 "the other side of *Main Street*." Ruth Suckow and Zona Gale depicted the struggle of women to forge identities in rural Iowa and Wisconsin. But the master was Willa Cather. In 1923, five years after *My Ántonia* and one year after her Pulitzer Prize-winning war novel, *One of Ours*, Cather completed *A Lost Lady*. The setting is Sweetwater, Nebraska. The "lost lady" is beautiful, witty Marian Forrester. "There could be," Cather wrote, "no negative encounter, however slight, with Mrs. Forrester. If she merely bowed to you, merely looked at you, it constituted a personal relation. Something about her took hold of one in a flash; one became acutely conscious of her, of her fragility and grace, of her mouth which could say so much without words; of her eyes, lively, laughing, intimate, nearly always a little mocking."[18]

She is married to Captain Daniel Forrester, a widower, twenty-five years her senior, who has helped build the Burlington Railroad across the plains. A man of wealth, integrity, and honor, he has shared the vitality and vision of the pioneers, reminiscing at a dinner party: "All our great west has been developed from such dreams; the homesteader's and the prospector's and the contractor's. We dreamed the railroads across the mountains just as I dreamed my place on the Sweet Water. All these things will be everyday facts to the coming generation, but to us . . ."[19]

The Forrester home is a place of gracious hospitality. Neighbors or visiting executives from the Burlington are always warmed by the sight of Marian Forrester, who, alerted by the sound of hoofbeats on the wooden bridge over the creek, waits at the door to greet them. They "could not imagine her in any dress or situation in which she would not be charming." Yet, her eagerness to welcome company reveals a restlessness and loneliness. Unlike Carol Kennicott, she risks an affair. Once, when the captain is away on business, young Niel Herbert, who adored Marian, impulsively picks some wild roses to leave on her bedroom windowsill. As he approaches he is stunned to hear the laughter of Frank Ellinger, a handsome Denver bachelor. In shock, Niel walks away, wondering bitterly: "Beautiful women, whose beauty meant more than it said. . . . was their brilliance always fed by something coarse and concealed? Was that their secret?"[20]

The fortunes of the Forresters and Sweet Water decline together. The captain, always a man of honor, insists on paying the depositors when his bank fails. Marian, facing straitened circumstances, supports his decision, but privately agonizes to Niel, "What will become of me. . . . I've always danced in the winter; . . . you wouldn't believe how I miss it. . . . I need it!" She cries out: "So that's what I'm struggling for—to get out of this hole . . . out of it! When I'm alone here for months together, I plan and plot. If it weren't for that . . ."[21] After Captain Forrester suffers a stroke and becomes increasingly immobilized, Marian turns for help to Ivy Peters, one of the new generation.

A lawyer and a speculator, Peters is one of the new breed "who had never dreamed anything." He is "an ugly fellow" who likes being ugly. "His eyes were very small and an absence of eyelashes gave his pupils the fixed, the unblinking hardness of a snake's or a lizard's." After the captain's death Marian is jilted by Frank Ellinger. Now drinking heavily, she sells part of her land to Peters and puts him in charge of her investments. Niel's last glimpse of her is in her kitchen; Ivy Peters stands behind her with his hands over her breast. "It was," Niel reflected, "what he most held against Mrs. Forrester; that she was not willing to immolate herself like the widow of all these great men, and die with the pioneer period to which she belonged; that she preferred life on any terms." He "went away with weary contempt for her in his heart." Leaving Sweet Water, he makes the "final break with everything that had been dear to him in his boyhood. The people, the very country itself, were changing so fast that there would be nothing to come back to." Years later he has news of Marian Forrester; she married a wealthy Englishman and is living in Argentina. She sends him a message: "things have turned out well for me."[22]

Marian is a survivor, a risk taker. Like Daisy Buchanan she needs beautiful things and the security of marriage and wealth. Like Carol Kennicott, she chafes at the isolation of a small prairie town, but she is interested in her neighbors; she enjoys people; she wins friends. The captain is honorable, but she is forced to be practical. When the world changes, she copes. Armed with neither the vision nor the exquisite sensibility of Cather's alter ego, Professor Godfrey St. Peter, in *The Professor's House*, she shares his knowledge "that life is possible, may be even pleasant, without joy, without passionate griefs."[23]

While Cather gave an added dimension to Lewis's sterile world of Main Street, Edith Wharton explored the New York society of Fitzgerald's sophisticates. In 1920 as Fitzgerald completed *This Side of Par-*

adise, Wharton was depicting *The Age of Innocence* of the 1870s. In 1925, when *The Great Gatsby* appeared, Wharton wrote *The Mother's Recompense* in an attempt, as one biographer explained, to "clarify her sense of herself as a woman and a writer of a certain age" and to test her relationship to the younger generation. Her success in straddling the generations was obvious in the critics' assessment that *The Mother's Recompense* made Wharton the equal of both John Galsworthy and F. Scott Fitzgerald.[24]

Wharton's heroine, Kate Clephane, had abandoned her marriage and her three-year-old daughter, Anne, when she was no longer able to tolerate "the thick atmosphere of self approval . . . which emanated from John Clephane like coal-gas from a leaking furnace." After living for two years with yachtsman Hilton Davies, she had settled in France, and just before the outbreak of World War I, had an affair with Christopher Fenno, at least ten years her junior. When the novel opens, Kate is living a careful, comfortable, but aimless life in an expatriate society of "frumps, hypocrites, and the good sort 'like herself.' " Two wires arrive. One announces the death of the family dowager, old Mrs. Clephane (John died years earlier); the other contains an invitation from her daughter Anne to return to be with her in the opulent Clephane home in New York. Kate sails at once.[25]

She has no difficulty recognizing her daughter in the crowd at the dock; "there was her whole youth, her whole married past, in that small pale oval—her own hair, but duskier; something of her smile too, she fancied; and John Clephane's straight rather heavy nose, beneath old Mrs. Clephane's awful brows." Kate is generously and fully accepted by Anne and is reestablished in the Clephane mansion. She eagerly observes the changes in society and custom. A "new tolerance" seems to be applied to everything. She wonders about the new generation: "What did they think? . . . they reminded her of a band of young entomologists, equipped with the newest thing in nets, but in far too great a hurry ever to catch anything." Her in-law, Lilla Gates, introduces her to the chatter of the flapper: "I hate talking. I only like noises that don't mean anything." Kate is struck by the "innocent uniformity" of the American face: "How many of them it seemed to take to make up a single individuality! . . . One may be young and handsome and healthy and eager, and yet unable, out of such rich elements, to evolve a personality. . . . Since Americans have ceased to have dyspepsia, they have lost the only thing that gave them any expression."[26]

Her daughter is an exception. Anne has beauty, talent, determination, and character. She is also in love, Kate finds to her horror, with Major Chris Fenno whom she had met while he was convalescing from his war wounds. When Fenno discovered Anne's wealth and identity, he ended his relationship with her. She had, however, pursued him and meant to have him. Distressed and puzzled by her mother's vehement opposition and her inability to explain, Anne cries in a heated exchange, "Can't we agree, mother, that I must take my chance—and that, if the risks are as great as you think, you'll be there to help me? After all, we've all got to buy our own experience, haven't we?"[27]

Convinced that the marriage must be stopped, Kate threatens that if Chris persists, she will tell Anne everything. But finally "the vehemence of Anne's passion . . . baffled them both; if he loved her as passionately as she loved him, was he not justified in accepting the happiness forced upon him? And how refuse it without destroying the girl's life?" In her despair, Kate turns to an Episcopal priest for help in advising "her friend." After insisting that the "friend" must tell her daughter and stop the marriage, he pauses and adds: "The thing in the world I'm most afraid of is sterile pain. . . . I should never want any one to be the cause of that." Kate, knowing it means she must leave her daughter again, blesses the wedding. She leaves for France the same evening, rejecting an offer of marriage and security from a long-time admirer and Anne's former guardian. The only way she can live in peace is to be sure in the knowledge that she has taken nothing.[28] It is the mother's recompense. It is an honorable and courageous decision beyond the ken of Daisy Buchanan.

Anita Loos provides a closer match to Fitzgerald's generation and to his fictional world. In 1926, Wharton reported the high point of her summer was reading the new best-seller *Gentlemen Prefer Blondes*. It was, she asserted, "the great American novel." Philosopher George Santayana was similarly enthusiastic. When asked to name the best philosophical work by an American, he did not hesitate to say *Gentlemen Prefer Blondes*. The diminutive Loos, with her short dark hair and zest for life, could have been the model for John Held's flapper cartoons. A scenario writer for D. W. Griffith and Douglas Fairbanks, she could hold her own in the quick exchanges at the Algonquin Round Table and in conversations with the redoubtable H. L. Mencken. Reportedly fascinated and somewhat piqued at the ability of a blonde to distract and bemuse Mencken, Loos sketched out a short story on the blonde mystique and sent it to the *American Mercury*. Mencken suggested that she try *Harper's Bazaar* instead, explaining: "Little girl. You're making fun of sex and that's never been done before in the U.S.A." In *Harper's Bazaar*, it would be lost among the ads and would not offend anyone. *Harper's Bazaar's* editor was so enchanted he suggested: "Take your blonde to Europe and let her have more adventures."[29] Thus was Lorelei Lee created.

Lorelei Lee lives in a New York apartment, supported by the button king of Chicago, Mr. Eisman. He is dedicated, as she explains in her diary account, to giving her an education: "I mean we always seem to have dinner at the Colony and see a show and go to the Trocadero and then Mr. Eisman shows me to my apartment. So of course when a gentleman is interested in educating a girl, he likes to stay and talk about the topics of the day until quite late, so I am quite fatigued the next day and I do not really get up until it is time to dress for dinner at the Colony." In between Eisman's visits, Lorelei likes to entertain "to have a good time before Mr. Eisman arrived." She makes her parties educational by inviting literary gentlemen. One English novelist becomes so smitten he is ready to divorce his wife and take over the education of Lorelei. She considers his proposal, but is exhausted by his endless talk. It wearies "your brain with things you never even think of when you are busy." Mr. Eisman comes to the rescue and sends her to Europe, accompanied by her friend Dorothy, to further her education.[30]

She faithfully records her experiences in her diary. London, she hates to tell Mr. Eisman, is "a failure because we know more in New York." Through an acquaintance made on the boat, she meets Sir Francis Beekman, Piggy, and educates him in generosity. She starts with a dozen orchids and works up to a diamond tiara, because "if you get a gentlemen started on buying one dozen orchids at a time, he really gets very good habits." Arriving in Paris, pursued by the angry Lady Beekman, Lorelei is anxious, for "a girl has to look out in Paris, or she would have such a good time . . . that she would not get anywheres. So I really think that American gentlemen are the best after all, because kissing your hand may make you feel very very good but a diamond and safire bracelet lasts forever."[31]

In Paris, she meets a wealthy, upright Presbyterian, Henry Spofford from Philadelphia. She and Dorothy join Henry, his mother, and her suspicious companion on trips to Munich and Vienna. She meets "Dr. Froyd" and has "quite a long talk." She writes in her diary: "So it seems that everybody seems to have a thing called inhibitions, which is when you want to do a thing and you do not do it. So then you dream about it instead. . . . I told him that I never really dream about anything. I mean I use my brains so much in the day time that at night they do not seem to do anything else but rest. . . . So then he asked me all about my life. . . . So then he seemed very very intreeged at a girl who always seemed to do everything she wanted to do."[32]

Returning to New York with Dorothy, she finally agrees to marry Henry. Mr. Eisman is mollified because he has educated her so well she is able to join an old Philadelphia family. Lorelei plans to use the Spofford money to back a Hungarian filmmaker she befriended. They will all go to Hollywood. She has always wanted a career in the cinema, and Henry can carry on welfare work with the Hollywood extras. "Everything," she confides to her diary, "always turns out for the best." The irresistible Lorelei Lee is dependent but not trapped. There seems always to be an English novelist or a new adventure ready for the taking. Henry Spofford is in Hollywood, happy and just where Lorelei wants him. She is unencumbered by scruple, guilt, or fine distinctions of right or wrong. She faces life with zest; she survives by her wits. Her theme song might have been the popular "Ain't We Got Fun."

Yet, as Fitzgerald pointed out, the rich were different. The ethnic and black women novelists explored the search for freedom and survival in the separate worlds of New York's lower East Side and Harlem. Creed and race were as crucial as gender in the struggle of their heroines for autonomy and identity.

Anzia Yezierska, a Jewish immigrant from Polish-Russia, was forty-five when she completed her powerful, autobiographical novel *Bread Givers* in 1925. She had worked in the sweatshops and laundries of the lower East Side, attended night classes at a settlement house, and then, scrimping and saving, took courses as a special student at Teachers College, Columbia University. In 1919, her "The Fat of the Land" won the O'Brien Prize for the best short story of the year. Her first book, a collection of short stories, *Hungry Hearts*, brought her prosperity in 1920 when the film rights were sold to Samuel Goldwyn for $10,000. Her heroine in the lead story, Shenah Pessah, a twenty-two-year-old janitress working for the old uncle who had paid her passage to America, is filled with yearning for life and love. She cries out: "I can't help it how old I am or how poor I am! I want a little life! I want a little joy!" Falling in love with an American, she determines to enter his world. "This fire in me," she cries, "it's not just the hunger of a woman for a man—it's the hunger of all my people back of me from all ages, for light, for the life, higher!" It is a hunger to be "a person that can't be crushed by nothing nor nobody—the life higher."[33] Her struggle foreshadows the fight of Sara Smolinsky for freedom and identity in *Bread Givers*.

The Smolinsky family—father Reb (the rabbi), a Talmudic scholar, mother Shenah, and four daughters, Bessie, Mashah, Fania, and Sara—occupy a two-room flat on Hester Street. The father and his books occupy the front room. The other room is kitchen, bedroom, and parlor. Reb Smolinsky, as Yezierska's own father, has chosen "to have his portion in the next world." His learning brings holiness and honor to the home but no income. The three older daughters support the household. When they are laid off, the youngest, Sara, goes into Hester Street to barter, Shenah Smolinsky takes in boarders, and the father and his books are settled with the rest of the family in one room. The clash of the Old World and the New erupts when suitors arrive. Berel Bernstein wants to marry Bessie, "the burden bearer"; the most reliable breadwinner, she would be a partner in setting up his new business. When Reb Smolinsky asks for money to start a business of his own as compensation for Bessie's lost wages, Bernstein explodes: "I'm marrying your daughter—not the whole family. Ain't it enough that your daughter kept you in laziness all these years? You want yet her husband to support you for the rest of your days? In America they got no use for Torah learning. In America everybody got to earn his living first. You got two hands and two feet. Why don't you go to work?" Equally outraged, Smolinsky rejects working "like a common thickneck," claiming, "My learning comes before my living."[34] Bernstein finds another wife.

Stung by the anger of his wife and dismay of his daughters, Smolinsky turns Old World matchmaker. For the beautiful Mashah, who loves a concert pianist, he finds Moe Mirsky, an alleged diamond merchant who turns out to be a struggling salesman. For Bessie, he brings Zalmon the fishmonger, a widower seeking a mother for his six children and a helper in the store. For Fania, who loves a poet, he finds a Los Angeles realtor. All are miserable, but yield out of hopelessness and a desire to escape the household. With his matchmaking money, Smolinsky is conned into buying a grocery store in Elizabeth, New Jersey, grandly sealing the purchase before his more business-minded wife can arrive. While Shenah and Sara work to bring in trade, Smolinksy lectures or haggles with the rare customer who wanders in. After one of these exchanges over two cents, Sara declares her independence: "I've got to live my own life. It's enough that Mother and the others have lived for you." "Chzufeh! You brazen one!" her father shouts. "The crime of crimes against God—daring your will against your father's will. In olden times the whole city would have stoned you!" "I'm not from the old country," replies Sara. "I'm American!"[35]

None of her sisters can help, so Sara, on her own, finds work in a laundry, rents a small room, and begins classes in night school. Her goal is set; she will be a teacher in the American New World. Hungry and exhausted, she comes home each night to the noise of the tenement. She describes her struggle: "The jarring clatter tore me by the hair, stretched me out of my skin, and grated under my teeth. I felt like one crucified in a torture pit of noise." But she rallies: "Stop all this sensitiveness, or you're beaten already before the fight is begun."

When her worried mother brings her a featherbed, Sara asks, "Won't you be proud of me when I work myself up for a school teacher in America?" They are all old maids, Shenah replies, "good enough for Goyim but not for you."[36] When her sister Fania sends a suitor from Los Angeles, Sara is tempted. But Max Goldstein talks too much business; he seems "to turn into a talking roll of dollar bills." Sara is determined not to be another piece of property. She will marry, but first she will make herself a person.[37] After her rejection of Max and possible income, her father appears. "It says in the Torah," he reminds her, "breed and multiply. A woman's highest happiness is to be a man's wife, the mother of a man's children. You're not a person at all."[38]

Finally, she earns enough credits to be admitted to college, and she works at a laundry to pay her tuition and board there. Older than the others, she is the only student from Hester Street, but she is sustained by her work, her books, and the encouragement of the dean. "Your place," he tells her, "is with the pioneers. And you're going to survive." At graduation, she wins $1,000 in an essay competition on "What College Has Done for Me." With money and a college degree, she returns to New York and a job teaching students from Hester Street.

Her happiness is shattered by the death of her mother, the remarriage of her father, and the arrival of his letter to her principal, Hugo Seelig, accusing her of letting him starve. He asserts: "If you have the fear of God in your heart, you will yourself see that at least half her wages should go to her poor old father who is a smarter man as she is a *teacherin*." Sara pours out her story to Seelig, telling how she has hardened her heart, how her father called her "blood and iron." Seelig comforts her: "You hard! You've got the fibre of a strong, live spruce

tree that grows in strength the more it's knocked about by the wind."
In the final sequence, Sara and Seelig invite the old man to live with
them and teach Seelig Hebrew. Sara, who has fought for her freedom
from the Old World of Hester Street, "felt the shadow still there. . . .
It wasn't just my father, but the generations who made my father
whose weight was still upon me."[39]

As Yezierska explored the pull of culture and creed, black novelists
Nella Larsen and Jessie Fauset wrote of the tension of gender and race.
W. E. B. Du Bois had worried that young Negro writers would follow
the trend of stressing the primitive or the underworld rather than por-
traying the truth about themselves and their class. Both Larsen and
Fauset were truth tellers. Through the power of their novels, both successfully overcame what Fauset described as the idée fixe of the white
publishing world that only the exotic or the violent would sell in a novel
about blacks.[40]

Born in the Virgin Islands, the daughter of a Danish mother and
black father, Larsen published two novels in the 1920s, *Quicksand* in
1928 and *Passing* in 1929. Both deal with the struggle of mulattoes to
find a physical, psychological, and spiritual home in a land rent by
racial hostility. In *Passing*, Larsen portrays the dilemma by comparing
the lives of three young women who could pass. Childhood friends
while growing up in Chicago, they meet again as married women and
discuss their families over tea. Gertrude has married a white butcher,
who is aware that she is a mulatto. They have twin boys. Both are
light-skinned, but Gertrude, who has been apprehensive throughout
her pregnancy about their color, is not willing "to chance" another.
Clare Kendry has passed and married a bigoted white businessman.
His nickname for Clare is "Nig," kidding that she has seemed to grow
darker since their wedding. He is clear about his feelings: "No niggers
in my family. Never have been and never will be." They have one
daughter who is "white." Irene Redfield has married a black physician.
Her concerns are those of a middle-class housewife in Harlem. Above
all she wants security, and "things left as they were." Certainly she is
not responsive to her husband's suggestion that they move to Latin
America where their two dark sons could grow up in a society that is
not so discriminatory against blacks. Through the interaction of Irene
and Clare, Larsen depicts black-white tensions and the agony of passing. Increasingly, Clare seeks the company of the Redfields and their
black friends. When Irene urges caution, Clare cries: "I can't, I
can't. . . . I would if I could, but I can't. You don't know. You can't

realize how I want to see Negroes, to be with them again, to talk with them, to hear them laugh." Brian Redfield understands: "It's always that way. . . . They always come back. I've seen it happen time and time again." Later, Clare again insists: "Can't you realize that I'm not like you a bit? Why, to get the things I want badly enough, I'd do anything, hurt anybody, throw anything away. Really, Rene, I'm not safe." Irene is at first suspicious and then convinced that Carol has decided that she wants Brian. In the final scene, when Jack Kendry, having discovered Clare's deception, confronts her at a Harlem party, Clare smiles coolly and, as Irene goes to her, falls or is pushed to her death through an open window. Irene wants "only to be tranquil. Only unmolested, to be allowed to direct for their own best good the lives of her sons and her husband."[41] In the final analysis, she too has been a risk taker. She survives but at a price.

In *Quicksand*, the mulatto's quest to belong, the search for self and home, is portrayed through Helga Crane. Helga, like Larsen, is the daughter of a black father and Scandinavian mother. At the opening of the novel, she is determined to leave her position at Naxas College, a black southern bastion of respectability and the status quo, white-style. Her decision has been triggered by the lecture of a visiting white preacher who asserted that "if all Negroes would only take a leaf out of the book of Naxas . . . there would be no race problem, because Naxas Negroes knew what was expected of them. They had good sense and they had good taste. They knew enough to stay in their places." Leaving Naxas means breaking her engagement to James Vayle, another member of the faculty. She has been concerned about fitting in with his "old family." "If you couldn't prove your ancestry and connections," she says, "you were tolerated, but you didn't 'belong.' "[42]

Not at home in the docile, respectable world of the southern black college, she moves to Chicago and, after a series of sharp rebuffs in her attempts to find a white-collar job, finally wins a position with a black lecturer, who takes her to Harlem and finds her work and friends. Helga is fascinated by the "continuously glorious panorama" of that city within a city. The "sober mad rush of white New York failed entirely to stir her." Yet she is restless.[43]

When her white uncle sends her money to travel to Denmark to live with her Aunt Katrina, she accepts. In the luxurious home of her aunt, Helga finds the "realization of day-dreams and longings. Always she had wanted, not money, but the things which money could give, leisure, attention, beautiful surroundings. Things. Things. Things." Her beauty and darkness are enhanced by the exotic wardrobe her aunt's family provides. High colors and low cuts emphasize the primitive. She is a social sensation, and wins and rejects an offer of marriage by a renowned Danish artist.

Harlem becomes home again: "*These* were her people. Nothing, she had come to understand now, could ever change that. Strange that she had never truly valued this kinship until distance had shown her its worth." She is also aware that Harlem is an enclave in hostile territory and reflects after Vayle arrives and again proposes marriage: "Marriage—that means children to me. And why add more suffering to the world: Why add any more unwanted, tortured Negroes to America? Why *do* Negroes have children? Surely it must be sinful. Think of the awfulness of being responsible for the giving of life to creatures doomed to endure such wounds to the flesh, such wounds to the spirit."[44] When she does find someone to love, the sensitive, highly educated former dean of Naxas, he is already married to a good friend. She considers returning to Denmark. But in a climactic scene, she stumbles out of a rainstorm into a church filled with writhing, weeping, shouting blacks, all chanting, "Less of self and more of Thee." She feels the "brutal desire to shout and to sling herself about." Fainting, she is taken home by the preacher, Rev. M. Pleasant Green.

Believing she has found a spiritual home, she marries the Reverend Green and returns to the poverty of his ministry in Alabama. Within twenty months she bears three children, twin boys and a girl. She is so weakened that her fourth child dies soon after birth. She calls out in her pain to God, but she knows now that "he wasn't there. Didn't exist." For Negroes, life "wasn't a miracle, a wonder . . . only a great disappointment." She longs to flee to the city and freedom, but the children hold her back. First, however, she must regain her strength, but "hardly had she left her bed and become able to walk again without pain . . . when she began to have her fifth child."[45]

The quicksand has been waiting for Helga since her own birth, and she passes on her bitter legacy to child after child. Yet within this grim naturalistic novel, Larsen allows Helga Crane the right and dignity of choice. She freely moves from Naxas to Chicago, Harlem, Denmark, and Alabama. But for her there is no home.[46]

In *Plum Bun*, Jessie Fauset also explored the possibility of freedom and survival for the black woman. Like Larsen, she tested the pull of race through the decision to pass made by her heroine, Angela Murray. The Murray family, Mattie and Junius and their two daughters, Angela

and Virginia, live on Opal Street in Philadelphia. It is "narrow, un-
sparkling, and uninviting . . . an unpretentious street lined with unpretentious little people." Mattie has been a lady's maid and Junius a
chauffeur when they meet. To Junius, Mattie is a "perfect woman,
sweet, industrious, affectionate, and illogical." To Mattie, he is "a God."
When she reads fairy tales to the children, she always ends, "And so
they lived happily ever after, just like your father and me." They are
determined that their daughters will not suffer their hardships and plan
for their careers in teaching.[47]

Unified by love, the family is quirkily divided by color. Mattie and
Angela are pale; Junius and Virginia, dark. On Saturday outings, they
pair by color and interest. Mattie, who loves to shop in the elegant
downtown stores and to have tea in first-class hotels, takes Angela and
passes. In one encounter Mattie and Angela ignore Junius and Virginia
when they are leaving a hotel. Guilt-ridden, Mattie later apologizes
only to be reassured by Junius: "My dear girl, I told you long ago that
where no principle was involved your passing means nothing to me.
It's just a little joke; I don't think you'd be ashamed to acknowledge
your old husband anywhere if it were necessary."

Angela, who "didn't see any sense in living unless you're going to be
happy," continually confronts the problem of mistaken racial identity.
An early and scarring encounter at school keeps being repeated. "You
never told me you were coloured," starts the dialogue. Angela's response is always, "Tell you I was coloured! Why, of course I never told
you that I was coloured. Why should I?" After her parents' deaths, she
moves to New York to study art where no one knows that she is "coloured." She changes her name to Angele Mory. Sitting on a bench in
Union Square, she dreams of her future: "If she could afford it she
would have a salon, a drawing room, where men and women, not necessarily great, but real, alive, free and untramelled in manner and
thought should come. . . . She would need money and influence—perhaps it would be better to marry a white man."[48]

Her classmates in the studio at Cooper Union bring her opportunities and advice. Paulette, the free spirit, knows what she wants and
uses her "wiles as a woman to get it." Martha Burden, addicted to
causes, gives her advice on winning a husband: "It is a game, and the
hardest game in the world for a woman, but the most fascinating." The
woman has "to be careful not to withhold too much and yet to give
very little. . . . Oh, Angele, God doesn't like women." Paulette introduces Angele to Roger Fielding. Like Clare Kendry's husband in *Pass-*

ing, he is white, handsome, and bigoted. He is also wealthy and immediately attracted by Angele's beauty and the sense of excitement about her. Angele sees that she is "swimming in the flood of excitement created by her unique position. Stolen waters are the sweetest." She thinks: "Here I am having everything that a girl ought to have just because I had sense enough to suit my actions to my appearance." When another art student, Anthony Cross, presses his suit, asking, "Could you for the sake of love, for the sake of being loyal to the purposes and vows of someone you loved, bring yourself to endure privation and hardship and misunderstanding?" he hasn't a chance.

Believing that Roger is going to propose marriage, Angele violates the family principle of passing. When she arrives at the train station to greet Virginia, who has come to New York to take an examination, she unexpectedly encounters Roger. Faced with a choice, she refuses to acknowledge her sister. In the aftermath her world disintegrates. Roger wants a mistress, not a wife, and she finally succumbs. When she reconciles with Virginia, she finds herself increasingly envious of her life in Harlem. When she finally realizes that she loves Anthony Cross, that a woman can be her true self with him, she discovers that he too is black and that he is engaged to Virginia. More than once she thinks of dying, "of the race of her parents and of all the odds against living . . . And she saw them as a people powerfully, almost overwhelmingly endowed with the essence of life. They had to persist, had to survive because they did not know how to die."[49]

Finally, she is given another opportunity to claim her race when she and a black student both win a competition and prize money for study in Paris. When the judges rescind the prize because of race, Angele tells the press that she too is black. She secures funds for travel to France. In the final scene on Christmas night, she is surprised by the arrival of Anthony Cross. Virginia has married her first love from Philadelphia. Everyone, as Mattie Murray would have ended, "lived happily ever after."

Unlike Helga Larsen or Clare Kendry, Angela Murray has the strength of family to sustain her. The resilience, courage, and dignity of her race become her strength. Her gender proves more burdensome.

While all these women novelists of the 1920s across generation, ethnicity, and class created characters who fought for freedom and survival, none achieved the power of Ellen Glasgow in *Barren Ground*. Glasgow was forty-seven in 1920; her first novel, *The Descendant*, had been published in 1897. She followed that with *Virginia* and *The Voice of the People*, inveighing against the southern code and its stranglehold on southern women; by the 1920s, she was writing of the commercialism and cruelty of the New South and mourning the loss of sensitivity and civility. A southern critic of her early work found her novels unfit reading for the "trusting wives of Southern gentlemen." H. L. Mencken wrote approvingly of her work in the *American Mercury*: "In her gallery all the salient figures of the Virginia zoology stalk about under glaring lights, and when she has done with them . . . there is little left to know about them—and not too much that is made known is reassuring."[50] In the 1920s she wrote two of her comedies of manners, *They Stooped to Folly* and *The Romantic Comedians*, a tale of amorous, elderly Judge Honeywell, who, widowed, resolutely refuses to marry his patient childhood sweetheart, but chooses youth instead and dances to exhaustion. Both novels are funny and wise, but they were only an interlude. All of her life and in all her writings, Glasgow unrelentingly searched for a meaning in life.

In 1925, she completed *Barren Ground*, the first of a trio of works that tested her theory of survival through irony and fortitude. In an introduction to a later edition, she wrote, "If I might select one of my books for the double-edged blessing of immortality, that book would be, I think, *Barren Ground*." Her heroine is Dorinda Oakley. The setting, Queen Elizabeth County in the Tidewater area, is "bare, starved, desolate." In the face of a dwindling yield each year, the farmers steadfastly refuse to change. Year after year, the land turns into "old fields" covered with broomsedge and pine and life-everlasting. The Oakley's Old Farm is a thousand acres of scrub pine and scrub oak "where a single cultivated corner was like a solitary island in some chaotic sea." Her father, Josiah, is a tireless laborer "but that destiny which dogs the footsteps of the ineffectual spirits pursued him from the hour of his birth." Her hard-working mother, Eudora, suppresses "religious mania." She never worries about anything smaller than eternal damnation. Dorinda, their only daughter, works to help out in Nathan Pedlar's store. Her monotonous life is changed by the arrival of young Dr. Jason Greylock. Returning home to care for his alcoholic father, Jason tries to reform the farming methods of the community. The hardest thing, he confides to Dorinda, is to believe that people "will fight to stay in a rut, but not to get out of it." He attaches himself to Dorinda, the one bright spot in the desolate area and finally proposes marriage. One week before the wedding, however, he is bullied into marrying the daughter of the most prosperous farmer in the area, jilting the now pregnant Dorinda.

Fleeing to New York, Dorinda loses her baby after a street accident. While convalescing, she works in a doctor's office and begins to read farm journals. She finally decides to return to Old Farm, declaring, "I can't stay away any longer. I'm part of it. I belong to the abandoned fields."[51]

Backed by a loan from her New York friends, she establishes a dairy herd and begins to transform Old Fields. She lives the adage of an old countryman, "Put yo' heart in the land. The land is the only thing that will stay by you." There is ceaseless effort in the next years, but the farm prospers. Dorinda reflects: "I was able to take risks because I was too unhappy to be afraid." She begins to go to church again, and gradually she is worn down by the persistence of Nathan Pedlar and agrees to marry him. Her wedding night finds her in the barns tending the cows. One man has "ruined her life; but no other man should interfere with it."[52]

As she faces middle age, she looks "exactly what she was in reality, a handsome, still youthful woman of thirty-eight, who had been hardened but not embittered by experience." Meanwhile, Jason Greylock's marriage disintegrates and he sinks into alcoholism. Dorinda has the satisfaction of buying the Greylock farm Five Oaks, and redoubling her efforts. Work sustains her; "if she had looked for it, she sometimes told herself, she could have found sufficient cause for unhappiness; but she was careful not to look for it." After losing the companionship of Nathan who has died a hero's death in a train accident, Dorinda takes in the dying Jason Greylock to see him through his last days. His death unleashes a torrent of hag-ridden dreams, but "in the morning the land which she had forgotten was waiting to take her back to its heart. Endurance. Fortitude. The spirit of the land was flowing into her, and her own spirit strengthened and refreshed, was flowing out again toward life. . . . While the soil endured, while the seasons bloomed and dropped, while the ancient, beneficent ritual of sowing and reaping moved in the fields, she knew that she could never despair of contentment. . . . At middle age, she faced the future without romantic glamour, but she faced it with integrity of vision."[53]

In her trenchant study, *Reinventing Womanhood*, Carolyn Heilbrun observed:

Woman's most persistent problem has been to discover for herself an identity not limited by custom or defined by attachment to some man. Remarkably, her search for identity has been even less successful within the world of fiction than outside it. . . . Men writers have created women characters with autonomy, with a self that is not ancillary, not described by a relationship—wife, mother, daughter, mistress, chief assistant. Woman writers, however, when they wished to create an individual filling more than a symbiotic role, projected their ideal of autonomy onto a male character.[54]

Not all male writers, she added, created "women heroes"; indeed American writers, with the rare exception of Henry James and Nathaniel Hawthorne, had not done so. Yet the women novelists of the 1920s also provide clear exceptions. Cather's Marian Forrester and Wharton's Kate Clephane are risk takers and survivors. In the determination of Sara Smolinski to have "the life higher," the recklessness of Clare Kendry in passing and in seeking the company of her own race, and the hard-won courage of Angela Murray, the fictional women achieve "the full range of human experience."[55]

Ellen Glasgow's Dorinda Oakley was the most fully drawn, the most fully autonomous. She existed "wherever a human being has learned to live without joy, wherever the spirit of fortitude has triumphed." Glasgow's answer to how to live was close to Hemingway's "grace under pressure." Her sense of the ironic closely paralleled his. Her fortitude, her vein of iron, was close to his stoic courage. The difference was endurance. It was the essential difference in the characters drawn by the men and the women novelists of the 1920s. The women, as Zelda Fitzgerald, not one of the survivors, wrote "do not die tomorrow—or the next day. They have to live on to any one of many bitter ends." In the works of the women novelists, they chose those ends—they forged their own freedom and survival.[56]

The first newspaper photograph taken of Anne Morrow after she announced her engagement to Charles Lindbergh in Mexico City.

CHAPTER TEN

Conclusion

The last ten years have seen an extraordinary flux in the position, the activities, and most of all in the inner attitudes of women. A natural impulse is to conjure with the word progress; to tell over the new legal freedoms and powers, and the new occupations of women, and to expound the achievements of outstanding individuals. But if this survey is to be a serious reckoning, it must first ask in what sense the quality of progress may be ascribed to these multitudinous changes, or, pressing further, in what progress in the woman movement may rightly be held to consist.

> Ethel Puffer Howes,
> *"The Meaning of Progress in the Woman Movement."*[1]

Women were major contributors to the velocity of change of the 1920s. Assessing the status of women in American society ten years after the suffrage victory, Ethel Puffer Howes's article in the *Annals* bristled with words conveying a sense of accelerated motion. When the Lynds concluded in *Middletown* that a citizen had "one foot on the relatively solid ground of established habits and the other fast to an escalator careening madly in several directions at a bewildering variety of speeds," they could have heightened the drama by making that citizen a woman. In no other decade of the twentieth century, until the 1970s, have women been so at the center of the major issues. Traditionally the anchors of those anchoring institutions for the individual and nation— the family, the churches, the schools—in the twenties, women were expected to maintain the "relatively solid ground of established habits" and at the same time to leap onto the fastest-moving escalators.

If, as Howes suggested, the natural impulse "to tell over the new legal freedoms and powers" is followed, a roller coaster is a more apt image than an escalator. After the heady momentum and the brave hopes of the suffrage victory, political progress proved difficult, uneven, halting, and, to many, deeply disappointing. The potential power of new women voters and the organization, networking, and effective lobbying of the social feminists proved a major force in maintaining the vestiges of the progressive movement and won the first federal social welfare legislation in the passage of the Sheppard–Towner Act. By mid-decade, the divisions between the social and radical feminists, a growing complacency in country and Congress, a continued stereotyping of feminists as "hard-favored, vinegar-faced shrews," and the indifference of the younger generation brought the twin defeats of the child labor and equal rights amendments. The reform impulse of the social feminists was stayed. Radical feminism, as one historian observed, of the quest for ERA, was "an idea whose time had not come, . . . [but] women in the 1920s were diverted, . . . not vanquished."[2] In the elections of 1928, women, though radically divided by ethnicity and issues, again showed their organizational muscle when aroused for a cause. They scored their greatest successes in their 1928 campaigns for office. Their great failure was in not gaining the interest or adherence of the younger generation to organization or cause. But their victories did regain some lost momentum; their network was intact and ready for action when called by Eleanor Roosevelt to help stem the disaster of the depression.[3]

Women's economic aspirations did not lag far behind their high political expectations. Yet the job market proved as problematic as the polling place. There was a continued movement of women into factories, offices, and professions, but there were few escalators that went to the top. In 1920, 86 percent of the 8.3 million working women clustered in ten occupations. In the factories, the expanded opportunities of the war quickly contracted. Women primarily worked in those industries that were extensions of their functions in the home—textiles, clothing, shoemaking, and food processing. Only one in thirty-four belonged to a union; their wages hovered at 52 to 55 percent of those of male workers. The major expansion for women came in white-collar occupations—at the telephone switchboard, in the department store, and at the office. New office technology and the emphasis on efficiency and scientific management compartmentalized work. Women, who were perceived as "tolerant of routine, careful, and manually dexterous," filled 52 percent of the clerical positions by 1930 in a rare instance of a shift from men's to women's work. Throughout the decade, as newspaper want ads graphically demonstrated, the world of work was segregated by gender. Women's work remained women's work.[4]

The professions as well as the marketplace were generally segregated by gender. In the traditional "soft" professions, women continued to dominate, forming in 1930 81 percent of the teachers; 78.7 percent of the social workers; 91.4 percent of the librarians, and 98.1 percent of the nurses. When women advanced in medicine, science, or law, they usually remained in feminized areas—pediatrics, home economics, or family law. In all of the professions and in business, professional women organized, networked, and endured. United in their professionalism, they divided by generation and expectation. The determined pioneers expected to sacrifice marriage for profession; the next generation, in their thirties and forties in 1920, strained to have a career and marriage. If forced to choose between the two, they frequently kept the career. The young generation, entering the professions during the decade, also hoped to "have it all," but began to discount the "rewards from a material success that must be accomplished at the expense of love."[5]

Marriage and family remained the primary goal and homemaker the primary occupation for most American women. In no institution were the changes they fashioned and experienced so radical or rapid. It was apparent, as sociologists Ernest R. Groves and William Ogburn pointed out in 1928, that old attitudes were "disintegrating more rapidly" than new post-Freudian ones were being formed. The family, to use the Lynds' image, was the most "madly careening" escalator. The married woman was to be a wife-companion, a knowledgeable consumer-in-chief, scientific homemaker, childbearer and child rearer. She was to master these roles while becoming more conscious of her sexual needs, grappling with the option of birth control, mechanizing her housekeeping, guarding against wreaking psychological mayhem on her children, and, increasingly, working outside the home to meet the economic necessities or consumer demands of her family. Across class, ethnicity, and creed the challenges varied, but they were unrelenting. The strain was most visible in the marriages of the younger generation. They wed with both higher expectations and lower tolerance. They demanded, as psychologist Beatrice Hinkle explained, "recognition as individuals first, and as wives and mothers second." They claimed "the right to dispose of themselves according to their own needs and capacities."[6]

In school, that other traditional anchor of individual and nation, women's expectations were also high. The daughters of immigrants saw high school as the door opening "the way to that Elysian field, the modern office."[7] In higher education, the surge in women's enrollments continued. By 1920, 431,000 women were enrolled in colleges and universities—43.7 percent of the total college population. As President William Allan Neilson of Smith College observed, the path blazed by the nineteenth-century pioneers had "become a highway," albeit still traveled by an elite group.[8] By 1920, the generations of women who had hungered for education and had fought for it were succeeded by a generation that took it for granted. The debates of the 1920s centered not on whether women should go to college, but on the kind of college education and for the kind of future it should prepare them.

In both the women's colleges and in the coeducational institutions, it was expected that women graduates would both marry and have a career. The academically rigorous Seven Sisters colleges, defensive at charges that their programs led only to a "spinster of art" degree, gathered statistics demonstrating the rising marriage rates of graduates. In the coed colleges and universities, which women chose in increasing numbers, undergraduate education was frequently separate, by field of study, and unequal, in the restrictions of dormitory life. One registrar waggishly divided subjects into those that were "useful full-blooded, and manly and those which were ornamental, dilettantish and feminine."[9] On all campuses, as Paula Fass has detailed, undergraduate men and women were challenging traditional values and forging new rules and new relationships; "they knew that they lived in a changing world that demanded new understanding, new conventions, and constant readjustments." "Their clothes, their music, their athletics, and their slang—merged into the consciousness of a decade," Fass concluded. "The adult population hounded their every step, and where some came to condemn, others stayed to imitate."[10]

The churches, which were cauldrons of change for women in the 1920s, sounded the alarm at the new manners and morals. Churchwomen, an increasing plurality in congregations though thwarted in their fight for an equal or at least more responsible role in church affairs, were called to extend their influence to curb the excesses of the flapper and to stand against the worst incursions of the "revolution in manners and morals." In their fight for the old morality and the American way, women divided. Generally Protestant, old stock, and rural America stood for Prohibition against the wet proclivities of Roman Catholic, newer, urban Americans. As the Ku Klux Klan reemerged, women joined as auxiliaries; lines were drawn on religious and racial grounds. Whether the guardians of morality or newer Americans and flappers challenging the old ways, women stood at the center of the struggles of a culture at the crossroads.

Women writers and artists were full partners in shaping and in reflecting the complex culture of the 1920s. They produced a rich and challenging cacophony in the cheekiness of Anita Loos, the eccentricities and experiments of Margaret Anderson, the edged humor and stark frankness of Dorothy Parker, the determined freedom of Isadora Duncan and Martha Graham, the surrealist paintings of Romaine Brooks, and the pale and commercial Hollywood images of the child-woman, vamp, and temptress. Novelists as diverse as Willa Cather, Edith Wharton, Anzia Yezierska, Jessie Fauset, Anita Loos, and Ellen Glasgow tellingly related changing generations, environments, and values. Their heroines, across generations, yearned for fulfillment, but above all, they were determined survivors. The young demanded the right to forge their own futures—from the urgency of Shenah Pessah's "hunger for light, for the life, higher" to Anne Clephane's reasoned query, "we've all got to buy our own experience, haven't we?" The older heroines endured, accepting with Cather that "life is possible, maybe even pleasant, without joy, without passionate griefs." At their best, they shared the fortitude of Dorinda Oakley and "faced the future without romantic glamour, but . . . with integrity of vision."[11]

The great gift from the women who had come of age in the struggles for suffrage and reform to the young generation of the 1920s was freedom of choice. They continued to expend their talents and use their networking in politics, the professions, and the churches to fight reverses and to win more modest victories throughout the decade. But above all, they maintained options for their successors. The young generation staked out their own ground; they too went where the "action" was. They sought meaning and value where "the solid ground" was shifting most precipitously. Educated to fuller expectations for marriage and for life, they found their hardest challenge was within—within the home, and, more profoundly, within themselves. Unlike their predecessors, united by cause or linked by organization, they faced that challenge on their own. Psychologist Beatrice Hinkle saw the "great inner meaning" of their struggle as "nothing less than the psychological development of themselves as individuals. . . . If they have individually failed to achieve their full destiny, their attitude is part of a great rolling tide which is bringing to birth a new woman."[12]

Across generations the women of the 1920s met the dual challenge of setting the course beyond suffrage and of crafting the self "beyond separate spheres." In their public and private lives they insisted on equality—of citizenship and personhood. They built a foundation that weathered the setback of the depression, the turmoil of World War II, and the challenge of affluence and the feminine mystique. Veteran reformer Mary Anderson lived to see the passage of equal pay legislation and the early skirmishes over Title VII of the Civil Rights Act of 1964. Alice Paul survived to recount on television the early struggles for ERA as Congress voted its support for the amendment. Their hard struggle with "the psychological development of themselves as individuals" was a necessary prelude to the emergence of the "different voice" in the 1960s, described by Carol Gilligan, offering women's experience in relationships, interdependence, responsibility, care, and nurturing as needed balance and perhaps even salvation to a nation rocked by division and war and challenged by a major revolt of the young generation.[13] The "great rolling tide" formed by the women of the twenties cut channels that were broad and deep.

The yearning, the challenge, the realism, and the courage of the women of the decade were movingly expressed in 1928 by Anne Morrow, a Smith undergraduate:

I must say over and over to myself. *Make your world count*—it is little, but you must find something there. I am trying to work it out. What do I want to do— what *can* I do? The nearest I can get to it is that perhaps I could be useful and happy trying to help people to appreciate (by teaching or some other way— writing, *perhaps* and perhaps through a family and children) the things I care most about: the beauty and poise and completion of flowers, or birds, or music, of some writing, of some people—glimpses of perfection in all of these.[14]

Later that same year, when she had decided to marry Charles Lindbergh, she wrote to a good friend, capturing the spirit and the qualities that linked the women of the 1920s: "if you write me and wish me conventional happiness, I will *never* forgive you. Don't wish me happiness—I don't expect to be happy, but it's gotten beyond that, somehow. Wish me courage and strength and a sense of humor—I will need them all."[15]

Notes and References

Preface

1. Paul A. Carter, *Another Part of the Twenties* (New York: Columbia University Press, 1977), x.
2. Estelle B. Freedman, "The New Woman: Changing Views of Women in the 1920s," *Journal of American History* 61 (September 1974):372.
3. Ibid., 373, 387.
4. E. E. Calkins, "The United States of Advertising," *Saturday Review of Literature* 5 (17 November 1928):679.

Chapter One

1. Frederick Lewis Allen, *Only Yesterday: An Informal History of the Nineteen-Twenties* (New York: Harper & Row, 1931), 281; Paula S. Fass, *The Damned and the Beautiful: American Youth in the 1920s* (Oxford: Oxford University Press, 1977), 3; William E. Leuchtenburg, *The Perils of Prosperity, 1914–32* (Chicago: University of Chicago Press, 1958), 11.
2. See Allen, *Only Yesterday*; Elizabeth Stevenson, *Babbitts and Bohemians: The American 1920's* (New York: Macmillan, 1967); Frederick Hoffman, "Philistine and Puritan in the 1920's," *American Quarterly* 1 (Fall 1949):242–63; Paul A. Carter, *The Twenties in America* (Arlington Heights, Ill.: AHM, 1975), 4; H. S. Commager and S. E. Morison, *The Growth of the American Republic* (New York: Oxford University Press, 1961), 653; Burl Noggle, "The Twenties: A New Historiographical Frontier," *Journal of American History* 8 (September 1966):314; George E. Mowry, ed., *The Twenties: Fords, Flappers & Fanatics* (Englewood Cliffs, N.J.: Prentice-Hall, 1963), 1.
3. Noggle, p. 299; Mark Sullivan, *Our Times: The United States, 1900–1925* (New York: Charles Scribners, 1935), 6:4; cited in Leuchtenburg, 11; Allen, 100–101.
4. Robert and Helen Lynd, *Middletown: A Study in American Culture* (New York: Harcourt Brace Jovanovich, 1956), 498, 493; Leuchtenburg, 204.
5. Burl Noggle, *Into the Twenties* (Urbana: University of Illinois Press, 1974); Geoffrey Perrett, *America in the Twenties: A History* (New York: Simon & Schuster, 1982), 29–31; Allen, 4–16. See Robert K. Murray, *Red Scare: A*

Study in National Hysteria, 1919–1920 (New York: McGraw Hill, 1964) for a good overview of the labor unrest and Bolshevist hysteria.

6. See Murray and Stanley Coben, "A Study in Nativism, The American Red Scare of 1919–20," *Political Science Quarterly* 79 (March 1964):52–75; Paul L. Murphy, "Sources and Nature of Intolerance in the 1920's," *Journal of American History* 51 (June 1964):60–76; Fred L. Paxson, "The Great Demobilization," *American Historical Review* 44 (January 1939):237–51; Allen, 40; David Shannon, *The Socialist Party of America: A History* (New York: Modern Library, 1955); James Weinstein, *The Decline of Socialism in America, 1912–25* (New York: Monthly Review, 1967).

7. See Robert L. Friedheim, *The Seattle General Strike* (Seattle: University of Washington, 1964).

8. David Brody, *Labor in Crisis: The Steel Strike of 1919* (Philadelphia: Lippincott, 1965). See also Murray.

9. Robert D. Worth, "The Palmer Raids," *South Atlantic Quarterly* 58 (January 1949):1–23.

10. See Herbert Ehrmann, *The Case That Will Not Die: Commonwealth vs. Sacco and Vanzetti* (Boston: Little, Brown, 1969) and Francis Russell, *Tragedy at Dedham* (New York: McGraw Hill, 1958).

11. Carter, 23; Leuchtenburg, 179–80.

12. Hicks, 110; Perrett, 337–38; Allen, 133.

13. Paul Carter, *Another Part of the Twenties* (New York: Columbia University Press, 1977); Leuchtenburg, 180; Preston W. Slosson, *The Great Crusade and After: 1914–1928* (New York: Macmillan, 1930), 140–41.

14. Slosson, 219–23, 241; Allen, 136; Carter, *Another Part of the Twenties*, 2.

15. Allen, 137; Leuchtenburg, 196–97; Perrett, 224, 231; Slosson, 313, 393.

16. Perrett, 19, 347; Leuchtenburg, 192–93; Slosson, 183–85. See also Alan Raucher, *Public Relations and Business* (Baltimore: Johns Hopkins University Press, 1968).

17. Morrell Heald, *The Social Responsibilities of Business, Company and Community, 1900–1960* (New York: Columbia University Press, 1970).

18. Hicks, 12–13; Slosson, 177–78.

19. Allen, 139; Leuchtenburg, 200; Hicks, 190–210.

20. Leuchtenburg, 188; Perrett, 49; Allen, 144–49; Purniton cited in Mowry, 4; James Truslow Adams, *Our Business Civilization* (New York: Albert & Charles Boni, 1929), 31.

21. Allen, 133; Perrett, 321–22; Hicks, 113–15; Slosson, 225.

22. Perrett, 250.

23. Irving Bernstein, *The Lean Years: A History of the American Worker, 1920–1933* (Baltimore: Penguin Books, 1966), 83–142.

24. Bernstein, 211–12, 366–77, 1–43; Perrett, 326–27.

25. Theodore Salutos and John D. Hicks, *Twentieth-Century Populism: Agricultural Discontent in the Middle West 1900–1939* (Lincoln: University of Nebraska Press, 1951), 87–110; Allen, 133; Arthur S. Link, "Federal Reserve Policy and Agricultural Depression of 1920–1921," *Agricultural History* 20 (July 1946):166–75.

26. Salutos and Hicks, 321–71.

27. Kenneth McKay, *The Progressive Movement of 1924* (New York: Octagon Books, 1947); James H. Shideler, "The Disintegration of the Progressive Party Movement of 1924," *Historian* 13 (Spring 1951):189–201; Leuchtenburg, 135.

28. Salutos and Hicks, 372–434; Carter, *The Twenties*, 41.

29. Leuchtenburg, 145–50.

30. Frederick J. Hoffman, *The 20's: American Writing in the Post War Decade* (New York: Free Press, 1962), 74–80; Loren Baritz, ed., *The Culture of the Twenties* (Indianapolis: Bobbs-Merrill Co., 1970), 1; Allen, 191.

31. Baritz, 116–17; Perrett, 266.

32. Hoffman, 21, 32.

33. Warren I. Susman, "A Second Country, the Expatriate Image," *Texas Studies in Literature and Language* 3 (Summer 1961):171–83; Baritz, 1; Malcolm Cowley, *Exile's Return* (New York: Viking, 1951).

34. Hoffman, 51.

35. Henry S. Canby, "The Young Romantics: An Interpretive Survey of Recent Fiction," *Century* 103 (February 1922):521; Baritz, p. xvi; John W. Aldridge, "Afterthoughts on the 20's," *Commentary*, November 1973, 37–39; Fass, 3, 26; Allen, 200.

36. Allen, 81–85, 98–101, 198–99; Slosson, 149, 282, 388; Leuchtenburg, 165; Perrett, 154, 222–23.

37. Perrett, 222–23; Carter, *Another Part of the Twenties*, 203–23.

38. Slosson, 108–9; Andrew Sinclair, *Prohibition: The Era of Excess* (Boston: Little, Brown, 1962); Warren E. Stickle, "New Jersey Democracy and the Urban Coalition, 1919–1932" (Ph.D. diss., Georgetown University, 1971).

39. David M. Chalmers, *Hooded Americanism: The First Century of the Ku Klux Klan, 1865–1965* (Chicago: Quadrangle, 1965); E. D. Cronon, *Black Moses: The Story of Marcus Garvey and the Universal Negro Improvement Association* (Madison: University of Wisconsin Press, 1955); Kenneth Jackson, *The Ku Klux Klan in the Cities, 1915–1930* (New York: Oxford University Press, 1968).

40. David Burner, *The Politics of Provincialism: The Democratic Party in Transition, 1918–1932* (New York: Alfred A. Knopf, 1968); Robert K. Murray, *The 103rd Ballot: Democrats and Disaster in Madison Square Garden* (New York: Harper & Row, 1976); J. Leonard Bates, "The Teapot Dome Scandal and the Election of 1924," *Mississippi Valley Historical Review* 60 (October 1954):303–22; Lee Allen, "The McAdoo Campaign for the Presidential Nomination in 1924," *Journal of Southern History* 29 (May 1963):211–38.

41. Leuchtenburg, 239–40; E. Moore, *A Catholic Runs for President* (New York: Ronald Press, 1956); Allen Lichtman, *Prejudice and the Old Politics: The Presidential Election of 1928* (Chapel Hill: University of North Carolina, 1979.)

42. Robert H. Elias, *Entangling Alliances with None: An Essay on the Individual in the American Twenties* (New York: Norton, 1973), 112; David Burner, *Herbert Hoover, a Public Life* (New York: Knopf, 1979).

43. Jerome M. Clubb and Howard W. Allen, "The Cities and the Election of 1928: Partisan Realignment?" *American Historical Review* 74 (Spring 1969):1205–20; Leuchtenburg, 202. See Lichtman for the fullest analysis.

44. Charles and Mary R. Beard, *America in Midpassage* (New York: Macmillan Co., 1939); Leuchtenburg, pp. 240–47; Allen, 266–81. See John K. Galbraith, *The Great Crash* (Boston: Houghton Mifflin Co., 1955).

45. Bernstein, 251; Beards, 11–16; Allen, 268–69; and Galbraith.

46. Carter, *Another Part of the Twenties*, 165.

47. Susman, 122–48; Hoffman, 30.

48. John William Ward, "The Meaning of Lindbergh's Flight," in Hennig Cohen, ed., *The American Culture: Approaches to the Study of the United States* (New York: Houghton Mifflin Co., 1968), 18–29; Plesur, 2; Allen, 183–84.

Chapter Two

1. Cornelia Bryce Pinchot, "In Search of Adventure," in Elaine Showalter, ed., *These Modern Women: Autobiographical Essays from the Twenties* (Old Westbury, N.Y.: Feminist Press, 1978), 126; Margaret Mead, *Blackberry Winter: My Earlier Years* (New York: Washington Square Books, 1972), 1.

2. Barbara Welter, "The Cult of True Womanhood, 1820–1860," *American Quarterly* 18 (Summer 1966):151–74.

3. Caroline Ticknor, "The Steel-Engraving Lady and the Gibson Girl," *Atlantic Monthly* 88 (July 1901):105–8.

4. Harriet L. Bradley, "The Return of the Gentlewoman," *Atlantic Monthly* 93 (March 1904):402; "Futurist Manners," *Atlantic Monthly* 112 (September 1913):112; Cornelia A. P. Comer, "The Vanishing Lady," *Atlantic Monthly* 108 (December 1911):721; Eliot Gregory, "Our Foolish Virgins," *Century* 43 (November 1901):3–15.

5. Margaret Deland, "The Change in the Feminine Ideal," *Atlantic Monthly* 105 (March 1910):291, 293.

6. "Mr. Grundy," "Polite Society," *Atlantic Monthly* 125 (May 1920):606. He provoked two articles in response: John F. Carter, Jr., "These Wild Young People," *Atlantic Monthly* 126 (September 1920):301–4 and "By a Last Year's Debutante," "Good-Bye Dear Mr. Grundy," *Atlantic Monthly* 126 (November 1920):642–46.

7. Preston W. Slosson, *The Great Crusade and After, 1914–1928* (New York: Macmillan, 1929), 157.

8. Beatrice M. Hinkle, "The Chaos of Modern Marriage," *Harper's* 152 (December 1925):9.

9. G. Stanley Hall, "Flapper Americana Novissima," *Atlantic Monthly* 129 (June 1922):780. Kenneth A. Yellis, "Prosperity's Child: Some Thoughts on the Flapper," *American Quarterly* 21 (Spring 1969):44–64, provides a thoughtful analysis of the surface fashions and underlying aspirations of the flapper.

10. Bromley and Pruette, cited in Showalter, 12–13, 16.

11. Leta S. Hollingworth, "The New Woman in the Making," *Current History* 27 (October 1927):20.

12. Anne Firor Scott, "Jane Addams," in *Notable American Women, 1607–1956*, ed. Edward T. James, Janet James, and Paul S. Boyer (Cambridge: Harvard University Press, 1971), 1:16–20; Allen Davis, *Spearheads for Reform: The Social Settlements and the Progressive Movement, 1890–1914* (Philadelphia: Temple University Press, 1967); Jane Addams, *Twenty Years at Hull House* (New York: Macmillan Co., 1910).

13. See Jill Conway, "Women Reformers and American Culture, 1870–1930," *Journal of Social History* 5 (Winter 1971–72):164–78.

14. Rosalind Rosenberg, *Beyond Separate Spheres: Intellectual Roots of Modern Feminism* (New Haven: Yale University Press, 1982), 5–6, 11–12; Carrol Smith-Rosenberg, *Disorderly Conduct: Visions of Gender in Victorian America* (New York: Alfred A. Knopf, 1985), 258.

15. Rosenberg, 18, 26.

16. Ibid., 197.

17. Ibid., 203.

18. Ibid., 159.

19. Ibid., 107.

20. Havelock Ellis, Introduction to *Sex in Civilization*, ed. V. F. Calverton and S. D. Schmalhausen (New York: Macmillan, 1929; AMS reprint, 1976), 21–22.

21. See Havelock Ellis, *Little Essays of Love and Virtue* (Garden City, N.Y.: Doubleday, Doran & Co., 1930) and his massive *Studies in the Psychology of Sex* (New York: Random House, 1936).

22. Waldo Frank, "The Perception of Power," in Loren Baritz, ed., *The Culture of the Twenties* (Indianapolis: Bobbs-Merrill, 1970), 381; Lucy Freeman and Herbert S. Strean, *Freud and Women* (New York: Frederick Ungar Publishing Co., 1981), 199.

23. The bourgeois analogy is from an unpublished article by Linda Turbyville, an anthropologist-historian at Georgetown University.

24. Baritz, xli; Perrett, 148.

25. Joseph Breuer and Sigmund Freud, *Studies on Hysteria*, trans. James Strachey (New York: Basic Books, 1957), 257; A. A. Brill, *Fundamental Conceptions of Psychoanalysis* (New York: Harcourt Brace & Co., 1921), 21–22.

26. Freeman and Strean, 198–99.

27. Anne Martin, "Women and 'Their' Magazines," *New Republic*, 20 September 1922, 92–94. Martin particularly criticized the magazines for promoting baby formula, when the data of the Children's Bureau so clearly showed the value of breast-feeding.

28. Floyd H. Allport, "Seeing Women as They Are," *Harper's* 158 (March 1929):397.

29. Ibid., 399–407.

30. Ibid., 408. An article by James H. Leuba, "The Weaker Sex: A Scientific Ramble," *Atlantic Monthly* 137 (April 1926):454–60, provides a full explication of the ongoing argument for inferiority and difference.

31. Carrie Chapman Catt, "Woman Suffrage Only an Episode in Age-Old Movement," and Charlotte Perkins Gilman, "Woman's Achievements Since the Franchise," *Current History* 27 (October 1927):1–6, 7–14.

32. The articles are compiled by Elaine Showalter, ed., *These Modern Women: Autobiographical Essays from the Twenties* (Old Westbury, N.Y.: Feminist Press, 1978), 3.

33. Ibid., 52.

34. Ibid., 5.

35. Ibid.

36. Ibid., 141.

37. Ibid., 5, 12–13, 192.

38. "Negro Womanhood's Greatest Needs," *Messenger* 9 (April, May, June 1923):109, 150, 198–199.

39. Nancy Norton, "Hazel V. Hotchkiss Wightman," in *Notable American Women: The Modern Period*, ed. Barbara Sicherman and Carol Hurd Green (Cambridge, Mass.: Harvard University Press, 1980), 731–32 (henceforth *NAWMP*); Ellen W. Gerber, Jan Felshin, et al., *The American Woman in Sport* (Reading, Mass.: Addison-Wesley Publishing Co., 1974), 129–30. In 1920 the *New York Times* reported there were 3 million women tennis players in the United States. Golf and tennis were the most popular female sports. In 1925, capping a $300,000 fund-raising drive sparked by golf champion Marion Hollins, the Women's National Golf and Tennis Club opened at Glen Head, Long Island.

40. "How a Girl Beat Leander at the Hero Game," *Literary Digest* 90 (21 August 1926):53.

41. Ibid., 58–60.

42. Claudia M. Oakes, *United States Women in Aviation 1930–1939* (Washington, D.C.: Smithsonian Institution Press, 1985), 24.

43. Kathleen L. Brooks-Pazmany, *United States Women in Aviation, 1919–1929* (Washington, D.C.: Smithsonian Institution Press, 1983), 1–27.

44. Katherine A. Brick, "Amelia Mary Earhart," in *NAWMP*, 538–39.

45. Ibid.

46. Mead, 55.

47. Ibid., 97, 109.

48. Ibid., 111, 117.

49. Ibid., 1.

50. Judith Schachter Modell, *Ruth Benedict, Patterns of a Life* (Philadelphia: University of Pennsylvania Press, 1983), 144.

51. Mead, *Blackberry Winter*, 1.
52. Margaret Mead, *Coming of Age in Samoa* (New York: Modern Library, 1953), 246.

Chapter Three

1. Carrie Chapman Catt cited in Robert A. Shanley, "The League of Women Voters—a Study of Pressure Politics in the Public Interest" (Ph.D. diss., Georgetown University, 1955), 25; Ruth Baker Pratt, "The Lady or the Tiger," *Ladies' Home Journal* 45 (May 1928):8, 119.
2. Eleanor Flexner, *Century of Struggle: The Women's Rights Movement in the United States* (Cambridge, Mass.: Harvard University Press, 1969), 320–23.
3. June Sochen, *Movers and Shakers: American Women Thinkers and Activists, 1900–1970* (Chicago: Quadrangle, 1973), 117.
4. Catt cited in Shanley, 25. See also Kathryn H. Stoner, *Twenty-Five Years of a Great Idea: A History of the National League of Women Voters* (Washington, D.C.: League of Women Voters, 1946), 7–8.
5. Shanley, 34–35; J. Stanley Lemons, *The Woman Citizen: Social Feminism in the 1920s* (Urbana: University of Illinois Press, 1973), 87–89. *Woman Citizen* article cited in William O'Neill, *Everyone Was Brave: A History of Feminism in America* (Chicago: Quadrangle, 1971), 51; Carole Nichols, *Votes and More for Women: Suffrage and After in Connecticut* (New York: Institute for Research in History and Haworth Press, 1983), 34.
6. O'Neill, 84–89, 98–99; Breckinridge, 15–25, 50–53, 65, 137–39; Anna Steese Richardson, "God Send a Leader of Women," *Collier's*, 27 October 1923, 7.
7. Sophonisba Breckinridge, *Women in the Twentieth Century: A Study of Their Political, Social, and Economic Activities* (New York: Arno Press, 1972), 270; Dorothy Johnson, "Organized Women as Lobbyists in the 1920's," *Capitol Studies* 1 (Spring 1972):41–59.
8. Breckinridge, 265; Joseph B. Chepaitis, "The First Federal Social Welfare Measure: The Sheppard-Towner Maternity and Infancy Act, 1918–1932" (Ph.D. diss., Georgetown University, 1968), 91–92.
9. Stanley Lemons, "The Sheppard-Towner Act: Progressivism in the 1920's," *Journal of American History* 3 (July 1969):776–86; Chepaitis, 12.
10. Chepaitis, 12–19, 129–36.
11. Cited by Chepaitis, 47–58; Minutes, 14 February 1921, Box 6, WJCC, Library of Congress.
12. Chepaitis, 57.
13. Chepaitis, 85–89; Correspondence of Mrs. John French, 27 May 1921, and Florence Kelley, 16 May 1921, Box 1, WJCC.
14. Florence V. Watkins to A. S. Buell, 1 September 1921, Box 1, WJCC.
15. Lemons, *The Woman Citizen*, 157–62; Chepaitis, 96.
16. Estelle Freedman, *Their Sisters' Keepers: Women's Prison Reform in Amer-*

ica, 1830–1930 (Ann Arbor: University of Michigan, 1981), 145–46; Sanford Bates, *Prisons and Beyond* (New York: Macmillan, 1936), 9–40; Barbara A. Filo, "Reclaiming Those Poor Unfortunates: The Movement to Establish the First Federal Prison for Women" (Ph.D. diss., Boston University, 1982), 210–33.

17. Helen E. Gibson, "Women's Prisons: Laboratories for Penal Reform," *Wisconsin Law Review*, no. 1 (1973):20–33; Freedman, 110–47.

18. Dorothy M. Brown, *Mabel Walker Willebrandt: A Study in Power, Loyalty, and Law* (Knoxville: University of Tennessee Press, 1984), 83–84.

19. Ibid.

20. Filo, 265–70.

21. *Federal Prisons*, General Federation of Women's Clubs pamphlet, President's File, Box 7, GFWC archives, Washington, D.C.

22. Brown, 84–85.

23. Ibid.

24. Mary Belle Harris, *I Knew Them in Prison* (New York: Viking Press, 1942), 254–55, 262, 274.

25. Walter I. Trattner, *Crusade for the Children: A History of the National Child Labor Committee and Child Labor Reform in America* (Chicago: Quadrangle Books, 1970), 171.

26. Report of the Lookout Committee, 29 May 1922, Box 6, WJCC.

27. Florence Kelley to Mrs. R. B. Hawes, 19 March 1924, Reel 48, NCL, Library of Congress. See also Trattner, 165–67; Mary Anderson, *Women at Work: The Autobiography of Mary Anderson as Told to Mary N. Winslow* (Minneapolis: University of Minnesota, 1951), 188–89; Lemons, *The Woman Citizen*, 219–25; Gladys Boone, *The Women's Trade Union League in Great Britain and the United States* (New York: Columbia University Press, 1942), 136–37.

28. Trattner, 169.

29. Florence Kelley to Mrs. Richardson, Jane Addams, Nelle Swartz, and Frances Perkins, October-December 1924, Reel 48, NCL.

30. Trattner, 176–78; Breckinridge, 262–63.

31. Mari Jo Buhle, *Women and American Socialism, 1870–1920* (Urbana: University of Illinois Press, 1981), 318–19; White cited in "Where Are the Prewar Radicals?" *Survey* 55 (February 1926):556.

32. Eleanor Flexner, *A Century of Struggle* (New York: Atheneum, 1968), 263–80; Sochen, 117–18; O'Neill, 126–28; Nancy F. Cott, "Feminist Politics in the 1920s: The National Woman's Party," *Journal of American History* 71 (June 1984):43–44.

33. Eastman cited in Susan D. Becker, *The Origins of the Equal Rights Amendment: American Feminism between the Wars* (Westport, Conn.: Greenwood Press, 1981), 168; Park cited in Sochen, 113; Cott, 47–49.

34. Elaine Showalter, *These Modern Women: Autobiographical Essays from the Twenties* (Old Westbury, N.Y.: Feminist Press, 1978), 4, 52–53; Cott, 44.

35. Maud Younger to Florence Kelley, 21 April 1921, and Florence Kelley

to Newton D. Baker, 3 June 1921, Reel 51/C4, NCL; Lemons, 188–89; Becker, 49.

36. Maud Younger to Woman's party state chairwomen, 20 September 1921, Reel 51/C4, NCL.

37. Ethel Smith to Florence Kelley, 10 October 1921; Ethel Smith to WTUL members, 30 September 1921, Reel 51/C4, NCL.

38. Florence Kelley to Sen. Charles Curtis, 21 October 1924; Florence Kelley to Mrs. Charles F. Edson, 19 October 1921; postcards, Reel 51/C4, NCL.

39. Maud Younger to Ethel Smith, 19 December 1921, Reel 51/C4, NCL.

40. Florence Kelley to Simeon D. Fess, 16 December 1921; M. Bruere to A. Burlingame, 14 March 1922; Molly Dewson, letter on organization, January 1922, Reel 51/C4, NCL.

41. Becker, 119–21; Lemons, *The Woman Citizen*, 191–92; *Equal Rights*, 26 May 1923, 115.

42. Senator Curtis to Florence Kelley, 5 December 1923, Reel 51/C4, NCL.

43. Becker, 93–94; Lemons, *The Woman Citizen*, 199–204.

44. Becker, 163.

45. Ibid., 166–68.

46. Ibid., 172.

47. Alice Paul, "Progress of Women's Efforts to Secure Equal Nationality Rights through International Law," *Congressional Digest* 9 (November 1930):279. Fanny Bunand-Sevastos, "What the Inter-American Commission of Women Has Accomplished," *Congressional Digest* 9 (November 1930):267–68.

48. Alice Kessler-Harris, *Out to Work: A History of Wage-Earning Women in the United States* (New York: Oxford University Press, 1982), 209; Becker, 204.

49. Charles DeBenedetti, *Origins of the Modern Peace Movement, 1915–1929* (Milwood, N.Y.: KTO Press, 1978), 24–25, 240–42.

50. Constance Drexel, "Have Women Failed as Citizens?" *Collier's* 71 (12 May 1922):5–6.

51. Anna Steese Richardson, "God Send a Leader of Women," *Collier's* 72 (27 October 1923):7–8.

52. DeBenedetti, 86–87, 113–41, 185; Charles Chatfield, *For Peace and Justice: Pacifism in America, 1914–1941* (Knoxville: University of Tennessee Press, 1971), 94.

53. Florence B. Boeckel, "Women in International Affairs," *Annals* 143 (May 1929):230–48.

54. DeBenedetti, 230.

55. Florence E. Allen, "The First Ten Years," *Woman's Journal* 15 (August 1930):32; DeBenedetti, 230.

56. Allen, 31.

57. Cited in DeBenedetti, 90.

58. Cited in Sochen, 117.

59. Phillip R. Shriver, "Harriet Taylor Upton," in *Notable American Women, 1607–1956*, ed. Ed T. James, Janet James, and Paul S. Boyer. (Cambridge, Mass.: Harvard University Press, 1971), 3:502–3 (henceforth *NAW*); Margot Jerrand, "Emily Newell Blair," in *NAWMP*, 82–83.

60. Elizabeth Fraser, "Here We Are—Use Us," *Good Housekeeping* 71 (September 1920):161.

61. Emily Newell Blair, "Women in the Political Parties," *Annals* 143 (May 1929):119.

62. Breckinridge, 275–78; Lemons, *The Woman Citizen*, 87.

63. "The Woman Politician Arrives," *Outlook*, 27 June 1928, 326.

64. Blair, 220–21.

65. Becker, 100.

66. Eunice F. Barnard, "Madame Arrives in Politics," *North American Review*, November 1928, 551–56; Martin Gruberg, *Women in American Politics: An Assessment and Sourcebook* (Oshkosh, Wis.: Academia Press, 1968), 152–55; Breckinridge, 296–97; Becker, 100.

67. Gruberg, 152–55.

68. Breckinridge, 332.

69. Marguerite M. Wells, "Some Effects of Woman Suffrage," *Annals* 143 (May 1929):207.

70. Stuart A. Rice and Malcolm M. Willey, "American Women's Ineffective Use of the Vote," *Current History* 20 (July 1924):641–47.

71. "Fooling the Women in Politics," *Ladies' Home Journal*, September 1923, 29, 159–60; Nichols, 50–52.

72. Blair, 227; Oliver McKee, Jr., "Ten Years of Women Suffrage," *Commonweal*, 16 July 1930, 298–300.

73. Rice and Willey, 641.

74. Charles Edward Russell, "Is Women Suffrage a Failure?" *Century Magazine* 107 (March 1924):724–30.

75. Cited in Glenda E. Morrison, "Women's Participation in the 1928 Campaign (Ph.D. diss., University of Kansas, 1978), 258.

76. Charles Merz, *The Dry Decade* (Seattle: University of Washington Press, 1969), 213–21.

77. Breckinridge, 286–87.

78. Morrison, 59–60, 80–100.

79. Ibid., 100–103.

80. Morrison, 215; Andrew Sinclair, *Prohibition: The Era of Excess* (Boston: Little, Brown, 1962), 342–43; David E. Kyvig, *Repealing National Prohibition* (Chicago: University of Chicago Press, 1979), 119.

81. Morrison, 207.

82. The Gentleman at the Keyhole, "Where Duty Lies," *Collier's*, 27 October 1928, 45.

83. Mabel Walker Willebrandt, *The Inside of Prohibition* (Indianapolis: Bobbs-Merrill, 1929), 303–17; Brown, 156–67.

84. *New York Times*, 22 September 1928; Alfred E. Smith, *Up to Now* (New York: Viking, 1929), 395–96.

85. Allan Lichtman, *Prejudice and the Old Politics: The Presidential Election of 1928* (Chapel Hill: University of North Carolina Press, 1979), 41–90.

86. Morrison, 45, 88, 135; Eunice F. Barnard, "Women in the Campaign," *Woman's Journal* 13 (December 1928):7–9, 44–55.

87. Breckinridge, 256; "Ten Years of Women Suffrage," *Literary Digest* 105 (26 April 1930):11.

88. Nancy Woloch, *Women and the American Experience* (New York: Knopf, 1984), 387; Vorse cited in Sochen, 99.

Chapter Four

1. Sophonisba P. Breckinridge, *Women in the Twentieth Century: A Study of Their Political, Social and Economic Activities* (New York: Arno, 1972), 126; "Women in Industry: The New Position of Women in American Industry," *Monthly Labor Review* 12 (January 1921):152–57; Julie A. Matthaei, *An Economic History of Women in America: Women's Work, the Sexual Division of Labor, and the Development of Capitalism* (New York: Schocken Books, 1982), 142.

2. Emily Newell Blair, "Where Are We Women Going?" *Ladies' Home Journal* 36 (March 1919):37, 85.

3. William Howard Taft, "As I See the Future of Women," *Ladies' Home Journal* 36 (March 1919):27, 113.

4. Mary Anderson, *Women at Work: The Autobiography of Mary Anderson*, as told to Mary N. Winslow (Minneapolis: University of Minnesota, 1951), 135; Alice Henry, *Women and the Labor Movement* (New York: Arno, 1971), 192–93.

5. Anderson, p. 104; Mary Van Kleeck, "Federal Policies for Women in Industry," *Annals of the American Academy of Political Science* 81 (January 1919):90–93 (henceforth *Annals*).

6. Anderson, 113.

7. Ibid., 173–74.

8. Henry, xii.

9. Theresa Wolfson, "Trade Union Activities of Women," *Annals* 143 (May 1929):120.

10. Irving Bernstein, *The Lean Years: A History of the American Worker, 1920–1933* (Baltimore: Penguin Books, 1966), 52–53, 62.

11. Robert K. Murray, *Red Scare: A Study of National Hysteria* (New York: McGraw-Hill, 1964), 7–9, 59–61, 64–65, 126–27, 135–43, 153–58.

12. Bernstein, 47–51.

13. Sophonisba P. Breckinridge, "The Activities of Women outside the

Home," in *Recent Social Trends in the United States* (New York: McGraw-Hill, 1933), 712–19; Leslie W. Tentler, *Wage-Earning Women: Industrial Work and Family Life in the United States, 1900–1930* (New York: Oxford University Press, 1979), 85; Matthaei, 194–95.

14. Alice Kessler-Harris, *Out to Work: A History of Wage-Earning Women in the United States* (New York: Oxford University Press, 1982), 212–13; *State Laws Affecting Women*, U.S. Department of Labor, Women's Bureau Bulletin no. 40 (Washington, D.C.: GPO, 1923–25); Florence Kelley and Marguerite Marsh, "Labor Legislation for Women and Its Effects in Earnings and Conditions of Labor," *Annals* 143 (May 1929):289–91.

15. Henry, 180–81; Anderson, 71.

16. Mary N. Winslow, "The Effects of Labor Legislation on Women's Work," *Annals* 143 (May 1929):284–85.

17. Mary D. Hopkins, *Employment of Women at Night*, U.S. Department of Labor, Women's Bureau Bulletin no. 64 (Washington, D.C.: GPO, 1922), 5–15, 32–49, 52–56.

18. *Effects of Labor Legislation on the Employment Opportunities of Women*, U.S. Department of Labor, Women's Bureau Bulletin no. 68 (Washington, D.C.: GPO, 1926), 10–16.

19. Kessler-Harris, 194; Kelley and March, 300.

20. Elizabeth Faulkner Baker, "At the Crossroads in the Legal Protection of Women in Industry," *Annals* 143 (May 1929):267–79.

21. Dr. Alice Hamilton, *Women Workers and Industrial Poisons*, U.S. Department of Labor, Women's Bureau Bulletin no. 57 (Washington, D.C.: GPO, 1925–27), 1–5; Emily C. Brown, *Industrial Accidents to Men and Women*, U.S. Department of Labor, Women's Bureau Bulletin no. 81 (Washington, D.C.: GPO, 1930), 18–25.

22. Brown, 18–25

23. Amy G. Maher, "Ohio's Women Workers," *Annals* 143 (May 1929):98–101.

24. Alice Rogers Hager, "Occupations and Earnings of Women in Industry," *Annals* 143 (May 1929):69–73; Breckinridge, 215; Nelle Swartz, "The Trend in Women's Wages, *Annals* 143 (May 1929):104–5; Henry, 135–36. See also Lillian Herstein, "Women Discuss Wages," *American Federationist* 36 (August 1929):949–59.

25. Anderson, 75, 151.

26. Tentler, 25.

27. Bernstein, 227–28; Philip Foner, *Women in the American Labor Movement* (New York: Free Press, 1980), 144.

28. Foner, 144–46; Bernstein, 231–34.

29. Anderson, 37.

30. Mary E. Dreier, *Margaret Dreier Robins: Her Life, Letters and Work.* (New York: Island Press Cooperative, 1950), 18–27; Gladys Boone, *The Women's*

Trade Union League in Great Britain and the United States (New York: Columbia University Press, 1942), 111, 118.

31. Boone, 11, 8–19; Anderson, 222–29; Kessler-Harris, 173–79.
32. Dreier, 153.
33. Boone, 123–29; Dreier, 153, 166–67; Anderson, 131–33.
34. Dreier, 179–84; Anderson, 125; Boone, 126–34.
35. Anderson, 125–27.
36. Foner, 125–33; Henry, 101. See also Nancy Schrom Dye, *As Equals and as Sisters: Feminism, the Labor Movement, and the Women's Trade Union League of New York* (Columbia: University of Missouri Press, 1980).
37. Dreier, 169–70; Henry, 98–101; Foner, 135.
38. Foner, 36–37; Anderson, 33.
39. Boone, 147–48.
40. Editorial, *American Federationist* 36 (August 1929):913.
41. Breckinridge, *Women in the Twentieth Century*, 166; Foner, 151–52.
42. Wolfson, 120–22, 126; Bernstein, 35; Tentler, 42.
43. Foner, 166–74.
44. Ibid., 162.
45. Foner, 199, 207; Wolfson, 127.
46. Foner, 186–93, 213–21.
47. Kessler-Harris, 240–43; Matilda Lindsey, "Southern Women in Industry," *American Federationist* 36 (August 1929):973–75; Foner, 226; Bernstein, 9.
48. Bernstein, 13.
49. Ibid., 13, 26; Foner, 228–30.
50. Bernstein, 20–25, 32–36; Foner, 2, 30, 31.
51. Henry, 203–5.
52. Ibid., 206.
53. *Negro Women in Industry in 15 States*, U.S. Department of Labor, Women's Bureau Bulletin no. 70 (Washington, D.C.: GPO, 1929), 5–11; Henry, 208–9.
54. Caroline Manning, *The Immigrant Woman and Her Job*, U.S. Department of Labor, Women's Bureau Bulletin no. 74 (Washington, D.C.: GPO, 1929).
55. Emily C. Brown, *Industrial Home Work*, U.S. Department of Labor, Women's Bureau Bulletin no. 79 (Washington, D.C.: GPO, 1929).
56. Grace L. Coyle, "Women in Clerical Occupations," *Annals* 143 (May 1929):180–81; Elyce J. Rotella, "From Home to Office: U.S. Women at Work 1870–1930" (Ann Arbor: UMI Research Press, 1981), 148–51.
57. "Those who Spin in Offices," *Delineator* 95 (November 1919):35–64.
58. Booth Tarkington, *Alice Adams* (New York: Grosset & Dunlap, 1924), 433–34.
59. Rotella, 115, 119.

60. Josephine Stricker, "A Women's Road to Success," *Delineator* 95 (October 1919):24; "A Woman's Preparation for Business," *Delineator* 95 (November 1919):25, 102; "To Thine Own Self Be True," *Delineator* 96 (February 1920):28; "Business Life: Is It Worth the Cost?" *Delineator* 96 (March 1920):28; Margery W. Davies, *Woman's Place Is at the Typewriter: Office Work and Office Workers, 1870–1930* (Philadelphia: Temple University Press, 1982) provides the most useful study for the feminization of the office force.

61. Kessler-Harris, 234.

62. Ernest R. Groves, "The Personality Results of the Wage Employment of Women Outside the Home and Their Social Consequences," *Annals* 143 (May 1929):341–42.

63. Ibid.

64. Breckinridge, "The Activities of Women Outside the Home," 118.

65. Cited in V. F. Calverton, "Careers for Women: A Survey of Results," *Current History*, January 1929, 636.

66. Mary N. Winslow, *Married Women in Industry*, U.S. Department of Labor, Women's Bureau Bulletin no. 38 (Washington, D.C.: GPO, 1924), 1.

67. Ibid., 4.

68. Gwendolyn Hughes Berry, "Mothers in Industry," *Annals* 143 (May 1929):317.

69. Breckinridge, "The Activities of Women outside the Home," 121.

70. Winslow, *Married Women in Industry*, 8. See also Agnes L. Peterson, "What the Wage-Earning Woman Contributes to Family Support," *Annals* 143 .(May 1929):79–93.

Chapter Five

1. Arthur W. Calhoun, *A Social History of the American Family: From Colonial Times to the Present* (Cleveland: Arthur H. Clarke, 1919), 199.

2. Ernest R. Groves and William F. Ogburn, *American Marriage and Family Relationships* (New York: Arno Press, 1976), 13.

3. Robert S. Lynd and Helen Lynd, *Middletown: A Study in American Culture* (New York: Harcourt Brace, 1956), 114–17; Frederick Lewis Allen, *Only Yesterday* (New York: Harper & Row, 1952), 71, 73.

4. Eleanor R. Wembridge, "Petting and the Campus," *Survey* 54 (July 1925):393; "Another Spinster" and "No Courtship at All," *Atlantic Monthly* 129 (February 1922):243–45.

5. Edgar A. Guest, "What I Shall Teach Bud and Janet about Marriage," *American Magazine* 97 (May 1924):109–10.

6. Groves and Ogburn, 134–89; U.S. Department of Commerce, *Statistical Abstract of the United States, 1930* (Washington, D.C.: GPO, 1930), 30–31.

7. Groves and Ogburn, 16–25; Sheila Rothman, *Woman's Proper Place: A History of Changing Ideals and Practices, 1870 to the Present* (New York: Basic

Books, 1978), 179; Nathalie Sedgwick Colby, "Marriage," *Atlantic Monthly* 133 (May 1924):668. See also Clara S. Littledale, "Living Happily Ever After," *Good Housekeeping* 74 (March 1922):15; Louis W. Waller, "On Being Happily Married," *Harper's* 144 (February 1922):394–96; Rothman 193. See also David Kennedy, *Birth Control in America: The Career of Margaret Sanger* (New Haven: Yale University Press, 1970).

8. Groves and Ogburn, 37.

9. Katharine B. Davis, "A Study of the Sex Life of the Normal Married Woman," *Journal of Social Hygiene* 9 (January 1923):1–26.

10. Ibid.; Katharine B. Davis, "A Study of the Sex Life of the Normal Married Woman," *Journal of Social Hygiene* 9 (March 1923):129–46.

11. Ibid.

12. Rothman, 188; Allen, 77; Dix cited in Lynd, 117.

13. Rothman, 180–84; Groves and Ogburn, 51.

14. Benjamin R. Andrews, "The Home Woman as Buyer and Controller of Consumption," *Annals* 143 (May 1929):41; Anna E. Richardson, "The Woman Administrator in the Modern Home," *Annals* 123 (May 1929):22; Elaine Showalter, ed., *These Modern Women: Autobiographical Essays from the Twenties* (Westbury, N.Y.: Feminist Press, 1978), 13. See also Groves and Ogburn, 22–23 and Winifred D. Wandersee, *Women's Work and Family Values, 1920–1940* (Cambridge, Mass.: Harvard University Press, 1981), 7–9.

15. Wandersee, 15–18, 24–26.

16. Lynd, 93–99.

17. Ibid., 100–106; Wandersee, 17; William F. Ogburn, "Decline of the American Family," *New York Times Magazine*, 17 February 1929.

18. Richardson, 25. See also Robert S. Lynd, "The People as Consumers," in *Recent Social Trends in the United States* (New York: McGraw-Hill, 1933), 2:857–911.

19. William F. Ogburn, "Marriage and the Family," in *Recent Social Trends in the United States* (New York: McGraw-Hill, 1933), 1:71–72; Barbara Ehrenreich and Deirdre English, *For Her Own Good: 150 Years of the Experts' Advice to Women* (Garden City, N.Y.: Anchor, 1979), 164–76; Wandersee, 8; Jo Ann Vanek, "Time Spent in Housework," in *A Heritage of Her Own*, ed. Nancy F. Cott and Elizabeth H. Pleck (New York: Simon & Schuster, 1979), 500.

20. Richardson, 22–23. See also Alice Ames Winter, "What Is Your Market Value, Madam?" *Woman's Home Companion* 50 (January 1923):18.

21. Dix cited in Ehrenreich and English, 168–69.

22. Ibid., 178–79.

23. Vanek, 502–6; Wandersee, 58.

24. Hildegard Kneeland, "Woman's Economic Contribution in the Home," *Annals* 143 (May 1929):33–40.

25. Richardson, 31.

26. Ernest R. Groves, "The Personality Results of the Wage Employment

of Women outside the Home and Their Social Consequences," *Annals* 143 (May 1929):339–43; Lynd, 26. See also Agnes L. Peterson, "What the Wage-Earning Woman Contributes to Family Support," *Annals* 143 (May 1929):79 and Wandersee, 59.

27. Lynd, 26–27; Wandersee, 2–3.

28. Gwendolyn H. Berry, "Mothers in Industry," *Annals* 143 (May 1929):317; Peterson, 82–83.

29. Barbara Klacynska, "Why Women Work: A Comparison of Various Groups in Philadelphia, 1910–1930," *Labor History* 17 (Winter 1976):73. For Italian-American families, see Virginia Yans-McLaughlin, "A Flexible Tradition: South Italian Immigrants Confront a New Work Experience," *Journal of Social History* 7 (Summer 1974):429–46.

30. Lorine Pruette, "The Married Woman and the Part-Time Job," *Annals* 143 (May 1929):301–14; Wandersee, 1, 63; Groves and Ogburn, 76–77.

31. Richard W. and Dorothy C. Wertz, *Lying-In: A History of Childbirth in America* (New York: Free Press, 1977), 150–56.

32. Lynd, 131; Rothman, 188–89; Nancy Woloch, *Women and the American Experience* (New York: Alfred A. Knopf, 1984), 412; *Statistical Abstract of the United States, 1930*, 85; Groves and Ogburn, 14.

33. Kennedy, 1–3, 16–17.

34. Kennedy, 11–12; James Reed, "Margaret Sanger," in *NAWMP*, 624; Rothman, 199–200.

35. Margaret Sanger, *Women and the New Race* (New York: Maxwell Reprint Co., 1966), 75; Linda Gordon, "Birth Control and Social Revolution," in Cott and Pleck, 458.

36. Sanger, *Women and the New Race*, 233–34; Gordon, 464–65.

37. Geoffrey Perrett, *America in the Twenties: A History* (New York: Simon & Schuster, 1982), 161–63; "Birth Control and Taboo," *New Republic* 29 (30 November 1921); "The Petition and Report of the Seven Bishops of the Administrative Committee of the National Catholic Welfare Council to His Holiness Pius IX," Archives of the Catholic University of America, (E74), 22–28.

38. Linda Gordon, *Woman's Body, Woman's Right: A Social History of Birth Control in America* (New York: Grossman Publishers, 1976), 464; W. R. Inge, "Control of Parenthood—Moral Aspects," *Nation*, 7 December 1921, 642–43.

39. Gordon, *Woman's Body, Woman's Right*, 262–63; Rothman, 205–7.

40. Margaret Sanger, "The Case for Birth Control," *Woman Citizen* 8 (23 February 1924):28.

41. Gordon, *Woman's Body, Woman's Right*, 259–60, 270; Rothman, 220–21.

42. Edward A. Ross and Ray E. Baber, "Slow Suicide among Our Native Stock," *Century* 107 (February 1924):504.

43. "Our Declining Birth-Rate," *Literary Digest* 76 (24 March 1923):12–13.

44. Gordon, *Woman's Body, Woman's Right*, 278–84; Margaret Sanger, *The Pivot of Civilization* (New York: Brentano, 1922), 22.

45. Rothman, 201–2; Gordon, *Woman's Body, Woman's Right*, 276–77.

46. Ibid., 271–77.

47. Katharine B. Davis, "A Study of the Sex Life of the Normal Married Woman," *Journal of Social Hygiene* 8 (April 1922):173–88; Gordon in Cott, 445.

48. Ehrenreich and English, 184–201.

49. Dr. Frank Crane, "Don't Be a Door Mat," *American Magazine* 94 (December 1922):53.

50. Ehrenreich and English, 75; Robert H. Elias, *Entangling Alliances with None: An Essay on the Individual in the American Twenties* (New York: W. W. Norton & Co., 1973), 2–7.

51. John B. Watson, *Psychological Care of Infant and Child* (New York: W. W. Norton & Co., 1928), 12.

52. Ibid., 8–9.

53. Ibid., 38–45.

54. Ibid., 70–85, 108–14.

55. Elias, 8.

56. Rothman, 216; Elizabeth Frazer, "Changing Johnny's Behavior," *Saturday Evening Post* 199 (14 August 1926):37, 165.

57. Beatrice Barmby, "What Are We Doing with Our Children?" *Ladies' Home Journal*, February 1922, 45.

58. Lynd, 149–52.

59. William L. O'Neill, *Divorce in the Progressive Era* (New Haven: Yale University Press, 1967), viii–x; James Cardinal Gibbons, "Divorce," *Century* 18 (May 1909):145–49.

60. Groves and Ogburn, 347–63; Katharine F. Gerould, "Divorce," *Atlantic Monthly* 132 (October 1923):460–70; "Is Marriage Breaking Down?" *Literary Digest* 76 (17 February 1923):36; Paula Giddings, *When and Where I Enter: The Impact of Black Women on Race and Sex in America* (New York: William Morrow & Co., 1984), 149.

61. Joseph F. Newton, "What God Hath Not Joined," *Atlantic Monthly* 131 (June 1920):721–27.

62. Richard Boardman, "Marriage—A Selective Process," *Atlantic Monthly* 132 (November 1923):627; "Beans as Breeders of Divorce," *Literary Digest* 4 February 1922, 33.

63. Leonard McGee, "Nine Common Causes of Unhappy Marriages," *American Magazine* 97 (March 1924):28; Lynd, 128–29.

64. *Statistical Abstract of the United States, 1930*, 91–92, 30; Lynd, 120–27; Newton, 721–22; B. Hall, "Shall I Divorce My Wife?" *Atlantic Monthly* 134 (August 1924):155–62; "Divorce," *Current Opinion* 73 (November 1923):58–81.

65. Lynd, 130.

66. "I Did Not Believe in Divorce," *Woman's Home Companion* 51 (May 1924):9, 53.

67. Lynd, 130; Ogburn, "Decline of the American Family."

Chapter Six

1. Jill K. Conway, "Perspectives on the History of Women's Education in the United States," *History of Education Quarterly* 14 (Spring 1974):1–12.

2. Caroline Pratt, *I Learn from Children* (New York: Cornerstone Library, 1948), 48.

3. *Abstract of a Survey of the Baltimore Public Schools 1920–1921*, George D. Strayer, director (Baltimore; Board of School Commissioners, 1921), 1:38–39, iii–vii.

4. Lawrence A. Cremin, *The Transformation of the Schools: Progressivism in American Education, 1876–1957* (New York: Alfred A. Knopf, 1969), 104–5, 136, 240–45.

5. Ibid., 282, 211–12, 249.

6. Ibid., 234.

7. Edward A. Krug, *The Shaping of the American High School 1920–31* (Madison: University of Wisconsin Press, 1972), 28, 34–35; Norris Hundley, Jr., "Susan Almira Miller Dorsey," *NAW*, 1:506–8.

8. Hundley, 507; Krug, 34–35; Robert Lynd and Helen Lynd, *Middletown* (New York: Harcourt Brace Jovanovich, 1956), 188–89.

9. Charles H. Judd, "Education," in *Recent Social Trends in the United States: Report of the President's Research Committee on Social Trends* (New York: McGraw-Hill Book Co., 1933), 1:325–27.

10. Krug, 3, 40–46, 120–23; Judd, 341.

11. Lynd, 184.

12. Krug, 24–25.

13. Ibid., 68.

14. Lynd, 194.

15. Krug, 4–6.

16. Thomas Woody, *A History of Women's Education in the United States* (New York: Science Press, 1929), 2:52–64, 81; Susan B. Carter and Mark Prus, "The Labor Market and the American High School Girl, 1890–1928," *Journal of Economic History* 42 (March 1982):163–71.

17. Lynd, 216.

18. Ibid.

19. Krug, 22–23, 131–38, 193.

20. Barbara Miller Solomon, *In The Company of Educated Women: A History of Higher Education in America* (New Haven: Yale University Press, 1985), 62–64; Judd, 340–41.

21. William Allan Neilson, "Overcrowding in Women's Colleges," *Nation* 120 (13 May 1925):539–40.

22. Solomon, 95.

23. Ibid., 146–47.

24. Ibid., 71–72.

25. Helen L. Horowitz, *Alma Mater: Design and Experience in the Women's Colleges from their Nineteenth Century Beginnings to the 1930s* (New York: Alfred Knopf, 1984), 277–79; Elaine Kendall, *"Peculiar Institutions," An Informal History of the Seven Sisters Colleges* (New York: G.P. Putnam's Sons, 1975), 151.

26. Liva Baker, *I'm Radcliffe! Fly Me!* (New York: Macmillan, 1976), 2; Freda Kirchway, "Too Many College Girls?" *Nation* 120 (3 June 1925):625–27.

27. Baker, 8; Kendall, 132; Mabel Newcomer, *A Century of Higher Education for American Women* (New York: Harper & Bros., 1959), 1–2.

28. Helen M. Bennett, "Seven Colleges—Seven Types," *Woman's Home Companion* 47 (November 1920):13.

29. Kendall, 179–80.

30. Frederick Rudolph, *The American College and University* (New York: Alfred A. Knopf, 1962), 452–54; Mabel Louise Robinson, *The Curriculum of the Women's College*, U.S. Bureau of Education, Bulletin no. 6 (Washington, D.C.: GPO, 1918), 107–9; Kendall, 170–71.

31. Solomon, 85.

32. Horowitz, 287–88.

33. Horowitz, 293; Kendall, 132–42; Edna Yost, "The Case for the Co-Educated Woman," *Harper's* 155 (July 1927):194–202.

34. W. Beram Wolfe, "Why Educate Women?" *Forum* 87 (March 1929):167.

35. Charles H. Selden, "Vassar," *Ladies' Home Journal* 43 (May 1925):15, 154–57; "Bryn Mawr," *Ladies' Home Journal* 44 (September 1925):32, 104–9.

36. Horowitz, 318.

37. Mary E. Woolley, "The College Girl Today and Yesterday," *Woman's Home Companion* 52 (October 1925):12, 100–2; Horowitz, 293; Kirchway, 597.

38. Kendall, 169.

39. Ibid., 286–87.

40. Kendall, 172–73; Solomon, 166; Baker, 86; Horowitz, 285–88; "The Languid Generation," *Nation* 117 (21 November 1923):572.

41. Kendall, 171–76.

42. Horowitz, 228.

43. Ibid., 319–50.

44. Jessica B. Peixotto, "The Case for Coeducation," *Forum* 70 (November 1923):2059–66.

45. Olivia Howard Dunbar, "Women at Man-Made Colleges," *Forum* 70 (November 1923): 2049–58; "Personal and Otherwise," *Harper's* 155 (September 1927):527–28; Wolfe, 168.

46. Dunbar, 2056–58; Bernard De Voto, "The Co-Ed, The Hope of Liberal Education," *Harper's* 155 (September 1927):452–59; Rollo Walter Brown, "Coeducation versus Literature," *Harper's* 148 (May 1924):785; Rudolph, 324.

47. Solomon, 81–82; Clarence C. Little, "Women and Higher Education," *Scribner's* 86 (August 1929):146–50; Howard H. Peckham, *The Making of*

the University of Michigan, 1867–1967 (Lansing: University of Michigan Press, 1967), 165.

48. Louis R. Wilson, *The University of North Carolina, 1900–1930: The Making of a Modern University* (Chapel Hill: University of North Carolina Press, 1957), 534–35; Peckham, 153–55.

49. Solomon, 159; George Callcott, *A History of the University of Maryland* (Baltimore: Maryland Historical Society, 1966), 292.

50. Paula S. Fass, *The Damned and the Beautiful: American Youth in the 1920s* (Oxford: Oxford University Press, 1977), 206.

51. Ibid., 182; Solomon, 106–7; Mabelle B. Blake, *Guidance for College Women* (New York: D. Appleton & Co., 1927), 85.

52. Fass, 139–69; Peckham, 155; Clifford S. Griffin, *The University of Kansas: A History* (Lawrence: University Press of Kansas, 1974).

53. Fass, 292–98, 196; "Women and the Weed," *Literary Digest* 87 (19 December 1925):312.

54. Fass, 311; Solomon, 159; Peckham, 166; Charles H. Selden, "Fashions in College Morals: Chicago," *Ladies' Home Journal* 43 (February 1926): 207–8.

55. Fass, 300–304.

56. Krug, 23.

57. Charles H. Selden, "Fashions in College Morals: Wisconsin," *Ladies' Home Journal* 43 (March 1926):222; Fass, 260–65, 277–78.

58. Callcott, 295–98.

59. Sister Mary Mariella Bowler, *A History of Catholic Colleges for Women in the United States of America* (Washington, D.C.: Catholic University of America, 1933); Sister M. Madeleva, *My First Seventy Years* (New York: Macmillan Co., 1939), 51–58.

60. Bowler, 90; Harold A. Buetow, *Of Singular Benefit: The Story of Catholic Education in the United States* (New York: Macmillan Co., 1970), 216.

61. Bowler, 85–87.

62. Ibid., 115; Edward J. Power, *Catholic Higher Education: A History* (New York: Appleton-Century-Croft, 1972), 318.

63. Jeanne L. Noble, *The Negro Women's College Education* (New York: Teachers College Columbia, 1956).

64. Elaine M. Smith, "Mary Mcleod Bethune," in *NAWMP*, 76–80.

65. Lucy D. Slowe, "Higher Education of Negro Women," *Journal of Negro Education* 2 (July 1933):352–58; Willare Range, *The Rise and Progress of Negro Colleges in Georgia, 1865–1914* (Athens: University of Georgia, 1951), 192; Noble, 28.

66. Slowe, 354; Solomon, 150; Noble, 27.

67. W. E. Bigglestone, "Oberlin College and the Negro Student, 1865–1940," *Journal of Negro History* 56 (July 1971):198–209.

68. Ibid., 210.

89. Ibid., 211–15.

70. Marita Bonner, "On Being Young—a Woman—and Colored," *Crisis* 31 (December 1925):63–65.

71. Solomon, 172–73.

72. Henry R. Carey, "Sterilizing the Fittest," *North American Review* 228 (November 1929):519; Henry R. Carey, "Career or Maternity?" *North American Review* 228 (December 1929):741.

73. William S. Sadler, "College Women and Race Suicide," *Ladies' Home Journal* 39 (April 1922):29; Mary Lee, "College Graduates and Civilization," *Harper's* 162 (May 1931):723.

74. Henry N. MacCracken, "Letter to a Gratified Husband," *Woman's Home Companion* 52 (March 1925):156–57; Katharine B. Davis, "Why They Failed to Marry," *Harper's* 156 (March 1928):460–69.

75. Davis, 460–61.

76. Park cited in Carey, "Career or Maternity," 738; Bessie Bunzel, "The Woman Goes to College," *Century* 117 (November 1928):26.

77. Solomon, 173–76; V. F. Calverton, "Careers for Women—A Survey of Results," *Current History*, January 1929, 633–38.

78. Catherine Filene, ed., *Careers for Women* (Boston: Houghton Mifflin Co., 1920); Miriam S. Leuck, "Women in Odd and Unusual Fields of Work," *Annals* 143 (May 1929):166–79; Sophonisba Breckinridge, *Women in the Twentieth Century: A Study of Their Political, Social and Economic Activities* (New York: Arno Press, 1972), 187.

79. Newcomer, 89.

80. Willystine Goodsell, "The Educational Opportunities of American Women—Theoretical and Actual," *Annals* 143 (May 1929):8; "Bryn Mawr Installs Miss Park," *School and Society* 16 (28 October 1922):492–93.

81. Herschel T. Manuel, "Save the Schools," *School and Society* 11 (24 April 1920):493–95; Breckinridge, 190–91; Kendall, 170–71.

82. Roy Lubove, *The Professional Altruist: The Emergence of Social Work as a Career 1880–1930* (Cambridge, Mass.: Harvard University Press, 1965), 106–9; Muriel W. Pumphrey, "Mary Ellen Richmond," in *NAW*, 3:152–53.

83. Lubove, 88–92.

84. Ibid. See also Roy Lubove, "Anna Beach Pratt," in *NAW*, 3:93–94.

85. Lubove, *The Professional Altruist*, 113–15.

86. June Axium, "Jessie Taft," in *NAWMP*, 673–75.

87. Lubove, *The Professional Altruist*, 127–36; Robert Mennel, "Miriam Van Waters," in *NAWMP*, 709–11; Breckinridge, 204–6.

88. Breckinridge, 203; Sigrid A. Edge, "Jeanne M. Flexner," in *NAW*, 1:633–34; Alma Kenny, "Anne Carroll Moore," in *NAWMP*, 489–90; Valmai Fenser, "Linda Anne Eastman," in *NAWMP*, 215–16.

89. Solomon, 126–27; Breckinridge, 201–2; Woody, 73.

90. Josephine A. Dolan, *Nursing in Society: A Historical Perspective* (Philadelphia: W. B. Saunders Co., 1973), 257–61.

91. Ibid., 268–70; Nancy Tomes, "Annie Warberton Goodrich," in *NAWMP*, 286–88; Virginia M. Dunbar, "Mary Adelaide Nutting," in *NAWMP*, 642–44.

92. Breckinridge, 59–60.

93. Ibid., 202; Robinson, 127.

94. Woody, 331; Breckinridge, 196–97; Emilie J. Hutchinson, "Women and the Ph.D.," *Journal of the AAUW* 22 (October 1928):20; Glenna Matthews and Gloria Valencia-Weber, "Against Great Odds: The Life of Angie Debo," *OAH Newsletter*, May 1985, 8.

95. Patricia A. Graham, "Expansion and Exclusion: A History of Women in American Higher Education," *Signs*, Summer 1978, 764–65; Woody, 329; Newcomer, 14; Hutchinson, 19–28.

96. Margaret W. Rossiter, *Women Scientists in America: Struggles and Stereotypes to 1940* (Baltimore: Johns Hopkins University Press, 1942), 134–35.

97. Marion Hawthorne, "Women as College Teachers," *Annals* 143 (May 1929):146–53.

98. Susan B. Carter, "Academic Women Revisited: An Empirical Study of Changing Patterns in Women's Employment as College and University Faculty, 1890–1963," *Journal of Social History* 14 (Summer 1981):675–99. See also Jessie Bernard, *Academic Women* (University Park: Pennsylvania State University, 1964).

99. Hawthorne, 153; Rossiter, 162.

100. Mary Ruth Walsh, *"Doctors Wanted" No Women Need Apply: Sexual Barriers in the Medical Profession, 1835–1975* (New Haven: Yale University Press, 1977), 185–86, 221–23, 262; Goodsell, 6; Breckinridge, 201–2.

101. Cynthia F. Epstein, *Women in Law* (Garden City, N.Y.: Anchor Books, 1983), 4; Woody, 373; Goodsell, 6; *Phi Delta Delta*, November 1973.

102. Dorothy M. Brown, *Mabel Walker Willebrandt: A Study in Power, Loyalty, and Law* (Knoxville: University of Tennessee Press, 1984).

103. Jeannette E. Tuve, *First Lady of the Law: Forence Ellinwood Allen* (Boston: University Press of America, 1984).

104. Anne S. Moore, "When Women Sit in Judgment," *Good Housekeeping* 70 (April 1920):46–47.

105. Estella M. Place, "Interesting Westerners," *Sunset* 61 (July 1928):46; Goodsell, 6.

106. Solomon, 130–31; William C. McLoughlin, "Aimee Semple McPherson," in *NAW*, 2:477–80.

107. Rossiter, 141–43.

108. Alice Kessler-Harris, *Out to Work: A History of Wage-Earning Women in the United States* (New York: Oxford University Press, 1982), 116.

109. Marion C. McCarroll, "Getting On in the World: Business Wants Housekeepers," *Saturday Evening Post* 199 (5 March 1927):194.

110. Alice A. Winter, "Business Plus," *Ladies' Home Journal* 43 (December 1926):106.

111. Alma L. Kenney, "Hattie Carnegie," in *NAWMP*, 135–36; Walter Fisher, "Sarah Breedlove Walker," in *NAW*, 3:533–35; Paula Giddings, *When and Where I Enter* (Toronto: Bantam Books, 1984), 187–89; Alma L. Kenney, "Helena Rubinstein," in *NAWMP*, 607–8; Albro Martin, "Elizabeth Arden," in *NAWMP*, 32–33.

112. Lillian M. Gilbreth, "Efficiency of Women Workers," *Annals* 143 (May 1929):61–64.

113. Marion McLean, "What Kind of Business Woman Am I?" *Delineator* 100 (June 1922):6.

114. Helen C. Bennett, "Does Business Give Women a Square Deal?" *American Magazine* 107 (February 1929):40–41, 96–104.

115. Anne W. Armstrong, "Are Business Women Getting a Square Deal?" *Atlantic Monthly* 140 (July 1927):28–36.

116. Breckinridge, 63–64; *A History of the National Federation of Business and Professional Women's Clubs, Inc.*, *1919–1944* (Washington, D.C.: National Federation of Business and Women's Clubs, 1979).

117. Elisabeth I. Perry, "Training for Public Life: ER and Women's Political Networks in the 1920's," in *"Without Precedent": The Life and Career of Eleanor Roosevelt*, ed. Joan Hoff-Wilson and Marjorie Lichtman (Bloomington: Indiana University Press, 1984), 28–46; interview with Grace B. Knoeller, July 1982, Upper Marlboro, Md.

118. Barbara J. Harris, *Beyond Her Sphere: Women and the Professions in American History* (Westport, Conn.: Greenwood Press, 1942), 121, 739–40; Frank Stricker, "Cookbooks and Law Books: The Hidden History of Career Women in Twentieth Century America," in *A Heritage of Her Own: Toward a New Social History of American Women*, ed. Nancy F. Cott and Elisabeth H. Pleck (New York: Simon & Schuster, 1979), 478–79.

119. Stricker, 488.

Chapter Seven

1. Sidney E. Ahlstrom, *A Religious History of the American People* (New Haven: Yale University Press, 1972), 895.

2. Paula S. Fass, *The Beautiful and the Damned* (Oxford: Oxford University Press, 1977), 42.

3. "The Case against the Younger Generation," *Literary Digest*, 17 June 1922, 51–52.

4. Ahlstrom, 896–97; C. Luther Fry and Mary F. Jessup, "Changes in Religious Organizations," in *Recent Social Trends in the United States* (New York: McGraw Hill, 1933), 2:1012.

5. Robert T. Handy, "The American Religious Depression, 1925–1935," *Church History* 29 (March 1960):3, 6.

6. Fry and Jessup, 1019; Ahlstrom, 899.

7. Ahlstrom, 905; Handy, 8.

8. Harry Emerson Fosdick, "Will Science Displace God?" *Harper's* 153 (August 1926):362–66; Frederick Lewis Allen, *Only Yesterday* (New York: Harper & Row, 1931), 166.

9. Ahlstrom, 910–15; Elizabeth Hovell Verdesi, *In But Still Out: Women in the Church* (Philadelphia: Westminster Press, 1976), 80–90.

10. Handy, 7; Allen, 163–64; Lynd, 315, 328–29, 347, 370; Fry and Jessup, 1060.

11. Lynd, 316, 342, 407; Handy, 7.

12. Fry and Jessup, 1020–21. There was a 55 percent membership nationwide.

13. Fry and Jessup, 1046–48; Kenneth S. Latourette, "What Is Happening to Missions?" *Yale Review* 18 (September 1928):75–78.

14. Latourette, 73; "The Amazing Growth of Missions," *Literary Digest* 84 (14 February 1925):31.

15. Thomas J. Jones, "A Good Word for Missionaries," *Current History* 24 (July 1926):539–41; Lawrence F. Abbott, "There Are Missionaries and Missionaries," *Outlook* 35 (19 September 1923):94; "A Missionary Sees It Through," *Literary Digest* 98 (1 September 1928):27; "New Difficulties for the Missionary," *Literary Digest* 83 (18 October 1924):34–35.

16. "Handicaps of a Missionary Wife," *Missionary Review of the World* 50 (January 1927):29–42; "The Other Things that Missionaries Do," *Literary Digest* 90 (21 August 1926):34–35; "A Missionary Sees It Through," *Literary Digest* 98 (1 September 1928):27; Latourette, 77–80.

17. Barbara Welter, "She Hath Done What She Could: Protestant Women's Missionary Careers in Nineteenth Century America," in *Women in American Religion*, ed. Janet W. James (Philadelphia: University of Pennsylvania Press, 1974), 119; Mrs. Charles K. Roys, "Women's Place in the Missionary Enterprise," *Missionary Review of the World* 48 (June 1915):451–54; Janet H. Penfield, "Women in the Presbyterian Church—An Historical Overview," *Journal of Presbyterian History* 55 (Summer 1977):107–9; Virginia L. Brereton and C. R. Klein, "American Women in Ministry: A History of Protestant Beginning Points," in James, 175.

18. Elizabeth H. Gripe, "Women Restructuring and Unrest in the 1920's," *Journal of Presbyterian History* 52 (Summer 1974):188–98; Brereton and Kline, 180–81.

19. Sharon Klingelsmith, "Women in the Mennonite Church," *Mennonite Quarterly Review* 54 (July 1980):169–205.

20. Lucy W. Peabody, "Women's Place in Missions Fifty Years Ago and Now," *Missionary Review of the World* 56 (December 1927):906–9.

21. Gripe, 196–98; Klingelsmith, 74; Mrs. Charles Roys, "Status of Women in Church," *Missionary Review* 47 (May 1924):383. See also Rosemary Ruether and Eleanor McLaughlin, *Women of Spirit: Female Leadership in the Jewish and Christian Traditions* (New York: Simon & Schuster, 1979), 27.

22. Penfield, 118–19; Verdesi, 91–95; R. Douglas Brackenridge, "Equal-

ity for Women: A Case Study in Presbyterian Policy, 1926–1930," *Journal of Presbyterian History* 58 (Summer 1980):144.

23. Verdesi, 96–101.

24. Brackenridge, 148–54; Verdesi, 103–8.

25. Ellen M. Umansky, "Women in Judaism: From the Reform Movement to Contemporary Jewish Religious Feminism," in Ruether and McLaughlin, 339–40; Norma F. Pratt, "Transitions in Judaism: The Jewish American Woman through the 1930's," in James, 225.

26. Ruether and McLaughlin, 20; Mary Ewens, O.P., "Removing the Veil: The Liberated American Nun," in Ruether and McLaughlin, 256–73; Mary J. Oates, "Organized Volunteerism: The Catholic Sisters in Massachusetts, 1870–1940," in James, 142; Joseph Creusen, S.J., and Adam C. Ellis, S.J., *Religious Men and Women in Canon Law* (Milwaukee: Bruce Publishing Co., 1958), 202–3. See also James J. Kenneally, "Eve, Mary, and the Historians: American Catholicism and Women," in James, 198.

27. Ruether and McLaughlin, 19–21; Fry and Jessup, 1055, Juli N. Budlong, "Aimee Semple McPherson," *Nation* 128 (19 June 1929):738; Morrow Mayo, "Aimee Rises from the Sea," *New Republic* 61 (25 December 1929):136–37; William G. McLoughlin, "Aimee Semple McPherson," in *NAW*, 2:477–80.

28. Mayo, 136–39; Budlong, 737; Bruce Bliven, "Sister Aimee, Mrs. McPherson (Saint or Sinner?) and Her Flock," *New Republic* 48 (3 November 1926):287; Sarah Comstock, "Aimee Semple McPherson: Prima Donna of Revivalism," *Harper's* 156 (December 1927):11; Shelton Bissell, "Vaudeville at Angelus Temple," *Outlook* 149 (23 May 1928):158; "Aimee Semple McPherson, Four Square!" *Sunset* 58 (February 1927):14–16.

29. Merrit Cross, "Alma Birdwell White," in *NAW*, 3:581–83; Joseph R. Washington, *Black Sects and Cults: The Power Axis in an Ethnic Ethic* (New York: Anchor, 1972), 65–67.

30. John Higham, *Strangers in the Land, Patterns of American Nativism, 1860–1925*, (New Brunswick: Rutgers University Press, 1955), 266.

31. "The Case against the Younger Generation," *Literary Digest*, 17 June 1922, 46.

32. Cited by Sister Mary Patrice Thaman, *Manners and Morals of the 1920s in the Religious Press* (New York: Bookman, 1954), 36–42.

33. Thaman, 39, 94; Preston W. Slosson, *The Great Crusade and After* (New York: Macmillan, 1931), 157.

34. Frederick L. Allen, *Only Yesterday* (New York: Harper & Row, 1931), 72–78, 86–87; Willard Thorp, "This Flapper Age," *Forum* 68 (August 1922):637–43; "The Pope's Appeal to Men to Reform Women's Dress," *Literary Digest* 72 (29 January 1927):27–28; McGovern, 326–27.

35. Thaman, 95.

36. Allen, 74–75; Thaman, 70–80.

37. Thaman, 48–52.

38. Ibid., 106–11; Allen, 84, 94; Charles A. McMahon, "Cleansing the

Movies," *NCWC Bulletin* 2 (February 1921):19; Charles A. McMahon, "The Problem of the Movies," *NCWC Bulletin* 2 (January 1921):16–17; McGovern, 331.

39. Thaman, 69–70; "Resolutions Adopted at 7th Annual Convention of the NCCW," *NCWC Bulletin* 11 (November 1927):18.

40. Ahlstrom, 915.

41. Higham, 291–92; Kenneth T. Jackson, *The Ku Klux Klan in the City, 1915–1930* (New York: Oxford University Press, 1967), 249; Myron A. Marty, *Lutherans and Roman Catholicism* (Notre Dame: University of Notre Dame Press, 1968), 9; *Baltimore Catholic Review*, 18 February 1927; John M. Mecklin, *The Ku Klux Klan: A Study of the American Mind* (New York: Russell & Russell, 1963), 157.

42. David M. Chalmers, *Hooded Americanism: The History of the Ku Klux Klan* (Chicago: Quadrangle, 1968), 293–94.

43. Cross, 581–83; Bishop Alma White, *Klansmen: Guardians of Liberty* (Zaraphath, N.J.: Good Citizen, 1926), 4; Alma White, *Heroes of the Fiery Cross* (Zaraphath, N.J.: Good Citizen, 1928), 28.

44. *Baltimore Morning Sun*, 21 November 1923.

45. Jackson, 70; *Constitution and Laws of the Women of the Ku Klux Klan adopted by First Imperial Klonvocation at St. Louis Missouri on the Sixth Day of January 1927.*

46. Jackson, 18–19; Chalmers, 46.

47. Chalmers, 240–41.

48. Chalmers, 170–73; Higham, 294.

49. Chalmers, 246–48.

50. *NCWC Bulletin* 2 (September 1920):20; "A Call to American Catholic Women," *NCWC Bulletin* 3 (September 1921):10–11.

51. See *NCWC Bulletin* for January, November, and December 1921 and December 1922.

52. Pratt, 210–21; Higham, 278–79.

53. Ahlstrom, 901–4; Chalmers, 248–49; Andrew Sinclair, *Era of Excess: A Social History of the Prohibition Movement* (New York: Harper & Row, 1962), vii, 5.

54. Sinclair, 67–69; Ruth Bordin, *Women and Temperance: The Quest for Power and Liberty: 1873–1900* (Philadelphia: Temple University Press, 1981), 156–58; Edith K. Stanley, *Ten Decades of White Ribbon Service 1883–1963* (Cincinnati: Revivalist Press, 1983), 6.

55. Joseph R. Gusfield, *Symbolic Crusade: Status Politics and the American Temperance Movement* (Urbana: University of Illinois Press, 1963), 123–24; Hays, 33–39, 144–45; Stanley, 55.

56. Charles Merz, *The Dry Decade* (Seattle: University of Washington Press, 1931), 140–41.

57. David E. Kyvig, *Repealing National Prohibition* (Chicago: University of Chicago Press, 1979), 119–23.

58. Sinclair, 5, 413; Ahlstrom, 902–4.

Chapter Eight

1. Malcolm Cowley, *A Second Flowering: Works and Days of the lost generation* (New York: Viking Press, 1973), 248–49.

2. Frederick J. Hoffman, *The Twenties: American Writing in the Postwar Decade* (New York: Viking Press, 1955), 26, 434.

3. Ibid., 40.

4. Cowley, 247.

5. Margaret Anderson, *My Thirty Years War: An Autobiography* (Westport, Conn.: Greenwood Press, 1971), 35. See also Mathilda M. Hills, "Margaret Anderson," in *NAWMP*, 21–23.

6. D. D. Paige, ed., *The Selected Letters of Ezra Pound, 1907–1941* (New York: New Directions Press, 1971), 346; Anderson, 178, 211; Hills, 21–23.

7. Charles Allen, Frederick J. Hoffman, and Carolyn F. Ulrich, *The Little Magazine* (Princeton: Princeton University Press, 1946), 20, 225; Hoffman, 205–8; Cheryl A. Wall, "Jessie R. Fauset," in *NAWMP*, 225–27.

8. George Wicks, "Natalie Clifford Barney," in *NAWMP*, 52–53.

9. Sylvia Beach, *Shakespeare and Company* (New York: Harcourt Brace, 1959); Herbert R. Haber, "Sylvia Beach," in *NAWMP*, 70–71. When Hemingway arrived in Paris in 1944 with the American liberation forces, he headed a column of soldiers marching down the rue l'Odeon and emotionally greeted Beach, who had closed the bookstore rather than sell Joyce to the Nazis.

10. Douglas Day, "Gertrude Stein," in *NAW*, 3:355–59; Catherine R. Stimpson, "Alice B. Toklas," in *NAWMP*, 693–94; Gertrude Stein, *The Autobiography of Alice B. Toklas* (New York: Vintage, 1966), 7.

11. Marianne Moore, "A Letter to Ezra Pound," in *Marianne Moore: A Collection of Critical Essays*, ed. Charles Tomlinson (Englewood Cliffs, N.J.: Prentice-Hall, 1969), 18; Caroline F. Ware, *Greenwich Village, 1920–1930* (Boston: Houghton Mifflin, 1935), 225, 236–44, 261–63.

12. Edna St. Vincent Millay, *A Few Figs from Thistles* (New York: Harper & Bros., 1922), 1; John Malcolm Brinnin, "Edna St. Vincent Millay," in *NAW*, 2:536–38; Allen Tate, "Miss Millay's Sonnets," *New Republic* 66 (6 May 1931):335–36; Carl Van Doren, "Youth and Wings: Edna St. Vincent Millay: Singer," *Century* 106 (June 1923):310–16. Elinor Wylie's life was the stuff of modern melodrama; see Judith Farr, *The Life and Art of Elinor Wylie* (Baton Rouge: Louisiana State University Press, 1983).

13. S. V. Baum, "Marianne Moore," in *NAW*, 2:490–94; Marianne Moore, *Observations* (New York: Dial, 1924); Tomlinson, ed. *Marianne Moore: A Collection of Critical Essays*; Hoffman, *The Twenties*, 208.

14. Ann Douglas, "Dorothy Rothschild Parker," in *NAWMP*, 522–25; John Keats, *I Might as Well Live: The Story of Dorothy Parker* (New York: Viking, 1952), 29–130; Dorothy Parker, *Enough Rope* (New York: Boni & Liveright, 1926), 85, 51, 69, 91, 61; Dorothy Parker, *The Collected Stories of Dorothy Parker* (New York: Modern Library, 1942).

15. Nathan I. Huggins, *Harlem Renaissance* (New York: Oxford University

Press, 1971), 3–15; Allan H. Spear, Introduction to *The New Negro: An Interpretation*, by Alain Locke (New York: Johnson Reprint, 1968); Locke, "The New Negro," in *The New Negro*, xi, 6, 15–16.

16. Huggins, 25, 56–59, 71–74, 89–99; Abby A. Johnson and Ronald M. Johnson, *Propaganda and Aesthetics: The Literary Politics of Afro-American Magazines in the Twentieth Century* (Amherst: University of Massachusetts Press, 1979), 54–72, 86–87.

17. Charlotte S. Rubinstein, *American Women Artists from Early Indian Times to the Present* (New York: Avon, 1982), 181–84; Paul Rosenfeld, "The Paintings of Georgia O'Keeffe," *Vanity Fair* 19 (October 1922):56, 112, 114.

18. Elmer S. Apter, "Katherine Sophie Dreier," in *NAWMP*, 202–4; Rubinstein, 163–64, 172–80, 193–96; Jane Grant, "Neysa McMein," in *NAW*, 2:476–77.

19. Rubinstein, 180–93.

20. Ibid., 202–7; Myrna G. Eden, "Malvina Cornell Hoffman," in *NAWMP*, 343–45; Rayford W. Logan, "Meta Vaux Warrick Fuller," in *NAWMP*, 255–56; Myrna G. Eden, "Anna Vaughn Hyatt Huntington," in *NAWMP*, 358–59.

21. Rubinstein, 172–76.

22. Adelyn D. Breeskin, "Beatrice Romaine Goddard Brooks," in *NAWMP*, 110–11; Rubinstein, 196–200.

23. Matilda Gaune, "Ruth Parker Crawford-Seeger," in *NAWMP*, 173–74; Christine Ammer, "Marion Eugenie Bauer," in *NAWMP*, 68–69; Eugenia Kaledin, "Mabel Wheeler Daniels," in *NAWMP*, 177–79; Gilbert Chase, *America's Music* (New York: McGraw-Hill, 1955), 581.

24. Josephine H. Love, "Hazel L. Harrison," in *NAWMP*, 317–19; Carol Neuls-Bates, "Ethel Leginska," in *NAWMP*, 415–16.

25. Janet Wilson James, "Grace Moore," in *NAW*, 2:524–26; "The New Etude Gallery of Musical Celebrities," *Etude* 47 (June 1929):437–38; Elaine Brady, "Mary Garden," in *NAWMP*, 259–66; Charles Jahant, "Geraldine Farrar," in *NAWMP*, 223–25; Henry T. Finck, "Geraldine Farrar's Career," *Vanity Fair* 19 (November 1922):57, 118, 120.

26. Charles Edward Smith, "Gertrude Pridgett Rainey," in *NAW*, 2:110–11; Larry Gara, "Bessie Smith," in *NAW*, 3:306–7; Robert Dierlam, "Helen Morgan," in *NAW*, 2:579–80; Anne C. Reed, "Florence Mills," *NAW*, 2:545–46; Chase, 464–65. Sophie Tucker was also at the peak of her career; however, she spent much of the 1920s in England.

27. "Isadora Duncan's Triumphs and Tragedies," *Literary Digest* 95 (8 October 1927):48–52; "Isadora Duncan's Artistic Credo," *Literary Digest* 95 (8 October 1927):28–29.

28. Walter Terry, *Miss Ruth: The "More Living Life" of Ruth St. Denis* (New York: Dodd, Mead, 1969).

29. Don McDonagh, *Martha Graham: A Biography* (New York: Praeger, 1973), 53, 63. Doris Humphrey also left the Denishawn Company in the 1920s

to form her own company; see Selma J. Cohen, "Doris Humphrey," in *NAWMP*, 356–58.

30. Elliott Norton, "Theresa Helburn," in *NAWMP*, 328–30; Dorothy L. Swerdlowe, "Edith Rich Isaacs," in *NAW*, 2:370–71.

31. Arthur E. Waterman, "Susan Glaspell," in *NAW*, 2:49–51; Carolyn G. Heilbrun, "Edna Ferber," in *NAWMP*, 227–29; Walter J. Meserve, "Rachel Crothers," in *NAWMP*, 174–76.

32. Paul Myers, "Katharine Cornell," in *NAWMP*, 167–69; Mabel Dodge Luhan, "On the Career and Character of Katharine Cornell," *Vanity Fair* 24 (July 1925):40, 78; Pat M. Ryan, "Ethel Barrymore," in *NAWMP*, 58–60; Ethel Barrymore, "My Reminiscences," *Delineator* 104 (January 1924):16–17; Clara M. Behringer, "Jeanne Eagels," in *NAW*, 1:537–38; Stark Young, "Jeanne Eagels in French," *New Republic* 50 (6 April 1927):94–95; Jim Haskins and Kathleen Benson, "Josephine Baker," in *NAWMP*, 40–41; Andre Lawson, "The Negro Dance under European Eyes," *Theater Arts Monthly* 11 (April 1927):282–93.

33. Dorothy Spinsley, "Languishing Romances," *Photoplay* 29 (September 1925):28.

34. Molly Haskell, *From Reverence to Rape: The Treatment of Women in the Movies* (New York: Holt Rinehart, 1974), 89; Robert Sklar, *Movie-Made America* (New York: Random House, 1975), 74–75; Marjorie Rosen, *Popcorn Venus* (New York: Avon Books, 1974), 100; Frances Clark, "Fighting the Sex Jinx," *Photoplay* 31 (January 1927):36. Elinor Glyn and Dorothy Arzner were two women directors.

35. Loos, 91–95; Ada Patterson, "The Gish Girls Talk about Each Other," *Photoplay* 20 (June 1921):29, 104–5; James R. Quirk, "The Enigma of the Screen," *Photoplay* 29 (March 1926):62–63. Rosen, 42–51.

36. Haskell, 58–60; Rosen, 113; *Collier's* 69 (10 June 1922):7; Mary Pickford, *Sunshine and Shadow* (New York: Holt, Rinehart, 1936), 83.

37. Mary Pickford, "Mary Is Looking for Pictures," *Photoplay* 28 (June 1925):39, 109; James R. Quirk, "The Public Just Won't Let Mary Pickford Grow Up," *Photoplay* 29 (September 1925):36–37.

38. Adela Rogers St. Johns, "Adela Rogers St. Johns's Story of the Married Life of Doug and Mary," *Photoplay* 31 (February 1927):35, 131–36; Alma Whitaker, "Mrs. Douglas Fairbanks Analyzes Mary Pickford," *Photoplay* 33 (March 1928):30–31, 127–28.

39. Arthur Lennig, "Theda Bara," *NAWMP*, 49–50.

40. John Gassner, "Alla Nazimova," *NAW*, 2:611–13; Alexander Kirkland, "The Woman from Yalta," *Theater Arts* 33 (December 1949):28–29; Herbert Howe, "A Misunderstood Woman," *Photoplay* 21 (April 1922):24–25.

41. Rudy Behlmer, "Clara Bow," *Films in Review* 14 (October 1963):451–65; Lois Shirley, "Empty Hearted," *Photoplay* 39 (October 1929):29, 128–29.

42. John Bainbridge, *Garbo* (Garden City: Doubleday, 1955), 73–121.

43. Sklar, 95; James B. Kennedy, "Drop the Pie," *Collier's* 83 (8 June 1929):28, 48; Adela Rogers St. Johns, "Gloria: An Impression," *Photoplay* 24

(September 1923):28–29; Gloria Swanson, "There is No Formula for Success," *Photoplay* 29 (April 1929):32–33, 117–19; James R. Quirk, "Everybody Calls Him Harry," *Photoplay* 28 (June 1925):34–35.

44. Rosen 85; Bainbridge, 109; Herbert Howe, "Why Many Movie Marriages Fail," *Photoplay* 28 (October 1925):30–31; 96, 100.

Chapter Nine

1. Sinclair Lewis, *Main Street* (New York: Harcourt, Brace & Howe, 1920), 452; Elaine Showalter, ed., *These Modern Women: Autobiographical Essays from the Twenties* (Old Westbury, N.Y.: Feminist Press, 1978), 24.

2. Lewis, 1–9.

3. Ibid., 58, 265–67.

4. Ibid., 155–56.

5. Ibid., 201, 354.

6. Ibid., 254, 271.

7. Ibid., 448.

8. Ibid., 451.

9. Cited in Frederick Hoffman, *The Twenties: American Writing in the Post-war Decade* (New York: Viking, 1955), 114, 131.

10. F. Scott Fitzgerald, *The Great Gatsby* (New York: Charles Scribner's Sons, 1925), 8–18.

11. Ibid., 17.

12. Ibid., 58–59.

13. Ibid., 25–28, 37.

14. Hoffman, 135–144, 154.

15. Ernest Hemingway, *The Sun Also Rises* (New York: Grosset & Dunlop, 1926), 24–28, 152–53.

16. Ibid., 252–54, 258–59.

17. Antoinette Frederick, "Fannie Hurst," in *NAWMP*, 359–61; Stephen G. Hyslop, "Ruth Suckow," in *NAWMP*, 666–67; Ida H. Washington, "Dorothy Canfield Fisher," in *NAWMP*, 235–36; Barbara Welter, "Mary Roberts Rinehart," in *NAWMP*, 577–79; Carolyn G. Heilbrun, "Edna Ferber," in *NAWMP*, 227–29.

18. Willa Cather, *A Lost Lady* (New York: Alfred A. Knopf, 1978), 31.

19. Ibid., 51.

20. Ibid., 6–7, 42, 83, 87.

21. Ibid., 124–25.

22. Ibid., 172, 232–33.

23. Willa Cather, *The Professor's House* (New York: Vintage, 1973), 282–84. See also E. K. Brown, *Willa Cather: A Critical Biography* (New York: Alfred A. Knopf, 1953), 239; Jennifer Bailey, "The Dangers of Femininity in Willa Cather's Fiction," *American Studies* 16 (September 1982):391–406.

24. R. W. B. Lewis, *Edith Wharton: A Biography* (New York: Harper & Row, 1975), 64–65, 424.

25. Edith Wharton, *The Mother's Recompense* (New York: D. Appleton, 1925), 3–4, 16.

26. Ibid., 36, 62–69, 83.

27. Ibid., 234.

28. Ibid., 266. Gertrude Atherton's *Black Oxen* (New York: Boni & Liveright, 1923) is the most dramatic study of generations in New York society.

29. Lewis, *Edith Wharton: A Biography*; Anita Loos, *A Girl Like I* (New York: Viking, 1966), 266–74.

30. Anita Loos, *Gentlemen Prefer Blondes* (New York: Liveright, 1973), 13–20.

31. Ibid., 83, 100.

32. Ibid., 155–56.

33. Jules Chametzky, "Anzia Yezierska," in *NAWMP*, 753–54; Anzia Yezierska, *Hungry Hearts and Other Stories* (New York: Persea Books, 1985), 64.

34. Anzia Yezierska, *Bread Givers* (New York: Persea Books, 1975), 48.

35. Ibid., 137–38.

36. Ibid., 164, 172.

37. Ibid., 172, 199.

38. Ibid., 206–7.

39. Ibid., 273–74, 296–97. In her introduction to the 1975 edition of *Bread Givers*, Alice Kessler-Harris observed that "freedom is at the pivot of this book as it was the driving force of Yezierska's life." She "freed herself from a tradition few of her countrywomen could ignore in that first generation, and she did it against the heaviest odds. But she paid an enormous price." *Bread Givers* was "part of her attempt to seek absolution."

40. Deborah E. McDowell, Introduction to *Plum Bun: A Novel without a Moral*, by Jessie R. Fauset (London: Pandora Press, 1985), 18.

41. Nella Larsen, *Passing* (New York: Arno Press, 1969), 59–60, 96, 129, 200.

42. Nella Larsen, *Quicksand* (New York: Negro Universities Press, 1969), 5, 19.

43. Ibid., 89–107.

44. Ibid., 213, 231.

45. Ibid., 275–302.

46. Nathan I. Huggins, *Harlem Renaissance* (New York: Oxford University Press, 1971), 157–58.

47. Fauset, 11–27.

48. Ibid., 43, 70.

49. Ibid., 309.

50. Marjorie R. Kaufman, "Ellen Glasgow," in *NAW*, 2:44–49; Ellen Glasgow, *A Certain Measure* (New York: Harcourt, Brace, 1938), 12; H. L. Mencken, "A Southern Skeptic," *American Mercury* 24 (August 1933):565.

51. Ellen Glasgow, *Barren Ground* (New York: Hill & Wang, 1977), 89–93.

52. Ibid., 284–85.

53. Ibid., 408.

54. Carolyn G. Heilbrun, *Reinventing Womanhood* (New York: W. W. Norton & Co., 1979), 72–73.

55. Ibid., 88.

56. Nancy Milford, *Zelda: A Biography* (New York: Harper & Row, 1970), 92.

Chapter Ten

1. Ethel Puffer Howes, "The Meaning of Progress in the Woman Movement," *Annals* 143 (May 1929):14.

2. Nancy F. Cott, "Feminist Politics in the 1920s: The National Woman's Party," *Journal of American History* 71 (June 1948):44; Susan D. Becker, *The Origins of the Equal Rights Amendment: American Feminism between the Wars* (Westport, Conn.: Greenwood Press, 1981), 62; Elaine Showalter, *These Modern Women: Autobiographical Essays from the Twenties* (Old Westbury: Feminist Press, 1978), 26.

3. See Susan Ware, *Women in the New Deal* (Cambridge: Harvard University Press, 1981).

4. Sophonisba P. Breckinridge, "The Activities of Women outside the Home," in *Recent Social Trends in the United States* (New York: McGraw-Hill, 1933), 712–19; Leslie W. Tentler, *Wage-Earning Women: Industrial Work and Family Life in the United States, 1900–1930* (New York: Oxford University Press, 1979), 85; Grace L. Coyle, "Women in Clerical Occupations," *Annals* 143 (May 1929):180–81; Elyce J. Rotella, *From Home to Office: US Women at Work 1870–1930* (Ann Arbor: UMI Research Press, 1981), 148–51.

5. Barbara J. Harris, *Beyond Her Sphere: Women and the Professions in American History* (Westport: Greenwood Press, 1942), 739–49; Frank Stricker, "Cookbooks and Law Books: The Hidden History of Career Women in Twentieth Century America," in *A Heritage of Their Own: Toward a New Social History of American Women*, ed. Elizabeth Pleck and Nancy F. Cott (New York: Simon and Schuster, 1979), 478–79.

6. Ernest R. Groves and William F. Ogburn, *American Marriage and Family Relationships* (New York: Arno Press, 1976), 13; Beatrice M. Hinkle, "The Chaos of Modern Marriage," *Harper's* 152 (December 1925):9.

7. Charles H. Judd, "Education," in *Recent Social Trends in the United States: Report of the President's Research Committee on Social Trends*, (New York: McGraw-Hill Book Co., 1933), 1:341.

8. William Allan Neilson, "Overcrowding in Women's Colleges," *Nation* 120 (13 May 1925):539–40.

9. Frederick Rudolph, *The American College and University* (New York: Alfred A. Knopf, 1962), 324; Rollo Walter Brown, "Coeducation versus Literature," *Harper's* 148 (May 1924):785.

10. Paula S. Fass, *The Damned and the Beautiful: American Youth in the 1920s* (New York. Oxford University Press, 1977), 375–76.

11. Ellen Glasgow, *Barren Ground* (New York: Hill and Wang, 1977), 408.

12. Beatrice Hinkle, "Why Feminism," in Showalter, 141.

13. For a fine summation of the women's movement post-1950, see the final chapters of Nancy Woloch, *Women and the American Experience* (New York: Alfred A. Knopf, 1984). See also Carol Gilligan, *In a Different Voice: Psychological Theory and Women's Development* (Cambridge: Harvard University Press, 1982), 150–174.

14. Anne Morrow Lindbergh, *Bring Me a Unicorn* (New York: Harcourt Brace Jovanovich, 1972), 131.

15. Ibid., 249.

A Note on Sources

In 1966 Burl Noggle, in a review of the historiography of the 1920s, called attention to two realities: the long and enduring reach of Frederick Lewis Allen's initial study of the decade, *Only Yesterday* (1931), and the need for new historical research ("The Twenties: A New Historiographical Frontier," *Journal of American History*, September 1966). The twenties had been richly chronicled by contemporaries. In addition to Allen, Preston W. Slosson, in *The Great Crusade and After 1914–1929* (New York: Macmillan Co., 1930), provided a sweeping survey of American society. Journalist Mark Sullivan in his *Our Times*, volume 6, provided a blow-by-blow report of the Harding election and scandals and a year-by-year account of headlines, music, and literature. Charles and Mary Beard completed their multivolume study of *The Rise of American Civilization* in 1933. There was then a hiatus. The twenties as a decade for historical study was accepted as either "done" or "out" until the 1950s and the Age of Affluence and Republican leadership prompted another look. William E. Leuchtenburg, in *The Perils of Prosperity, 1914–1932* (Chicago: University of Chicago Press, 1958), completed one major overview. While he placed added emphasis on America abroad, he fairly closely mirrored Allen's topics, if not his interpretations. It was not until the 1960s that John D. Hicks, in *Republican Ascendancy* (New York: Harper and Row, 1960), and Paul A. Carter, in *The Twenties* (Arlington Heights: AHM, 1968), broke the Allen mold. (In *Republican Ascendancy*, there was not one reference to women in the index.) In the 1970s, Paul Carter's *Another Part of the Twenties* (New York: Columbia University Press, 1977) and in the 1980s, Geoffrey Perrett's *America in the Twenties: A History* (New York: Simon and Shuster, 1982) have answered the call for further analysis of this complex decade. They have all benefited from the research and reports compiled by Robert S. and Helen Lynd in *Middletown: A Study in American Culture* (New York: Harcourt Brace, 1956) and *The Report of the President's Commission on Recent Social Trends in the United States* (New York: McGraw-Hill, 1933), two major starting points for any research on the 1920s.

In 1974, Estelle Freedman completed a survey of the historiography of "The New Woman" of the 1920s (*Journal of American History* 41 [Sept. 1974]) and concluded, as had Burl Noggle, that it was time to stop reiterating and to begin researching. The women, who had been mainly relegated to chapters on the revolution in manners and morals or depicted as retreating from politics back into the family, where they took up the happy life of consumers, did not receive a more searching examination until the late 1960s. During the twenties there had been a flurry of articles and series in magazines on the new woman. In 1926 and 1927, Freda Kirchway published a series on "These Modern Women" in *Nation* (reprinted in *These Modern Women: Autobiographical Essays from the Twenties*, edited by Elaine Showalter [Old Westbury: Feminist Press, 1978]). The May 1929 issue of the *Annals of the American Academy of Political Science* devoted to women, provided a wide variety of articles on women in politics and on the job. In October 1927, *Current History* also carried a series of articles on the "new woman." Sophonisba Breckinridge, who researched the chapter on women for the Presidents Research Commission, published a monograph in 1933, *Women in the Twentieth Century: A Study of Political, Social, and Economic Activities* (New York: Arno Press, 1970). In the late 1960s the most important resource for historians working in history of women of the 1920s began to be compiled, the invaluable *Notable American Women, 1607–1956*. This three volume work edited by Edward T. and Janet James and Paul S. Boyer (Cambridge: Harvard University Press, 1971) and the later *Notable American Women: The Modern Period* (Cambridge: Harvard University Press, 1984), edited by Barbara Sicherman and Carol Hurd Green, have been major catalysts for further study in women's history. Three useful overviews of women in the 1920s, all with different interpretations of their fate beyond suffrage are William L. O'Neill's *Everyone was Brave: The Rise and Fall of Feminism in America* (Chicago: Quadrangle Books, 1969), William Chafe's *The American Woman: Her Changing Social, Economic and Political Roles 1920–1970* (New York: Oxford University Press, 1972), and June Sochen's *Movers and Shakers: American Women: Thinkers and Activists, 1900–1970* (New York: Quadrangle, 1973). Both Shiela Rothman's *Woman's Proper Place: A History of Changing Ideals and Practices, 1870 to the Present* (New York: Basic Books, 1975) and Nancy Woloch's *Women and the American Experience* (New York: Alfred A. Knopf, 1984) are comprehensive and thoughtful surveys. For similar comprehensiveness on the black experience, Paula Giddings's *When and Where I Enter: The Impact of Black Women on Race and Sex in America* (New York: Bantam Books, 1984) is the most useful. Two monographs that grapple with the intellectual roots and the crisis in feminism in the 1920s are Rosalind Rosenberg's *Beyond Separate Spheres: Intellectual Roots of Modern Feminism* (New Haven: Yale University Press, 1982) and Carol Smith-Rosenberg's *Disorderly Conduct: Visions of Gender in Victorian America* (New York: Alfred A. Knopf, 1985).

The study of women in politics in the 1920s should begin with Eleanor Flexner's pioneering study *Century of Struggle: The Women's Rights Movement in the United States* (Cambridge: Harvard University Press, 1959). Breckinridge's *Women in the Twentieth Century* was supplemented by Martin Gruberg's *Women in American Politics* (Oshkosh: Academia Press, 1968). For the social feminists, the best study remains J. Stanley Lemons's *The Woman Citizen: Social Feminism in the 1920's* (Urbana: University of Illinois Press, 1973). For the National Woman's Party, Susan D. Becker's *The Origins of the Equal Rights Amendment: American Feminism between the Wars* (Westport: Greenwood Press, 1981) and Nancy F. Cott's "Feminist Politics in the 1920s: The National Woman's party" (*Journal of American History* 71 [June 1984]) are the most recent and helpful.

Three studies provide fine overviews of the experience and history of women on the job: Alice Kessler-Harris, *Out to Work: A History of Wage-Earning Women in the United States* (New York: Oxford University Press, 1979); Lois W. Tentler, *The Wage-Earning Woman: Industrial Work and Family Life in the United States, 1900–1930* (New York: Oxford University Press, 1982); and Julie A. Matthai, *An Economic History of Women in America: Women's Work, the Sexual Division of Labor and the Development of Capitalism* (New York: Schocken Books, 1982). For women in the labor movement, Irving Bernstein's *The Lean Years: A History of the American Worker, 1920–1933* (Baltimore: Penguin Books, 1966) and Philip Foner's *Women in the American Labor Movement* (New York: Free Press, 1980) are the most comprehensive. The feminization of the office is analyzed by Margery W. Davies in *Woman's Place Is at the Typewriter: Office Work and Office Workers, 1870–1930* (Philadelphia: Temple University Press, 1982) and Elyce J. Rotella in *From Home to Office: US Women at Work 1870–1930* (Ann Arbor: UMI Research Press, 1981). Mary Anderson's *The Autobiography of Mary Anderson* (Minneapolis: University of Minnesota Press, 1951) and Mary E. Dreier's biography of her sister, *Margaret Dreier Robins: Her Life, Letters and Work* (New York: Island Press Cooperative, 1950) provide good accounts of the leadership and frustrations of the WTUL.

The classic study of the family in the 1920s is Ernest R. Groves and William F. Ogburn's *American Marriage and Family Relationships* (New York: Arno Press, 1976). For birth control, in addition to Margaret Sanger's autobiographies and writings, David Kennedy's *Birth Control in America: The Career of Margaret Sanger* (New Haven: Yale University Press, 1970) and Linda Gordon's *Woman's Body, Woman's Right: A Social History of Birth Control in America* (New York: Grossman's Publishers, 1976) are thorough. For the tensions of married working women, Winifred D. Wandersee's *Women's Work and Family Values, 1920–1940* (Cambridge: Harvard University Press, 1981) is unmatched. Barbara Ehrenreich and Deirdre English survey the theories on child rearing in *For Her Own Good: 150 Years of the Experts' Advice to Women* (Garden City: Anchor, 1979).

Developments in the schools are most fully surveyed by Lawrence A. Cremin's *The Transformation of the Schools: Progressivism in American Education 1876–1957* (New York: Alfred A. Knopf, 1969). For the high school, Edward A. Krug's *The Shaping of the American High School 1920–1931* (Madison: University of Wisconsin Press, 1922) remains the classic. For women's higher education, Thomas Woody's *A History of Women's Education in the United States* (New York: Science Press, 1929) and Mabel Newcomer's *A Century of Higher Education for American Women* (New York: Harper & Bros., 1959) remain useful. The two most thorough and insightful recent studies on the women's colleges are Barbara Miller Solomon's masterful *In the Company of Educated Women: A History of Higher Education in America* (New Haven: Yale University Press, 1985) and Helen Horowitz's *Alma Mater: Design and Experience in the Women's Colleges from Their Nineteenth Century Beginnings to the 1930s* (New York: Alfred A. Knopf, 1984). For black colleges, Jeanne L. Noble's *The Negro Women's College Education* (New York: Teachers College Columbia, 1956) provides a good survey. Sister Mary Mariella Bowler, in *A History of Catholic Colleges for Women in the United States of America* (Washington: Catholic University of America, 1933), does the same for the Catholic institutions. Updated studies are needed in both of these areas. Undergraduate life is covered with zest and thoroughness by Paula S. Fass in *The Damned and the Beautiful: American Youth in the 1920's* (Oxford: Oxford University Press, 1977). For a recent history of the challenges to professional women, Barbara J. Harris's *Beyond Her Sphere: Women and the Professions in American History* (Westport: Greenwood Press, 1978) is comprehensive. A model of professional history is Mary Ruth Walsh's *"Doctors Wanted" No Women Need Apply: Sexual Barriers in the Medical Profession, 1835–1975* (New Haven: Yale University Press, 1977).

For the history of American religion, Sidney E. Ahlstrom's *A Religious History of the American People* (New Haven: Yale University Press, 1972) is the major comprehensive overview. There is, however, little on women, a reflection perhaps of their status in the churches. Rosemary Reuther and Elinor McLaughlin, in *Women of Spirit: Female Leadership in the Jewish and Christian Traditions* (New York: Simon & Schuster, 1979), provide a fine collection of recent work of scholars in church history. *Women in American Religion*, edited by Janet W. James (Philadelphia: University of Pennsylvania Press, 1974) is another highly useful work. Of all of the denominations, the Presbyterians have the most thorough histories of women in the church. Elizabeth Howell Verdesi's *In But Still Out: Women in the Church* (Philadelphia: Westminster Press, 1976) surveys the progress and regression of women Presbyterians. Sister Mary Patrice Thaman's study of *Manners and Morals of the 1920s in the Religious Press* (New York: Bookman, 1954) is a fine survey of the literature. Throughout the 1920s, *Literary Digest* carried a feature on religious news. Joseph R. Gusfield's *Symbolic Crusade: Status Politics and the American Temperance Movement* (Urbana: University of Illinois Press, 1963) and David E. Kyvig's *Repealing National Prohibition* (Chicago: University of Chicago Press, 1979) describe the cultural tensions that created and then ended Prohibition.

For the literature of the 1920s, a good starting point is Frederick J. Hoffman's *The Twenties: American Writing in the Postwar Decade* (New York: Viking, 1955). For art, Charlotte S. Rubinstein's *American Women Artists from Early Indian Times to the Present* (New York: Avon, 1982) is invaluable. For film, Molly Haskell's *From Reverence to Rape: The Treatment of Women in the Movies* (New York: Holt Rinehart, 1974) and Marjorie Rosen's *Popcorn Venus* (New York: Avon Books, 1974) provide interesting assessments in spite of the rakish titles. A quick tour of Broadway is possible through the multivolume *The Best American*

Plays (1920–1929), edited by Burns Mantle. Nathan I. Huggins's *Harlem Renaissance* (New York: Oxford University Press, 1971) is a good overview but it should be read in tandem with Alain Locke's *The New Negro: An Interpretation* (New York: Johnson Reprint, 1968).

For the cultural history of the 1920s, there is a massive resource in the magazines. *Vanity Fair,* the *New Yorker,* the *American Mercury,* and the *Messenger* all began during this decade. The reissue of Bessie Smith's blues recordings and the jazz of Jelly Roll Morton and Duke Ellington should be listened to, for, as Burl Noggle points out, the 1920s had a style and a rhythm all their own.

Index

Stoddard, Lothrop, 116
Strayer, George, 129
street car conductors, 83
Stricker, Josephine, 96
strikes and work stoppages, 3, 4–5, 12–13, 81, 90–94
summer schools for women in industry, 86–87, 92
The Sun Also Rises (Hemingway), 226–27
Susman, Warren, 25–26
Sutherland, George, 83, 85
Swanson, Gloria, 217–18
Swarts, Maud, 87
Swartz, Nelle, 85

Taft, Jessie, 35, 153
Taft, William Howard, 78, 85
Taggard, Genevieve, 202
Talbot, Marion, 35
Tammany Hall politics, 22, 70
Tarkington, Booth, 96
Tate, Allen, 201
Taylor, Frederick W., 7
teachers, 128, 130, 131, 142, 146, 151–52, 155–57, 177, 235–36, 247
tennis, 42–43
textile industry, 13, 82, 90, 93
theatre, 211–13, 216, 221
theology, 160, 170
This Side of Paradise (Fitzgerald), 18, 225
Thomas, M. Carey, 86–87, 136, 137, 150
Thompson, Helen, 35–36
Thompson, Randall, 207
Ticknor, Catherine, 30
tobacco industry, 8, 82, 93, 94, 182–83
Toklas, Alice B., 199
Towle, Charlotte, 152–53
Towner, Horace, 52
Trinity College (Washington, D.C.), 144–45
Tyler, Elizabeth, 186

Underwood, Oscar, 22
union organization, 86–87, 89, 91, 92–93
Unitarians and Unitarian Church, 168
United Brotherhood of Carpenters and Joiners, 89
United States Civil Service, 160–61

United Textile Workers, 13, 91–93
Upton, Harriet Taylor, 51, 55, 61, 66, 79
urban life, 11, 20, 22, 102, 131, 184, 190–91, 222, 225, 248

Van Doren, Irita, 198
Van Kleeck, Mary, 78, 79
Van Vechten, Carl, 204
Van Waters, Miriam, 153, 160
Vassar College, 134, 136, 138, 149–50
Versailles (peace treaty), 3, 87
vocational training, 154
Voluntary Parenthood League, 116
Vorse, Mary Heaton, 73–74
Votaw, Heber, 55
voting rights, 49, 51, 141, 159–60, 245–46, 249

Wadsworth, James, 51
Walker, C. J., 162
Wallace, Henry C., 14, 15
War Work Council (YWCA), 77
Ware, Carolyn, 200
warfare, outlawing war, 65
Washington Conference for the Limitation of Armaments (1921), 64–65
Watkins, Florence V., 52, 53
Watson, John B., 119–20
Way Down East (Griffith), 214
Weinstock, Anna, 92
Wellesley College, 138, 150
Welsh, Lilian, 158
Welter, Barbara, 29–30
Wesleyan Teachers College (Nebraska), 142
Wharton, Edith, 229–31, 249
Wheeler, Burton K., 15, 58
White, Bp. Alma, 179–80, 185, 188
White, Kent, 180
White, Sue Shelton, 41
White, William Allen, 59, 186, 228
white collar work, 95–97, 246
White-Williams Foundation, 153
Whitney, Gertrude Vanderbilt, 205–6
Whitney, Richard, 25
wife and husband, 103, 104, 105, 109, 123–24, 247
Wiggins, Ella May, 93